Building on Frege

Building on Years

Building on Frege
New Essays on Sense, Content, and Concept

edited by
Albert Newen
Ulrich Nortmann
Rainer Stuhlmann-Laeisz

CSLI
Publications
Center for the Study of
Language and Information
Stanford, California

Library of Congres Cataloging-in-Publication Data
Building on Frege: new essays about sense, content, and concepts /
[edited by] Albert Newen, Ulrich Nortmann, Rainer Stuhlmann-Laeisz.
    p. cm.
    Papers presented at a meeting.
    Includes bibliographical references and index.
    ISBN 1-57586-311-1 (alk. paper) – ISBN 1-57586-312-X (pbk. : alk.
paper)
    1. Frege, Gottlob, 1848-1925. I. Newen, Albert. II. Nortmann, Ulrich,
1956- III. Stuhlmann-Laeisz, Rainer.
    B3245.F24 B85 2001
    193–dc21   2001025229

Please visit our web site at
http://cslipublications.stanford.edu/
for comments on this and other titles, as well as for changes
and corrections by the authors, editors and publisher.

Chapter 2, "Frege, Lotze, and the Continental Roots of Early Analytic Philosophy"
by Gottfried Gabriel, from *From Frege to Wittgenstein*, edited by Erich H. Reck,
copyright ©2001 by Oxford University Press, Inc. Used by permission of Oxford
University Press, Inc.

Chapter 4, "Frege on Apriority" originally appeared in *New Essays on the A priori*,
edited by P. Boghossian, C. Peacocke, Oxford: Clarendon Press, copyright ©2001 by
Tyler Burge.

Chapter 13, "The Context Principle". A German version of this paper was published
under the title "Das Kontextprinzip" in *Gottlob Frege: Werk und Wirkung*, edited
by G. Gabriel, U. Dathe, Paderborn: Mentis, 2000.

Contents

Contributors   vii

Preface   ix

Introduction   xi

I. Frege and the Philosophical Tradition

1 Frege – A Platonist or a Neo-Kantian?   3
   WOLFGANG CARL

2 Frege, Lotze, and the Continental Roots
   of Early Analytic Philosophy   19
   GOTTFRIED GABRIEL

3 How Do We 'Grasp' a Thought, Mr. Frege?   35
   WOLFGANG MALZKORN

4 Frege on Apriority   53
   TYLER BURGE

II. Sense and Propositional Content

5 Sense and Objectivity in Frege's Logic   91
   GILEAD BAR-ELLI

6 Fregean Senses and the Semantics of Singular Terms   113
   ALBERT NEWEN

v

7   Frege on Identity, Cognitive Value, and Subject Matter   141
JOHN PERRY

8   How to Kripke a Frege-Russell   159
ROSEMARIE RHEINWALD

9   Concepts and Their Modes of Presentation   175
ULRICH NORTMANN

10 Modes of Presentation: Perceptual vs. Deferential   197
FRANÇOIS RECANATI

III. Empty Names and the Context Principle

11 Sense Without Reference   211
R. M. SAINSBURY

12 How Can "a exists" Be False?   231
EDGAR MORSCHER

13 The Context-Principle   251
RAINER STUHLMANN-LAEISZ

IV. Concepts

14 Constituents of Concepts: Bolzano vs. Frege   267
WOLFGANG KÜNNE

15 Concepts are Beliefs about Essences   287
ULRIKE HAAS-SPOHN AND WOLFGANG SPOHN

V. Sets, Truth and Logic

16 Concepts of a Set   319
FRANZ VON KUTSCHERA

17 Is Logic the Science of the Laws of Truth ?   329
UWE MEIXNER

Contributors

GILEAD BAR-ELLI: Department of Philosophy, The Hebrew University of Jerusalem, Jerusalem 91000, Israel.

TYLER BURGE: Department of Philosophy, University of California, 405 Hilgard Avenue, Los Angeles CA 90024-1451, USA.

WOLFGANG CARL: Philosophisches Seminar, Universität Göttingen, Humboldallee 19, 37073 Göttingen, Germany.

GOTTFRIED GABRIEL: Institut für Philosophie, Universität Jena, Zwätzengasse 9, 07740 Jena, Germany.

ULRIKE HAAS-SPOHN: Institut für maschinelle Sprachverarbeitung, Universität Stuttgart, Anzenbergstr. 12, 70174 Stuttgart, Germany.

WOLFGANG KÜNNE: Philosophisches Seminar, Universität Hamburg, Von-Melle-Park 6, 20146 Hamburg, Germany.

WOLFGANG MALZKORN: Philosophisches Seminar, LFB III, Universität Bonn, Lennéstr. 39, 53113 Bonn, Germany.

UWE MEIXNER: Universität Regensburg, Institut für Philosophie, 93040 Regensburg, Germany.

EDGAR MORSCHER: Institut für Philosophie, Universität Salzburg, Franziskanergasse 1, A-5020 Salzburg, Austria.

ALBERT NEWEN: Philosophisches Seminar, LFB III, Universität Bonn, Lennéstr. 39, 53113 Bonn, Germany.

ULRICH NORTMANN: Philosophisches Institut, Postfach 151150, Universität des Saarlandes, 66041 Saarbrücken, Germany.

JOHN PERRY: Department of Philosophy, Stanford University, Stanford, California 94305, USA.

FRANÇOIS RECANATI: Institut Jean Nicod (CNRS/EHESS), 1bis, rue Lowendal, 75007 Paris, France.

ROSEMARIE RHEINWALD: Philosophisches Seminar, Westfälische Wilhelms-Universität, Domplatz 23, 48 143 Münster, Germany.

R. M. SAINSBURY: Department of Philosophy, King's College London, London WC2R 2LS, Great Britain.

WOLFGANG SPOHN: Fachbereich Philosophie, Universität Konstanz, Postfach D21, 78457 Konstanz, Germany.

RAINER STUHLMANN-LAEISZ: Philosophisches Seminar, LFB III, Universität Bonn, Lennéstr. 39, 53113 Bonn, Germany.

FRANZ VON KUTSCHERA: Institut für Philosophie, Universität Regensburg, 93040 Regensburg, Germany.

Preface

The 8th of November, 1998, marked 150 years since Gottlob Frege's birth. To commemorate this anniversary, and to appreciate the lasting influence of this outstanding philosopher-logician's work on subsequent developments in philosophy, three members of the former Institute for Logic and Foundational Research (*Seminar für Logik und Grundlagenforschung*)[*] in Bonn (Germany), Rainer Stuhlmann-Laeisz, Albert Newen, and Ulrich Nortmann, "grasped the thought" of realizing a conference on Frege and on work in contemporary philosophy inspired by him.

The meeting took place from the 7th to 10th of October, 1998, in the Gustav-Stresemann-Institute in Bonn. The organizers were assisted by Ms. Ute Halfar-Schneiders, by Rimas Čuplinskas, Markus Schrenk, and Sven Walter, to whom they are grateful. They are also indebted to the German Research Foundation (DFG) for its generous financial support, as well as to the *Bouvier*-booksellers, the *General Anzeiger* (a leading local newspaper), and the DSL-bank for their kind contributions. Finally, we would like to thank Wilko Ufert and Eva Wilhelmus for their assistance in producing the final layout, and our publishers, *CSLI Publications*, for their active support.

This volume presents a selection of essays based on papers read in the Stresemann-Institute, and some additional material. We hope that the contributions will give a vivid picture not only of several current issues in the interpretation of Frege's writings, but also of more systematic considerations, either criticizing some of the proposals put forward by Frege, or intending to further develop what Frege set on foot.

---

[*] Presently: Institute of philosophy, department III (*Philosophisches Seminar, Lehr- und Forschungsbereich III*)

Introduction

With many, Frege counts for a modern Platonist. There are quite a few passages in his writings which can be quoted in support of such an assessment, and in sum they even today seem to make a strong case for adopting an ontology which is Platonistic in the broader sense. In particular, there is a passage in Frege's essay "On Thoughts" (*Der Gedanke*) telling that a "third realm" has to be acknowledged – a realm which is meant by Frege to include entities neither of the psychic variety nor accessible to the (outer) senses.

It is *Wolfgang Carl's* aim in his opening contribution entitled "Frege – a Platonist or a Neo-Kantian?" – one among a group of four articles exploring, among other things, the place of Frege in the history of philosophy – to show that the label "Platonist" does not really capture the special touch of Frege's position. No more does, according to Carl, the rival (yet in connection with Frege less familiar) label "neo-Kantian".

Carl starts by discussing the issue of Frege and Platonism. The residents of the "third realm" (which are meant to be all kinds of senses (*Sinne*) of linguistic expressions (including thoughts), and the usually recognized objects of mathematical investigation) are characterized by Frege as being neither subjective nor real. (Cf. On Sense and Reference, p. 30; On Thoughts, p. 76 seq.) Opposing the most obvious reading, Carl proposes not to take Frege's subjective-objective-distinction as an ontologically anchored classification of different types of entities, plausibly involving different kinds of being. Instead, the distinction relates, as Carl argues, to different types of discourse (so that it gets more of the taste of an epistemological than of an ontological dichotomy): in discourse about mathematical objects, e.g., it does not matter what any person *believes* to be true, or whatever ideas or mental images she associates with the linguistic expressions involved; in this sense, properly conceived mathematical discourse is objective. On Carl's view, Frege's primary concern is the accentuation of this epistemic side of the coin as opposed to the ontological one. Assuming a ranking of sides like that, Carl feels already justified in denying Frege's philosophy the Platonistic character – where he relies on a rather demanding notion of Platonism advocated by E. Reck.

In addressing the question whether Frege's philosophical approach is appropriately qualified as neo-Kantian in spirit, Carl reviews tenets of three leading members of the German neo-Kantian school: W. Windelband, H. Rickert, and H. Cohen. In comparing Frege to them, he finds a common element in all four thinkers' shared anti-psychologism. On the other hand, he points to a difference (which again, in his eyes, is sufficient to deny, with regard to Frege's thinking, the appropriateness of the label at issue): whereas for neo-Kantians acts of thinking essentially include, according to Carl, mental representations, Frege conceives thoughts (being items to be "grasped" in thinking) as the potential contents of *sentences*, thus relating them, and therewith thinking, to the realm of semantical entities, and loosening the connection of both with the sphere of the subjective. For Carl, this move of Frege's is in accordance with the spirit of the "context principle" whose adoption, in Frege's treatise on "The Foundations of Arithmetic" (*Die Grundlagen der Arithmetik*), is appreciated as a remedy against confusing the search for the content of a linguistic expression with the search for an idea (understood as a mental being, a *Vorstellung*) associated with it.

Gottfried Gabriel contradicts Carl in defending the thesis (attributed by Gabriel to H. Sluga) that "Frege's efforts are part of the neo-Kantian tradition." In support of this thesis he mentions, among other things, that the context principle adopted by Frege (saying that one should not ask for the content of a word in isolation, but only in the context of a complete sentence containing that word) was a semantical version of a metaphysical principle, in the final analysis going back to Hegel, which Frege took over from H. Lotze, the founder of neo-Kantianism. So with Carl, on the one hand, the way in which Frege puts to work in "The Foundations of Arithmetic" the *content* of the principle (namely as a means of demarcating an objectivist semantical approach from a subjectivist account of the contents of thinking) serves as evidence for the claim that there is a point where Frege's and the neo-Kantian ways diverge. Taking into account the *genesis* of the very same principle, Gabriel claims, on the other hand, to have revealed a common root in both party's thinking. In addition, Gabriel sides with Carl in assessing both party's shared anti-psychologism as a point of convergence.

In tracing the context principle back to the 'continental' philosophers Hegel and Lotze, while also finding it at work in the writings of thinkers of the analytical provenance like Frege, Wittgenstein, and more recent advocates of holistic approaches, Gabriel also claims to have pinpointed a continental root of analytical philosophy (as it is signaled by the title of his contribution).

Concerning the context principle, the moral to be drawn from Stuhlmann-Laeisz's contribution (chap. III) will however be that not too important a role in Frege's thinking should be granted to this principle.

Regarding the issue of Frege and Platonism, there is a remarkable point of agreement with Carl and Gabriel. Like Carl, Gabriel is inclined to interpret the peculiarity of those assumed residents of Frege's "third realm" which are thoughts not so much as a matter of particular ontological status but prefers to couch it in epistemological terms: the much stressed independence of the contents of human thinking, i.e. of thoughts, is not ontologically conceived as an independent existence, but logically as an independence in being valid: what individuals *believe* to be true is taken not to the slightest degree to matter for the validity of a thought. But for Gabriel, this kind of independence postulated by Frege (which in Gabriel's eyes marks another correspondence of Frege's and the neo-Kantians' ways) is sufficient to qualify Frege's philosophy as a form of Platonism (as "transcendental Platonism", to be precise). Here, he relies on a weaker notion of Platonism than Carl does.

Interestingly, a number of observations made by Gabriel on neo-Kantian value theory and the related terminology could offer an explanation for Frege's practice, when intending to talk about true or false sentences or thoughts, to choose the terms "truth *value*" (*Wahrheitswert*) and *Bedeutung* (the latter term conveying the idea of importance, and of being of value).

From the articles by Carl and Gabriel it is already plain to see that a crucial element in Frege's thinking is the conviction that human beings are capable, by way of thinking or "grasping thoughts" (as Frege used to express it), to enter into a relation with residents of the "third realm". In his already mentioned essay "On Thoughts", and in particular on p. 75 thereof, Frege presents himself as facing a problem with the possibility of such a relation. Thereby he foreshadows a question which is among the most discussed in today's philosophy: how can a mental state or process be endowed with a content which is, among other things, suited to be expressed by a sentence? In fact, *Wolfgang Malzkorn* proposes to analyze a person's grasping of a thought as that person's having an idea (in the sense of being in a particular mental state) which in turn has the thought involved as its content. The question what this relation between an idea and a thought consists of he leaves to be tackled.

Malzkorn's proposal regarding the grasping of thoughts is connected with an analysis he gives of the abovementioned passage from "On Thoughts" – a passage where Frege is trying to allay anticipated doubts about the view that grasping of thoughts is possible. The passage, and espe-

cially the contained assertion that for visual perception of things (as an example) to occur it be required that something non-sensible is added to a
given visual impression, is apt to ring Kantian bells, as E. Picardi elsewhere
expresses it. So, an analysis of the passage in question again raises the
question how Frege relates to Kant and Kantianism. Malzkorn rejects Kantian readings and offers an alternative interpretation according to which the
"non-sensible something" Frege has in mind would be "a certain faculty to
process sense-impressions of actual things and thus turn them into sense-
perceptions of those things."

The Frege-Kant-relation is also a theme in *Tyler Burge's* contribution.
Here, the object is to compare the notions of apriority found in Frege, Kant,
and Leibniz.

There is an enduring systematic interest in a clarification of the notion
of *a priori* truth because, to mention one point, it pertains to the still controversial epistemic status of mathematics. Not least owing to Frege's foundational work, it is clear that a clarification of the latter requires a clarification of the status of those set theoretical axioms which as we know permit
the derivation of wide parts of mathematics. Since Gödel accomplished the
proof of his incompleteness results, we know in addition that no consistent
and recursive first order theory including a sufficient portion of arithmetic
can comprise the totality of propositions recognized by mathematicians as
validly established. Hence the nature of validity and truth in mathematics,
which Frege believed to have settled for the field of arithmetic (until he was
confronted with Russell's paradox), remains an intriguing issue.

Having experienced the breakdown of his original project of a foundation of arithmetic, Frege stuck to his view (presented by Burge as a central
element in Frege's rationalism) that logic and mathematics are disciplines
of an *a priori* character. Only the more specific belief that truth in arithmetic is analytical truth he felt forced to drop. The established propositions of
(Euclidian) geometry he had always believed to be *synthetic a priori* truths,
here in agreement with Kant. Burge shows that in "The Foundations of
Arithmetic", Frege uses a notion of apriority which seems queer from a
standpoint widely adopted today. The point is that Frege wishes to call a
(mathematical) proposition an *a priori* truth if a (canonical) proof exists of
this proposition which starts from basic principles being *general*, and neither admitting nor being in need of a proof themselves. It is this emphasis
on the generality of the first principles, in combination with the assumption
that a certain natural, canonical order of justification exists, which on
Burge's view marks a common feature of the conceptions of apriority found
in Frege and Leibniz. "Frege's Leibnizian conception of apriority takes
generality of justificational starting point to be fundamental", as Burge puts
it. In his eyes, this means an opposition to Kant who primarily links apriority to justificational independence of sense experience while not at all

excluding particular acts of intuiting (if only the intuitions are "pure") relating to particulars, especially to particular geometrical objects, and carrying *no* generality with them. Burge prefers Kant's conception of apriority to Frege's. One reason is that he believes *cogito*-sentences (reporting the occurrence of certain of a speaker's mental events in a first-person perspective), and possibly other indexical sentences like "I'm here now", to be apriorily true, following S. Kripke. According to Frege's conception, however, such sentences seem to be bound to lack apriority due to their (presumptive) underivability from general laws.

The verbal agreement of Frege and Kant with respect to the claim that Euclidian geometry consists of *synthetically* true assertions (as a consequence of the justificational dependence on pure intuition of the basic principles in this field) actually is, according to Burge, not more than a verbal agreement. The reason is that in this connection Frege, as Burge understands him, has in mind only intuitive acts being devoid of any reference to particulars and particular constructions in (pure) space, in keeping with his generality-based conception of apriority.

While the first group of articles, apart from discussing a variety of Fregean themes, serve to locate Frege's thinking in the network of a broader philosophical tradition, the next group go into the details of a special, and venerable, subject anew tapped by Frege: the semantical content of expressions, and in particular their sense (meaning, *Sinn*).

Gilead Bar-Elli points to the distinctness of two conceptions of sense employed by Frege. The core idea of the first conception is to consider a sense a mode of presentation of something. According to the second conception, which is somewhat reminiscent of the context principle (as spelt out for the level of senses; cf. the distinctions made in Stuhlmann-Laeisz's contributuion), senses are primarily conceived as parts of thoughts: the sense of an expression α contributes to a thought which is expressed by a sentence containing α. Bar-Elli argues in favour of the first conception. In his eyes, the ways objects are given to us are fundamental for the objectivity of truths relating to them. In geometry, objects are given by intuition, and the basic axioms are justified, and therewith shown to be objective, or objectively true, by an appeal to intuition. In fact, Burge's discussion of Frege's claim that the assertions of Euclidian geometry are *a priori* truths raises the question how Frege would want to justify the underlying general principles, which he thinks admit of no further proof. Bar-Elli's answer: those principles express at least some basic aspects of the modes the geometrical objects are presented to us in intuition.

Things are similar in arithmetic, according to Bar-Elli: numbers are given to us as logical objects, and their special mode of being presented suffices for justifying the basic arithmetical truths. Bar-Elli also explains how logical objects come to be given: the decisive move is from an equivalence of functions to the sameness of the respective course of values, following Frege's basic law No. V. Bar-Elli ends up with a sort of reconciliation of the two concepts of sense under consideration: objectivity of a truth is objectivity of a thought which is composed of senses which are modes of presentation guaranteeing objectivity.

A starting point for *Albert Newen*'s considerations is Frege's view that the meaning (= the Fregean sense) of a subsentential expression occurring in a given sentence can be thought of in terms of what the expression contributes to the thought expressed by the sentence. Given this background assumption (which is also taken into account in Bar-Elli's article), the leading question of Newen's article is: what precisely does a proper name, or an indexical, contribute to the thought expressed by an utterance of a sentence containing that term, and how should the meaning of such a term be construed?

The answer stresses that, from a systematic point of view, the meaning of a singular term is a multi-dimensional entity (a "vector") comprising a number of different possible contributions to the semantic content of utterances of sentences containing that singular term. Which part of the vector is, so to speak, activated in constituting the content of an utterance depends on the peculiarities of the respective communicative situation. Accordingly, Newen's approach denies a strict separation between the semantics and the pragmatics of singular terms.

John Perry rejects a certain move Frege made in "On Sense and Reference" (*Ueber Sinn und Bedeutung*). The move consists in subjecting the possession of "proper" cognitive value by a true identity statement "$a = b$" to the condition that each of the terms "a" and "b" presents (*gibt*) the common reference in its own peculiar way.

Perry argues that in order to meet the phenomena, one should better take the concept of the (conceptual) content of expressions as employed by Frege in the "Conceptual Notation" (*Begriffsschrift*) as a starting point, and fan out conceptual content into three directions – finally arriving at *three* propositions associated with an identity statement all of which can have proper informational value. The first one is what Perry calls the "subject matter proposition" associated with "$a = b$" (it corresponds to what is otherwise known as the Russellian proposition belonging to the statement in question). The second one has to be the pertinent "modes of designation proposition", and the third one figures as the associated "modes of presentation proposition." Concerning these matters, there is a remarkable convergence of Albert Newen's and John Perry's ideas.

Frege had a problem with relating an intersubjectively stable sense to genuine proper names (*eigentliche Eigennamen*, cf. On Sense and Reference, p. 27, fn. 2), as opposed to definite descriptions. In fact one would ask how to think of the way Aristotle is "given" by the name "Aristotle" (setting aside the problem that, in a sense, Aristotle no longer exists, so that there is nothing left to be "given" to anybody).

There is an obvious reaction to the problem: assume *direct reference* for genuine proper names, that is, take it that they refer directly to an individual, not requiring a mediating sense; there is no sense associated with them. An essentially equivalent option consists in simply equating senses of proper names with their reference.

A crucial point in *Rosemarie Rheinwald*'s considerations is the insight that the latter option is supported by conceiving the meaning (= the Fregean sense) of a proper name, following a Carnap-Church-Kaplan-thread (as it is also followed in Nortmann's contribution), as the function defined on the set of all possible worlds which assigns to each world the (fixed) extension of the name. Assuming along with S. Kripke that proper names are rigid designators, there is in fact only one value being assigned to all arguments, that is we have a constant function. Simply identify such a function with its only value, and you are in agreement with Rheinwald who says: "Since the function is constant, I propose to identify the meaning of a proper name with its reference."

Given this proposal, Rheinwald argues that a Fregean semantics as formalized *à la* A. Church is in combination with the rigidity-thesis by and large equivalent to Russell's "constituent thesis". The latter is the thesis that individuals (as they can be designated by proper names) can figure as constituents of propositions. At any rate, the constituent thesis is true from a Fregean point of view provided that senses of proper names *are* the referents of those names. Defending moreover the thesis that Russell, properly understood, did *not* hold a description theory of ordinary proper names, Rheinwald finally arrives at a localization of Frege's semantics which finds expression in the equations: Frege-Church + rigidity thesis = Russell = Kripke.

Ulrich Nortmann's subject is the sense of predicates. At the beginning of his contribution, he rejects a principle of exclusive designation to the effect that functions can be designated *only* by expressions which are themselves in need of completion (*ergaenzungsbeduerftig*, as Frege used to express it). Thereby the ground is cleared for talking in the familiar ways about concepts in the later sections of the paper. In addition, the stage is set for a discussion of the "function theory of the *Sinn* of predicates" (P. Geach). According to this theory, the sense of a predicate is a function which takes senses of names of individuals as arguments and maps each of them to the thought expressed by the sentence which results from combining the respective name with the given predicate. Sect. 2 contains some speculations about what Frege could have gained even for his logicist project if he had adopted a more critical attitude towards said principle.

Then the main questions of Nortmann's contribution are tackled: can one have a distinctively Frege-style semantic approach which at the same time has been modernized along Carnapian lines by drawing on Carnapian intensions, and what could one say about the senses of predicates in such a theory? The first question is answered positively, and a special kind of composition-function is introduced in dealing with the second question.

In the final section, some consequences are drawn, based on the answer to the second question, for the interpretive hypothesis (criticized by M. Dummett) that the function theory of the sense of predicates is at least compatible with Frege's views.

Frege assumed that each concept expression refers to a single concept which is its Fregean meaning (= *Bedeutung*), and which is associated with the expression as such, not varying with respect to distinct epistemic conditions different utterers might be in. Here, Frege is at variance with the intuitively plausible view (which is also supposed in Haas-Spohn's and Spohn's exposition) that it must be possible for each member of a party of speakers of differing degrees of competence concerning a certain subject matter to associate his/her own special concept with a single concept expression. It was H. Putnam who, in this context, coined the formula of the "division of linguistic labour." A physician, it seems, will be in the possession of a concept of arthritis which need not coincide with the arthritis-concept employed by his/her arthritis-patient not endowed (let us assume) with the appropriate medical knowledge.

It is *François Récanati*'s concern in his contribution to embed the sketched view into the framework of a Frege-style semantics by postulating and exploring a special type of mode of presentation: the "deferential" type.

Récanati maintains (in a sense keeping a Fregean course) that the "content" of the arthritis-concept employed by the patient who suffers from but is not really informed about that disease is *the same* as the "content" of the arthritis-concept of the physician in charge. A possible analysis says that one and the same Fregean concept (the concept of arthritis) is involved here, but that it is given to the patient in a *deferential* mode, namely as: the concept which the physician associates with the expression "arthritis." The achievement of successfully referring is, so to speak, *deferred* to the physician as the utterer who is competent on the relevant score.

Récanati proceeds by comparing the deferential mode of presentation with indexical ways of presentation. For the reference of the demonstrative expression "this house over there" to be determined it is required that the utterer has perceptive access to it. In a similar vein, Récanati's patient will manage to refer only if he/she utters "arthritis" in a context which is such that in it, he/she is in contact with a person figuring as the expert-utterer.

The papers by Sainsbury, Morscher, and Stuhlmann-Laeisz deal again with special issues in Fregean semantics. When Frege wrote "On Sense and Reference", there was no doubt with him that there can be names endowed with sense (*Sinn*) but lacking reference (*Bedeutung*): empty proper names, in Sainsbury's words. Frege's view is not unproblematic (as already indicated above) if you think of senses as being modes of presentation of something: when there is nothing there, then there can't be a particular way to give something either which would serve as the sense to be associated with an expression. (But remember that from Bar-Elli's article it is clear that there is also another notion of sense to be found in Frege.)

An opposite view is Russell's: the meanings of proper names are exhausted by the particulars designated by the names; accordingly, an expression void of designation cannot be a (meaningful) name at all. Such an approach to the semantics of expressions used as names is called "object-based" in *Mark Sainsbury's* contribution. Causal theories of the semantics of names *à la* S. Kripke would also have to be classified as "object-based", since they take as essential for name-using original baptisms which in turn presuppose the existence of something to be baptized.

Sainsbury opposes to both versions of object-based accounts, as well as to "informational accounts" (in his words) which tend to equate names with descriptions. He offers an alternative account which in the main characteristic is similar to Kripke's but dispenses with generally taking those events which name-using practices originate from to be acts of baptizing *something*. In short, the idea is (cf. sect. 3.1 of Sainsbury's article): adopt Kripkean ideas of transmission while eliminating the object. This alternative account is Fregean insofar as it does not bind the understood use of an expression as a name, and thereby (one would add) the expression's possession of meaning, to the existence of a referent. On the other hand, it is in a sense *non*-Fregean in leaving room for the possibility that there is no *common* piece of information whose possession would be required for each of a party of speakers to be credited with an understanding of a given name. (A case for this is made in sect. 3.3 of Sainsbury's essay.) No doubt, however, the latter option is to a certain extent foreshadowed by Frege when he talks, as already mentioned, about possible variations of the senses of names like "Aristotle" in "On Sense and Reference".

In Sainsbury's eyes, object-based accounts are deficient for various reasons. One reason is, as Sainsbury illustrates, that a characterization of a certain historical-philological research project as addressing the question who *Homer* was (if anyone) would count as natural and quite intelligible notwithstanding the possibility that the name "Homer" finally proves to be empty. Further arguments in favour of a not object-based approach are drawn from the efficiency which Sainsbury's account shows in the analysis of several natural language phenomena involving what he calls "name-using practices" (such as "fusion", "confusion", and "fission" as explained in sections 3.4 to 3.6).

Frege did not have a real problem with negative existential statements which contain as their grammatical subject a string consisting of an indefinite article and a predicate, such as "A *perpetuum mobile* does not exist." In cases like that, there was no question for Frege that the logical subject existed; on his view, the logical subject is a concept here, and the point of the statements in question is to express that that concept is empty (i.e., no individual falls under the concept).

Things look different, however, when negative singular existential statements are to be taken into account. They mean a real problem for the Fregean, because their truth seems to imply that their respective grammatical subject is an empty name, which in turn would imply that, referring to nothing, they *lack* a truth value. Singular existential statements are the subject of *Edgar Morscher*'s contribution from sect. 8 onwards. Morscher's starting point is the following task: try to find a well formed formula of first order predicate logic with identity (i.e. of PL1=, using Morscher's abbreviation) which is neither logically true nor logically false, and which can claim in other respects as well to be an acceptable explication of "*a* exists" (with "*a*" being a singular term). An obvious candidate like $\exists x(x = a)$ will not do, since this formula is PL1=-valid (whereas existence, as one would reasonably argue, must as a rule be a matter of contingent fact).

Morscher proceeds by discussing several solutions to the problem proposed in recent literature (by J. Hintikka, B. van Fraassen, B. Skyrms, S. Lehmann and others), and finally ends up with what he calls the "classical solution" (because it can be traced back to Bolzano): in contexts of type "*a* exists", singular terms "*a*" refer to what normally is their sense; the statements in question say about the involved sense that it is not empty, but that there is a corresponding referent. The classical solution (so Morscher argues) has to be supplemented, however, by a fairly up-to-date conception of senses which frames them, for instance, in a possible-worlds-setting (as Nortmann seeks to do for the senses of predicate expressions).

When Frege wrote down "The Foundations of Arithmetic", it apparently seemed somewhat difficult to him to present the figures and their natural-language counterparts ("one", "two", ...) as meaningful and referring singular terms. According to one of the notions of sense found in Frege, senses are modes of presentation of something, and not without plausibility Frege asks (The Foundations of Arithmetic, §62) how it was possible for a number to be presented to a human being if it is to be conceived as an abstract object, hence as something which surely cannot be given through perceptual experience. He even goes to the point of conceding (not yet explicitly distinguishing between sense and reference) that a number-expression might lack designation outside a complete sentential context (Foundations, §60). In fact one could argue from a later standpoint, underlining the fact that sentences of the type

"the number belonging to the concept F is the same
as the number belonging to the concept G"

can be rephrased as

"there is a bijection relating the F-things to the G-things",

that apparent designators of numbers are incomplete symbols, actually empty names which can be explained away in context. Frege is anxious to avoid consequences like that, and he seems to succeed by relying on the method of explicitly (not contextually) defining number-expressions he presents in "Foundations", §68.

Rainer Stuhlmann-Laeisz observes, however, that Frege's definitional procedure is impaired by an internal difficulty. As he points out, Frege's explicit definition of cardinal numbers:

the number belonging to the concept F is the extension of the concept (or equivalently, of the property) of being equinumerous with F

presupposes the concept of the extension of a concept, and therewith (in the light of "The Basic Laws of Arithmetic") the concept of the course of values of a function. Thence it follows, Stuhlmann-Laeisz argues, that this explicit definition affords no solution to the "Julius Caesar-problem", i.e. the problem of how to enable one at least in principle to decide of any given object whether it is a number or not. For in order to accomplish this task, one would have to be in the position to decide of any object whether it is a course of values (of any function) or not. This however cannot be managed on the base of a mere explication of the identity of the courses of values of any two given functions; nor can it be managed on the base of an explicit definition of courses of values which follows the paradigm of the above-mentioned number-definition, since such a definition of courses of values is bound to be circular.

For these reasons, Stuhlmann-Laeisz sums up, the Julius Caesar-problem was ultimately unsolvable for Frege. So he was in effect forced to stick to his contextual definition of numbers as a second-best solution – acknowledging *faute de mieux* a context principle for this special case of introducing the numbers. But Frege was not inclined, Stuhlmann-Laeisz contends, to see a virtue in accepting a general context principle.

A fourth group of articles are again concerned with concepts. But here the focus is more on concepts as such, not so much on their potential functioning in a semantical framework. *Wolfgang Künne* points out that Frege at least partly endorsed what Bolzano completely rejected, namely the "Canon of Reciprocity (CR)" of the logical tradition. (CR) can be split into two claims concerning any pair of concepts x and y: firstly, if the extension of x is a (proper) part of the extension of y, then the content of y is a (proper) part of the content of x; the second claim is the converse of the first one. As to the first one (which was explicitly supported by Frege), Bolzano knew significant counterexamples. These depend, however, on his special notion of *being part* according to which, for instance, the concept *woman* would be a component of *relative of a woman*. A line of defence open to Frege is to require as necessary for the content of y to be part of the content of x that every individual falling under x *must* also fall under y. This condition is also necessary for the concept y's being a Fregean "mark" (*Merkmal*) of x. This strategy is not suited, however, for a defence of the second half of (CR). Bolzano attacked it by pointing to concepts of which the one is comparatively abundant, containing the other one as a more terse component, as e.g. with *equilateral triangle which is equiangular* ($= y$) and *equilateral triangle* ($= x$). Here, the content of x is part of the content of y, and every object falling under y must also fall under x; nevertheless, the extension of y is identical with that of x , hence it is not a (proper) part of the latter.

Ulrike Haas-Spohn and *Wolfgang Spohn* start from externalism, i.e. from the view (propagated by T. Burge and H. Putnam) that meanings are not in the head, and the beliefs of an epistemic subject are not completely determined by the subject's internal states. Nevertheless they express their conviction that there is a certain species of close relatives of meanings and belief contents which *can* be completely "in the head" – "narrow contents", as they call them.

Frege found himself in a historical situation in which he encountered strong psychologist tendencies in theories of language, logic and mathematics. Accordingly he was so eager to stress the intersubjective and objective character of thoughts, and of meanings in general, that theorizing about subjective relatives of (potentially) intersubjectively shared contents was not his concern. This bias, which was certainly fruitful in Frege's times, has been counterbalanced by more recent developments in semantical theory which Haas-Spohn's and Spohn's considerations fit in. In their present article, the authors' aim as partial internalists is to offer a conception of narrow concepts individual and general, i.e. of the narrow (subjective) contents associated with singular terms and with predicates. In basing their proposal on D. Kaplan's character-theory, they seek to avoid on the one hand what they call "Schiffer's problem" (this is the problem of how to reach that aim without drawing on functional roles); on the other hand, they seek a course enabling them to avoid both horns of what they call "Block's dilemma" (which are syntacticism, or the boiling down of concepts essentially to words, and holism so excessive that it gets any little change in a person's beliefs entail a change of her concepts).

Roughly spoken and simplified, Haas-Spohn's and Spohn's proposal is (expressed for the case of a singular term "*a*"):

> The concept which a subject s associates with *a* in a situation is a function assigning to each possible (and subject-centered) world the set of objects existing in that world which, according to the subject's judgement in that situation, could be the object which *a* refers to in the reference situation.

To be identical with the relevant object is possible (in a certain sense) precisely for those objects which share the relevant object's *essential* properties. So the gist of the proposal can be expressed as the idea that, in the special case mentioned, a subject's individual concept associated with *a* is constituted by that subject's beliefs about the *essence* of the individual which the term *a* refers to.

Récanati analyzes the subject-relativity which is also Haas-Spohn's and Spohn's concern in a way which leaves room for talking of the sameness of the "content" of concepts employed by distinct subjects, and which makes the variation across subjects a matter of differing modes of presentation. Haas-Spohn's and Spohn's account is in a more radical fashion subjectivist. Their proposal gives rise to the question, however, how to draw the line between subjects counting as competent speakers, and subjects not so qualifying. Is there an upper limit to the eventual absurdity of the beliefs about essences involved? As it stands, the proposal admits every belief system whatsoever.

Set theory and (classical, Fregean) logic form the pillars which a wide range of contemporary mathematics can be based upon. So it is crucial for an assessment of the epistemic status of mathematics to get clear about the nature of these disciplines, or to try to shape them in a philosophically satisfactory way.

Burge argues in his article that a theory of sets starting with a supply of *ur*-elements, and raising a universe of sets on it, would not have been to Frege's taste (at least when he wrote "The Foundations of Arithmetic"). The reason is that such *ur*-elements would count as particulars, and that assertions about irreducible particulars would presumably lack the generality which Frege demands, according to Burge, of the principles of an *a priori* theory. Instead, a system of set theory shaping sets as extensions of concepts, and starting with an empty set determined by some empty concept, might be much more to the taste of the Fregean due to the generality he would grant to concepts.

It is precisely this idea, meeting the supposed Fregean demand, which leads *Franz von Kutschera* in formulating a new system of set theory – a system which on the other hand bears a nominalistic stamp, and in so far would seem to deviate from Fregean ideas, as a result of von Kutschera's finally working with extensions of *predicates* instead of extensions of concepts. In contrast to Carl, von Kutschera does not hesitate to classify Frege as a Platonist for his realist attitude towards concepts which according to von Kutschera is involved in his realism towards sets: "if sets are extensions of concepts then realism as to sets implies realism as to concepts", he writes.

The system labeled "Ω" in von Kutschera's contribution is introduced by way of a step by step comparison with G. Boolos's iterative set theory as presented in Boolos's article from the early seventies, "The Iterative Concept of Set". According to von Kutschera, Boolos's system, even though a step in the right direction, sticks to a collective notion of set, as opposed to the markedly constructive character claimed by von Kutschera for his own conception. Insofar as the extensions of predicates employed by von Kutschera are merely "relative" extensions, the relevant predicates being restrictively defined for objects on the levels of a certain hierarchy similar to that which underlies Boolos's approach, von Kutschera's construction incorporates elements of the latter.

Uwe Meixner presents several respects in which Frege's characterization of logic as the science of the laws of being true seems mistaken – and this not only in a present-day perspective, but also from a Fregean viewpoint itself. Regarding the latter, Meixner is right to point out: for a long stretch, Frege propagated the logicist thesis; had this thesis been true, it would have been correct to view even arithmetic, ultimately, as a science of the laws of truth – an assessment which Frege hardly would have supported.

Even if the scope of Frege's characterization of logic is limited to classical elementary logic (while intuitionist logic, e.g., and systems strong enough to afford the development of larger parts of elementary number theory are excluded), it remains subject to criticism as it is advanced in sect. 9 of Meixner's contribution: it is possible to explicate classical validity and implication (on the level of propositional logic) within an intensionalistic framework, doing completely without the concept of truth; nevertheless, this concept can be regained within such a framework by appropriate definition (again in opposition to Frege for whom truth was undefinable).

Albert Newen

Ulrich Nortmann

Rainer Stuhlmann-Laeisz

Part I

FREGE AND THE PHILOSOPHICAL TRADITION

1

Frege – A Platonist or a Neo-Kantian?

WOLFGANG CARL

Frege is one of the most studied and debated philosophers of the last hundred years. However, there is no general agreement about his philosophical significance. One major strand in the current Frege-interpretation attributes a certain metaphysical or ontological point of view to him, called 'realism' or 'platonism'. A second major interpretation strategy is to situate him in the historical context of his time and to underline the affinities between Frege and a philosophical movement called 'Neo-Kantianism'. Because Neo-Kantianism is well-known for its anti-metaphysical stance, the historical interpretation of Frege's work is in direct conflict with the ontological or metaphysical interpretation. Indeed, the two interpretations tend to be inconsistent with each other. What I want to show is that neither interpretations really capture what is peculiar to Frege's philosophical reasoning. I will start by considering the view – outlined recently by Tyler Burge – that Frege is a Platonist.

The term 'Platonism', as it is used here, was established – as far as I know – by Paul Bernays in 1934. In a paper entitled 'Sur le platonisme dans les mathématiques', Bernays claims that a Platonist "postulates the existence of a world of ideas which contains all objects and relations of mathematics" (Bernays 1978: 68). It is the postulated existence of logical objects like numbers which invites us to consider Frege as a Platonist. However, Frege's Platonism is not restricted to numbers; as Tyler Burge points out correctly, Frege was a Platonist about truth values, functions and thought contents as well. (cf. Burge 1992: 349) If he was committed to Platonism at all, it extends beyond the realm of mathematics; and his reasons for such a commitment could not have been purely mathematical. Thus, we have to ask what reasons Frege could have had for committing himself to such an extended Platonism.

As is well known, Frege holds that numbers, functions and thoughts are imperceptible, non-spatial, atemporal and causally inert. According to Burge, he is thereby committed to Platonism, taken to be the doctrine which "regards some entities as existing non-spatially and atemporally." (Burge 1992: 353) – One might point out that Frege himself does not use the term 'entity' at all – and he could not do so (cf. Ricketts 1986: 87f.) –, nor does he talk about the *existence* of objects or thoughts. – However, it is not just the assumption of such entities which paves the way to Platonism, because, as Burge himself points out, "Platonism has no monopoly on claims to lawlike or intersubjective objectivity of non-spatial, atemporal entities." (Burge 1992: 352) Thus, to be a Platonist, one also has to reject the idea that "the nature or existence of these atemporal entities is to be regarded as in any way dependent on something mental, linguistic, communal, or on anything like a practice or activity that occurs in time." (Burge 1992: 353)

The idea that numbers, thoughts and truth values are independent of things mental, linguistic or conventional plays a crucial role in Frege's account of the objective. Is this idea operative in Burge's definition of Platonism? In a draft of a 'Logik' written around 1897 Frege explains his idea of independence by distinguishing two cases. Firstly, what is true is independent of our recognizing or acknowledging it as true. Frege argues for this independence by pointing out that otherwise our taking something to be true would imply that it is true. "There would be no science, no error and no correction of error, properly speaking, there would be nothing to be true in the ordinary sense of the word. For this is so closely bound up with that independence of being recognized as true which we are emphasizing here, that it cannot be separated from it." (Frege 1969: 144; Frege 1979: 133) The notion of independence involved here is required for making sense of the very notions of truth and error. Whoever accepts these notions must make room for such an independence. Secondly, Frege claims: "In order to be true, thoughts – e.g. laws of nature – not only do not need to be recognized by us as true: they do not have to have been thought by us at all." A thought, being true, doesn't require that it is entertained by anybody. What this kind of independence amounts to can be seen by pointing out that a law of nature is discovered by us, not invented by us. Frege concludes "that the laws of nature ... are valid at all times and not just since they were discovered." In other words: the validity of a claim to knowledge doesn't depend on the context of its discovery. Frege has a further reason for underlining the possiblity of discovery as a salient feature of our concept of knowledge: it excludes the idea that cognition – "Erkenntnis" – is conceived "as an activity that creates what is known" (Frege 1893: XXIV; Frege 1964: 23). Knowledge doesn't produce its own object.

Independence is used by Frege to justify basic features of our concept of knowledge or cognition. There is nothing distinctively Platonistic in this concept, as can be seen from Kant's rejection of an "intellectus archetypus" as a model for our knowledge. If Platonism is not necessary for an adequate account of knowledge one might wonder why Frege should be committed to it. Burge claims that "Platonism rejects any deeper philosophical commentary that would indicate that the nature or existence of these atemporal entities is to be regarded as in any way dependent on something mental, linguistic, communal ... ." (Burge 1992: 353) However, the dependence Frege wants to exclude is really quite specific, namely that which holds between a person and his ideas: "A thought does not belong in the peculiar way to the person who thinks it, as does the representation to the person who has it: everyone who grasps the thought encounters it in the same way, as the same thought." (Frege 1969: 145; Frege 1979: 133) The independence Frege has in mind is very restricted: a thought is not dependent on something mental that is "inexpressible in words" and essentially private. (Frege 1884: 35) Frege claimed that thoughts are independent of anything mental, because he wanted to block the way to solipsism and to idealism in something like the strong Berkeleyan sense. But the rejection of these doctrines does not yet amount to Platonism.

Burge holds that "the lack of qualification in Frege's claims of independence" of a thought being true in the passages just quoted is a decisive reason for calling Frege a Platonist. (Burge 1992: 357) However, given that the notion of independence at issue is already so specific there is no need for qualification, and, given the rather innocent or obvious things Frege wants to establish by his notion of independence – to give an account of the possibility of error and truth "in the ordinary sense of the word" – it is most implausible to cite such independence as a reason for crediting Frege with any far-reaching metaphysical point of view at all. It is not difficult to understand why one would stick with the notion of independence in the attempt to identify Frege's metaphysical point of view. For by sticking to independence we seem to raise ontological questions about the *existence* of thoughts and other abstract objects and whether such things depend on our conceptual frameworks, cognitive activities, etc. However, if one looks at Frege's own attempts to characterize his philosophical views, one realizes that such ontological questions do not play any role at all. Frege's self-characterization has two well-known, closely related strands: Firstly, he acknowledges a domain of things objective, but not real, and secondly, he claims that we must accept a "third realm".

I have argued elsewhere that the distinction between the three realms is part of Frege's answer to the central question of the second part of his essay called 'The Thought', that is: what can be the object of my knowledge? I have also argued that the real point of the distinction is to distinguish between different kinds of access to different domains of knowledge. No particular ontology is involved in this. (cf. Carl 1994: 197-201) I will not pick up this issue again, but will confine myself to Frege's claim that there is a domain of things which are objective but not real – a claim stated in the 'Preface' of the first volume of 'The Basic Laws of Arithmetic'. As is well known, one of the major issues of the 'Preface' is Frege's concern with "the corrupting incursion of psychology into logic". (Frege 1893: XIV; Frege 1964: 12) He thinks that his own views can be summarized and generalized by saying that one has to acknowledge a domain of things which are objective, but not real. What his claim amounts to can be explained only by looking at the various objections raised against psychologism in logic.

It is important to realize that, at the outset, Frege mentions a view about logical laws shared by his opponents – the view that such laws are "guiding principles for thinking in the attainment of truth". Frege himself accepts this view, but he believes that one has to be more precise and aware of distinctions to be drawn. Such guiding principles are instrumental rules defined by the aim of attaining the truth. All genuine laws can be used in the following way: they require that our thinking conforms with them if we hope to reach any truth in the field that they govern. For giving an account of the *logical* laws one has to consider laws of thinking – "Denkgesetze" –, that is "the most general laws, which prescribe universally the way in which one ought to think if one is to think at all". (Frege 1893: XV; Frege 1964: 12) If our aim is to attain the truth, these laws must play a constitutive role in our thinking. They are "prescriptions about asserting ... judging, inferring". (Frege 1918: 58; Frege 1977: 1)

Frege thinks the prescriptive character of the laws of logic is "only too easily forgotten". (Frege 1893: XV; Frege 1964: 12) if one takes their generality not as a constitutive mark of thinking aiming at the truth, but as a descriptive feature of thinking as a "mental process" which is not necessarily directed towards the truth as its goal. We forget the prescriptive character of the laws of logic, when we take them to be descriptive laws of psychology. Psychological laws are not prescriptive with regard to our practice of asserting and inferring; they are not guiding principles for evaluating this practice, but rather laws which explain how thinking as a mental process occurs. It is essential for considering thinking according to the laws of psychology that it can not be taken as part of a practice which aims at truth. Frege calls this kind of thinking "taking something to be true". Thus, thinking as a part of a practice aiming at the truth and thinking as just taking something to be true form the distinctive fields of logic and psychology respectively. The laws of logic cannot be reduced to the laws of psychology, because our practice of asserting and inferring cannot be reduced to our taking something to be true. For otherwise, "truth has not here been given its proper place". (Frege 1918: 58; Frege 1977: 1) Our aiming at the truth, a constitutive feature of that practice, cannot be accounted for as long as one considers thinking only as a mental process which happens to occur according to certain regularities.

At this point Frege distinguishes between being true and being taken to be true, "whether by one or many or everybody", and claims that the former cannot be reduced to the latter. (Frege 1893: XV; Frege 1964: 13) Michael Dummett takes this claim as an affirmation of Frege's "realist stance", that is as a metaphysical claim concerning the independence of knowledge and reality. (Dummett 1981: 433f.) However, what Frege has in mind can be seen from the example he gives: "If it is true that I am writing this in my chamber on the 13th of July, 1893, while the wind howls out-of-doors, then it remains true even if all men should subsequently take it to be false." (Frege 1893: XVI; Frege 1964: 13) What is true is not beyond any reasonable or justified belief; it is rather something that is, as a matter of fact, taken to be false by people lacking the appropriate evidence – people who were not present, have forgotten it, etc. – while Frege himself, having that evidence, knows that it is true and takes it to be true. The distinction between being true and being taken to be true is not a gap between world and mind, but rather indicates that our beliefs or thinking aiming at the truth has to be governed by the appropriate rules, including the logical laws. Being taken to be true does not entail being true. It is the very notion of thinking directed towards the truth which requires this independence.

This independence holds as well for the laws of logic themselves. Because they are not psychological laws, "natural laws of what human beings take to be true" (Frege 1893: XVI; Frege 1964: 14), and because they are concerned with truth connections which hold independently of our taking them to be true, they can be compared with "boundary stones set in an eternal foundation, which our thought can overflow, but never displace." (Frege 1893: XVI; Frege 1964: 13) Leaving aside for a moment what Frege means by "foundation" here, we can take the laws of logic to be "boundary stones" to the extent that they guide all thought directed towards the truth and yield a standard by which to evaluate all judgment and inference. We can "overstep these stones" by thinking in a way that runs afoul of the standard set by logic, but we cannot thereby "displace" them.

But what about the foundation of the logical laws? What sort of "eternal foundation" does Frege imagine? It is well known that Frege distinguishes between justifying a logical law by reducing it to other more basic logical laws, and justifying the basic laws themselves which cannot be done by logic. That said, Frege does mention a non-logical justification for the basic laws: we must accept these laws, unless "we wish to reduce our thought to confusion and finally do without all judgment whatever." (Frege 1893: XVII; Frege 1964: 15) Speaking in his own voice, Frege is pointing to the constitutive role of logical laws which establish the very possibility of all thinking directed towards the truth. Thus, Frege's boundary stones, i.e. the basic laws of logic, are not set in a foundation as in any kind of Platonic cloud-cuckoo-land. On the contrary, they are set in a foundation firmly planted in the ground – in the business of evaluating judgments and drawing inferences.

Frege points out that the source of his controversy with the psychologists is a difference in conceptions of truth. For him truth is something objective and independent of the judging subject, while the psychological logicians reject this claim. Is Frege's claim to be taken as an admission of Platonism, as the expression of a belief in a realm of a certain kind of entities? As Frege explicitly points out, the dispute is about the notion of truth. It is a dispute about something both parties are supposed to accept, it is not about any kind of entity which is accepted on the one side and rejected on the other. Frege himself is inclined to consider the dispute about truth in "more general terms". Thus, the issue seems to be whether we will accept "a domain of what is objective and unreal" or whether we will reject such a domain by identifying what is unreal with what is subjective. (Frege 1893: XVIII; Frege 1964: 16) What is the issue?

Frege has two distinctions in mind, the distinction between the real and the unreal and the distinction between the objective and the subjective. According to the psychological logicians, the two distinctions are one and the same. Thus, the objective is supposed to coincide with the real, while the subjective is supposed to coincide with the non-real. But Frege rejects this; he denies that the real and the objective must always go hand in hand and he sees no reason to conflate the non-real with the subjective. Frege himself associates the subjective with the psychological, and distinguishes this pair from the objective which he associates in turn with the logical. This is indeed the first of the three guiding principles in the 'Foundations of Arithmetic': "always to separate sharply the psychological from the logical, the subjective from the objective." (Frege 1884: X)

By connecting the subjective with the psychological and the objective with the logical Frege wants to establish a domain of reference for the kind of evidence appropriate for statements about objects in that domain. Thus, he argues against the view that numbers are subjective by pointing out that statements about numbers are not based upon "the description of mental processes which precede the delivery of a judgment of number". (Frege 1884: 34) Such a judgment "can never be adduced in proof of any proposition of arithmetic; it acquaints us with none of the properties of number". (Frege 1884: 34) Whatever is a concern for psychology is subjective:

whether or not something is a concern for psychology depends on the appropriate evidence accepted for a certain class of statements. According to Frege, this evidence has something to do with "what belongs to the mental life of an individual and merges with other ideas with which it is associated according to the laws of psychology ... ." (Frege 1893: XVIII; Frege 1964: 16)

Frege associates the objective with the logical, without identifying them. Thus he says that the distinction between the subjective and the objective "is as justified as the distinction between psychology and logic". (Frege 1884: 37n.) As we know from the 'Preface' of the first volume of the 'Basic Laws' the distinction between psychology and logic is concerned with what is subjective on the one hand and a realm of discourse on the other, in which agreement and disagreement of beliefs are possible and logic has to play its appointed role as "arbiter in the conflict of opinions". (Frege 1893: XIX; Frege 1964: 17) The objective is whatever can be scrutinized according to the laws of logic.

The distinction between the subjective and objective is not concerned with an ontological classification of different kinds of entities. Rather it is supposed to distinguish between different kinds of discourse in terms of the appropriate evidence. In this respect numbers and the North Sea are comparable (cf. Frege 1884: 34) – not because they share some salient ontological features, but because neither the one nor the other is a concern for psychology: statements about numbers and statements about the North Sea are not based upon statements about mental states.

This brings us back to Frege's claim that there is a domain of things objective, but unreal. It is important to understand that this claim does have various ontological commitments. As we have seen, the objective includes physical objects, numbers and thoughts, while the subjective comprises various mental states, their representational content, and the people who find themselves in those states as well. However, neither the objective nor the subjective defines any particular class of entities or determines any special kind of existence. Frege is not at all concerned with the ontological commitments which go hand in hand with acknowledging a domain of what is objective. This domain does not form any well-defined and distinctive class of entities, but rather it has something to do with "what is subject to laws, what can be conceived and judged, what is expressible in words". (Frege 1884: 35) What holds for the objective also holds for the distinction between the real and the unreal. Reality is not to be equated with existence, as Dummett correctly points out, (cf. Dummett 1981: 120) and to say that something is unreal is not to make any particular ontological claim, but is rather to say something about the limits of the realm of causal interactions.

By acknowledging a domain of what is objective, but unreal, Frege does not want to characterize the difference between himself and the psychological logicians in terms of ontology. It would be misleading to say that, according to Frege, there are things the psychological logician does not accept. What he rejects is the idea that "something being independent of the judging subject has to be real, i.e. has to be capable of acting directly or indirectly on the senses." The domain of whatever is independent in this sense is a domain of whatever allows for the distinction between recognizing something as true and its being true. By rejecting the idea that this domain has to be identified with the domain of physical, medium-sized objects one commits oneself to an ontology which extends beyond the realm of physical objects. This amounts to a rejection of empiricism, but being an anti-empiricist is not the same as being a Platonist.

Erich Reck has argued that what is peculiar to Platonism is a "clean separation of metaphysics, semantics, and epistemology" and a particular order of explanation, moving from metaphysics to epistemology. (Reck 1997: 131) But Frege's acknowledgement of a domain of things objective, but unreal, proceeds just in the reverse order: the possibility of knowledge and shared language is considered as basic, and the metaphysics or ontology is determined by whatever is required to account for this. Given Reck's conception of Platonism which is philosophically more demanding than the one to be found in Burge, Frege is not a Platonist. Quite generally speaking, Frege's concern is the very possibility of logic, and, as Frege himself points out, logic has no need of metaphysics, it is rather the other way round. (cf. Frege 1893: XIX; Frege 1964: 17f.) So much for Platonism and the metaphysical interpretation of Frege's work. Let me now turn to the rival historical interpretation - the attempt to situate Frege in the larger philosophical context of Neo-Kantianism.

Those who call Frege a Neo-Kantian do not want to claim that he was a member of a school of professional philosophers which for various reasons since 1875 were called in that way. (cf. Holzhey 1984) The idea is rather that Frege's underlying philosophical assumptions can be spelled out in terms of the philosophy of his day. However, one might wonder whether the idea of underlying or tacit assumptions is really appropriate. Frege's critical assessment of philosophers of his days is quite explicit and well-known: Cohen, Erdmann and Husserl were the target of his devastating criticism. This suggests that Frege's own philosophical views were quite different and even strongly opposed to those of his contemporaries. However – so the argument goes – this impression is misleading, because Frege and his opponents shared a common philosophical background which is recognisably Neo-Kantian. Thus, Gottfried Gabriel has claimed that Frege's "basic epistemological view" ("erkenntnistheoretische Grundposition") is that of Neo-Kantianism. (Gabriel 1986: 84) Gabriel justifies his claim by pointing out the affinities between the views held by Neo-Kantian philosophers and those held by Frege. Thus, Frege and the Neo-Kantians alike made a sharp distinction between the context of discovery and the context of justification; they called attention to the difference between arithmetic and geometry in terms of their foundations, and strongly opposed the empiricism that was in vogue among some of their contemporaries. However, these points of contact show only that Frege was addressing the very same issues as the Neo-Kantian philosophers, and that he came up with answers comparable with theirs. What these points of contact do not show is whether Frege and the Neo-Kantians arrived at their conclusions in anything like the same way. I believe we cannot appreciate the distinctive features of Frege's thoughts, if we are content only to review and catalogue his conclusions, without also trying to understand how Frege was led to them. In other words, we must investigate his arguments. These arguments account for the peculiarity of Frege's thought and distinguish it from Neo-Kantian philosophy. Moreover, they account for Frege's special significance for the philosophy of this century, which Neo-Kantianism does not seem to have.

I will consider the issue of psychologism in logic as an example. Neo-Kantian philosophers were as strongly opposed to psychologism as Frege, who was convinced that it was "the labyrinth of philosophy". (Frege 1893: XIVn.; Frege 1964: 12n.) I will examine three different views about psychologism in logic or epistemology stated by leading Neo-Kantian philosophers and go on to consider Frege's views in the 'Foundations of Arithmetic'.

In their criticism of psychologism Neo-Kantian philosophers were not only concerned with logic and its proper role, but with the task of epistemology as well. Logic and epistemology were not taken to be different disciplines, and the objections raised against the attempt to psychologize logic brought into focus quite general epistemological issues. In a paper of 1882 entitled 'Was ist Philosophie?', Windelband tries to establish the claim that philosophy is the "theory of science". (Windelband 1882: 22) Such a theory is not a "genetic explanatory science of scientific thought" (Windelband 1882: 22) to be found in psychology and in a theory of cultural history, because we have to distinguish between what is taken to be true by the scientific community on the one hand and what ought to be recognized as true on the other. (cf. Windelband 1882: 23) According to Windelband, we want to know why scientific knowledge has a value which extends beyond its genesis. Like Frege, Windelband points out that a causal genetic explanation of our beliefs can be given not only for our true beliefs, but for our false beliefs as well. (cf. Windelband 1882: 24) Psychology explains the origins of our beliefs, while philosophy is concerned with its truth values (cf. Windelband 1882, 27). This way of describing the difference between philosophy and psychology leads to a quite general and fundamental distinction between "judgment and assessment" ('Urteil und Beurteilung'). (cf. Windelband 1882: 29ff.) Judgments express the connection between the contents of representations, while assessments are concerned with the evaluation of what is represented. There are different kinds of assessments depending on the point of view of the evaluation; I confine myself to evaluations of true and false. Windelband claims that philosophy is concerned with evaluations or assessments more precise: about the "absolute validity" of these assessments. What is the problem?

We have beliefs, and we just can't help it. Believing something involves an assessment that one's representations of the matter are true or false – so claims Windelband. This claim cannot be relativized to persons, but is supposed to hold for everybody. (cf. Windelband 1882: 37) Windelband points out that it does not matter whether this claim can be validated or not; what matters, is that "the evaluation of our representations from the point of view of truth presupposes an absolute measure which is valid for all people." (Windelband 1882: 37) This validity is not "a factual one, but an ideal one ... , something which ought to be the case." (Windelband 1882: 42)

The normative feature inherent in all assessments is, according to Windelband, a basic feature of our consciousness, "Normalbewußtsein", as he puts it, and which he distinguishes from our empirical consciousness. (Windelband 1882: 44) While psychology is concerned with empirical consciousness, (cf. Windelband 1882: 53) philosophy is concerned with the normative features of our evaluations. Again, this account is suggestive of Frege's distinction between logical laws as being prescriptive and psychological laws as being descriptive laws of our thinking. However, I think such a comparison is rather misleading, because it conceals a more basic dissimilarity. Nevermind the greater clarity and precision of Frege's writing compared with the dull and tedious prose of Windelband. The issue is rather the general policy followed by them in their attempts to demarcate the proper place of psychology: while Windelband tries to show that psychological descriptions and explanations make a contribution to an analysis of what he calls "consciousness" without, however, exhausting the matter, Frege argues that, with regard to logic and epistemology, psychological considerations are completely irrelevant, leading to confusions and mistakes. While Windelband claims that there is nothing wrong with psychology, as long as it is confined to its proper realm, Frege wants to point out that it is fundamentally misguided.

Rickert, in his paper 'Zwei Wege der Erkenntnistheorie', published in 1909, distinguishes between thinking and cognition ("Erkenntnis"): "By thinking we mean any mental event which can be true or false, and cognition is distinguished from thinking in general by being true thinking ("wahres Denken")." (Rickert 1909: 169) Epistemology is supposed to be the science of thinking so far as it is true. Rickert does not clarify the notion of 'true thinking': he claims that "for being true the activity of thinking has to be something more than a mental process and, therefore, to contain something that is not just merely thinking". (Rickert 1909: 170) The idea of a process containing something or other does not seem to be very helpful nor does it become clear what "being more than a mental process" is supposed to be. Making a quick run is, after all, an activity of running, although it is not merely running. However, Rickert is convinced that the distinction between thinking and true thinking is quite sufficient for drawing a "sharp" distinction between epistemology and empirical psychology: "The truth as being the reason for calling thinking cognition is not a mental fact; it is nothing at all which can be explored with regard to its being by psychology." (Rickert 1909: 172) According to Rickert, treating epistemology as a kind of empirical psychology leads to the decomposition of the concept of cognition and to the rejection that there is any true thinking at all. His point seems to be that, although cognition or true thinking is a kind of thinking and, therefore, a mental fact, its being true cannot be explained by reference to our mental states. There is no way of distinguishing between true thinking and false thinking by means of psychology.

Cohen attempts in the book 'Logik der reinen Erkenntnis', published in 1902, to draw a boundary between logic and psychology by sticking with the distinction between thinking and representation. (cf. Cohen 1902: 19) The notion of thinking has to be taken in a special way: a theory of thinking is nothing less than a theory of cognition. (cf. Cohen 1902: 12) While Rickert appeals to the notion of truth, Cohen sticks with some kind of unity of cognition: Although "thinking as a cognitive process" – "Vorgang des Erkennens" – is a process of consciousness" and, therefore, within the reach of psychology, it is "the unity of the content of cognition" which cannot be explained in psychological terms. (Cohen 1902: 4) If one considers this unity as a constitutive feature of cognition itself, a psychological theory of our mental states cannot be a complete and adequate account of thinking as cognition. The contrast between thinking and representation outlined by Cohen has to be considered in the following way: thinking as cognition has a psychological aspect, but a psychological theory cannot account for what is peculiar to this kind of thinking. Thus, the contrast mentioned amounts to nothing more than to the rejection that they are identical. (cf. Cohen 1902: 21) Logic cannot be reduced to psychology, because "the creative power of thinking revealed by logic" (Cohen 1902: 29) is beyond the scope of a psychological theory of mental states and events.

Having summarized these various arguments against psychologism by three leading Neo-Kantian philosophers, one can discern at least three assumptions shared by them all. Firstly, thinking and cognition can certainly be characterized in psychological terms, i.e. in terms of representations or mental processes. But, secondly, psychological considerations do not exhaust everything there is to say about thinking or cognition. There has to be some other consideration as well. The distinction between logic or epistemology on the one hand and psychology on the other hand tends to be a distinction between different aspects of cognition. And, thirdly, there is no difference between what is accessible by thinking and what can be given by representations, although there is a sharp distinction between the content of our thinking or representations and the peculiar stance assumed by thinking called "evaluation" (Windelband), "accepting or rejecting" (Rickert) or "the activity of pure thinking". (Cohen)

Frege's anti-psychologism can be described in many ways: He rejects the idea that the logical laws are descriptive psychological laws of thinking. He opposes himself to the conflation of being true and of taking something to be true. He sticks with the distinction between causes which merely give rise to judgments and the reasons, which justify judgments, and he clearly distinguishes between the meaning of an expression and the representations associated with it. Thus, psychologism is a rather diffuse matter, and some of the targets of Frege's criticism where the same as those of some of the Neo-Kantian philosophers of his day. However, there is one salient feature of Frege's arguments, and this is the very kernel of his criticism to which nothing corresponds in Neo-Kantianism, and it is this feature which defines the nature of Frege's philosophical thought. What I have in mind are the first two principles of the 'Foundations', or to be more precise: the connection between them. The first principle requires "always to separate sharply the psychological from the logical, the subjective from the objective", while the second principle states that one has to ask for the meaning of the words only in the context of a proposition and not in isolation. (Frege 1884: X)

Frege calls attention to the connection between the two principles in the following way: "If the second principle" – that is the famous context-principle – "is not observed, one is almost forced to take as the meaning of words mental pictures or acts of the individual minds, and so to offend against the first principle as well." (Frege 1884: X) If to violate the second principle is to offend against the first, then to accept the first is to accept the second. Why is there any connection between separating the psychological from the logical and asking for the meaning of a word only in the context of a proposition? The connection Frege has in mind can be clarified by spelling out what it is to consider a word in isolation. According to him, one is inclined to regard the representations associated with the word as its meaning. What is wrong with that? Frege claims several times that we are not able to think without representations (cf. Frege 1884: 71; Frege 1969: 6, 115; Frege 1979: 5, 105), but he also claims that these representations do not matter at all for what we are thinking about. Thus, although our thinking is accompanied by representations, the content of our thinking does not need to fit the content of our representations. Frege concludes that the fact that we can not form any representation to associate with a word is no reason at all for denying it a meaning. In other words: that a word has a meaning does not imply that there is any representation of it. For fixing the meaning we do not need to rely on our representations, and often we cannot.

However, this is only a negative claim which has to be supplemented by a positive account, given by the context-principle. The real point of this procedure can be clarified by asking why we do not have to care about representations at all. Frege hints at an answer to our question by raising another: "How, then, are numbers to be given to us, if we cannot have any representations or intuitions of them?" (Frege 1884: 73) His answer to that question is the following: "Since it is only in the context of a proposition that words have any meaning, our problem becomes this: to define the sense of a proposition in which a number word occurs." (Frege 1884: 73) This procedure can be generalized: to consider the sense of a proposition is the only way of providing epistemic access to whatever can be grasped without relying upon representations, i.e. to whatever can be grasped only by thinking. Thus, the context-principle is a means of having access to whatever can be thought about. It is the intimate connection between thinking and using sentences which leads Frege to the view "that the proper means of expression for a thought is a sentence. But a sentence is hardly an appropriate vehicle for conveying a representation". (Frege 1969: 143; Frege 1979: 131) Thus, the distinction drawn by the first principle – namely to separate sharply between the objective and the subjective – has to be explained in terms of the difference between thought and representation, and the connection between the first and the second principle is based upon the view that thoughts can only be expressed by sentences. To ask for the meaning of a word in the context of a sentence is to ask for its meaning as a "logical element in the judgment" (Frege 1884: 71) and there is no other way of making that request if the meaning of a word is supposed to play the role of a constituent of a thought.

The fundamental objection raised by Frege against psychologism is that thoughts and representations are completely different. Given the further assumption that thoughts can only be expressed by sentences we get to Frege's idea of the objective as something that is "conceptual, judgeable, what can be expressed by words". (Frege 1884: 35) This, in turn, leads to the idea that representations are non-conceptual and cannot be conveyed by linguistic means. The salient feature of Frege's idea is that representations are essentially subjective: different persons cannot have the same representations, and one can know only one's own representations. Representations cannot, therefore, be objective in the sense of being the same for different persons (cf. Frege 1884: 37), and they are private. If the distinction between thought and representation is explained in Frege's terms of what is objective and what is subjective, psychologism drifts into idealism and solipsism. (cf. Frege 1893: XIX; Frege 1964: 17) This is a very radical conclusion, which, as far as I know, none of the Neo-Kantian philosophers argued for in their criticism of psychology. However, it is not Frege's radical conclusion which distinguishes his criticism of psychologism from the objections raised by the Neo-Kantians. It is rather the starting point of Frege's reasoning, lying in the connection between the first and the second principle, which shows what is peculiar to his position.

Frege's starting point can be spelled out as two claims: firstly, there is something logical or objective which can be grasped only by thinking, and secondly, the only way to determine what is thought of is to consider propositions. As Frege puts it: "The expression in language for a thought is a proposition." (Frege 1969: 189; Frege 1979: 174) The distinction between logic and psychology is cashed out in terms of thinking and having representations. The same approach is to be found among Neo-Kantian philosophers. What is peculiar to Frege is the idea that the distinction between thinking and having representations has to be explained as a difference in content as well as a difference in the way they are expressed. It is this move that leads to the contrast between what has to be expressed by sentences and is intersubjectively accessible on the one hand and what is subjective and private on the other hand. Given this contrast, to consider thoughts is to consider the propositions expressing them, which in turn requires a semantic analysis of language. Given the difference between thinking and having representations as a difference in content, the psychological approach can't be a way of taking account of what is accessible by thinking. While Neo-Kantian philosophers always sustained the traditional view that thinking has something to do with representations, but cannot be reduced to them, Frege broke completely with this tradition by separating sharply between thought and representation; and by connecting thinking with the use of sentences, he provided a new foundation for the philosophical analysis of thought and cognition. The project of a semantic analysis of language did not occur to the Neo-Kantian philosophers, because they did not explore the connection between thinking and the use of sentences. Thus, they missed what is central to Frege's anti-psychologism: to distinguish between thought and representation by means of the contrast between what is objective and intersubjectively accessible by the use of a language on the one hand and what is subjective and private on the other hand. Frege's analysis of thinking and cognition converges on a semantic account of sentences. This is the program defined by the connection between the first and the second principle of the 'Foundations'. There is nothing comparable in the Neo-Kantianism of his day; and to call him a Neo-Kantian is to miss what is the very centre of his philosophical project.

The question raised by the title of my paper is concerned with a classification of Frege's philosophical views in terms of systematic philosophy and the history of philosophy. If I am right they are both wrong, but obviously not for the same reasons. However, there is a comparable mistake in both current approaches to Frege.

To call him a Platonist is to place him in the context of a systematic conception of philosophy which takes metaphysics or ontology as its starting point. But there is no such conception to be found in Frege. By denying that he is a Platonist I don't want to suggest that he is an Idealist. The currently much favoured alternatives 'Platonism vs. Idealism' or 'Realism vs. Anti-realism' don't fit Frege, because he wasn't engaged in this kind of abstract philosophical discourse, but rather in spelling out what he considered to be the necessary condition of perspicuousness in philosophical reasonings concerning logic. (cf. Frege 1893: XII; Frege 1964: 9) And it is a very dubious assumption to take for granted that all philosophical reasoning has to be either realist or anti-realist, platonist or idealist. To make the same point in other words: there is a kind of low-level philosophical reasoning which aims at clarification and solving problems without addressing the thick and abstract metaphysical issues. Frege's philosophical contributions are just of this kind.

To call Frege a Neo-Kantian is to place him in a context of the history of philosophy, – of the philosophy of his day. I have argued that this attempt fails, because it doesn't catch what is really peculiar to him. What distinguishes his philosophical reasoning from the views of his contemporary philosophers gets lost in this way; it cannot be identified – neither in terms of the assumptions they shared nor in terms of the conclusions they wanted to draw. It is rather the network of arguments developed by Frege that defines what is peculiar to his philosophical reasoning. Thus, the two labels mentioned in the title of my paper don't fit him, because they are labels which subsume his philosophical reasoning under categories wellknown from philosophy and its history, and thereby, leave out what is really new in his philosophical thought and quite essential to it.

References

Bernays, P. 1978. Über den Platonismus in der Mathematik. Translated into German by P. Bernath. *Das Universalien-Problem (=Wege der Forschung* Vol. 83), ed. W. Stegmüller, 64-83. Darmstadt: Wissenschaftliche Buchgesellschaft. (original publication in French: 1935. Sur le platonisme dans les mathématiques. *L'Enseignement mathématique* 34: 52-69.)

Burge, T. 1992. Frege on Knowing the Third Realm. *Frege: Importance and Legacy.* ed. M. Schirn, 347-68. Berlin, New York: de Gruyter 1996.

Carl, W. 1994. *Frege's Theory of Sense and Reference: Its Origins and Scope.* Cambridge: Cambridge University Press.

Cohen, H. 1902. *Logik der reinen Erkenntnis.* Berlin: Cassirer.

Dummett, M. 1981. *The Interpretation of Frege's Philosophy.* Cambridge, Mass.: Harvard University Press.

Frege, G. 1884. *Die Grundlagen der Arithmethik. Eine logisch mathematische Untersuchung über den Begriff der Zahl.* Breslau: Koeber. (reprint: 1961. Hildesheim: G. Olms.)

Frege, G. 1893. *Grundgesetze der Arithmetik. Begriffsschriftlich abgeleitet,* Vol. I. Jena: Pohle. (reprint: 1962. Hildesheim: G. Olms.)

Frege, G. 1918. Logische Untersuchungen. Erster Teil: Der Gedanke. *Kleine Schriften,* G. Frege, ed. I. Angelleli, 342-362. Hildesheim, Zürich, New York: G. Olms [2]1990. (cited above with the page numbers of the original publication 1918/19, in *Beiträge zur Philosophie des deutschen Idealismus* 1: 58-77.)

Frege, G. 1964. *The Basic Laws of Arithmetics. Exposition of the System,* ed. and transl. M. Furth, Berkeley and Los Angeles: University of California Press.

Frege, G. 1969. *Nachgelassene Schriften,* ed. H. Hermes, F. Kambartel und F. Kaulbach. Hamburg: Meiner.

Frege, G. 1977. *Logical Investigations,* ed. P.T. Geach, transl. P.T. Geach and R.H. Stoothoff. Oxford: Blackwell.

Frege, G. 1979. *Posthumous Writings,* ed. H. Hermes, F. Kambartel, and F. Kaulbach, translated by Peter Long and Roger White. Oxford: Blackwell.

Gabriel, G. 1986. Frege als Neukantianer. *Kant-Studien* 77: 84-101.

Holzhey, H. 1984. Neukantianismus. *Historisches Wörterbuch der Philosophie,* eds. J. Ritter and K. Gründer, col. 747-754.

Reck, E. 1997. Frege's Influence on Wittgenstein: Reversing Metaphysics via the Context Principle. *Early Analytic Philosophy. Frege, Russell, Wittgenstein. Essays in Honor of Leonard Linsky.* ed. W. Tait, 123-185. Chicago and La Salle, Ill.: Open Court.

Rickert, H. 1909. Zwei Wege der Erkenntnistheorie. Transscendentalpsychologie und Transscendentallogik. *Kant-Studien* 14:169-228.

Ricketts, T. 1986. Objectivity and Objecthood: Frege's Metaphysics of Judgment. *Frege Synthesized.* eds. L. Haaparanta and J. Hintikka, 65-95. Dordrecht: D. Reidel.

Windelband, W. 1882. Was ist Philosophie? *Präludien. Aufsätze und Reden zur Einführung in die Philosophie,* W. Windelband, Vol. I, 1-54. Tübingen: Mohr [4]1911.

2

Frege, Lotze, and the Continental Roots of Early Analytic Philosophy

GOTTFRIED GABRIEL

The title of my essay implies the thesis that at least *early* analytic philosophy has its roots in the tradition of continental philosophy, especially in the philosophy of Hermann Lotze. Indeed this is the thesis I want to argue for. The thesis itself is not really new. As far as Frege is concerned it has been presented before by Hans Sluga in various papers as well as in his book on Frege (Sluga 1980). This book was the starting point of a controversy between Sluga and Michael Dummett about a crucial point of understanding Frege (Dummett 1981). I do not want to go into the details but, in developing my own position, it might be helpful to say a few words about this controversy. I agree with Dummett that some of Sluga's interpretations of Frege are not correct and that Sluga was misled by such interpretations in his evaluation of Frege as a philosopher. On the other hand I agree with Sluga's general picture of Frege's philosophical background. I do not accept all of the details, but I think his thesis that Frege's efforts are part of the Neo-Kantian tradition is correct. Neo-Kantianism is to be understood as an alternative to German speculation in the tradition of Hegel, on the one hand, and to British empiricism in the tradition of Hume and Mill, on the other hand. Hermann Lotze, Frege's teacher at the University of Göttingen, can be regarded as the founder of Neo-Kantianism.

Agreeing with Sluga on these points does not imply accepting his bold assertion that Frege turns out to be a transcendental idealist. We should realize that to be a Neo-Kantian does not mean to be a Kantian in all respects. The Neo-Kantians worked in the spirit of Kant's philosophy, but they very often, and sometimes fundamentally, disagreed with the letter of his works. For example, most of them did not accept the thing in itself. What most of the Neo-Kantians shared with Kant was his apriorism. This apriorism links them together in their fight against every kind of naturalism with respect to the foundation of science (including logic, ethics and aesthetics). But neither was it on the question of idealism or realism where they agreed with one another. So it seems to me that Dummett's and Sluga's controversy about whether Frege was a realist or a transcendental idealist is not posed very well. Concerning Frege's philosophical background other questions are much more central. This becomes clearer when we compare Frege with the Neo-Kantians *in detail*. And it is *here* where one can find a deficiency in Sluga's argument: Although his thesis that Frege belongs to the Neo-Kantian tradition seems to be correct, he does not really *show* that Frege was a Neo-Kantian. His thesis might be true but he didn't prove it. The evidence he presents is too thin. In so far as this is the case we have to concede to critics (like Dummett) that they are right not to be convinced.

What I want to do is to make Sluga's thesis more defensible, and to present some more historical evidence for it. Mainly, I will compare some of Frege's views with those of the two Neo-Kantians Otto Liebmann (1840-1912) and Wilhelm Windelband (1848-1915). What seems to me important here is the fact that both were influenced by Hermann Lotze, especially Windelband, who wrote his doctoral thesis at the University of Göttingen under Lotze 1870, shortly before Frege moved from Jena to Göttingen. Lotze was indeed a central figure in the whole intellectual scene before the unfortunate separation of continental and analytic philosophy. Especially the University of Jena became a center of Lotze-Studies (cf. Kreiser 1984, 23). Therefore, to understand Frege and the roots of analytic philosophy we have to go back to this scene. It will turn out that Lotze's influence was not restricted to Germany, indirect reactions can even be found in the logical atomism of Russell and Wittgenstein.

1   The Philosophy of Hermann Lotze

It was J. Passmore (1966, 49) who called Lotze the most 'pillaged' philosopher of the 19th century. If we ask about Lotze's importance we have to take into account especially his *Logic* which impressed a whole generation of *academic* philosophers. In this connection we have to realize that though Lotze's *Mikrokosmus* was much more popular because it includes a complete 'Weltanschauung', its influence was restricted to popular philosophy, whereas academic philosophy was much more interested in Lotze's *System of Philosophy* (*System der Philosophie*). This *System* includes as its first part the *Logic*, as its second part the *Metaphysics*. Its third part on ethics, aesthetics, and philosophy of religion did not appear because of Lotze's sudden death in 1881. For more historical and biographical details see Pester (1997).

There is at least one Lotzean concept which unites continental and early analytic philosophy, namely the concept of validity. Of course, the *concept* itself, i.e., the distinction between the genetic point of view of *psychological* explanation and the foundationalist point of view of *logical* validity can already be found in Kant and Herbart and even in Leibniz, but it was Lotze who took up this tradition and established the distinction by introducing the term 'validity' (*Geltung*). He prepared the logical discussion of 19th century philosophy to argue against naturalistic tendencies which reduced thinking to processes of ideas (*Vorstellungsverläufe*). In doing so Lotze provided later philosophers like Frege, Windelband and Husserl with anti-psychologist arguments. On the other hand we have to keep in mind that anti-psychologism is not opposed to psychology. Lotze belongs to the classic authors of psychology as well, but he was, at the same time, completely aware of the categorical difference between psychology and logic.

The concept of validity became the leading concept in the logical and epistemological doctrines up to the thirties of our century, until *Lebensphilosophie* and existential hermeneutics succeeded to dominate German philosophy. Although the central role of the concept of validity is not restricted to the German-speaking philosophical world, it is this German tradition about which I mainly want to talk. Concerning logic and epistemology we may divide this tradition into two lines, namely the Neo-Kantian and the phenomenological line. Both lines go back to Lotze. To be more correct, for there are two schools of Neo-Kantianism, it is the so-called south-west German school of Neo-Kantianism which is influenced directly by Lotze: Besides Wilhelm Windelband and Otto Liebmann, there are Heinrich Rickert, Bruno Bauch, Emil Lask and the early Martin Heidegger. The sociologist Max Weber also came into contact with this tradition via Rickert. The members of the so-called Marburg school seem to have been influenced only indirectly. Concerning the phenomenological tradition we have to note that Franz Brentano was in contact with Lotze, and that his disciples Carl Stumpf, who was the teacher of Edmund Husserl, and Anton Marty were students of Lotze too.

The most influential part of Lotze's *Logic* was the epistemology in the third book. This book includes in its second chapter (*The World of Ideas*) Lotze's reconstruction of Plato's theory of ideas in terms of the concept of validity. Let us have a more detailed look at this chapter. Lotze tries to defend Plato against the old Aristotelian accusation that he (Plato) had hypostasized ideas into real existing things. His argument runs as follows:

> While Plato by [...] describing the Ideas, takes security for their independent validity, he has at the same time abundantly provided against the confusion of the validity thus implied with that wholly distinct reality of Existence which could only be ascribed to a durable thing. When he places the home of the Ideas in a super-celestial world, a world of pure intelligence [...], when again more than this he expressly describes them as having no local habitation, such language makes it abundantly clear to any one who understands the mind of Greek Antiquity, that they do *not* belong to what we call the real world. To the Greek that which is not in Space is not at all, and when Plato relegates the Ideas to a home which is not in space, he is not trying to hypostasize that which we call their mere validity into any kind of real existence, but on the contrary he is plainly seeking to guard altogether against any such attempt being made. (Lotze 1980, § 318; references are to numbers of paragraphs.)

We do not have to establish that this is a correct interpretation of Plato. From a logical point of view I myself like it very much, but we have to keep in mind that the non-conceptual, contemplative aspect of intellectual intuition (*intellektuelle Anschauung*) in Plato is neglected by Lotze. Anyway, what this interpretation achieved was the reunion of Platonic and Kantian philosophy in an epistemological position which might be, and in fact was, called 'transcendental Platonism'. I think that the position of Frege and some Neo-Kantians (like Windelband, Rickert and Bauch) can be described exactly in this way. Transcendental Platonism is Platonistic because it accepts contents of thinking (thoughts) which are independent of the individual thinking subjects, and it is transcendental (as opposed to transcendent) because the independence is not thought of as an ontological one of existence, but a logical one of being valid.

To put this idea into the form of a transcendental argument, we may give the following explanation: Logic starts with making a 'distinction of value' between 'truth and untruth' (Lotze 1980, § II). True and untrue, or false, cannot appear as properties of *processes* of thinking, but only of *contents* of thinking. To talk about truth and falsehood necessarily presupposes – as a *conditio sine qua non*, i. e., as a 'condition of possibility' in the Kantian sense – that we have first grasped the same cognitive content and are discussing the same thought. To take this consequence seriously we have to accept that a thought cannot be a psychological item, because such a view would imply that different individual subjects are not able to participate in the same cognitive content or thought.

The independence of thoughts thus means nothing more than stating the following categorical fact: An item which we want to value as true or false, i.e., an item which is meant as the 'bearer' of a truth-value, cannot have individual psychological existence. On the other hand, this does not imply that we have to search for some kind of *existence* different from psychological existence. Such an attempt is out of place, and insisting on such an attempt is a category mistake. Cognitive content does not exist; it is valid (or not valid). To be *valid* does not imply *to be*. To give a short and handy characterization of this position we might explain it by converting the well-known Quinean slogan 'no entity without identity' into the additional slogan 'but identity without entity'. It is a transcendental condition of talking about truth and falsity that the bearer of a truth-value remains identical, but it is not necessary to accept this bearer as an ontological entity. Lotze's conception of validity 'as a form of Reality (*Wirklichkeit*)' presupposes 'the eternally self-identical significance of Ideas', but it does not include the 'Being or Existence (*Sein*)' of these Ideas and their conceptual content (Lotze 1980, § 317). Reality (*Wirklichkeit*) could come in here only either on the level of psychological events or on the level of logical validity. To give a more complete account let us take a look at a famous and often quoted passage:

> For we call a thing Real which is, in contradistinction to another which is not; an event Real which occurs or has occurred, in contradistinction to that which does not occur; a relation Real which obtains, as opposed to one which does not obtain; lastly we call a proposition Really true which holds or is valid as opposed to one of which the validity is still doubtful. (Lotze 1980, § 316)

This quotation implies the following categorical distinctions:

Reality (*Wirklichkeit*)
of things (*Dinge*): they are (or exist)
of events (*Ereignisse*): they happen (or occur)
of relations (*Verhältnisse*): they obtain
of propositions (*Sätze*): they are valid (or hold).

These modes of reality are conceived of as independent from each other; it is not possible to explain one by reducing it to any other. What is missing in this scheme is the 'self-identical' content of propositions themselves. Using Lotze's own terminology, which is not completely coherent here, we might say that he accepts for thoughts as the meanings of propositions the status of *objectivity* (Lotze 1980, § 3), which is simply the negation of subjectivity, namely the independency of these contents from singular subjects which might conceive these contents. The self-identical contents in themselves are objective but not real. They can get reality either in psychological realization as events or in being 'really true', i.e. valid.

It should be clear that Lotze here prepared the categorical basis for the separation of logical investigations from psychological ones. The self-identical content of propositions later appeared for instance as *Gedanke* (Frege), *Sinngebilde* (Rickert), *Objektiv* (Meinong), *ideal identischer Inhalt*

(Husserl) or *logischer Inhalt* (Heidegger). Concerning Lotze himself, we have to add that he was not completely clear about the fact that the content has to be accepted as the same even if it is not valid or true. 'The conception of Validity', Lotze explains, 'at once excludes the substance of the valid assertion from the reality of actual being and implies its independence of human thought' (Lotze 1980, § 316). The English translation here is a little bit artificial. The expression 'the substance of the valid assertion' corresponds to nothing else but 'valid content *(geltender Inhalt)*' in the German original. What is problematic here is the implicit restriction to *valid* assertions or contents, for the self-identity of the content does not depend on its validity. A content which is not valid has to be the same too; otherwise we could not apply the categorical predicate 'invalidity' to it. The transcendental condition of self-identity holds not only for valid but also for invalid contents. This point was made clear by Frege in his article 'On Negation', as well as in the further development of logical value-theory.

This development may be divided into two strands. First there is the south-west German school of Neo-Kantianism which extended Lotze's conception of validity *(Geltung)* by building on its basis a comprehensive value-theory that included the normative disciplines of logic, ethics and aesthetics with their differentiation in regions of values. Considered from a historical point of view, this universal value-theory was a philosophical response to Nietzsche's nihilistic *Umsturz der Werte*. Neo-Kantianism tried to substitute Nietzsche's will to power *(Wille zur Macht)* by a Kantian will to value *(Wille zum Wert)*. Windelband used the phrase 'will to truth *(Wille zur Wahrheit)*'. In contemporary philosophy we find a revival of this debate in J. Habermas' defense of a discourse-theoretical variant of the Neo-Kantian value-theoretical program against Nietzschean Postmodernism. Habermas' distinction between different claims of validity *(Geltungsansprüche)* goes back to Neo-Kantian concept, via the sociologist Max Weber.

Besides this Neo-Kantian development of Lotzean ideas we have already mentioned the phenomenological tradition, which, at least in its beginning, was mainly concerned with logical (and ontological) questions. It was the phenomenologist Husserl who, following Fregean insights, made the Lotzean distinction between objective (but not real) contents of thought and real events of thought the starting point of his logical investigations. The very early Heidegger, who was a disciple of both Husserl and the Neo-Kantian Rickert, formulated this starting point in a way which shows very clearly the decisive influence of Lotze's distinctions on the antipsychologist program. He wrote in 1912:

> Grundlegend für die Erkenntnis der Widersinnigkeit und theoretischen Unfruchtbarkeit des Psychologismus bleibt die Unterscheidung von psychischem Akt und logischem Inhalt, von realem in der Zeit verlaufenden

Denkgeschehen und dem idealen außerzeitlichen identischen Sinn, kurz die Unterscheidung dessen, was 'ist', von dem, was 'gilt'. Dieser reine, in sich Bestand habende Sinn ist Gegenstand der Logik, und damit wird ihr von Anfang an der Charakter einer empirischen Disziplin genommen. (Heidegger 1978, 22).

I think this statement is very interesting because Heidegger, who at that time called Lotze's *Logic* the 'fundamental book (*Grundbuch*)' of modern logic (Heidegger 1978, 23, footnote 9), later became (under the influence of the *Lebensphilosophie*) the most radical critic of his own tradition. When we read in *Sein und Zeit* his polemics against the value-theory of his time, which culminates in calling 'validity' a 'word-idol (*Wortgötze*)' (Heidegger 1979, 155-56), we should remember Heidegger's beginnings. It seems to me that Lotze's platonistic departure from a restriction to existing things was at least one necessary step into the direction of Heidegger's critique of the ontology of *Vorhandenheit*. This would explain why even in later years he recommended Lotze's *Logic* to beginners in philosophy. An astonished looking student, G. Picht, was informed by Heidegger that beginners should realize what hard work his (Heidegger's) own thinking had had to go through (Picht 1977, 201). If we take this statement by Heidegger seriously, it seems to imply a general advice: Before reading Heidegger first study Lotze's *Logic* or, at least, do not read Heidegger without studying Lotze! Now I want to show that for a better understanding of Frege we should read Lotze at least *after* studying Frege.

2   Frege and the Neo-Kantians

As we have already seen, Lotze used the word 'logic' in the broader sense of the 19th century, thus as including epistemology. To show how Lotze's conception of validity has influenced logic and epistemology of continental *and* analytic philosophy, we should now consider some aspects which both Neo-Kantians and Frege took over from Lotze. I will start with Otto Liebmann, the originator of the Neo-Kantian slogan 'back to Kant'.

Liebmann was a colleague of Frege's at the University of Jena from 1882 to 1911. In 1900 Frege was involved in a discussion and correspondence with the son of Otto Liebmann, Heinrich Liebmann (later professor of mathematics at the University of Heidelberg), about Hilbert's *Grundlagen der Geometrie*. My comparison of Frege and Otto Liebmann concerns Frege's *Grundlagen der Arithmetik* and Liebmann's *Zur Analysis der Wirklichkeit*.

The fact that Frege refers to Kant directly in *Grundlagen* might be the reason why it has been overlooked that Frege's views are similar to those of Liebmann. And indeed Frege does not even mention his elder contemporary, i. e., Liebmann's name appears nowhere in Frege's works. (Hermann Lotze and Wilhelm Windelband met the same fate.) It might be interesting here to mention that Frege had indeed read Liebmann's *Analysis der Wirklichkeit*. Frege borrowed Liebmann's work from the Jena University library when he was writing his *Grundlagen* (Kreiser 1984, 25-26). This fact should serve to remind us that the absence of names does not imply the absence of influence or of agreement. Now let's get into the texts of Liebmann and Frege.

First of all, we find agreement between them on the conception of the apriori. Against empiricism and its overvaluation of induction, Liebmann (1900, 208) maintains that induction is impossible without 'general fundamental truths' (*allgemeingültige Fundamentalwahrheiten*). In the same vein, Frege declares in his *Grundlagen*:

> If we recognize the existence of general truths at all, we must also admit the existence of such primitive laws, since from mere individual facts nothing follows, unless it be on the strength of law. Induction itself depends on the general proposition that the inductive method can establish the truth of a law, or at least some probability for it. If we deny this, induction becomes nothing more than a psychological phenomenon, a procedure which induces men to believe in the truth of a proposition, without affording the slightest justification for so believing. (Frege 1953, 4, footnote)

We can find the source of Liebmann's and Frege's view of induction in Lotze's *Logic*:

> It is clear therefore that the attempt to derive the entire body of general knowledge from experience, that is to say from a mere summing up of particular perceptions, breaks down. We have invariably to help ourselves out by assuming at one point or another some one of those self-evident principles, some principle to which when once its content has been thought we at once concede with intuitive confidence that universal validity to which it makes claim. (Lotze 1980, § 330, last section)

The quotation from Frege above refers to the Lotzean distinction between questions of genesis (*Genese*) and questions of validity (*Geltung*). Epistemology is not concerned with the genetic-psychological question of how it is that we accept some propositions as true. Rather epistemology deals with the question of the validity of these propositions, that is, with the question of the justification of a true proposition. Like Kant, Lotze and the Neo-Kantians conceded that from a genetic point of view all knowledge might have its origin in experience. But they deny that this shows that all knowledge is empirical. When we seek to justify the foundation of knowledge we have to accept propositions which are non-empirical apriori truths. In this sense Frege points out in *Grundlagen*:

> By this I do not mean in the least to deny that without sense impressions we should be as stupid as stones, and should know nothing either of numbers or of anything else; but this psychological proposition is not of the slightest concern to us here. Because of the ever-present danger of confus-

ing two fundamentally different questions, I make this point once more. (Frege 1953, 115, footnote)

It is the same confusion which Liebmann addresses by distinguishing psychological laws from laws of knowledge (*Erkenntnisgesetze*). For him the psychological laws are natural laws of the changing content of the mind, whereas the laws of knowledge are norms which must be followed if we want to reach the truth (Liebmann 1900, 251-52).

So far we have considered the general basic consensus between Frege and the Neo-Kantians in the tradition of Hermann Lotze. A more specific agreement between Liebmann and Frege emerges when we look at their views about mathematics. Here they both disagree with Kant in a significant respect: the status of arithmetic in relation to geometry. As is well known, Frege agrees with Kant's view that geometry is an apriori synthetic science. Frege's reason is that insight into the validity of the geometrical axioms is impossible without intuition. But unlike Kant, Frege wants to demonstrate in his *Grundlagen* that arithmetic is a branch of logic and therefore an *analytic* apriori science. Frege tries to make this so called 'logicism' of the *Grundlagen* plausible by considering the differences between the domain that is 'governed' by the truths of arithmetic and that governed by the truths of geometry (Frege 1953, § 14). He states that the domain of geometry is (in opposition to the temporally intuitable) 'all that is spatially intuitable' (*das räumlich Anschauliche*). This includes the actual as well as the fictitious. This assignment of domains amounts to a restriction of geometry in relation to arithmetic. Frege argues:

> The truths of arithmetic govern all that is numerable. This is the widest domain of all; for to it belongs not only the actual, not only the intuitable, but everything thinkable. (Frege 1953, 21)

For Frege these considerations were helpful in making the logicist program plausible *before* carrying it out. So he concludes with the suggestive question: 'Should not the laws of number, then, be connected very intimately with the laws of thought?' Now, Frege starts his attempt to draw arithmetic into the domain of non-intuitive conceptual (pure logical) thinking with a short treatment of non-euclidean geometry. Frege states that a non-euclidean space cannot be intuited, but can be thought. Among his arguments is the following: to assume the negation of an axiom of euclidean geometry does *not* involve thought in self-contradiction; whereas assuming the negation of any basic law of arithmetic does. Frege's treatment of non-euclidean geometry seems to be inspired directly by Otto Liebmann who defended non-euclidean geometry from a Kantian (!) point of view. Liebmann distinguishes between 'logical necessity' and 'necessity of intuition'. He says that the negation of an intuitively necessary proposition is not a contradiction, it is merely not intuitable. Pointing out that he agrees with Kant essentially, Liebmann maintains that the axioms of (euclidean) geometry are non-logical necessities that are nevertheless unavoidable for beings with intuitive capacities like ours; in this sense they are apriori intuitions. And because they are apriori *intuitions*, they are subjective. Of course, Kant would not have agreed with this last point.

I think Frege agrees with all points of this reformulation of Kant, even with the last one, namely the view that the euclidean axioms are subjective. This can be seen in Frege's definition of objectivity, which includes independence of intuition (Frege 1953, § 26, last sentence). Dummett (1982) has argued against Sluga that Frege's view of geometry is not really Kantian. In a way, Dummett is right here and Sluga is perhaps too vague. It turns out that Frege was not a Kantian, but a *Neo*-Kantian.

Liebmann's discussion of geometry concludes with some views on the relationship between arithmetic (*Größenlehre*), logic, and geometry which we have already found in Frege's *Grundlagen*. For Liebmann, the 'extension or domain of validity' of arithmetic and logic is broader than that of euclidean geometry. Whereas the latter is valid only for an intelligence with the same type of intuition, arithmetic and logic are valid for all intelligent beings whatever (Liebmann 1900, 254). Consequently, both Frege and Liebmann come to the same judgment about actual and possible beings whose laws of logic and arithmetic (not of geometry) would contradict ours. One would have no choice but to regard them as 'mad (*verrückt*)' (Liebmann 1900, 253; Frege 1962, vol. 1, XVI).

We can conclude our comparison between Liebmann and Frege with an amusing example of an implicit agreement. This agreement consists in some polemic remarks against German physiological materialism (represented, for example, by Vogt, Moleschott, Büchner). From a Neo-Kantian point of view, this position is a good example of confusing the question of validity with questions of genesis as a consequence of confusing the laws of thought with its natural physiological conditions. Liebmann asks polemically: 'What have the protein, potash and phosphorous in the brain-substance [...] got to do with logic?' (Liebmann 1900, 540). And in the 'Introduction' to the *Grundlagen* Frege exclaims ironically: 'Otherwise, in proving Pythagoras' theorem we should be reduced to allowing for the phosphorous content of the human brain.' (Frege 1953, VI). Without mentioning the name, Liebmann and Frege here obviously (obviously at least for their readers in the 19th century) refer to a slogan of Jacob Moleschott, who wrote in his *Der Kreislauf des Lebens*: 'No phosphorous no thought'.

Looking for further circumstantial evidence for Frege's connection to Neo-Kantianism we now come to Windelband. Several of Liebmann's and Frege's Neo-Kantian positions also appear in Windelband's writings. For instance, we can find the distinction between genesis and validity (Windelband 1915, vol. 1, 24) and the view that induction is impossible without non-empirical presuppositions which must, without proof, be acknowledged as general laws (Windelband 1915, vol. 2, 107) or, as Frege puts it in the *Grundlagen*, 'which neither need nor admit of proof (*die selber eines Beweises weder fähig noch bedürftig sind*)' (Frege 1953, § 3). By the way, this formulation is an acknowledged quotation from Lotze (1874, § 200). It goes back to Leibniz and corresponds with the conception of axioms in Aristoteles' *Analytica posteriora*. What is said about general laws holds in particular of the laws of logic which both Windelband and Frege consider to be unprovable presuppositions of *all* thought (*Denken*).

Nevertheless Windelband demands, and Frege develops, an argument for why we must accept the laws of logic. As Windelband and Frege stress, this argument itself cannot be a logical one (i. e., it cannot give a logical reason). Following Windelband's presentation it is a teleological one of the following form: *If* we want to fulfil the purpose of thought, that is, truth, we are forced to accept the laws of logic (Windelband 1915, vol. 2, 109). Frege refers to this kind of transcendental argumentation, which he delegates to epistemology (cf. Gabriel 1996), when he says:

> We are compelled to make judgments by our own nature and by external circumstances; and if we do so, we cannot reject this law – of Identity, for example; we must acknowledge it unless we wish to reduce our thought to confusion and finally renounce all judgment whatever. (Frege 1982, 15)

Though Frege 'neither dispute[s] nor support[s] this view', he in fact accepts it:

> This impossibility of our rejecting the law in question hinders us not at all in supposing beings who do reject it; where it hinders us is in supposing that these beings are right in so doing, it hinders us in having doubts whether we or they are right. At least this is true of myself.

The basis of Windelband's transcendental-teleological argumentation is his theory of values. Windelband is the founder of the value-theoretical *Südwestdeutsche* school of Neo-Kantianism. He used the term 'truth-value' (*Wahrheitswert*) before Frege (Windelband 1915, vol. 1, 32). It should be added that Liebmann (1900, 252-53), too, considers truth as 'value'. Also, once more the trail goes back to Lotze who speaks of the 'value-difference' (*Wertunterschied*) between truth and untruth (Lotze 1874, 4). Frege was not concerned with all of the values value-theory treats, but only with the value 'true'. Yet, in the opening passage of 'Der Gedanke' he refers to the same triad of values as Windelband: 'Just as the word 'beautiful' points the way for aesthetics and 'good' for ethics, so does 'true' for logic.' Moreover, Frege states an 'affinity' of logic with ethics (Frege 1979, 4) and thus follows the Windelbandian connection of the teleological and the value-theoretical aspects of truth: 'Like ethics, logic can also be called a normative science. How must I think in order to reach the goal, truth?' (Frege 1979, 128).

Seen against the background of the Neo-Kantian value-theoretical tradition, even Frege's problematic connection between truth-value and *Bedeutung*, that the *Bedeutung* of a sentence is its truth-value, becomes more plausible (Gabriel 1984). Finally let us have a look at the indirect reception of Lotze's philosophy in logical atomism (Russell, Wittgenstein).

3 Monism, Logical Atomism, and the Fregean Context-Principle

So far we have considered the influence of Lotze's *Logic*. Lotze's *Metaphysics* was influential in some respects too, but more in the English Neo-Hegelian tradition than in the German Neo-Kantian tradition. To give some hints concerning the British reception of Lotze's philosophy, we have to note that the English translations of Lotze's *Logic* and *Metaphysics* were prepared by the Neo-Hegelians, especially by B. Bosanquet, who was the editor of both books (the translation was initiated by T. H. Green). The Neo-Hegelians mainly agreed with Lotze on his ontological holism which consists of the thesis that the being of things (*das Sein der Dinge*) means standing-in-relation (*in Beziehung stehen*). They took this conception as the basis of their holistic monism; compare for instance Bradley's view that 'reality is not made up of separate objects with relations among them' (Hylton 1990, 54).

It is interesting and amusing to look at the reception of this holistic thesis in British philosophy. Holism was criticized as a result of Hegelian monistic idealism by Bertrand Russell from a logical atomistic point of view, or, to put it the other way round, Russell tried to overcome the Hegelianism of his own time by means of logical atomistic arguments against holistic implications of Hegelianism. Following the *modus tollens*, a theory which implies a wrong thesis is itself wrong. As Russell declares in *The Philosophy of Logical Atomism*: 'The logic which I shall advocate is atomistic, as opposed to the monistic logic of the people who more or less follow Hegel.' (Russell 1972, 32). Compare also later his emphasis concerning his logic as opposed to monistic logic:

> The acquaintance with the simpler is presupposed in the understanding of the more complex, but the logic that I should wish to combat maintains that in order thoroughly to know any one thing, you must know all its relations and all its qualities, all the propositions in fact in which that thing is mentioned; and you deduce of course from that that the world is an interdependent whole. It is on a basis of that sort that the logic of monism develops. (Russell 1972, 59)

Although Russell is arguing here against the Hegelianism of his time, the position described is, in some respects, similar to that of Lotze who, as a disciple of C. H. Weiße, was in contact with Hegelianism. The irony is now that analytic philosophy, following the Anti-Hegelian tradition, which iden-tifies the birth of analytic philosophy with Russell's break with Hegelianism, had to rediscover holism via the Fregean context-principle, 'nach der Bedeutung der Wörter muss im Satzzusammenhange, nicht in ihrer Vereinzelung gefragt werden' (Frege 1986, 10). The context-principle appears as a semantic version of a metaphysical Hegelian principle which Frege took over from his teacher Lotze, while restricting it to propositions. Frege did not defend a holism outside of propositions, that is, he did not hold a coherence theory of truth.

It is the same in the case of Wittgenstein (in the *Tractatus*). Here the formulation of the context-principle is the following: 'Only propositions have sense; only in the nexus of a proposition does a name have meaning.' (Tractatus 3.3). In Wittgenstein's ontological way of speaking an object can occur only within a state of affairs and cannot exist on its own (Tractatus 2.0121). The independence of things is only a relative one:

> Things are independent in so far as they occur in all possible situations, but this form of independence is a form of connexion with states of af-fairs, a form of dependence. (It is impossible for words to appear in two different rôles: by themselves, and in propositions.) (Tractatus 2.0122)

As a consequence Wittgenstein acknowledges that objects do have in-ternal properties and that these properties are essential ones: 'If I am to know an object, though I need not know its external properties, I must know all its internal properties.' (Tractatus 2.01231).

Wittgenstein does not go as far as Bradley and Lotze. For Lotze (1872, 483) the possibility of understanding the world-process (*Weltlauf*) is grounded in thorough-going (*durchgängigen*) relations which connect all objects with one another (*welche alle Dinge miteinander verknüpfen*). Witt-genstein does not defend the holistic chain of all beings, but he accepts the chain of beings *inside* a state of affairs: 'In a state of affairs objects fit into one another like the links of a chain.' (Tractatus 2.02). So Wittgenstein's holistic internalism is restricted to states of affairs and thus to elementary propositions. But we have to realize that his logical atomism only works on the higher level of complex propositions.

Wittgenstein's view that things have only a relative independency ap-pears almost in the same formulation already in Lotze's writings. This be-comes quite clear if we compare the German originals:

> Das Ding ist selbständig, insofern es in allen möglichen Sachlagen vor-kommen kann, aber diese Form der Selbständigkeit ist eine Form des Zu-sammenhangs mit dem Sachverhalt, eine Form der Unselbständigkeit. (Es ist unmöglich, daß Worte in zwei verschiedenen Weisen auftreten, allein und im Satz.) (Tractatus 2.0122)

Allerdings müssen die Dinge sein, um sich aufeinander beziehen zu kön-
nen; aber dies noch beziehungslos gedachte Sein, das wir uns als Grund
der Möglichkeit des bezogenen vorstellen, ist nicht eine für sich vorkom-
mende Wirklichkeit, aus der die Dinge in gegenseitige Beziehungen tre-
ten, und in welche sie sich aus allen Beziehungen zurückziehen könnten;
vielmehr besteht es nur latent in den Formen des bezogenen Seins, unab-
trennbar von diesen [...]. (Lotze 1872, 483-84, cf. 473: compare Lotze
1884, §§ 13-14)

If we take into account the reception of ideas, we can see that even
Wittgenstein's use of the context-principle is indirectly connected with
Hegel-Lotzean holism. Against this background it is less astonishing to find
common views between English Neo-Hegelians and Frege (Manser 1984,
307-8). Both learned from Lotze or at least from the widespread discussion
about Lotze's philosophy. In the case of the context-principle we have a
good example of how it can happen that historical ignorance forces one to
discover old ideas in a new way. At least we see that in the *history* of ideas
holism might be an adequate approach: everything seems to be connected
with everything, even such things as continental and analytic philosophy.*

References

Dummett, M. 1981. *The Interpretation of Frege's Philosophy*. Cambridge, Mass.:
Harvard University Press.

Dummett, M. 1982. Frege and Kant on Geometry. *Inquiry* 25: 233-254.

Frege, G. 1953. *The Foundations of Arithmetic*, ed. J. L. Austin. Oxford: B. Blackwell.

Frege, G. 1962. *Grundgesetze der Arithmetik*, I-II. Darmstadt: Wissenschaftliche
Buchgesellschaft.

Frege, G. 1979. *Posthumous Writings*, ed. H. Hermes/F. Kambartel/F. Kaulbach,
transl. P. Long/R. White. Oxford: B. Blackwell.

Frege, G. 1982. *The Basic Laws of Arithmetic*, ed. M. Furth. Berkeley: University of
California Press.

Frege, G. 1986. *Die Grundlagen der Arithmetik*. Centenarausgabe, ed. C. Thiel.
Hamburg: F. Meiner.

Gabriel, G. 1984. Fregean Connection: *Bedeutung*, Value and Truth-Value. In C.
Wright, ed. *Frege. Tradition & Influence*. Oxford: B. Blackwell, pp. 188-193.

Gabriel, G. 1996. Frege's 'Epistemology in Disguise'. In M. Schirn, ed. *Frege:
Importance and Legacy*. Berlin/New York: W. de Gruyter, pp. 330-346.

Heidegger, M. 1978. *Frühe Schriften* (= Gesamtausgabe, vol. 1). Franfurt a. M.:
Klostermann.

Heidegger, M. 1979. *Sein und Zeit*, 15th ed. Tübingen: Max Niemeyer.

---

* I am grateful to Erich H. Reck for correcting my English.

Hylton, P. 1990. *Russell, Idealism, and the Emergence of Analytic Philosophy*. Oxford: Clarendon Press.

Kreiser, L. 1984. G. Frege *Die Grundlagen der Arithmetik* – Werk und Geschichte. In G. Wechsung, ed. *Frege Conference 1984*. Berlin: Akademie-Verlag, pp. 13-27.

Liebmann, O. 1900. *Zur Analysis der Wirklichkeit*, third ed. Strassburg: Karl I. Trübner.

Lotze, H. 1872. *Mikrokosmus. Ideen zur Naturgeschichte und Geschichte der Menschheit*, vol. 3, second ed. Leipzig: S. Hirzel.

Lotze, H. 1874. *Logik. Drei Bücher vom Denken, vom Untersuchen und vom Erkennen*. Leipzig: S. Hirzel.

Lotze, H. 1884. Metaphysik. Drei Bücher der Ontologie, Kosmologie und Psychologie. Leipzig: S. Hirzel.

Lotze, H. 1980. *Logic*, I-II, ed. B. Bosanquet, second ed. Repr. New York/London: Garland Publishing.

Manser, A. 1984. Bradley and Frege. In A. Manser/G. Stock, eds. *The Philosophy of F. H. Bradley*. Oxford: Clarendon Press, pp. 303-317.

Passmore, J. 1966. *A Hundred Years of Philosophy*, second ed. London: Duckworth.

Pester, R. 1997. *Hermann Lotze. Wege seines Denkens und Forschens*. Würzburg: Königshausen & Neumann.

Picht, G. 1977. Die Macht des Denkens. In G. Neske, ed. *Erinnerungen an Martin Heidegger*. Pfullingen: Neske, pp. 197-205.

Russell, B. 1972. *Russell's Logical Atomism*, ed. D. Pears. London: Fontana/Collins.

Sluga, H. 1980. *Gottlob Frege*. London/Boston/Henley: Routledge & Kegan Paul.

Windelband, W. 1915. *Präludien*, I-II, fifth ed. Tübingen: I. C. B. Mohr (P. Siebeck).

Wittgenstein, L. 1966. *Tractatus Logico-Philosophicus*, ed. D. F. Pears/B. F. McGuinness. London: Routledge & Kegan Paul.

3

How Do We 'Grasp' a Thought, Mr. Frege?

WOLFGANG MALZKORN

1 Introduction

Gottlob Frege's essay *Thoughts* which was published in 1918 is subtitled 'A Logical Investigation' and was followed by a series of three other 'Logical Investigations': the 1919 essay *Negation*, the 1923 essay *Compound Thoughts* and the posthumeous fragment *Logical Generality*. In all of these papers Frege is concerned with the foundations of classical sentential and first order predicate logics; in *Thoughts* he focuses primarily on ontological and epistemological questions which are - in Frege's approach - closely related to the foundations of logic. For Frege logic is the science of the 'laws of truth', and truth and falsity are properties of thoughts;[1] therefore, as part of his investigations in the foundations of logic he has to deal with the following ontological question in particular: 1. What are thoughts and what is their ontological status? As a consequence of his answer to this question he has to deal with the epistemological question: 2. How can we get knowledge of thoughts?

---

[1] Cf. Frege 1918/9, p. 58, pp. 60-1, and Frege 1893, pp. xiv-xvii. Page numbers always refer to the original edition, if not indicated otherwise.

In dealing with the first of these questions Frege develops his well-known theory of the three ontological realms. He divides the universe of all things into (a) the realm of the concrete (physical) objects, (b) the realm of psychological entities (*e.g.* ideas, attitudes, sense-impressions *et cetera*) and (c) the realm of abstract objects (*e.g.* numbers, the truth-values *et cetera*). To distinguish the second realm from the first and the third realms Frege uses an ontological criterion: psychological entities exist only in dependence of subjects to whose mental states they belong, whereas the actual things and the abstract objects exist independently of subjects. In short terms: psychological entities are *subjective*, concrete (physical) objects and abstract objects are *objective*. In order to distinguish the elements of the first realm from those of the third realm Frege refers to an epistemological criterion: concrete (physical) objects are perceptible by the senses, while abstract objects are not. In this regard, abstract objects and psychological entities are similar. A subject *has* ideas, attitudes, sense-impressions *et cetera*, but it does not perceive them. Yet, as Frege indicates by using the word 'actual' ('wirklich') and by some explicit remarks, this epistemological criterion presupposes an ontological criterion: the elements of the first realm are perceptible by the senses because they can be *immediate causes* of certain effects, *i.e.* because they are actual ('wirklich'), whereas the elements of the third realm cannot be *immediate causes* of anything.[2] Therefore, I take Frege's distinction of the three realms as a basically *ontological* distinction.[3]

Thoughts are abstract objects; on the one hand, they are objective, on the other hand, they are not perceptible by the senses because they cannot have *immediate* causal effects on sensual subjects. Yet, we must be able to get epistemic access to thoughts since otherwise knowledge would be impossible at all. This becomes obvious as soon as we consider Frege's definition of facts as true thoughts.[4] If we did not have any epistemic access to thoughts, we would not have any epistemic access to facts either. But, knowledge of facts is exactly what we are usually aiming at.

Though Frege concedes that we have epistemic access to thoughts, *i.e.* that we can 'grasp' thoughts, as he calls it, he does not explain the grasping of a thought very well. However, Frege has noticed himself that the *relation* of grasping, in which a subject can come to stand to a thought, may seem to

---

[2] I am opposing here Wolfgang Carl's view who tries to construe Frege's distinction between the three realms as an epistemological distinction; cf. W. Carl 1994, p. 196. I should like to add that my interpretation is completely consistent with Frege's claim that our grasping of a thought can be a cause of something (cf. Frege 1918/9, pp. 76-7).

[3] Cf. Frege 1918/9, pp. 67-9

[4] Cf. Frege 1918/9, p. 74

be obscure, particularly because, according to his theory, this relation has to serve as a bridge over the 'deep gap' between the realm of actual things (including sensual beings) and abstract objects. He says:

> A thought belongs neither to my inner world as an idea, nor yet to the external world, the world of things perceptible by the senses.
>
> This consequence, however cogently it may follow from the exposition, will nevertheless perhaps not be accepted without opposition. It will, I think, seem impossible to some people to obtain information about something not belonging to the inner world except by sense-perception.[5]

Thus, according to Frege, the relation of grasping (thoughts) is a basic prerequisite of human knowledge, on the one hand, but may seem to be 'impossible', on the other hand. The tension that raises from this situation makes it interesting and worthwhile to look more closely to the relation of grasping (thoughts). Moreover, a closer look to the relation of grasping (thoughts) may shed some light on Frege's account of knowing abstract objects in general.

2   Frege on Grasping Thoughts

Towards the end of his essay *Thoughts* Frege compares the grasping of thoughts with sensual knowledge of actual things und thus tries to point out an important issue about the relation of grasping (thoughts). Since the passage being in question contains one of the most explicit remarks Frege has ever made on this subject and since it has been treated as a key to an understanding of the relation of grasping thoughts by some commentators, I shall quote it at full length. It follows immediately on the passage quoted at the end of the preceding section of this paper.

> Sense-perception indeed is often thought to be the most certain, even the sole, source of knowledge about everything that does not belong to the inner world. But with what right? Sense-perception has as necessary constituents our sense-impressions and these are a part of the inner world. In any case two men do not have the same sense-impressions though they may have similar ones. Sense-impressions alone do not reveal the external world to us. Perhaps there is a being that has only sense-impressions without seeing or touching things. To have visual impressions is not to see things. How does it happen that I see the tree just there where I do see it? Obviously it depends on the visual impressions I have and on the particular sort which occur because I see with two eyes. On each of the two retinas there arises, physically speaking, a particular image. Someone else

---

[5] Cf. Frege 1918/9, p. 75. In quoting from this work I usually follow the translation by P. T. Geach and R. H. Stoothoff (in Frege 1977), although I shall modify it whereever I judge it to be appropriate.

sees the tree in the same place. He also has two retinal images but they differ from mine. We must assume that these retinal images determine our impressions. Consequently the visual impressions we have are not only not the same, but markedly different from each other. And yet we move about in the same world. Having visual impressions is certainly necessary for seeing things, but not sufficient. What must still be added is not anything sensible. And yet this is just what opens up the real world for us; for without this non-sensible something everyone would remain shut up in his inner world. So, perhaps, since the decisive factor lies in the non-sensible, something non-sensible, even without the co-operation of sense impressions, could also lead us out of the inner world and enable us to grasp thoughts. Besides our inner world we should have to distinguish the external world proper of sensible, perceptible things and the realm of what is not sensibly perceptible. We should need something non-sensible for the recognition of both realms; but for the sense-perception of things we should need sense-impressions as well, and these belong entirely to the inner world. So the distinction between the ways in which a thing and a thought are given mainly consists in something which is assignable, not to either of the two realms, but to the inner world. Thus I cannot find this distinction to be so great as to make impossible that a thought which does not belong to the inner world, can be given to us. (Frege 1918/9, p. 75)

It is beyond any doubt that this passage would be the key to an understanding of Frege's account of how we grasp thoughts, *if* Frege intended to give a *comprehensive* answer to this question here and *if* he had in mind a *particular* 'non-sensible something' which is just waiting to be revealed by an ingenius commentator. But, did Frege really intend to give a *comprehensive* answer to the question of how we grasp thoughts, here? Did he really have in mind a *particular* 'non-sensible something', that 'could [...] lead us out of the inner world and enable us to grasp thoughts'? Did he, for some unknown reason, decide not to tell us what exactly he had in mind? Did Frege want to make a contribution to epistemology here, at all? - Before I shall try to answer these questions and give my own interpretation of the passage just quoted, I shall first discuss some competing interpretations.

3   Some Competing Interpretations

3.1. Stuhlmann-Laeisz's Interpretation

I start my survey of competing interpretations with Rainer Stuhlmann-Laeisz's commentary on the passage in question because it is the most unassuming one.[6] Stuhlmann-Laeisz tries to make sense of Frege's words without relying on sources of knowledge which are not explicitly men-

---

[6] Cf. R. Stuhlmann-Laeisz 1995, pp. 91-95

tioned by Frege. According to Stuhlmann-Laeisz Frege was deceived (or tried to deceive the reader) by an ambiguity of his own words and thus came to postulate a 'non-sensible something' that enables us to grasp thoughts. But, let us look on Stuhlmann-Laeisz's interpretation step by step: In the passage in question Frege opposes a possible sensualistic position, which in connection with his doctrine of the three realms amounts to the consequence that thoughts do not exist at all or that they exist in such a way that we cannot have any knowledge of them. In order to refute that position, Frege looks for another way to connect the inner world (the second realm) with the other realms, besides sense-perception. To this aim he tries to soften up the opposition between the realm of actual things and the third realm. He claims that it is only a necessary but not a sufficient condition for a person to see an actual thing, that that person has a sense-impression of the thing. Something must be added. 'What must still be added is not anything sensible' (see quotation above). According to Stuhlmann-Laeisz the word 'sensible' in this sentence refers to something which belongs to the inner world. Consequently, 'what must still be added', either belongs to the first realm or to the third realm. Since the second alternative seems to be out of question, Stuhlmann-Laeisz choses the first alternative. 'What must still be added' to a person's sense-impression of an actual thing is the thing itself. However, when Frege continues his argument, saying that '[s]o, perhaps, since the decisive factor lies in the non-sensible, something non-sensible, even without the co-operation of sense-impressions, could lead us out of the inner world and enable us to grasp thoughts' (see quotation above), Stuhlmann-Laeisz takes him to use the word 'non-sensible' to refer to a means to grasp thoughts. So, Frege fell a victim of his own equivocation of the words 'sensible' and 'non-sensible', respectively, and thus failed to establish an analogy between perceiving actual things and grasping thoughts. Consequently, he also failed to establish the existence of a 'non-sensible' means to grasp thoughts.

Is this interpretation compelling? I think the answer is 'no', and here is why. (i) Frege mentions two reasons for his claim that *actual things and a person's sense-impressions caused by them* are necessary but not sufficient for that person to see those things. The first reason is: 'Perhaps there is a being that has only sense-impressions [*sc.* caused by actual things] without seeing or touching [*sc.* those] things' (see quotation above).[7] The second reason is: the (visual) sense-impressions, which are determined by the two retinal images which anyone of us has (except for blind or one-eyed peo-

---

[7] Here, Frege uses the words 'seeing' and 'touching' in the strong sense of getting knowledge of things by means of the visual or haptic senses, respectively.

ple), must be processed to see *one* actual thing at a certain place.[8] Obviously, it is not the case that actual things would improve the situation of a possible being 'that has only sense-impressions [*sc.* caused by those things] without seeing or touching [*sc.* the] things'. Nor do actual things help a person to process his/her sense-impressions of them in order to perceive them. The actual things are already in the picture and, therefore, do not need to be added. (ii) As Frege tells us, the adjective 'sensible' must not be applied to elements of the inner world. As we cannot have sense-impressions of the elements of the third realm, we cannot have sense-impressions of the elements of the inner world. We cannot *perceive* ideas, attitudes, sense-impressions *et cetera*, we simply *have* them.[9] Therefore, the elements of the inner world are not sens*ible*. Frege usually applies the adjective 'sensible' only to elements of the first realm, *i.e.* to actual things, and he continues to do so in the passage being in question, when, towards the end of that passage, he mentions 'the external world proper of sensible, perceptible things' (see quotation above). For this reason, Stuhlmann-Laeisz's interpretation of the word 'sensible' in Frege's sentence 'What must still be added is not anything sensible' is not convincing. If, however, we take the word 'sensible' in this sentence in its usual meaning, then we have no reason to suppose any equivocation in Frege's argument whatsoever. (iii) As it will be shown below, we can make sense of the passage being in question, taking the word 'sensible' in its usual meaning. Therefore, there is no need to assume that Frege made such an obvious mistake as Stuhlmann-Laeisz suggests.

3.2. Carl's Interpretation

Wolfgang Carl's interpretation of the passage being in question can be found in the eighth chapter of his book *Frege's Theory of Sense and Reference*; the chapter is entitled 'Frege's contributions to epistemology'.[10] It starts with the following general statement:

---

[8] A diligent and close reading of the passage in question reveals that Frege puts much emphasis on the spatial order of the things we see: 'How does it happen that I see the tree just there where I do see it? Obviously it depends on the visual impressions I have and on the particular sort which occur because I see with two eyes. On each of the two retinas there arises, physically speaking, a particular image. Someone else sees the tree in the same place. He also has two retinal images but they differ from mine. Consequently the visual impressions we have are not only not the same, but markedly different from each other. And yet we move about in the same world' (see quotation above). This may be taken as a hint that for Frege visual knowledge of things (i.e. seeing things) involves putting those things in a spatial order.

[9] Cf. Frege 1918/9, p. 67

[10] Cf. W. Carl 1918/9, pp. 186-211

Frege was particularly opposed to empiricism and psychologism, which, according to him, are connected with each other and lead in the long run to idealism. His own philosophical position as it emerges from his criticism of empiricism and psychologism can be described as an epistemology devoted to maintaining the objectivity of knowledge founded on the human capacity for grasping thoughts. (Carl 1994, p. 186)

According to Carl, in the passage being in question Frege gives an account of perceptual knowledge that 'forms a part of a critical examination of the empiricist view that sense perception is "the most certain, even the sole, source of knowledge about everything that does not belong to the inner world"'.[11] To this aim Frege states that having sense-impressions is not the same as perceiving outer objects; it is not even a sufficient but only a necessary condition for having access to the outer world. A non-sensible component has to be added to the sense-impression of an object in order to perceive the object. 'This non-sensible component of the perception of a material object consists in grasping a thought, because sense perception is taken to be a source of knowledge and knowledge issues in judgement that requires grasping of a thought acknowledged to be true. [...] This view can be aptly compared with Kant's claim that intuitions require concepts (1787, B74-5)'.[12] In taking Frege to think that sense-perception involves grasping a thought and acknowledging it to be true, Carl follows Michael Dummett.[13]

Be that as it may, what can be said about Carl's interpretation of the passage being in question? - (i) Unlike Carl I do not think that it is Frege's primary aim in that passage, simply to attack empiricism in general. Frege's primary aim is not an epistemological one. To the contrary, he tries to refute a strong sensualistic position because it jeopardizes his claim that thoughts are objective and non-actual. (ii) Carl truly asserts that sense-impressions are not sufficient for the perception of objects because they need to be processed by the mind. He points out correctly, that, according to Frege, having sense-impressions of a thing is not the same as perceiving a thing since (a) Frege judges it to be possible that there is a being that has sense-impressions of a thing without perceiving it and since (b) a visual impression of a thing normally consists in having *two* retinal images, which is not

---

[11] Cf. W. Carl 1994, p. 194. For the passage quoted by Carl see my quotation above.

[12] ibid. - Two pages later Carl gives a slightly different characterization of the 'non-sensible component' of a perception of an actual object: 'Thus, our access to the outer world requires a variety of cognitive processes and an integration of different sources of knowledge. [...] The 'non-sensible' that [...] is required for perceiving an outer object is just an abbreviation of a variety of cognitive processes that include our capacity to grasp a thought and to make a judgement and our knowledge of the laws of nature' (p. 196).

[13] Cf. M. Dummett 1991, p. 273; see also T. Burge 1996, p. 349 n.6, 356

the same as seeing *one* thing (at a certain place). (iii) Even if it is true that for Frege a sense-perception involves grasping a thought, Carl is wrong about the 'non-sensible component'. If he were right in assuming that that 'non-sensible component [...] consists in grasping a thought' (see above), he would have to accuse Frege either of an equivocation different from that which Stuhlmann-Laeisz detects or of presenting a triviality which begs the question. For, Carl either would have to maintain that the 'non-sensible something' that enables us to grasp a thought is completely different from the 'non-sensible component' that enables us to perceive a thing, or he would have to claim that Frege tells us that for grasping a thought it is necessary and sufficient to grasp the thought. Since Carl does not comment on the remainder of the passage being in question, where Frege talks about grasping thoughts, we do not know which alternative he would prefer. But, it is certain, that none of these alternatives would be helpful to understand Frege's argument.

3.3. The Kantian Interpretation

A Kantian perspective on the passage being in question has, for example, recently been taken by Eva Picardi in her article Frege's Anti-Psychologism.[14] Picardi starts her comments on that passage by asserting that 'his [sc. Frege's] claim [...] that perceptual experience involves a non-sensible element [...] ring[s] a familiar (Kantian) bell' (Picardi 1996, p. 313). Some pages later she explains the passage 'roughly as follows: a non-sensible element, belonging presumably to the third realm and therefore itself thought-like in character, has to be acknowledged, for it is its presence that discloses the outer world and turns sense-impressions into perception and judgement. Perhaps the mutual understanding which we seem to reach through language is made possible by the presence of this non-sensible element: it turns our apprehension of the sentences of natural language (conceived as physical entities) into a grasp of the thoughts they help to convey' (Picardi 1996, p. 321-2). However, at the end of her article Picardi tells us that she wants to leave unanswered the question '[w]hether this non-sensible element is to be construed as a thought-like ingredient, or as the faculty of reason tout court' (Picardi 1996, p. 328). Yet, though Picardi does not intend to answer this question, the way she puts it is interesting per se.

I should like to make three comments here, of which two are more specific and one more general. (i) Picardi's interpretation of Frege's 'non-sensible elements' which are necessary to perceive actual things as well as to grasp thoughts seems to be the strongest interpretation, yet. Picardi seems

---

[14] For a more spelled-out Kantian interpretation see Gerold Prauss 1976, pp. 42-6

to imply that the (type of) 'non-sensible something' that is a necessary component of sense-perception is *the same* (type of) 'non-sensible something' that enables us to grasp a thought. I am not sure that Picardi is wrong in this point but I am also not sure that Frege intended to say what Picardi seemingly takes him to say. If Picardi is right, Frege must have had in mind a specific (type of) 'non-sensible something'. But, why did he not call it by its name, then? (ii) Picardi seems to confine the problem of grasping thoughts to the problem of 'our apprehension of the sentences of natural language (conceived as physical entities)' which 'help to convey' thoughts (see above). However, in my opinion Frege does not only address the problem of grasping thoughts that are conveyed to us by means of tokens of sentences of natural language, but the more general problem of grasping thoughts at all. If Dummett, Carl and Burge are right in assuming that for Frege any sense-perception involves grasping a thought, then any sense-perception can serve as an example of grasping a thought which is *not* conveyed by means of a sentence of natural language (conceived as a physical entity). (iii) Frege's claim that sense-perception involves a 'non-sensible element' does *not* ring a *Kantian* bell. If it did, we would have to think of the 'non-sensible element' either as a Kantian category of reason or as the faculty of reason *as Kant construed it*. It is well-known, however, that for Kant the faculty of reason (or, more accurately, the faculty of understanding) *constructs* the objects of our external world (from intuitively given material) by means of the categories. It is in this sense, that 'intuitions require concepts' (see my quotation from Wolfgang Carl's book above). Thus, the existence and specific nature of the objects of our external world depend on (the specific nature of) our cognitive faculties. Therefore, according to Kant, the objects of our external world are, in Frege's terminology, not objective. This, however, is certainly not Frege's view, as I have shown above.[15] Moreover, Frege did not share Kant's theory of abstract objects (*e.g.* mathematical objects), although there may be some agreements with Kant on the sources of geometrical knowledge.[16] Consequently, Frege did not have in mind Kant's theory of reason or any particularly Kantian part of it when he wrote the passage being in question.[17] Of course, this

---

[15] Since I do not agree with G. Prauss that in the passage being in question Frege jeopardizes the foundations of his own theory by coming close to a Kantian, non-Platonist view (see Prauss 1976, pp. 34, 42-6), my argument opposes Prauss' interpretation, as well.

[16] See, for example, Frege 1884, sections 13-4, pp. 19-21, and section 89, pp. 101-2

[17] I find myself in complete agreement with Tyler Burge's comment on Hans Sluga's reading of Frege as a Kantian idealist: 'Frege nowhere asserts or clearly implies that he maintains any sort of idealism - Kantian or otherwise - about the physical objects studied by the physical sciences. [...] It is dubious historical methodology to attribute to a philosopher with writings that stretch over decades, a large, controversial doctrine, if he nowhere clearly states it in his

does in no way exclude that Frege alluded to our faculty of reason neutrally construed.

4 An Alternative Interpretation

Every diligent reader of Frege's writings will notice that sometimes Frege rediscusses a claim that he has already made and well argued for, in order to add an auxiliary argument. Thereby, he mostly tries to prevent a possible objection or simply to destroy remaining doubts. The passage in question here is just intended to deliver such an auxiliary argument for the claim that thoughts are objective but not sensible, *i.e.* that they belong to 'a third realm'. (Notice, that even the word 'thought' by itself suggests an alternative view, since it has a subjective connotation.) It is the primary aim of the whole passage to give additional support to that claim, and we have to keep this in mind when reading or interpreting the passage.[18] Frege tries to defend his claim against the following *indirect* argument: Suppose, first, that thoughts are objective (*i.e.* not elements of my inner world) and not sensibly perceptible. Suppose, further, that it is 'impossible [...] to obtain information about something not belonging to the inner world except by sense-perception' (*i.e.*, that '[s]ense-perception [...] is the sole [,] source of knowledge about everything that does not belong to the inner world', see quotations above). Then, we would have no knowledge of thoughts and, since facts are true thoughts, no knowledge of facts either. But, we have knowledge of facts, *et cetera* ... .

Frege does not, as Wolfgang Carl thinks, intend to give an argument against empiricism in general and thus to enter an epistemological debate about such a philosophical position. He simply opposes, as Rainer Stuhlmann-Laeisz points out correctly, a strong sensualistic position which applies its epistemological restrictions even to what we nowadays call *propositions* and which threatens his theory of the three realms, which was developed by him in order to provide an ontological basis for his foundational investigations in logic. As the history of twentieth century philosophy shows there is a whole variety of empiricist positions which are consistent with Frege's assumption of objective and not sensibly perceptible thoughts.

---

writings. If Frege had believed in any such idealism about physical objects [...], he would have surely said he did' (T. Burge 1996, p. 355).

[18] My interpretation is supported (a) by the introduction to the passage (see the first quotation in this article), (b) by the intermediate result that '[b]esides our inner world we should have to distinguish the external world proper of sensible perceptible things and the realm of what is not sensibly perceptible' (see quotation above), and (c) by the conclusion Frege draws: 'I cannot find this distinction to be so great as to make impossible that a thought which does not belong to the inner world, can be given to us' (see quotation above).

Frege attacks the sensualistic position, at which he aims, by showing that even our knowledge of the external world relies on more than sense-impressions: 'Sense-impressions alone do not reveal the external world to us' (see quotation above). For reasons I have explained in my discussion of Stuhlmann-Laeisz's and Carl's interpretations, Frege maintains that sense-impressions caused by actual things are necessary but not sufficient to obtain perceptual knowledge of those things: 'Having visual impressions is certainly necessary for seeing things but not sufficient' (see quotation above). Something must be added; since the sensible thing is already in the picture, that 'something' cannot be anything sensible. Consequently: 'What must still be added is not anything sensible. And yet this is just what opens up the real world for us; for without this non-sensible something everyone would remain shut up in his inner world' (see quotation above). What kind of 'non-sensible something' can Frege possibly mean? If Frege meant an element of the inner world besides our sense-impressions, a sensualist would still have been able to get his head out of the noose since such a sensualist has no problems with the elements of our inner world. If Frege meant a thought or another element of the third realm, he would, as I have emphasized against Carl, simply have begged the question. The only alternative, that makes any sense to me, is that Frege had in mind a certain faculty to process sense-impressions of actual things and thus turn them into sense-perceptions of those things. Such a faculty would indeed be a cognitive faculty and it would correctly be called 'non-sensible', but it would not need to be the Kantian faculty of reason, as I have pointed out against Picardi.

Having established the claim that even sense-perceptions cannot simply be construed as a kind of wax impressions of actual objects, Frege then argues for the *very possibility* that there might be something similar, that enables us to grasp thoughts': 'So, *perhaps*, [...], something non-sensible, even without the cooperation of sense-impressions, could also lead us out of the inner world and enable us to grasp thoughts. [...] We *should* need something non-sensible for the recognition of both realms' (see quotation above, italics added). The fact that Frege explicitly includes the case in which we grasp a thought 'without the cooperation of sense-impressions' shows that he does not only consider thoughts about actual objects, but also logical or mathematical thoughts. It shows also that Frege is not concerned about the question, how we grasp a thought from a sentence (conceived as a physical entity) that we hear or read, as Picardi implies.

However, Frege does not intend to go beyond that result. He does not explain the 'non-sensible something' that enables us to grasp thoughts nor does he give any comprehensive genetic account of our knowledge of thoughts. He goes just as far as to tell us: 'To the grasping of thoughts there must [...] correspond a special mental capacity, the power of thinking' (Frege 1918/9, p. 74); but he does not care to specify that mental capacity. His primary task here is not an epistemological one. He abandons his argumentation about the relation of grasping thoughts, satisfied that he has destroyed a possible doubt about the ontological status of thoughts. This is as far as Frege needs to go in (the foundations of) logic, as is clearly expressed in the posthumous fragment *Logic*, where Frege states that the grasping of a thought (*e.g.* the law of gravitation)

> is a process which lies on the very confines of the mental and cannot be completely understood from a psychological standpoint since it concerns something essential which is not mental in a proper sense, namely the thought. Perhaps this process is the most mysterious of all. But, we do not have to care about it in logic since it is a mental process. It is enough for us to know that we can grasp thoughts and acknowledge them to be true; how this is done, is a different question. (Frege 1969a, p. 157, my translation)

Does Frege tell us more about the relation of grasping (thoughts) at different places, or do we have to be content with what he tells us in the passage just analyzed?

5   Ideas and Thoughts

In two subsequent footnotes to his article *Thoughts* Frege explains why he choses the metaphorical expression 'grasp' as a name for the relation in which a person can stand to a thought. In the first of these footnotes he states:

> A person sees a thing, has an idea, grasps or thinks a thought. When he grasps or thinks a thought he does not create it but only comes to stand in a certain relation to what already existed - a different relation from seeing a thing or having an idea. (Frege 1918/9, p. 69)

To think a thought is not to create it; thoughts are objective and can, therefore, not be created by thinking subjects. To grasp an actual thing does also not include an act of creation; the thing has existed before I grasp it. But my grasping it puts me in a close relation to it and gives me some kind of access to it, as Frege adds in the second footnote:

> The expression 'grasp' is as metaphorical as 'content of consciousness'. The nature of language does not permit anything else. What I hold in my hand can certainly be regarded as the content of my hand; but all the same it is the content of my hand in quite another and a more extraneous way than are the bones and muscles of which the hand consists or again the tensions these undergo. (Frege 1918/9, p. 74)

Although a person who grasps a thought 'is the owner of the thinking, not of the thought',[19] the thought is - according to Frege's comparison - a *content* of the persons mind in the same (*weak*) sense as what I hold in my hand is the *content* of my hand. How can that happen? Frege does not provide us with an explicit answer to that question in his article *Thoughts*; there, he gives only a hint, where we have to look for an answer:

> Although the thought does not belong *with* the contents of the thinker's consciousness, there must be something in his consciousness that is aimed at the thought. But this should not be confused with the thought itself. Similarly Algol itself is different from the *idea* someone has of Algol. (Frege 1918/9, p. 75, italics added)

Here, Frege invokes the distinction between Algol and the idea someone has of Algol to explain the difference between a thought and that, what is aimed at the thought in the consciousness of someone who grasps the thought. I would like to argue that it is the thinker's *idea* of the thought, what is aimed at the thought in the thinker's consciousness. There are some passages in different works of Frege where this becomes clear. Consider, for example, the following passages from Frege's *Review of Husserl's Philosophy of Arithmetic* and from the fragment *Logic*:

> [O]ne and the same thought can be grasped by many men. The constituents of the thought, and *a fortiori* things themselves, must be distinguished from the ideas that accompany in some mind the act of grasping the thought.[20]
>
> Human thinking is originally intermingled with having ideas and feelings. It is the aim of logic to separate the purely logical. This is not to say, that we should *think without having ideas, which is impossible*, but that we should carefully distinguish between the logical and the ideas and feelings which accompany it. One problem is, that we think in some language and that grammar, which has the same significance for language as logic has for judgements, intermingles the psychological with the logical.[21]

---

[19] Cf. Frege 1918/9, p. 75

[20] Frege 1894, p. 318. My translation follows that of P. T. Geach (in: P. T. Geach/ M. Black 1960), except for some corrections I have made. - The view that our ideas mediate our knowledge of facts was shared by most of the philosophers of Frege's time and also by two philosophers who supposedly had great influence on Frege: Kant and Bolzano. (I should like to add the remark that Kant's influence on Frege is well documented by Frege's writings, whereas in the case of Bolzano there are striking agreements, but there is no proof that Frege ever read his works.) However, for Kant and Bolzano ideas are not subjective in Frege's sense, but intersubjectively accessible.

[21] Cf. Frege's 1969a, p. 154 (my translation, italics added). It should also be noted that in his essay Thoughts Frege claims that the grasping of a thought 'is a process in the inner world of the thinker' (p. 76). And in On Sense and Reference Frege tells us that regarding linguistic expressions we have to distinguish between (i) the reference of the expression, (ii) its meaning

Once we concede that it was Frege's view that a person's idea(s) of a thought is/are the medium of his/her grasping of the thought, we have found a way to remove the apparent obscurity from the relation of grasping to some extent by reducing it to two different relations. Although Frege does not explicitly say so, we can conceive of the relation of grasping as a *product* of (i) the relation of having (ideas) and (ii) the relation of being the content (in the weaker sense) of (an idea). Writing 'aHv' for '(person) a *has* (the idea) v' and 'vCg' for '(thought) g is the content of (the idea) v', we can explain a person a's grasping a thought g ('aGg') by the following formula:

$$\forall a,g(aGg \equiv \exists v(aHv \wedge vCg))$$

or, equivalently, but in the language of the logic of relations: G = H|C.[22]

However, one could oppose this claim by arguing that a person's having a certain idea must be construed as an *act* or a *procedure* rather than as a relation between a person and another entity (the idea). I do not want to refute this objection here on systematic grounds, nor do I even want to enter a systematic discussion about the question underlying it. My answer is simply that the objection does not agree with Frege's view. In his ontological distinction of the three realms Frege obviously treats ideas as some kind of entities, and in the first of the two footnotes which I have quoted above he explicitly characterizes a person's having an idea as a relation. Consequently, I find myself in complete accordance with Frege.

Yet, what is the advantage of reducing the relation of grasping (thoughts) to the relations of having an idea and of being the content of an idea, respectively? - As I have shown above, in his article *Thoughts* Frege worries about the apparent obscurity of the relation of grasping (thoughts) since that obscurity could cast some doubts on the objectivity and non-perceptibility of thoughts. However, neither the relation of having an idea seems to be as obscure as the relation of grasping, nor does the relation of

---

(sense), and (iii) the idea which someone has when he uses the expression. 'The reference and sense of a sign are to be distinguished from the associated idea. [...] We can [...] recognize three levels of difference between words, expressions or whole sentences. The difference may concern at most the ideas, or the sense but not the reference, or, finally, the reference as well' (Frege 1892, pp. 29-30; my translation follows that of M. Black in: P. T. Geach/ M. Black 1960). Consequently, we can have different ideas to grasp (think) one thought. Moreover, different people have always different ideas when grasping one and the same thought.

[22] As I have shown above, in Frege's view the relation of seeing a thing ('aSc') is not reducible in the same way to the relation of having a sense-impression ('aHi') and the relation of being a sense-impression of a certain thing ('iEc'), but, at least, we have: $\forall a,c(aSc \supset \exists i(aHi \wedge iEc))$. According to Frege, the reverse implication is not true (see above).

being the content of an idea.[23] So, by reducing the relation of grasping (thoughts) to those other relations Frege could have - at least to some extent - removed the apparent obscurity of the former relation. To use a metaphor: the relations of having an idea and of being the content of an idea build the two parts of a bridge over the 'deep gap' between the first realm (to which thinking subjects usually belong) and the third realm, and the idea serves as the pillar in the middle of the bridge.

Of course, not any question about the relation of grasping (thoughts) is answered by this reduction. By no means I want to identify the 'non-sensible something' that, according to Frege, enables us to grasp a thought with the idea that mediates the grasping of the thought. So, there still remains the question, how it is possible, that a person has an (adequate) idea of a certain thought. Presupposing the reduction of the relation of grasping (thoughts), which I have suggested above, the point can be made that Frege's argument about the 'non-sensible something' addresses exactly that question. But, as I have shown above, it was not Frege's intention to give a comprehensive account of that 'non-sensible something'. In principle, Frege's argument is consistent with a variety of epistemological explanations of how it is possible for us to have (adequate) ideas of facts or thoughts. It is consistent with an evolutionary explanation (which says, roughly, that we come to have adequate ideas of facts or thoughts because of the mechanisms of evolution) as well as with a theory of a certain cognitive apparatus that is apt to preserve the adequacy of our ideas as well as with several other possible explanations.[24] This, in turn, shows, that Frege did not offer an answer to that question in his article *Thoughts* (nor elsewhere, as to my knowledge).

Finally, did Frege's well-known decisive anti-psychologism prevent him from introducing the reduction which I have suggested above? A persuasive investigation into the very foundations of Frege's anti-psychologism has recently been presented by Eva Picardi. According to Piccardi, the basic error of psychologism in Frege's view is 'a mistaken picture of language which turns the objectivity of sense and the communication of thoughts into a mystery'.[25] The confusion of logical laws with psychological laws on the side of psychologism is just another aspect of that 'mistaken picture of language' and results from a wrong, extremely naturalistic conception of truth. The psychological logicians, who are at-

---

[23] It is, for example, by no means obscure that I have an idea of a particular fact (*i.e.* of a particular true *thought*), though it might be in need of a further *epistemological* explanation.

[24] However, such a theory would have to explain the 'affinity in human ideas' that Frege assumes in his 1892, p. 31.

[25] Cf. Picardi 1996, p. 308

tacked by Frege, try to reduce the concept of truth to the concept of general intersubjective agreement. Such a conception of truth ends up in an extreme form of subjectivism regarding the meaning of linguistic expressions. Thus, Frege's conception of truth is the basis of his criticism of psychologism in the field of logic as well as of his criticism of psychologism in the field of the theory of meaning (sense).[26] – I do not see any conflict between the reduction model which I have presented above and Frege's objective conception of truth. Consequently, there should be no conflict between that reduction model and Frege's conception of logical laws or Frege's theory that our sentences have an objective meaning (*i.e.* thoughts). There should not be any such conflict, and I do not see any such conflict. A thought as the meaning of a sentence does not become subjective by being the content (in the weak sense) of anyone's ideas; hence, neither does truth become a property of subjective entities, nor do the logical laws become laws of such entities. Therefore, my answer to the question raised above is negative: Frege's anti-psychologism did not prevent him from introducing the reduction model I have suggested above. So, the question remains open, why Frege did not introduce that model.*

References

Bolzano, B. 1929-31: *Wissenschaftslehre*, 4 volumes, ed. by W. Schultz. Hamburg: Meiner

Burge, T. 1996: Frege on Knowing the Third Realm; in: M. Schirn (ed.): *Frege: Importance and Legacy*: 347-368

Carl, W. 1994: *Frege's Theory of Sense and Reference. Its Origins and Scope.* Cambridge: Cambridge University Press

Dummett, M. 1991: Thought and Perception: The Views of Two Philosophical Innovators. In: M. Dummett: *Frege and other Philosophers*. Oxford: Clarendon Press, 263-288

Frege, G. 1884: *Die Grundlagen der Arithmetik (The Foundations of Arithmetik)*. Breslau

Frege, G. 1892: Über Sinn und Bedeutung (On Sense and Reference). In: *Zeitschrift für Philosophie und philosophische Kritik. Neue Folge* 100: 25-50

Frege, G. 1893: *Grundgesetze der Arithmetik (Basic Laws of Arithmetic)*, vol. I. Jena: H. Pohle

---

[26] Picardi thus opposes Philip Kitcher's claim (in Kitcher 1979) that Frege's criticism of psychologism rests on epistemological considerations following Kant.

* I would like to thank Gottfried Gabriel, Ulrich Nortmann, Rainer Noske, Christian Thiel and Ed Zalta for valuable remarks and suggestions.

Frege, G. 1903: *Grundgesetze der Arithmetik* (*Basic Laws of Arithmetic*), vol. II. Jena: H. Pohle

Frege, G. 1894: Rezension von: E.G. Husserl, Philosophie der Arithmetik I (Review of Husserl's Philosophy of Arithmetic). In: *Zeitschrift für Philosophie und philosophische Kritik. Neue Folge* 103: 313-332

Frege, G. 1918/9: Der Gedanke. Eine logische Untersuchung (Thoughts). In: *Beiträge zur Philosophie des deutschen Idealismus* 1: 58-77

Frege, G. 1918/9a: Die Verneinung. Eine logische Untersuchung (Negation). In: *Beiträge zur Philosophie des deutschen Idealismus* 1: 143-157

Frege, G. 1923: Logische Untersuchungen. Dritter Teil: Gedankengefüge (Compound Thoughts). In: *Beiträge zur Philosophie des deutschen Idealismus* 3: 36-51

Frege, G. 1969: Logische Allgemeinheit (Logical Generality). In: *Nachgelassene Schriften*; ed. by H.Hermes, F.Kambartel und F.Kaulbach. Hamburg: Meiner, 278-283

Frege, G. 1969a: Logik [1897] (Logic). In: *Nachgelassene Schriften*; ed. by H.Hermes, F.Kambartel und F.Kaulbach. Hamburg: Meiner,

Frege, G. 1977: *Logical Investigations*, trans. and ed. by P. T. Geach and R. H. Stoothoff. Oxford

Gabriel, G. 1996: Frege's 'Epistemology in Disguise'. In: M. Schirn (ed.): *Frege: Importance and Legacy*: 330-346

Geach, P.T./Black, M. (eds.) 1960, *Translations from the Philosophical Writings of Gottlob Frege*. Oxford: Oxford University Press

Kant, I. 1787: *Kritik der reinen Vernunft* (*Critique of Pure Reason*). Riga: Johann Friedrich Hartknoch, first edition 1781, second edition 1787

Kitcher, Ph. 1979: Frege's Epistemology. In: *The Philosophical Review* 87: 235-262

Kutschera, F. von 1989: *Gottlob Frege*. Berlin-New York: De Gruyter

Picardi, E. 1996: Frege's Anti-Psychologism. In: M. Schirn (ed.): *Frege: Importance and Legacy*: 307-329

Prauss, G. 1976: Freges Beitrag zur Erkenntnistheorie. Überlegungen zu seinem Aufsatz 'Der Gedanke'. In: *Allgemeine Zeitschrift für Philosophie* 1: 34-61

Schirn, Matthias (ed.) 1996: *Frege: Importance and Legacy*. Berlin-New York:De Gruyter

Sluga, H. 1980: *Gottlob Frege*; London: Routledge & Kegan Paul

Stuhlmann-Laeisz, R. 1995: *Gottlob Freges »Logische Untersuchungen«. Darstellung und Interpretation*. Darmstadt: Wissenschaftliche Buchgesellschaft

4

Frege on Apriority

TYLER BURGE

Frege's logicism incorporated both a set of purported proofs in mathematical logic and an investigation into the epistemology of arithmetic. The epistemological investigation was for him the motivating one. He saw his project as revealing 'the springs of knowledge' and the nature of arithmetical justification. Frege maintained a sophisticated version of the Euclidean position that knowledge of the axioms and theorems of logic, geometry, and arithmetic rests on the *self-evidence* of the axioms, definitions, and rules of inference.[1] The account combines the traditional rationalist view that beliefs that seem obvious are fallible and understanding is hard to come by, with his original insistence that understanding depends not primarily on immediate insight but on a web of inferential capacities.

Central to Frege's rationalism is his view that knowledge of logic and mathematics is fundamentally apriori. In fact, near the end of *The Foundations of Arithmetic* he states that the purpose of the book is to make it probable that 'the laws of arithmetic are analytic judgments and consequently apriori.'[2] In this essay I want to discuss Frege's conception of apriority,

---

[1] Burge, (1998a).

[2] Frege (1884), section 87. (Translations are mine. I have consulted Austin's free but often elegant renderings. I will henceforth cite this book by section under the abbreviation "FA" in the text.) Frege's view of analyticity has been more often discussed than his view of apriority. Essentially he takes a proposition to be analytic if it is an axiom of logic or derivable from axioms of logic together with definitions. He rejects conceptions of analyticity that would tie it to containment or to emptiness of substantive content.

with particular reference to its roots in the conceptions of apriority advanced by Leibniz and Kant.

Frege advertised his notion of apriority as a 'clarification' of Kant's notion. It is well known that Frege did not read Kant with serious historical intent. But even allowing for this fact, his advertisement seems to me interestingly misleading. I believe that his notion is in important respects very different from Kant's and more indebted to Leibniz.

1   Frege and His Predecessors' Characterizations of Apriority

Frege's only extensive explication of his conception of apriority occurs early in *The Foundations of Arithmetic*. He begins by emphasizing that his conception concerns the ultimate canonical justification associated with a judgment, not the content of truths:

> These distinctions between a priori and a posteriori, synthetic and analytic, concern, as I see it,* not the content of the judgment but the justification for the judgment-pronouncement [*Urteilsfällung*]. Where there is no such justification, the possibility of drawing the distinctions vanishes. An a priori error is thus just as much a non-entity [*Unding*] as a blue concept. When a proposition is called a posteriori or analytic in my sense, this is not a judgment about the conditions, psychological, physiological, and physical, which have made it possible to form the content of the proposition in our consciousness; nor is it a judgment about the way in which another has come, perhaps erroneously, to believe it true; rather, it is a judgment about the deepest ground upon which rests the justification for holding it to be true.
>
> *(Frege's footnote): By this I do not, of course, want to assign a new sense but only meet [*treffen*] what earlier writers, particularly Kant, have meant. (*FA*, section 3.)

Frege writes here of apriori judgments. But afterwards he writes of apriori propositions and then apriori truths, and eventually (*FA*, section 87, cf. note 1) apriori laws. These differences are, I think, not deeply significant. Judgments in Frege's sense are idealized abstractions, commitments of logic or other sciences, not the acts of individuals. Individuals can instantiate these judgments through their acts of judgment, but the abstract judgments themselves seem to be independent of individual mental acts. Truths and judgments are, of course, different for Frege. But the difference in Frege's logic concerns only their role in the logical structure. Some truths (true antecedents in conditionals) are not judged. They are not marked by the assertion sign. But everything that is judged is true.[3]

Only truths or veridical judgments can be apriori for Frege. He writes that an apriori error is as impossible as a blue concept. Frege justifies his claim that only truths can be apriori by claiming that apriority concerns the nature of the justification for a judgment. Of course, some ordinary judgments can be justified without being true. But Frege seems to be focused on justifications – deductive proofs from self-evident propositions – that cannot lead judgment into error. Here Frege signals his concern with canonical, ideal, rational justifications, for which the truth-guaranteeing principles and proofs of mathematics and logic provide the paradigm.

In predicating apriority of truths and judgments, understood as canonical commitments of logic and mathematics, Frege is following Leibniz.[4] Leibniz gave the first modern explication of apriority. He maintained that a truth is apriori if it is knowable independent of experience.[5] Since Leibniz explicitly indicates that one might depend psychologically on sense experience in order to come to know any truth, he means that a truth is apriori if the justificational force involved in the knowledge's justification is independent of experience.

Like Leibniz, Frege conceives of apriority as applying primarily to abstract intentional structures. Leibniz applied the notion not only to truths but

---

[3] This doctrine is of a piece with Frege's view that (in logic) inferences can be drawn only from truths. Here he means not that individuals cannot infer things from falsehoods, but rather that the idealized inferences treated in logic proceed only from true axioms. Inferences for Frege are steps in proofs that constitute ideal, correct justifications that exhibit the natural justificatory order of truths. Michael Dummett seems to me to get backwards Frege's motivations for the view that proofs have to start from true premises and that one should not derive a theorem by starting with a supposition. Dummett claims that Frege believed that a complete justification must derive from premises of which no further justification is possible *because* of his rejection of inference from reductio or from other suppositions. Cf. Dummett, (1991: pp. 25-6). It seems clear that Frege rejected such inference because he thought of proofs as deductive arguments that reveal natural justificatory order. I do not see that this view is incompatible with allowing 'proofs' in *the modern sense* that proceed without axioms, by natural deduction. Frege's conception of proof is very different from the modern one. It is concerned with an ideal, natural order of justification. Leibniz also thought of reductios as second-class proofs because they do not reveal the fundamental order of justification. Cf. Leibniz, (1705; 1765; 1989: III, iii, 15). Cf. also Adams, (1994: pp. 109-110). I believe that Dummett may be right in holding that Frege's actual mathematical practice may have been hampered by too strict a focus on the justificatory ideal.

[4] Frege makes explicit his dependence on Leibniz on these matters in Frege (1884 section 17): 'we are concerned here not with the mode of discovery but with the ground of proof; or as Leibniz says, "the question here is not about the history of our discoveries, which differs in different men, but about the connection and natural order of truths, which is always the same".' Frege draws his quotation of Leibniz from Leibniz (1705; 1765; 1989: IV, vii, 9).

[5] Cf. Leibniz, (1705; 1765; 1989: IV, ix, 1, 434); Leibniz (1989: 'Primary Truths', p. 31); Leibniz (1989: 'On Freedom', p. 97).

to proofs, conceived as abstract sequences of truths.[6] Frege assumes that all justifications are proofs, indeed deductive proofs. The apriority of a justification (a series of truths constituting a deductive argument) resides in the character of the premises and rules of inference – in the 'deepest ground [justification, reason, *Grund*] on which a judgment rests'. Like Leibniz, Frege thinks that there is a natural order of justification, which consists in a natural justificatory order among truths.

Frege's definitional explication of apriority continues directly from the passage quoted above:

> Thus the question is removed from the sphere of psychology and referred, if the truth concerned is a mathematical one, to the sphere of mathematics. It comes down to finding the proof and following it back to the primitive truths. If on this path one comes only upon general logical laws and on definitions, one has an analytic truth, bearing in mind that one must take account also of all propositions upon which the admissibility of a definition depends. If, however, it is impossible to carry out the proof without making use of truths which are not of a general logical nature, but refer to the sphere of a special science, then the proposition is a synthetic one. For a truth to be aposteriori, it must be that its proof will not work out [*auskommen*] without reference to facts, i.e., to unprovable truths which are not general [*ohne Allgemeinheit*], and which contain assertions about determinate objects [*bestimmte Gegenstände*]. If, on the contrary, it is possible to derive the proof purely from general laws, which themselves neither need nor admit of proof, then the truth is apriori. (*FA*, section 3.)[7]

Several points about this famous passage need to be made at the outset. Frege distinguishes apriori from analytic truths. Analytic truths derive from general *logical* truths together perhaps with definitions. Apriori truths derive from general laws, regardless of whether they are logical, which neither need nor admit of proof. It is clear that Frege regards all analytic truths as apriori. The relevant logical truths are laws. It is also clear that Frege regards some apriori truths as not analytic. Truths of geometry are synthetic apriori, thus not analytic.

Although Frege uses the language of giving a sufficient condition in explaining 'analytic', 'synthetic', and 'apriori', he uses the language of giving a necessary condition in the case of 'aposteriori'. But Frege elsewhere (e.g. *FA*, section 63) uses 'if' when he clearly means 'if and only if'. And I

---

[6] Cf. Leibniz, (1989: 'First Truths'), and Leibniz (1714, section 45). There are also occasional attributions of apriority to knowledge or acquaintance. But Leibniz is fairly constant in attributing apriority primarily to truths and proofs.

[7] Austin's translation mistakenly speaks of giving or constructing a proof, which might suggest that the definition concerns what is possible for a human being to do. In fact, Frege's language is abstract and impersonal. His account concerns the nature of the mathematical structures, not human capacities. Austin translates 'bestimmte Gegenstände' as 'particular objects'. In this, I think that he is capturing Frege's intent, but I prefer the more literal translation.

believe on a variety of grounds that Frege sees himself as giving necessary and sufficient conditions, probably even definitions, for all four notions. I will mention some of these grounds.

In the passage from section 3 that precedes this passage, and which I quoted above, Frege states that judgments concerning all four categories are judgments about 'the deepest ground upon which rests the justification for holding [the relevant proposition] to be true'. This is a characterization of the nature and content of the judgment, not merely a characterization of a necessary or a sufficient condition. The subsequent individual characterizations of the four categories characterize the nature of the deepest grounds for a predication of each category. Thus they seem to be characterizing the nature of the judgments predicating the categories ('analytic', 'apriori', and so on), not merely one or another condition on their truth.

Frege's characterization of analytic judgments is clearly intended to provide necessary as well as sufficient conditions. His characterization is traditional and may be seen as a gloss on Leibniz's view of analyticity. The parallel in language between the characterization of analytic judgments and the characterization of apriori judgments counts towards regarding both as necessary and sufficient. As we shall see, the characterization of apriori judgments is one that Leibniz held to be necessary and sufficient, at least for finite minds. This was known to Frege. If he had meant to be less committal than Leibniz on the matter, it would have been natural for him to have said so.

In the fifth sentence of section 13 of *Foundations*, Frege tries to reconcile his account of intuition as singular with the view that the laws of geometry are general. Frege believed that the laws of geometry are general, that they are about a special domain of (spatial) objects, and that they do not need or admit of proof. He is assuming that arithmetic and geometry are both apriori, but that they differ in that geometry rests on intuition and is synthetic. I think that Frege is attempting to deal with the worry that since geometrical laws rest on intuition, they must rest on particular facts. This would not be a worry unless Frege regarded it as a necessary as well as sufficient condition on the apriority of geometry that its proofs rest on general laws that neither need nor admit of proof.

Frege's solution is roughly that intuition in geometry does not make reference to particular objects, and the geometric proofs begin with self-evident general principles, though they rest in some way, not well articulated (and which we shall discuss later), on the 'not really particular' intuition. Frege is clearly trying to explicate intuition's role in geometry in a way that leaves that role compatible with taking geometrical proofs to be grounded purely in general geometrical laws. Presumably intuition is meant to be part and parcel of the self-evidence of the general laws.

I do not think that Frege quite solves the problem, particularly inasmuch as he intends to agree with Kant. As I shall later argue, Frege is trying to marry a Leibnizean conception of apriority with Kant's account of synthetic apriority in geometry while siding with Leibniz about the analyticity of arithmetic. The marriage is not a complete success.

There is, of course, a parallel worry that runs as an undercurrent through Frege's mature work. The worry is that the attempt to derive arithmetic from general logical laws (which is required for it to be analytic apriori) is incompatible with the particularity of the numbers. How does one derive particularity from generality in arithmetic? The issue is signalled at the end of *Foundations*, sect. 13. This worry centers ultimately on Law V, which is the bridge in Frege's mature theory from generality to particularity. Again, this issue is naturally seen in the light of the demand that in being analytic apriori, arithmetic must derive ultimately from logical laws that are purely general.

For these and other reasons, I shall assume that Frege's characterization of apriority in *Foundations*, sect. 3 is intended as a necessary and sufficient condition. In fact, I think he views it as a definition.

The notion of a fact about a determinate object in Frege's explication of aposteriori truth in the passage from section 3 is reminiscent of Leibniz's identification of aposteriori truths with truths of 'fact', as contrasted with truths of reason.[8] Frege and Leibniz agree in not seeing truths of reason as any less 'factual' than truths of fact. The point is not that they are not factual, but that they are not 'merely' factual, not merely contingent happenstance. They are principles that are fundamental or necessary to the very nature of things. The point that apriori truths are *general* is basic to the Leibniz-Frege conception of apriority. I will return to this point.

Frege departed from Leibniz in thinking that apriori truths include both truths of reason and synthetic apriori truths that involve a combination of reason and geometrical spatial intuition. In this, of course, Frege follows Kant. I believe, however, that Frege's departure from Leibniz on this point is not as fully Kantian as it might first appear. I shall return to this point as well.

Mill had claimed that all justification ultimately rests on induction.[9] Turning Mill virtually on his head, Frege holds that empirical inductive justification is a species of deductive proof, which contains singular statements together with some general principle of induction as premises (*FA*: sect. 3). He does not make clear what he considers the form of the deduction to be. And he does not indicate in his definition of aposteriori truths how he thinks singular judgments about 'facts' are justified. Presumably he

---

[8] Cf. e.g. Leibniz, (1705; 1765; 1989: IV, vii, 9, 412; IV, ix, 1, 434).

[9] Mill (1843: II, VI, 1).

thinks the justification depends in some way on sense experience. It seems likely that he regarded sense-perceptual observations of facts as primitively justified aposteriori. For our purposes, it is enough that Frege thought that justifications relevant to apriori truths are either deductive proofs or self-evident truths. Such justifications have to start with premises that are self-evident and general.

Frege assumed that all apriori truths, other than basic ones, are provable within a comprehensive deductive system. Goedel's incompleteness theorems undermine this assumption. But insofar as one conceives of proof informally as an epistemic ordering among truths, one can perhaps see Frege's vision of an epistemic ordering as worth developing, with appropriate adjustments, despite this problem.[10]

Frege writes that the axioms 'neither need nor admit of proof'. This phrase is indicative of Frege's view of proof as a canonical justificational ordering of truths, or ideal judgments, that is independent of individual minds or theories. Any truth can be 'proved' within some logical theory, in the usual modern sense of the word 'prove'. But Frege conceived of proof in terms of natural or canonical justification. He saw some truths as fundamental 'unprovable' truths, axioms or canonical starting points in a system of ideal canonical justification. Such primitive truths do not need proof in that they are self-evident or self-justifying. And they cannot be justified through derivation from other truths, because no other truths are justificationally more basic. Thus they do not admit of proof in his sense. The formula of basic truths and axioms neither needing nor admitting of proof can be found *verbatim* in Leibniz, from whom Frege surely got it.[11]

In introducing his conception of apriority, Frege follows the traditional rationalist practice of indicating the *compatibility* of apriority with various sorts of dependence on experience. In particular, Frege notes that a truth can be apriori even though being able to think it, and learning that it is true, might each depend on having sense experience of facts.[12] Whether a truth

---

[10] Michael Dummett, (1991: pp. 29-30), in effect makes this point. Dummett errs, however, in thinking that Frege is concerned with what is knowable by *us* (cf. *ibid*, pp. 24, 26, 28-9). There is no such parameter in Frege's account. The natural order of justification among truths is conceived as a matter that is independent of whether *we* can follow it.

[11] Leibniz, (1705, 1765, 1989: e.g. IV, ix, 2; 434). The formula also occurs in Lotze. Perhaps Frege got the phrase from Leibniz through Lotze. Cf. Lotze, (1880, 1888: section 200). Frege seems, however, to have read Leibniz' *New Essays*. I discuss this notion of proof and Frege's view of axioms in some detail in Burge (1998a).

[12] Cf. this section of the passage quoted above: 'When a proposition is called a posteriori... in my sense, this is not a judgment about the conditions, psychological, physiological, and physical, which have made it possible to form the content of the proposition in our consciousness; nor is it a judgment about the way in which another has come, perhaps erroneously, to believe it true; rather, it is a judgment about the deepest ground upon which rests the justification for holding it to be true.'

is apriori depends on the nature of its canonical justification. Thus one could need to see symbols or diagrams in order to learn a logical or mathematical truth. One could need sense experience – perhaps in interlocution or simply in observing various stable objects in the world – in order to be able to think with certain logical or mathematical concepts. Perhaps, for example, to count or to use a quantifier, one needs to be able to track physical objects. But these facts about learning or psychological development do not show that the propositions that one thinks, once one has undergone the relevant development, are not apriori. Whether they are apriori depends on the nature of their justification. Frege thinks that such justification in logic and mathematics is independent of how the concepts are acquired, and independent of how individuals come to recognize the truths as true.

In his discussion of Mill's empiricism, Frege reiterates the point:

> If one calls a proposition empirical because we have to have made observations in order to become conscious of its content, one does not use the word 'empirical' in the sense in which it is opposed to 'apriori'. One is then making a psychological statement, which concerns only the content of the proposition; whether the proposition is true is not touched. (*FA*, section 8).[13]

The key element in the rationalist approach is this distinction between questions about the psychology of acquisition or learning and normative questions regarding the nature of the justification of the propositions or capacities thus learned.

I say 'propositions or capacities'. Frege follows Leibniz in predicating apriority of propositions, or more particularly, truths, or sequences of truths – *not* capacities, or mental states, or justifications associated with types of propositional attitudes. Apriority ultimately concerns justification. But Leibniz and Frege share the view that apriority is a feature of an ideal or canonical way of justifying a proposition. For them, a proposition is either apriori or aposteriori, but not both, depending on the nature of the ideal or canonical justification associated with it.[14]

---

[13] Frege fixes here on truth, not justification. I think that he is assuming that one learns something about the nature of apriori truths by understanding the proof structure in which they are embedded; and this proof structure constitutes their canonical justification. Cf. Frege (1884: section 105). Substantially the same distinction between the nature of a truth (and ultimately its justification) and the ways we come to understand the relevant proposition or to realize its truth is made by Leibniz, (1705, 1765, 1989: Preface, pp. 48-9; IV, vii, 9); and by Kant (1781, 1787: A1, B1).

[14] Some modern philosophers who take apriority to be predicated primarily of propositions call a proposition apriori if it *can* be justified apriori. Apriori justification is then explained in some non-circular way. Cf. Kripke (1972, p. 34). This formulation avoids commitment to that way's being canonical or ideal. But it also leaves out a serious commitment of such rationalists as Leibniz and Frege. For them, apriori justification is the best and most fundamental sort of justification. When something can be known or justified apriori, that is the canonical way.

In this, Leibniz and Frege diverge from one distinctive aspect of Kant's thinking about apriority. Like Leibniz and Frege, Kant predicates apriority in a variety of ways – to intuitions, concepts, truths, cognition, constructions, principles, judgments. But whereas Leibniz and Frege predicate apriority primarily of truths (or more fundamentally, proofs of truths), Kant predicates apriority primarily of cognition and the employment of representations. For him apriori cognition is cognition that is justificationally independent of sense-experience, and of "all impressions of the senses".[15] Apriori cognition is for Kant cognition whose justificational resources derive purely from the function of cognitive capacities in contributing to cognition. Apriori employment of concepts (or other representations) is employment that carries a warrant that is independent of sensory experiences. Aposteriori cognition is cognition which is justificationally derivative, in part, from sense experiences.

Both conceptions are ultimately epistemic. Frege very clearly states that his classification concerns 'the ultimate ground on which the justification for taking [a truth] to be true depends' (*FA*: section 3). Both sharply distinguish epistemic questions from questions of actual human psychology. Both take apriority to hinge on the source or method of warrant.

One might think that the main difference lies in the fact that Kant acknowledges more types of warrant as sources of apriority. Leibniz and Frege allow self-evidence and proof. Kant allows, in addition, constructions that rest on pure intuition and reflection on the nature of cognitive faculties.

I think, however, that this difference is associated with a fundamentally different orientation toward apriority. Frege and Leibniz explicate the nature of apriority in terms of a deduction from general basic self-evident truths. All that matters to apriority is encoded in the eternal, agent-independent truths themselves. For deductive proof turns entirely on such contents. An individual's being apriori justified consists just in thinking through the deductive sequence with understanding.

For Kant, the apriority of mathematics depends on possible constructions involving a faculty, pure intuition, that does not directly contribute components of truths, the conceptual components of propositions or thoughts. According to Kant, the proofs in arithmetic and geometry are not purely sequences of propositions. The justifications, both in believing axioms and in drawing inferences from them, must lean on imaginative constructions in pure intuition, which cannot be reduced to a sequence of truths. The intuitive faculty contributes singular images in apriori imagination. Not only are these not part of an eternal order of conceptual contents. The proofs themselves essentially involve mental activity and make essential reference, through intuition, to particulars. For Kant these particulars

---

[15] Kant, (1781, 1787: B2-3).

are aspects of the mind. So the structure of a mathematical proof makes essential reference to possible mental particulars. It is not an eternal sequence of truths that are fundamentally independent of particulars.

Kant's conception of synthetic apriori cognition thus depends on an activity, a type of synthesis involved in the making of intuitive constructions in pure imagination. It is significant that, unlike Leibniz and Frege, he makes no appeal to self-evidence. That is, he does not claim that the evidence for believing the basic truths of geometry and arithmetic is encoded in the truths. In arithmetic he does not even think that axiomatic proof is the basis of arithmetical practice.[16]

This orientation helps explain Kant's tendency to predicate apriority of cognition rather than truths. It is also at the root of his concentration, in his investigation of apriori warrant, on the functions and operations of cognitive capacities, not on the nature of conceptual content and the relations among truths. The orientation makes the question of what it is to *have* a justification much more complex and interesting than it is on the Leibniz-Frege conception. And it ties that question more closely to what an apriori warrant is.

Kant's shift in his understanding of apriority from the content of truth and of proof-sequences of propositions to the character of cognitive procedures opens considerably more possibilities for understanding sources of apriority, and for seeing its nature in capacities and their functions, or even in specific acts or mental occurrences, rather than purely in propositional forms. Kant's account does not depend on empirical psychology, but it does center on a transcendental psychology of the cognitive capacities of any rational agent.[17]

---

[16] Kant (1781, 1787: A164/B205).

[17] The relation between the two approaches is complex and needs further exploration. But it is worth remarking that Kant's approach has this advantage of flexibility: For Leibniz and Frege, a truth is either apriori or aposteriori. It is apriori if its canonical or ideal mode of justification is apriori. Its canonical mode of justification is apriori if it is situated in a natural proof structure either as a primitive truth – which does 'not need or admit of proof' – or as a deductive consequence from primitive truths and rules of inference. On Kant's conception, a truth can be known or justifiably believed either apriori or aposteriori, depending on what form of justificational procedure supports it for the individual. For on this conception, apriority is predicated not primarily of truths but of modes of justification, or even states of cognition. Kant did not make use of this flexibility. Its possibility is, however, implicit in his conception.

Michael Dummett, (1991: p. 27), writes 'it is natural to take Frege as meaning that an a priori proposition may be known a posteriori: otherwise the status of the proposition would be determined by any *correct* justification that could be given for it.' He goes on to discuss whether there are any propositions that can be known only apriori. I have no quarrel with Dummett's substantive discussion. But his historical reasoning is off the mark. Frege's characterization takes apriority to apply to truths or idealized judgments. There is no relativization to particular ways of knowing those truths. A truth or judgment-type is either apriori or not. A truth or judgment is apriori if its best or canonical justification proceeds as a deductive proof from general principles that neither need nor admit of proof. Dummett fails to notice that there

A second way in which Frege diverges from Kant is that his explanation of apriority in *The Foundations of Arithmetic* section 3 makes no mention of sense experience. Instead he characterizes it in terms of the generality of the premises of its proof.[18] Both Leibniz and Kant characterize apriority directly in terms of justificational independence of experience. Unlike Leibniz, Kant consistently takes experience to be *sense* experience. Since any modern notion of apriority seems necessarily tied somehow with justificational independence of experience, Frege's omission is, strictly speaking, a mischaracterization of the notion of apriority.[19]

From one point of view, this omission is not of great importance. Frege evidently took his notion of apriority to be equivalent with justificational independence of sense experience. His discussion of Millian empiricism follows his definition of apriority by a few pages. In those sections he repeatedly writes of 'observed facts', apparently picking up on the notion of fact that appears in his definition of aposteriority (*FA*: sections 7-9). He seems to assume that mere 'facts' – unprovable truths that are not general – – can enter into justifications only through observation.[20] So a proof's depending on particular facts would make it rest on sense-experience. Moreover, his criticism of Mill explicitly takes 'empirical' to be opposed to 'apriori' (*FA*: section 8).

---

is no clear meaning within Frege's terminology for a question whether a truth can be known both apriori and aposteriori. That question can be better investigated by shifting to a Kantian conception of apriority. Dummett slides between the two conceptions. Frege could certainly have understood and accepted the Kantian conception; but he did not use it or propose it.

Dummett's reasoning to his interpretation is unsound. Suppose for the sake of argument that we reject the view that an apriori proposition can be known aposteriori. (I myself would resist such a rejection.) We might allow that there are empirical justifications for something weaker than knowledge for all propositions. For example, we might strictly maintain the Leibniz-Frege conception and insist that apriori truths can be known only apriori. Then it simply does not follow that the status of the proposition would be determined by any correct justification that could be given for it. The status would still be determined by the best justification that could be given for it. Oddly, Dummett clearly sees that this is Frege's conception elsewhere – Dummett (1991: p. 23).

[18] As Dummett notes, Frege's definition of 'apriori' is cast in such a way that the premises of apriori proofs are counted neither apriori nor aposteriori. Dummett (1991: p. 24). I think that Dummett is correct in thinking this an oversight of no great significance. It would be easy and appropriate to count the primitive truths and rules of inference apriori.

[19] There are differences between Leibniz's and Kant's accounts on this point that are relevant, but which I intend to discuss elsewhere. Leibniz often characterizes apriority in terms of justificational independence of experience. Leibniz sometimes allows intellectual apprehension of intellectual events to count as 'experience'. Kant firmly characterizes apriority in terms of justificational independence of *sense* experience. Kant's specification has important consequences, and makes his view in this respect the more modern one. It was taken up by Mill, the positivists, and most other twentieth century empiricists. For purposes of epistemological discussion, 'experience' has come to mean *sense experience*.

[20] Precisely the same inference can be found in Leibniz (1705; 1765; 1989: Preface 49-50).

In *Foundations of Arithmetic* section 11, Frege infers from a proof's not depending on examples to its independence of 'evidence of the senses'. The inference suggests that he thought that a proof from general truths necessarily is justificationally independent of sense experience. At the beginning of *The Basic Laws of Arithmetic* he states the purpose of *The Foundations of Arithmetic* as having been to make it plausible that arithmetic is a branch of logic and 'need not borrow any ground of proof whatever from either experience or intuition.'[21] Here also Frege assumes that a proof's proceeding from general logical principles entails its justificational independence from experience or intuition. Frege commonly accepts the Kantian association of intuition (in humans) with sensibility, so here again it is plausible that he meant by 'experience' 'sense experience'.

In very late work, forty years after the statement of his definition, Frege divides sources of knowledge into three categories: sense perception, the logical source of knowledge, and the geometrical source of knowledge. He infers in this passage from a source's not being that of sense perception that it is apriori.[22]

So Frege took his definition of apriority in terms of derivation from general truths to be equivalent to a more normal definition that would characterize apriority in terms of justificational independence from sense experience. Still, the non-standardness (incorrectness) of Frege's definition is interesting on at least two counts. First, its focus on generality rather than independence from sense-experience reveals ways in which Frege is following out Leibnizean themes but in a distinctively Fregean form. Second, the definition is backed by a presupposition, shared with Leibniz, that there is a necessary equivalence between justifications, at least for finite minds, that start from general principles and justifications that are justificationally independent of sense experience. It is of some interest, I think, to raise questions about this presupposition.

2   Apriority and Generality

Let us start with the first point of interest. Leibniz and Frege both see apriori truth as fundamentally general. Apriori truths are derivable from general, universally quantified, truths. Both, as we have seen, contrast apriori truths with mere truths of fact. Leibniz held that mere truths of fact are contingent, and that apriori truths are necessary. He took necessary truths to be either general or derivable from general logical principles together with

---

[21] Frege (1893a,b, 1902a,b: section 0). Compare this characterization of the earlier book's purpose with the one quoted from Frege (1884: section 87 cf. note 1 above). It is possible that the latter characterization constitutes a correction of the mischaracterization of apriority in Frege (1884, section 39).

[22] Frege (1979: pp. 267ff., 276-7); Frege (1983: pp. 286ff., 296-7).

definitional analyses and logical rules of inference. So for Leibniz the apriori – aposteriori distinction lines up with the necessary – contingent distinction, and both are closely associated with Leibniz's conception of a distinction between general truths and particular truths.[23]

It is tempting to regard Frege in the same light. As we have seen, Frege even defines apriority in terms of derivability from general truths and aposteriority in terms of derivability from particular truths. But there is little evidence that Frege associated apriority or generality with necessity. In fact, modal categories are strikingly absent from Frege's discussion.

We can gain a more refined understanding of Frege's differences from both Leibniz and Kant by contrasting his terminology with Kant's. Kant's conception of apriority, as we have seen, is explicitly defined in terms of a cognition's independence for its transcendental or epistemological genesis and its justification from sense experience. But he cites two other properties as marks (*Merkmale*) or sure indications (*sichere Kennzeichen*) of apriority. One is necessity. The other is strict generality (or universality) (*strenge Allgemeinheit*).[24]

---

[23] Leibniz, (1705; 1765; 1989: Preface 49-50; IV, vii, 2-10, 408-13; IV, xi, 13, 445-6). The characterization of Leibniz's view that I use in this section, which brings it very close to Frege's, depends on laying aside Leibniz' views of God's cognition. The characterization seems to me true for Leibniz's view of finite, human cognition, but less obviously true of his view of divine cognition. Leibniz thought that God could have apriori knowledge of contingent truths through infinite analysis. By analyzing the infinitely complex individual concepts of conungently existing individuals, God could know all truths about them. Cf. 'Necessary and Contingent Truths' in *Leibniz: Logical Papers*, Parkinson trans. and ed. (Oxford, Clarendon Press, 1966): pp. 97ff. In discussing God's infinite analyses, Leibniz lays no explicit weight on the generality of the apriori truths. It is not clear that Leibniz thought that for God apriority is ultimately general. What Leibniz emphasizes is analysis of contents in such a way as to resolve them into identities. There is little discussion of the nature of the contents, where they come from, how they are determined. Whether these truths, which are knowable apriori through formal analysis by God, are ultimately singular is open to question. On the other hand, Leibniz thought that even individuals are reflections of a plan of God's. It therefore seems possible that contingent singular identities, on Leibniz's view, are ultimately instantiations of some general rational plan, which might have the status of a general law. Cf. *Discourse on Metaphysics* section 6. Leibniz sees singular identities in logic and mathematics as resolvable into identities that instantiate general necessary truths. These are truths that are knowable apriori by finite minds. In this Leibniz and Frege are one. Regardless of whether he thought that a generalization lay at the bottom of infinite analysis of contingent truth, Leibniz is also kin to Frege in his emphasis on the idea that apriority lies in formal structure. I am indebted for these qualifications to John Carriero.

[24] Kant (1781, 1787: B3-4; cf. A2; A91-2/B124). The same point is made in Kant (1790), section 7 (*Akademie Ausgabe* V, 213). There Kant calls comparative generality 'only general' (*nur generale*), and strict generality 'universal' (*universale*). Compare Leibniz, (1705; 1765; 1989: IV, ix, 14, 446): 'The distinction you draw [between particular and general propositions] appears to amount to mine, between 'propositions of fact' and 'propositions of reason'. Propositions of fact can also become general, in a way; but that is by induction or observation, so that what we have is only a multitude of similar facts...This is not perfect generality, since we cannot see its necessity. General propositions of reason are necessary...'

There are two points to be noted about these remarks. One is that Kant provides these marks or indications not as elements in the definition of apriority, but as signs, which according to his theory are necessarily associated with apriority. In fact, in providing these signs, he takes them to be sufficient for apriority. He does not, in these famous passages, claim that they are necessary conditions.[25] The reason why on his view apriori judgments are associated with necessity and strict generality, is not that these associations follow from his definition or conception of apriority. The associations derive from further commitments in Kant's system.

Kant explains strict generality itself in terms of modality. Kant contrasts strict generality with comparative or assumed generality. Comparative generality holds only as far as we have observed.[26] A judgment thought in strict generality 'permits no possible exception'. Kant infers from this that such a thought is taken as holding absolutely apriori.

Neither Kant nor Leibniz gives any hint of defining apriority in terms of generality. Both appeal, however, to generality in their elucidations of apriority. Frege's use of generality (*Allgemeinheit*) in his definition is surely inherited from them. Like them he believed that apriority is deeply connected with some form of generality of application, or universal validity. But he interpreted and used his notion of generality differently. He departs from both Leibniz and Kant in *defining* apriority in terms of generality. He departs from both in saying little about the relation between apriority and

---

[25] I think that Kant believed that necessity was (necessarily) necessary as well as sufficient for the apriority of a judgment. He clearly believed that being, or being derivable from, a strictly general proposition is sufficient for the apriority of a judgment. Kant surely believed that all apriori judgments are true without any possible exceptions. Whether he believed that all apriori judgments have to be derivable from judgments that are in the form of universal generalizations is more doubtful. I shall discuss this matter below. Whether strict generality was only a sufficient condition (a mark) of apriority, not a necessary one – or whether it was both necessary and sufficient, but understood in such a way as not to entail the logical form of a generalization – is a complex question that I shall leave open. What is certain is that Kant's views on the relation between apriority and both necessity and strict generality depend not merely on his definition or conception of apriority, but on other elements in his system. I believe that rejecting Kant's positions on these relations is compatible with maintaining his conception of apriority.

[26] Cf. n. 24. Strictly speaking comparative generality and strict generality do not seem to be exhaustive categories. It would appear that there are propositions that are comparatively general but which are not true accidental generalizations (there is a counterinstance that simply has not been found); yet true accidental generalizations are not necessary truths. This is because it is possible for there to be true accidental generalizations which have no counter-instances yet observed. (I leave open whether there are also empirical laws which are general but which are not strictly general, in Kant's sense.) It is possible, of course, that Kant means the 'we' in 'what we have so far observed' in a loose and highly idealized sense. It is conceivable that he intended comparative generality to include all possible actual observations by 'us'. Given his idealism, he would take this as equivalent to the empirical truth of the generalization. This is a matter that could bear more investigation.

necessity. Indeed, his conception of generality differs from both in that he does not connect it to modal notions, seen as independent notions, at all.

Frege does comment on the relation between generality and necessity very briefly in *Begriffsschrift*. He associates generality with the logical form of the contents of judgments. He claims that apodictic judgments differentiate themselves from merely assertoric ones in that they suggest the existence of general judgments from which the proposition can be inferred. He then writes:

> When I designate a proposition as necessary, I thereby give a hint about the grounds of my judgment. But since the conceptual content of the judgment is not thereby touched, the form of the apodictic judgment has no significance for us.[27]

Frege seems to think that necessity is not represented in logical form, but is to be explained in terms of a pragmatic suggestion regarding the epistemic grounds for a judgment. Generality for Frege (in the sense relevant to this context) is simply universal quantification. What makes a truth apriori is that its ultimate grounds are universally quantified. So Frege seems to explicate necessity in terms of apriority. Apriority is the notion that Frege attaches in *Foundations of Arithmetic* to the condition he envisages here in the *Begriffsschrift* of a judgment's having its ground in general propositions. If anything, Frege explains necessity in terms of the (ordinary) generality of the grounds of the proposition. This contrasts with Kant's explaining (strict) generality in terms of necessity.

I think that Frege was trying to get the effect of the difference between accidental generalizations and empirical laws, on one hand, and necessary generalizations, on the other, while avoiding explicit introduction of independent modal notions. His notion of generality is the simple one of universal quantification. Not just any general truth is apriori, however. Only general truths that are self-evident axioms, or first-truths, or which are derivable from self-evident axioms, or first-truths, are apriori. Apriori generalizations are generalizations whose *ultimate justification* does not rest on particular truths.

Frege does use the notion of law in his characterization of apriority: 'If...it is possible to derive the proof purely from general laws, which themselves neither need nor admit of proof, then the truth is apriori' (*FA*, section 3).[28] Empirical laws need and admit of 'proof', in that they need justification from statements of observation about particulars. It is common to hold that the notion of law contains or implies modal notions. That may well be. But I believe that Frege thought of laws in terms of basic principles in a

---

[27] Frege (1879), section 4. The issue is discussed briefly by Gabriel (1996).

[28] I believe that Frege's use of 'possible' in this remark is dispensable. It is possible to derive the proof in his sense if and only if there is a proof.

system of scientific propositions – either an empirical science or a deductive science – not (at least not officially) in terms of any modal or counterfactual element. Empirical laws are basic principles of idealized empirical scientific systems of true, grounded propositions. But they are not basic in the order of justification: singular observational statements (along with an apriori principle of induction) are supposed to be justificationally prior. Apriori laws differ in just this respect.

So the key idea in distinguishing empirical laws and accidental generalizations from apriori truths is taking apriority to be justificational derivation from general truths, which themselves are self-evident and do not need or admit of proof. Frege's notion of *generality* is fundamentally less modal than Kant's notion of strict generality or universality. It is simply that of universal quantification, where quantification is understood to be unqualifiedly general – to range over *everything*. Apriority is understood in terms of the priority of generality in justification.[29]

I have no doubt that Frege worked with an intuitive notion of logical validity. This enters his formulation of rules of inference. But the universal validity of *logical* laws is supposed to lie in their applicability to *everything* – which includes mathematical and geometrical objects and functions. The mathematical objects provide a sufficiently large and strict subject matter to enable true quantifications in logic and mathematics to have some of the force and effect of necessary truths that purport to quantify over possible objects or possible worlds. This force and effect seems to suffice for Frege's purposes. Frege seems to avoid invocation of an independent notion of modality and of merely possible objects, in epistemology, metaphysics, and logic.

Leibniz took all truths to be deducible in principle from truths of logic. On his view, it is a mere weakness of the finite human intellect that requires it to invoke empirical experience to arrive at ordinary truths about the physical world. Frege joined the rest of mankind in regarding Leibniz's view as overblown (*FA*: section 15). Of course, he agreed with Leibniz in holding that arithmetic is derivable from logic. Logic is naturally seen as a canon of general principles associated with valid inference. Here Frege sided with Leibniz against Kant in holding that one can derive truths about particular, determinate objects – the numbers – from purely general logical principles. Frege specifically states his opposition to Kant's view that without sensibility, no object would be given to us (*FA*, section 89). He argues that he can derive the existence of numbers from purely general logical laws. In this, of course, he failed. But the Leibnizean idea of obtaining

---

[29] Frege has another concept of 'generality', of course, by which he distinguishes arithmetic and logic, which are completely general in their domain of applicability, from geometry, which applies only to space.

truths about particular determinate objects from general, logical, apriori principles is fundamental to his logicist project.

It seems to me likely that Frege's opposition to iterative set theory partly derives from the same philosophical picture.[30] Iterative set theory naturally takes objects, the ur-elements which are the members of sets, as primitive. They may be numbers or unspecified ur-elements, but they are naturally taken as given. Frege thought that an apriori discipline has to start from general principles. And it would be natural for him to ask where the ur-elements of set theory come from. If they were empirical objects, they would not be given apriori. He regarded the null set as an indefensible entity from the point of view of iterative set theory. It collects nothing. He thought a null entity (a null extension) is derivable only as the extension of an empty concept. If one took the numbers as primitive, one would not only be giving up logicism. One would be assuming particular objects without deriving their existence and character from general principles – thus controverting Frege's view of the nature of an apriori subject. If one could derive the existence of numbers from logical concepts, one would not need set theory to explain number theory or, Frege thought, for any other good purpose. Thus it would have been natural for him to see set theory as raising an epistemic puzzle about how its existence claims could be apriori, inasmuch as they appear to take statements about particulars as primitive or given.

Leibniz actually *characterizes* reason as the faculty for apprehending apriori, necessary truths. These include for him all mathematical truths. As I have noted, Leibniz regards all necessary truths as ultimately instances of, or derivative from, *general* logical principles together with definitional analyses and logical rules of inference.[31] Generality for Leibniz is a hallmark of human reason. Principles of identity and non-contradiction underly and provide the logical basis for proof of mathematical truths. As noted, Frege agrees that arithmetic is thus derivative from general logical principles. He takes arithmetic to be an expression of pure reason, and its objects given directly to reason through logical principles (*FA*, section 105).

Kant famously separates apriority and necessity from pure reason in the sense that he holds that some apriori, necessary truths, the synthetic ones, can be known only by supplementing reason with the products of a non-rational faculty for producing singular representations – intuition. For Kant intuition is essentially a faculty for producing *singular* representations. It is

---

[30] Frege (1884: sects. 46-54; 1893,a,b, 1902a: 30; 1893; 1902b: I, 2-3; 1984: pp. 114, 209, 228; 1967: p. 104-5, 209-210). The latter passage especially seems to find the problem in the assumption of single things at the base of set theory. The idea that concepts are general and objects must be derivative from principles governing concepts guided his opposition.

[31] Leibniz (1705; 1765; 1989: Preface, 49-50; I, i, 19, 83; IV, vii, 2-10, 408-13; IV, vii, 19, 424; IV, xi, 13, 445-446). On these matters, see Margaret Wilson, 'Leibniz and Locke on "First Truths"', *Journal of History of Ideas* 28 (1967), pp. 347-366. Cf. note 23.

part of his view that synthetic cognition of objects, including synthetic apriori cognition in arithmetic and geometry, must partly rest its justification on the deliverances of intuition. Hence the justification must rest partly on singular representations, and perhaps propositions or thoughts in singular form as well.

Of course, Frege disagrees with Kant about arithmetic. He holds that arithmetic is not synthetic, but analytic – at least in the sense that it is derivative from general logical principles without any need to appeal to intuition. But Frege purports to agree with Kant about geometry (*FA*, section 89). He agrees that it is synthetic apriori. It is synthetic in that it is not derivable from logic. The logical coherence of non-Euclidean geometries seemed to confirm its synthetic character. Frege also purports to agree that geometry rests on pure apriori intuition.[32] He agrees with Kant in counting intuition a faculty different from the faculty of thought (e.g. FA 26, 90). Frege's agreement with Kant that apriori truths of geometry rest on intuition, a faculty for producing singular representations, puts some pressure on Frege's view that apriori truths must rest on fundamentally general laws. As we shall see, there is some reason to think that Frege's relation to Kant on this matter is not as straightforwardly one of agreement as he represents it to be.

3 Generality and Independence of Sensory Warrant

Let us now consider the second point of interest in Frege's characterization of apriority. This is his presumption that his characterization of apriority in terms of the primacy of generalizations in proof is equivalent with the usual post-Kantian characterization in terms of justificational independence from sense experience.

There are at least three areas where both the general characterization and Frege's assumption of equivalence can be challenged. One has to do with certain types of self-knowledge, and perhaps more broadly, certain context-dependent truths. One has to do with geometry. One has to do with arithmetic. I will not go into these issues in depth. But I hope that broaching them will be of both historical and substantive value.

Frege exhibits no interest in *cogito* judgments: judgments like the judgment that I am now thinking. But his characterization of apriority immediately rules them aposteriori, in view of the singularity of their form and their underivability from general laws. Now the question of whether *cogito* judgments are in fact aposteriori is a complex one.

---

[32] Unlike Kant, Frege gives no clear evidence of believing that all synthetic apriori principles rest on intuition. He holds that the principle underlying (non-mathematical) induction is synthetic apriori, but he gives no reason to think that it rests on intuition. This point is made by Michael Dummett (1982: p. 240).

Leibniz is in accord with Frege in counting them aposteriori. He counts them primitive, self-evident truths which nevertheless depend on 'experience'.[33] What Leibniz means by 'experience' is not very clear. His view suffers by comparison to Kant's in its vastly less developed conception of cognitive faculties and of the nature of experience. Sometimes Leibniz associates experience with sense experience. But it appears that he sometimes uses a very broad conception of experience that would include any direct awareness of an object or event, whether or not this awareness proceeds through one of the senses. Thus 'experience' for Leibniz, at least at times, seems to include not only what we would count sense experience but intellectual 'experience' as well. A conception of apriority as independence from experience in this broad sense would be defensible. Its counting instances of the *cogito* 'aposteriori' would also be defensible.

Frege consistently associates experience with *sense experience*. If he were to relax this association, it would be open to him to side with Leibniz (or one side of Leibniz) here against Kant in counting non-sensory intellectual awareness of particular intellectual events as experience.[34] Such a conception would, however, sever the connection between apriority and independence of the experience of the senses. Frege seems to accept this connection. It has dominated conceptions of apriority since Kant. What seems to me thoroughly doubtful is that our cognition of instances of the *cogito* (and perhaps other indexical thoughts such *as I am here now* or *I exist*) is justificationally dependent on sense experience. Such cognition seems to depend only on intellectual understanding of the thought content in an instance of thinking it. Contingent, singular truths seem to be apriori in the sense that our warrant to accept them is justificationally independent of sense experience.

If these points are sound, they raise interesting questions about the relation between apriority, reason, and generality. It seems to me natural – at least as a working conjecture – still to regard reason (with Leibniz and Kant) as essentially involved in supplying general principles and rules of inference. A warrant can, however, be justificationally independent of sense experience if it gains its force from either reason or understanding. And understanding essentially involves singular elements. The view is fundamentally Kantian: Reason is essentially general. Understanding, because of its interdependence with non-rational capacities, is sometimes understanding of truths in singular form

---

[33] Leibniz (1705; 1765; 1989: IV, vii, 7, p. 411; IV, ix, 3, p. 434; cf. IV, ii, 1, p. 367).

[34] Kant also thought that instances of the *cogito* produce no 'apriori' cognition. But this view cannot be directly derived from his characterization of apriority alone, as it can be from Leibniz's characterization. Rather Kant's view depends on his very complex (and I think mistaken) theory of the justificational dependence of cognition of one's thoughts in time on inner sense, which ultimately depends, albeit indirectly, for its justificational force on outer sense. I shall not discuss this Kantian view here.

that cannot be proved from general truths. Warrant can be apriori if it derives from reason or from understanding, if it does not depend on sense experience for any of the force of its epistemic warrant.

I believe that Kant was mistaken, however, in holding that understanding can yield non-logical cognition only if it applies to the form or deliverances of sensory capacities (and non-logical *apriori* cognition only if it applies to their form). I believe that understanding is capable of yielding non-empirical and non-sensible cognition of thoughts in singular form that are not derivable from general ones. One can, for example, know by intellection and understanding alone that certain of one's intellectual mental events are occurring (or have occurred), or that one is thinking. No invocation of sensible intuition or the form of one's sensory capacities is needed for the justification that underwrites the relevant knowledge. It seems to me plausible that our understanding sometimes applies to intentional contents that are tokens, instances of indexicals, in singular form.[35]

Perhaps to account for the apriority of our warrant for believing such instances, the warrant must be seen as deriving *partly or in some way* from something general. For example, to understand the self-evidence of an instance of *I am now thinking*, one must understand *I* according to the general rule that it applies to whomever is the author of the thought that contains its instantiation. One must understand a similar general rule for *now*. Thinking according to such rules, one can realize that any instance of *I am now thinking* will be true. This is an entirely general insight. It seems to me plausible to consider a logic for the *forms* of such indexicals as an expression of reason. Here the generality of reason would not reside in the form of the propositional content (which is singular), but in the generality of the rules governing its application. The semantical rule is in general form.[36]

But the realization of the truth of an *instance* of the *cogito* cannot be derived purely from these generalities. It cannot be derived purely from a logic of indexicals or from anything purely general. It must involve an awareness in understanding of an actual event of thinking and a recognition of its content. Thus the warrant cannot rest purely on an inference from general principles. There is something irreducibly singular in the application of the understanding. The warrant depends essentially for its force on the exercise of this singular application. Although the truth – the instance of the *cogito* – would count as aposteriori on Leibniz's conception and on Frege's conception, it is plausibly apriori on the Kantian conception: The warrant for an instance of thinking it is justificationally independent of sense experience. The warrant depends for its force purely on intellectual understanding applied to a singular instance of a *cogito* thought. (Cf. n. 34).

---

[35] Cf. Burge (1996; 1998b).

[36] For an example of a logic of such singular indexicals, see Kaplan (1989).

4   Apriority, Particularity, and Geometry

I turn now to Frege's application of his characterization of apriority to geometry. Frege accepted Kant's doctrine that Euclidean geometry is synthetic apriori. Frege meant by 'synthetic' here *not derivable from logic*. Frege also maintains with Kant that geometry rests on sensible geometrical spatial intuition. With Kant, Frege held the now discredited view that Euclidean geometry is both apriori and apriori-applicable to physical space. It is now tenable to hold that Euclidean geometry is apriori only if one considers it a pure mathematical discipline whose proper application, or applicability, to physical space is a separate and empirical question. I want, however, to discuss the issue of the epistemic status of Euclidean geometry from Frege's perspective.

What did Frege mean by his agreement with Kant about the epistemology of Euclidean geometry? There is no firm evidence that Frege accepted Kant's idealist conception of physical space. Frege's whole philosophy, especially in his mature period, seems out of sympathy with the explanation of apriority in terms of the mind's imposing its structure on the physical or mathematical worlds.[37] Frege articulated his agreement with Kant by agreeing that geometry is based on, or has its 'ground' in, pure intuition (*FA*, sections 12, 89).[38]

For Kant, pure intuition is both a faculty and one product of the faculty. Intuition is a faculty for singular, immediate representations. It represents singular elements of (or in) space or time without being mediated by any further representations that apply to the same semantical values or referents. Pure intuition is the faculty itself, considered independent of any passively received, sensational content. For Kant intuition could be either an intellectual faculty (in which case its exercises would always be pure), or a sensible one.[39] We humans have, according to Kant, only sensible intuition. Pure sensible intuition is the structure of the faculty which is constant regardless

---

[37] For an elaboration of some aspects of this theme, see Burge (1998a).

[38] Cf. also 'On a Geometrical Representation of Imaginary Forms in the Plane' in Frege (1984: p. 1; or 1967: p. 1); 'Methods of Calculation based on an Extension of the Concept of Quantity' in Frege (1984: p. 56; or 1967: p. 50).

[39] Frege shows a certain superficiality in his reading of Kant in Frege (1884: section 12). There he first notes that in his *Logic* Kant defines an intuition as a singular representation, noting that there is no mention there of any connection with sensibility. He further notes that in the Transcendental Aesthetic part of *Critique of Pure Reason* the connection is added (*hinzugedacht*), and must be added to serve as a principle of our cognition of synthetic apriori judgments. He concludes that the sense of the word 'intuition' is wider in the *Logic* than in the *Critique*. But it is not wider. In both books intuition is characterized in terms of singularity (and in the *Critique* sometimes in terms of immediacy as well). Cf. Kant (1800: section I.1; 1781; 1787: A320/B376-7). Kant intentionally leaves sensibility out of the characterization of the notion in both books because he takes intellectual (non-sensible) intuition to be one possible type of intuition – possible in principle, though not for humans.

of what sensational contents one receives in sense-perceptual experience or produces in empirical imagination.

Kant also believed that pure sensible intuition could itself yield pure representations as product – pure formal intuitions.[40] Such representations are representations of elements in the structure of space and time. Given his idealism, these elements were supposed to be features of the structure of the faculty of sensible intuition. Intuitions of all sorts are characterized by Kant as being objective representations that are both immediate and singular.[41]

If one strips this view of its idealist elements, one can regard pure sensible intuition as a faculty for intuiting the pure structure (not of the faculty itself but) of mind-independent space and time. Frege shows no interest in pure temporal intuition. Of course, in his mature period he rejects Kant's view that arithmetic rests on pure temporal intuition, or intuition of any sort. He believed, however, that we have a capacity for pure spatial intuition. He believed that Euclidean geometry is in some way grounded in exercises of this capacity. Like Kant, Frege associates the capacity for pure intuition (in humans at least) with sensibility – the capacity for having sense experiences. He distinguishes it from a capacity for conceptual thought (*FA*: section 14).

What interests me is Frege's understanding of the singularity of pure intuition and its relation to his characterization of apriori truths as following from general principles that do not need or admit of proof. He cites and does not reject Kant's conception of intuitions as individual representations (*FA*: section 12). He regards the axioms and theorems of Euclidean geometry as apriori. So he thought that they are, or follow from, general principles that do not need or admit of proof. The proof must work out without reference to unprovable truths which are not general and which contain assertions about determinate objects [*bestimmte Gegenstände*]. Kant takes intuitions to play a role in the warrant of some geometrical axioms and rules of inference. What is the epistemic role in Frege's view of pure intuitions – which for Kant are certainly singular, not general – in warranting the axioms of geometry?

Frege is aware of this question. He speaks to it in section 13 of *The Foundations of Arithmetic*. He writes,

> One geometrical point, considered in itself, is not to be distinguished any way from any other; the same applies to lines and planes. Only if more points, lines, planes are comprehended at the same time in an intuition, does one distinguish them. From this it is explicable that in geometry general propositions are derived from intuition: the intuited points, lines, planes are really not particular (*besondern*) at all, and thus they can count

---

[40] Kant (1781, 1787: B160).

[41] Kant (1781, 1787: A320/B377).

as representatives of the whole of their kind. But with numbers it is different: each has its own particularity (*Eigentumlichkeit*).[42]

Frege does not use language in this passage that connects precisely with the language of his characterization of apriority.[43] Perhaps he simply believed that since the relevant objects of intuitions are not 'particular' (*besondern*), they are not 'determinate objects' (*bestimmte Gegenstände*). (Cf. the definition of aposteriority.) Or perhaps he believed that pure intuition's contribution to the justification of general truths lies not in its representation of determinate objects (the individual lines and planes that it represents), but of aspects of them that are not particular to those objects. He may have thought that although we must be presented with particulars in pure intuition, the warranting power of the intuition lies *only* in geometrical properties that are invariant under Euclidean transformations. In either case, Frege does not give a precise explanation of how intuition helps 'ground' (*FA* section 12) our knowledge. Hence Frege gives no precise explanation of how his view of the apriority of geometry is compatible with his view of its depending on pure intuition – a faculty for singular representation.

Nevertheless, the main thrust of the passage seems to be to downgrade the role of the particularity of the geometrical objects, and of the singularity of thoughts about them, in the 'derivation' of general truths. In fact, Frege says that the objects of pure intuition in geometrical imagination are not genuinely particular. He seems to see the lines that he regards as objects of intuition as types. So they can serve as representatives whose characteristics that are shareable with relevantly similar objects are all that matter for arriving at general propositions. It is difficult to see here how Frege's view relates to Kant's, even bracketing the fact that Frege does not advocate Kantian idealism.

Let us approach this question by first comparing the just quoted passage from Frege with a passage in Leibniz. Leibniz writes:

> But I do not agree with what seems to be your view, that this kind of general certainty is provided in mathematics by 'particular demonstrations' concerning the diagram that has been drawn. You must understand that geometers do not derive their proofs from diagrams, although the expository approach makes it seem so. The cogency of the demonstration is independent of the diagram, whose only role is to make it easier to understand what is meant and to fix one's attention. It is universal propositions,

---

[42] Frege does not make it clear why it matters that one can distinguish the objects of intuition from one another only if they are comprehended in a complex intuition, or why this fact shows that the objects are not really particular at all.

[43] In a paper on Hilbert, Frege seems to sympathize with the idea that axioms assert basic facts about intuition. But he is focused on Hilbert's view that axioms both assert and define things. Frege's main point is that axioms cannot do both; he clearly believes that they assert something. There is little in the passage to help us with his attitudes toward the singularity of intuitions or their precise role in the epistemology of geometry. Cf. Frege (1984: pp. 275-7; 1967: pp. 264-6).

i.e. definitions and axioms and theorems which have already been demon-
strated, that make up the reasoning, and they would sustain it even if there
were no diagram.[44]

Leibniz holds that the singular elements introduced through reliance on
a diagram are inessential to a proof or derivation of the general propositions
of geometry. Frege's passage does not squarely advocate Leibniz's position. But Frege seems to be explaining away the elements of singularity in
his conception of pure intuition in order to avoid acknowledging that the
general truths of geometry are derivative in any way from singular elements
in intuition. This direction of thought about (pure) geometry seems to me
reasonable and plausible. But it is questionable whether Frege's view is
really compatible with Kant's.

Kant sees himself as fundamentally at odds with Leibniz about geometry. He takes the role of pure intuition in geometry to be to produce an irreducibly singular element into mathematical understanding, reasoning, and
justification. The problem for making these comparisons cleanly is that
Kant's own view, though developed in great detail and subtlety, is not entirely clear or agreed upon.

I shall, however, sketch my view of it. Kant takes pure intuition in geometry to be intuitions of determinate objects. The objects of intuition are
particulars, such as line-drawings, or even possible line-drawings, in pure
geometrical intuition – pure imagination. (They can also be carried out in
empirical intuition, on paper; but only non-empirical formal aspects of the
empirical intuition play any role in mathematical understanding, reasoning,
and justification.) From these objects one abstracts objects of a more general kind – 'the triangle', for example – which are the objects of mathematical reasoning.[45] These latter objects are forms within the structure of space
or time – on Kant's idealist view, forms of spatio-temporal intuition itself.

Theoretical cognition for Kant is fundamentally cognition of objects.
Kant thought that pure mathematics has objects, and that those objects are
not contingent, empirical objects.[46] 'Determination' (*Bestimmung*) is a fundamental term in Kant's epistemology. Objects of successful theoretical
cognition – the sort yielded in geometry – are necessarily determinate, or
objects of determinate concepts, specific, non-vague concepts. They are
abstracted from determinate particulars that are referents of pure intuition.
The abstracted objects are determinate formal objects – spatial shapes, like

---

[44] Leibniz (1705; 1765; 1989: IV, i, 360-1).

[45] Kant (1781, 1787: A713-4/B741-2; A723/B751).

[46] The point is denied in Friedman (1992: chs. 1 and 2). There are, however, numerous passages
in which Kant makes it clear that he believes that pure mathematics has objects which are *not* the
empirical objects experienced in space and time. For one such passage, see Kant (1781, 1787:
A723/B751). I will develop these points in some detail in future work on Kant.

triangles, and lines, planes, volumes. They form the subject matter of Euclidean geometry. The principles of geometry are about these objects. And thoughts about them are supported and guided by pure intuition about particular instances of these determinate objects. The role of intuition, hence the role of representation of *particulars*, is ineliminable from Kant's account of our understanding and warrant for pure geometry.

A passage in Kant that is comparable to the passages in Frege and Leibniz that we have just quoted is as follows:

> Mathematical cognition [is reason-cognition out of] the construction of concepts. To construct a concept means to exhibit the intuition corresponding to it. For construction of a concept therefore a non-empirical intuition is required, which consequently as intuition is a single object (*einzelnes Objekt*), but nonetheless, as the construction of a concept (of a general representation), it [the intuition] must express in the representation general [or universal] validity (*Allgemeingültigkeit*) for all possible intuitions, which belong under the same concept. Thus I construct a triangle by exhibiting the object corresponding to this concept, either through mere imagination in pure intuition, or in accordance therewith also on paper through empirical intuition, but in both cases purely apriori, without having had to borrow the pattern for it from any experience. The single drawn figure is empirical, yet it serves to express the concept without impairing its universality (*Allgemeinheit*); for in the case of this empirical intuition we look only at the action of the construction of the concept, to which [concept] many determinations [*Bestimmungen*] – for example, the magnitude of the sides and angles – are completely indifferent, and therefore we abstract from these differences, which do not alter the concept of triangle.... mathematical cognition [considers] the general in the particular (*Besonderen*), in fact even in the individual (*Einzelnen*), although still apriori and by means of reason, so that just as this individual is determined under certain general conditions of construction, the object of the concept, to which this individual corresponds only as its schema, must be thought as universally (*allgemein*) determined.[47]

Frege's claim that 'the intuited points, lines, planes are really not particular (*besonders*) at all' is definitely not compatible with Kant's view. Kant maintains that the referents of intuition are always particular or singular.[48] He takes the singularity of the intuition to be essential to the normative, justificational account of mathematical cognition. He takes abstraction from certain particularities inherent in the single object presented in pure intuition (or even in empirical intuition) to be necessary to understanding

---

[47] Kant (1781, 1787) A713-4/B741-2. The translation 'we look at' and 'we abstract from' is necessary for smooth rendering in English, but the German uses an impersonal passive construction in both cases.

[48] Actually for Kant the immediate referents of intuitions are property instances or mark-instances had by particular objects. And objects include parts of space and time as well as physical objects. But these are subtleties that we need not go into here.

the mathematical concept (the general concept, triangle) and to doing pure geometry. But the singularity of the intuition is irreducibly part of the justification of mathematical cognition.

Frege explains the general validity of geometrical truths by maintaining that the particularity of pure intuition is only apparent. They can therefore 'count as representatives of the whole of their kind'. Like Kant, he sees the particulars as serving as representatives or stand-ins for more general features. He does not explain what role the singular aspects of intuition play in the process. But unlike Kant, he appears to be committed to thinking that they play no role in mathematical justification. This would explain his departure from Kantian doctrine in his claim that the intuited lines and so forth are not really particular at all. Unlike Kant, Frege is not interested in the particularity of mental acts in his explanation; this is a sign of his lack of commitment to Kantian idealism. He sees intuition as presenting typical geometrical structures which have no intrinsic individuality.

Kant explains the general validity of geometrical truths by maintaining that the particularity is genuine and ineliminable but is *used* as a schema. One abstracts from particular elements of the objects of intuition in forming a general object of the geometrical concept (and geometrical principle).

Like Frege, Kant does not make completely clear the role of the particular in warranting and guiding universal principles and inferential transitions. He seems to think that the particularistic elements in mathematical reasoning ground it in particular elements of space and time that reveal mathematical structures with maximum concreteness, and thus safeguard mathematical reasoning from the dangers that even transcendental philosophy is faced with. Kant seemed to think that mathematics' concern with particularity helps explain its certainty. But it *is* clear that he thought that the role of the particular is not to be explained away or seen as merely apparent. It is hard to escape the view that for Kant, in contrast to Frege, synthetic apriori propositions in geometry are grounded not in general propositions but in possible or actual particularistic judgments that are guided and supported by intuitions about particular, determinate objects of pure geometrical intuition. Although there are ways of understanding Frege's own view so as to render it internally consistent, and even perhaps sound, it is doubtful that it is consistent with Kant's.

Frege is aware of a need to discount the role of the particular, individual, or singular in geometrical warrant. If the general propositions rested, justificationally, on singular propositions, they could not be apriori in his sense.

Kant holds that the principles of geometry are strictly general or universally valid. He thinks that the basic principles are in the form of generalizations. But he does not hold that the root of geometrical warrant – the apriority of geometry – lies in generality. The synthetic apriori axioms – and the inferential transitions – in pure geometry rest on non-general representations, pure intuitions. His examples of pure intuition supplementing our conceptions to yield warranted belief commonly involve propositions used singularly about particular geometrical constructions in Euclidean space.[49]

Kant claims that the successive synthesis of the productive imagination in the generation of figures – a process of singular representation – is the basis of axioms and inferences in Euclidean geometry. Although the axioms are general, their warrant does not rest on general propositions or general thoughts alone.[50]

There is a way of construing Frege's introduction of the notion of apriority that would reconcile his view with Kant's. Recall that Frege writes: 'If...it is possible to derive the proof purely from general laws, which themselves neither need nor admit of proof, then the truth is apriori' (*FA*: section 3.) Geometrical proof, in the modern sense of 'proof', starts with geometrical axioms. These are general. Thus for Frege 'proof' in geometry rests on general truths, axioms. One might hold that Kant realized as well as anyone that geometrical proofs begins with the axioms. On his own view, the axioms are general (universally quantified). Thus interpreted, there is no disagreement.

What makes this resolution unsatisfying to me is that neither Frege nor Kant utilized precisely this modern notion of proof. For Frege, proof is canonical justification. The axioms are, on his view, general, self-evident, and in need of no warrant from anything further. For Kant the axioms and proofs in geometry are warranted through their relations to actual or possible line-drawings in pure intuition – thus through their relation to singular representations.[51] These representations must (to represent their objects at all) be conceptualized and backed by propositions or judgments in singular form.

---

[49] Kant (1781, 1787: A220-1/B267-8; A234/B287).

[50] Of course, in his theory of arithmetic, Kant denies that arithmetical propositions are derivable from axioms – hence from anything general – at all. He seems to regard the singular arithmetical operations and equations as basic. Cf. Kant (1781, 1787: A164-6/B204-6). Frege effectively criticized this extreme rejection of the role of axioms and proof in arithmetic. Frege (1884: section 5). He is of course right in rejecting Kant's view that intuition enters into the justification of *inferences* in geometry and arithmetic. The issue of whether particularity is basic to mathematical justification is independent of whether justification of mathematical propositions (commonly) involves proof, and even of whether particularity enters the justification through non-conceptual intuition or directly from understanding. For a fine discussion of Kant's view of the role of intuition in inferences, see Friedman (1992: chs.1 and 2). I believe that in supporting his sound view that Kant believed that intuition is necessary to mathematical inference, Friedman underplays the role of intuition in providing a basis for at least some of the axioms of Euclidean geometry. I think that Kant thought that intuitive constructions are as much a part of geometrical warrant and practice as commitment to the axioms is. Indeed the two go together.

[51] Ultimately for Kant the warrant presupposes the point that space is a form of our intuition of physical objects. Cf. Kant (1781, 1787: A46-8/B64-6; B147). Hence the warrant for geometry (and indeed all of mathematics) depends on the alleged fact that its applicability to the world of experi-

So, Frege's notion of proof is one of canonical justification, not merely deductive sequences of thoughts. And on Kant's view axioms and proofs in geometry require warrant from pure intuition, which is essentially a faculty of singular representation. Unlike Frege, Kant is not wedded to a view of apriority that takes it to be founded in generality.[52] For Kant, synthetic apriori cognition is cognition that is grounded in the particular. For Kant the use of pure intuition is an integral part of geometrical practice and the mathematical understanding of the axioms and inferences themselves. Thus insofar as it is possible to compare like to like – Frege's epistemological conception of proof with Kant's conception of justificational reasoning within geometry – the views of the two epistemologies appear quite different.

As I have emphasized, Frege leaves it unclear exactly what role intuition plays. But he implicitly denies a basic Kantian doctrine in holding that the objects of intuition are either not particular, or not fundamental to warrant in geometry. His picture of the role of particular elements in intuition seems in this respect to be more Leibnizean than Kantian. There is no evident room on his view to give intuition (as a singular representation) a warranting role.

I believe that Frege's verbal agreement with Kant about geometry is thus misleading. Frege accepts the language of Kant's doctrine of pure intuition – as applied to geometry. But it is doubtful that he can consistently accept all that Kant intends by this doctrine, and maintain the centrality of generality in his conception of apriority. Frege's Leibnizean conception of apriority takes generality of justificational starting point to be fundamental. He uses Kant's terminology of pure intuition, but he divests it of any commitment to referential singularity or reference to particulars, at least in its role in grounding geometrical principles. He retains Kant's view that intuition is essentially a non-rational (non-logical) faculty, thus appealing to intuition in order to explain his non-logicist, non-Leibnizean view of geometry. In this way he holds together a Leibnizean conception of apriority with a Kantian rejection of logicism about geometry. The fact that Frege provides a less detailed account of geometry, and less full explication of his term 'intuition', than Kant does, is explained by Frege's preoccupation with the mathematics of number.

There is a further aspect of Frege's account of intuition in geometry that renders it very different from Kant's. Kant takes intuition to be a type of

---

ence is guaranteed through its having as its subject matter the forms of our experience. This is part of Kant's 'transcendental deduction' of the objectivity of mathematics. I have little sympathy for this side of Kant's view, which in large part depends on his transcendental idealism.

[52] In fact, he contrasts apriori cognition in mathematics with apriori cognition in philosophy by insisting on the central role of particularity in the justification of mathematical cognition. Cf. Kant (1781, 1787: A164/B204; A713-5/B741-3).

objective representation.[53] Frege holds that intuition is not objective. In fact, he explains objectivity partly in terms of independence from intuition, which he regards as essentially subjective (*FA*: section 26). In this passage, Frege makes his notorious claim that what is intuitable is not communicable. He sets out the thought experiment according to which what one being intuits as a plane another intuits as a point. He holds that since they can agree on geometrical principles (despite their subjective differences), their agreement is about something objective – about spatial structures that are subject to laws. Here again, it appears that particularistic aspects of intuition play no substantive role in Frege's account of the warrant for believing geometrical principles.

This doctrine of the subjectivity of spatial intuition is certainly not Kantian. Indeed, Kant characterizes intuition as an objective representation, in explicit contrast with subjective representations (sensations).[54] It is true that from a transcendental point of view, Kant regards space itself and hence pure apriori intuition as a form of our 'subjective' constitution.[55] This is part of Kant's transcendental deduction of the objectivity of geometry. Kant thinks that only because, from the transcendental point of view, space, geometry, and apriori intuition are *all* to be construed idealistically as forms of the subject, can one account for the objectivity of apriori principles – and indeed the objectivity of pure intuition – in geometry about space. From the 'empirical point of view' – the point of view of the practice of ordinary science and mathematics – apriori intuition, geometrical principles, and space itself are all objectively valid and in no way confined to individuals' subjectivity.

Frege appears to have thought that the ability of mathematicians to produce logically coherent non-standard geometries shows that one can conceive (though not imagine or intuit) the falsity of Euclidean geometry. He thought that our grasp of the self-evidence of the axioms of Euclidean geometry depends on some non-rational, or at least non-logical, capacity that he termed 'intuition'. The elements intuited that are captured by the axioms are common to all – and in fact can be grasped in thought even by subjects whose subjective intuitions differ from ours.[56] So particularistic aspects of the intuitions seem to play no role in their warranting the axioms.

Frege calls Euclidean axioms self-evident. This view is in some tension with his appeal to intuition as ground for the axioms. The warrant ('evi-

[53] Kant (1781, 1787: A320/B376-7).

[54] Kant (1781, 1787: A320/B377).

[55] Kant (1781, 1787: A48/B65).

[56] This explication is well-expressed by Dummett (1982: p. 250). I believe also that Dummett is correct in arguing that there is substantial evidence against the view that Frege accepted Kantian idealism about space. For an excellent, general discussion of Frege's views on geometry, see Tappenden (1995).

dence') for believing the axioms seems not to rest purely in the senses of the axioms themselves. At least, one can apparently conceive of them as being false if one abstracts from spatial intuition. So the notion of self-evidence must be understood to include support from capacities whose deliverances are not entirely assimilated into the senses of the axioms themselves, or at least provides a support for them that is needed as supplement to any conceptual grasp of them that would abstract from such support.[57] Perhaps general features associated with what mathematicians intuit, but *only* general features, play a role in warranting the axioms.

Both Kant and Frege held that Euclidean geometry yields apriori knowledge of physical space. As noted, this view is now untenable. What remains philosophically interesting is the epistemology of *pure* geometry. Warrant for mathematicians' belief in pure geometry seems to be apriori. Understanding the axioms seems sufficient to believe them. But what does such understanding consist in? Geometrical concepts appear to depend in some way on a spatial ability. Although one can translate geometrical propositions into algebraic ones and produce equivalent models, the meaning of the geometrical propositions seems to me to be thereby lost. Pure geometry has some spatial content, even if it involves abstraction from the exact empirical structure of physical space. Perhaps there is something in common to all legitimate spatial notions that any pure geometry makes use of. Whether the role for a spatial ability in our warrant for believing them is particularistic and non-conceptual – as Kant claims – or fully general and conceptual – as Leibniz, and seemingly Frege, believe – seems to me to invite further investigation.

I believe that Kant is likely to be right about the dependence of our understanding of pure geometries on our representation of spatial properties through sensory, non-rational capacities. Frege appears to have sided with Kant on this matter. I think that Kant is probably wrong in holding that a non-conceptual capacity, pure intuition, plays a warranting role in geometrical understanding, much less geometrical inference. Leibniz's view of warrant as deduction from basic (conceptually) understood truths of pure

---

[57] It is not entirely clear to me what Frege, in his mature *post-Foundations* work, thought the relation between intuition and the senses of geometrical propositions is. The subjective elements in intuition are surely not part of the senses. Whether he thought that in conceiving non-Euclidean geometries and regarding them as logically consistent yet incompatible with Euclidean geometry, we give different senses to the key terms ('straight') or give the same sense but somehow abstract from intuitive support is not clear to me. Frege seems to have thought that sometimes intuitions are used in symbolic ways, as representations of something other than what is intuited, in geometrical reasoning. For example, in discussing generalizations of geometry beyond Euclidean space to a space of four dimensions, Frege says that intuition is not taken for what it is but as symbolic for something else (Frege 1884: section 14). He may have seen the same sort of process as involved in conceiving Euclidean geometry false in the context of reasoning within non-Euclidean geometry. This is a matter that invites further investigation.

geometry seems closer to a sound modern mathematical epistemology. Like Kant, Frege appears to give pure intuition a role in warranting at least belief in the axioms of geometry. (I know of no evidence that Frege agreed with Kant that intuition is essential to warranting geometrical inference.) But Frege gives pure intuition a role in geometrical warrant only after removing the key Kantian feature of singularity of reference from this role. Moreover, Frege's view of the relation between the role of intuition in geometrical warrant and the alleged subjective character of intuition is left unclear.

It seems to me that conceptual understanding of the axioms of the various pure geometries suffices to warrant one in believing those axioms, as propositions in pure mathematics. Intuition in the Kantian sense seems to play a role in the fixing of geometrical content, but not in the warrant for believing the axioms or rules of inference.

5 Apriority, Particularity, and Arithmetic

I turn finally to the application of Frege's account of apriority to arithmetic. It is, of course, central to Frege's logicist project that truths about the numbers – which Frege certainly regarded as particular, determinate, formal objects (e.g. *FA*: sections 13, 18) – are derivative from general logical truths. The attempt to extract the existence and properties of particular objects from general principles centers, unfortunately, in Frege's defective Axiom V. There is a wide range of difficult issues here, and I cannot engage them seriously in this essay. But I want to broach, very briefly, some further points regarding Frege's characterization of apriority.

Suppose that Frege is mistaken, and arithmetic is not derivable in an epistemically fruitful way from purely general truths. Suppose that arithmetic has the form that it appears to have – a form that includes primitive singular intentional contents or propositions. For example, in the Peano axiomatization, arithmetic seems primitively to involve the thought that 0 is a number. And in normal arithmetical thinking we seem to know intentional contents that have singular form ($0 + 1 = 1$, for example) without deriving them from general ones. If some such knowledge is primitive – underived from general principles –, then it counts as aposteriori on Frege's characterization. This would surely be a defect of the characterization. The knowledge does not seem to rest on anything other than arithmetic understanding. This seems to be intellectual understanding. The justification of the knowledge does not involve sense experience in any way. Even though the knowledge does not seem to rest on pure sensible intuition, or on anything having essentially to do with perceptual capacities, it may be irreducibly singular.[58] Indeed it seems to be irreducibly singular from an epistemic point of view, regardless of whether it concerns (as it appears to) abstract but particular objects. At any rate, the failure of Frege's logicism gives one reason to worry whether apriority and generality coincide, even in the case of arithmetic. It seems to me, even after a century of reductive attempts, that we need a deeper investigation into the epistemology of arithmetic.

I think that from an epistemological perspective, arithmetic should be distinguished from set theory, second order logic, and various other parts of logic and mathematics. The enormous mathematical interest of the logicist project, and other reductive enterprises that have dominated the 20th century, should not be allowed to obscure the fact that our understanding and hence our mode of knowing these other theories is different from our understanding of arithmetic. It seems to me even that the typical Peano formulation of arithmetic in terms of the successor function is epistemologically different from the formulation in terms of Arabic numerals on a base ten, which most of us learned first. Mathematical equivalence does not entail sameness of sense (in Frege's sense), and hence sameness of cognitive mode of presentation.

6   Summary

It is time to summarize. Frege's characterization of apriority in terms of generality is a mischaracterization. Apriority bears an essential connection to justificational independence from experience. In modern times, 'experience' has come to mean *sense* experience. But Frege's characterization raises fundamental questions about the relation between apriority and generality. Frege followed a Leibnizean conception that assumed a close coincidence between the two notions.

If one thinks of experience sufficiently broadly (so as to include 'intellectual experience' not just sense experience), some of the pressure against the coincidence can be dissipated. Such a conception may have been one of Leibniz's conceptions of experience, and the associated conception of apriority may therefore have been Leibnizean as well. Such a conception could treat the instances of the *cogito* and other token, indexically based, self-evident truths as aposteriori. This is because the conception construes apriority in a way that excludes from the apriori even justificational dependence on purely intellectual 'experience'. Given a Kantian conception of apriority, which is more in line with the dominant modern conception, self-knowledge and knowledge of certain other indexical-involving truths can

---

[58] In fact, our knowledge of set theory, while apriori, also seems to make primitive reference to particular sets, as noted earlier. Whereas Frege blamed set theory, rejecting it altogether, I am inclined to fault Frege's conception of apriority.

be apriori. For warrant seems to derive purely from intellectual understanding. It in no way rests on sense perception.

Problems with geometry and arithmetic remain. Leibniz, Kant, and Frege all maintained that geometry and arithmetic are apriori. If the position is carefully confined to *pure* geometry and arithmetic, it seems highly plausible. I believe, however, that we do not understand very well the role of spatial abilities in the content and justification of pure geometries. So I think that it is not fully clear whether justification in pure geometry rests on purely general propositions, although it seems to me likely that it does. The case of arithmetic is, I think, more serious as a possible counterexample to the claim of a coincidence between apriority and the primacy of generalizations in canonical justification. For arithmetic is apparently committed to basic truths in singular form, in its most natural and straightforward formulations.

I think that Frege is right to reject Kant's claim that the deliverances of a non-conceptual faculty, pure intuition, are *justificationally* basic in the warrant for arithmetic. But Kant may nevertheless have been right to hold that although cognition of arithmetic is apriori, cognition (or propositions) in singular form can be justificationally basic. One's justification derives from an understanding that encompasses singular intentional contents. On such a view, some apriority would be non-logical, and would not derive purely from *general* principles of pure reason. In arithmetic apriori knowledge would derive from intellectual, non-sense-perceptual understanding of necessary, non-context-dependent, singular intentional contents. I think that we should investigate in more depth the innovation that Kant offered: apriority that does not rest on logical or other general principles. I recommend doing so without assuming that apriori theoretical cognition must be constrained, as Kant insisted, by relation to sensibility. I recommend doing so without presuming that we must invoke Kant's notion of pure sensible intuition. I believe that we can follow Leibniz and Frege in avoiding essential reliance on pure intuition in arithmetic, without following them in insisting that generality lies at the base of all apriori warrant. Kant's conception of underived, singular understanding which is nevertheless apriori seems to me worth pursuing.*

---

* I gave a shorter version of this paper at a conference on Frege in Bonn, Germany, in October 1998. I am indebted to John Carriero, Wolfgang Künne, Christopher Peacocke, Rainer Stuhlmann-Laeisz, and Christian Wenzel for comments that led to improvements. In the text I use 'apriori' and 'aposteriori' as single English words. In quotations from Frege, Kant, and Leibniz, I use the Latin phrases 'a priori' and 'a posteriori'. I use 'apriority' instead of the barbaric 'aprioricity'. The latter is the misbegotten result of drawing a mistaken parallel to 'analyticity'. It would be appropriate to the form 'aprioric' which of course has no use. 'Aprioricity' bears no natural relation to 'apriori'. Quine pointed this out to me several years back.

References

Adams, R. M. 1994, *Leibniz: Determinist, Theist, Idealist.* Oxford, Oxford University Press.

Burge, T. 1992, Frege on Knowing the Third World, *Mind* 101 pp. 633-650.

Burge, T. 1996, Our Entitlement to Self-Knowledge, *Proceedings of the Aristotelian Society.*

Burge, T. 1998a, Frege on Knowing the Foundation, *Mind* 107 pp. 305-347.

Burge, T. 1998b, Memory and Self-Knowledge, *Externalism and Self-Knowledge*, eds. Ludlow and Martin. Stanford, CSLI Publications.

Dummett, M. 1982, 'Frege and Kant on Geometry' *Inquiry* 25 pp. 233-254.

Dummett, M. 1991, *Frege: Philosophy of Mathematics.* Cambridge, Mass., Harvard University Press.

Frege, G. 1879, *Begriffsschrift.*

Frege, G. 1884, *The Foundations of Arithmetic.*

Frege, G. 1893, 1902, *The Basic Laws of Arithmetic.*

Frege, G. 1893b, 1902b *Grundgesetze der Arithmetik.*

Frege, G. 1967, *Kleine Schriften,* ed. Angelelli. Hildesheim, Georg Olms.

Frege, G. 1979 *Posthumous Writings*, eds. Hermes, Kambartel, Kaulbach. Chicago, University of Chicago Press.

Frege, G. 1983, *Nachgelassene Schriften.* Hamburg, Felix Meiner.

Frege, G. 1984, *Collected Papers* ed. McGuinness. Oxford, Basil Blackwell.

Friedman, M. 1992, *Kant and the Exact Sciences.* Cambridge, Mass., Harvard University Press.

Gabriel G. 1996, Frege's "Epistemology in Disguise", *Frege: Importance and Legacy,* ed. Schirn. Berlin, Walter de Gruyter.

Kant, I. 1781, 1787, *The Critique of Pure Reason.*

Kant, I. 1790, *The Critique of Judgment.*

Kant, I. 1800, *Jäsche Logic.*

Kaplan, D. 1989, A Logic of Demonstratives, *Themes from Kaplan*, eds. Almog, Perry, and Wettstein. New York, Oxford University Press.

Kripke, S. 1972, *Naming and Necessity.* Cambridge, Mass., Harvard University Press.

Leibniz, G.W., 1966, *Leibniz: Logical Papers*, trans. and ed. Parkinson. Oxford, Clarendon Press, 1966.

Leibniz, G.W. 1714, *Monadology.*

Leibniz, G.W. 1705; 1765; 1989, *New Essays on Human Understanding* (New York, Cambridge University Press.

Leibniz, G.W. 1989, *Philosophical Essays*, eds. Ariew and Garber. Indianapolis, Hackett Publishing Company.

Lotze, R.H. 1880, *Logik.* Leipzig.

Lotze, R.H. 1888, *Logic*, trans. Bosanquet. Oxford 1888, repr. New York 1980.

Mill, J.S. 1843, *System of Logic.*

Schirn, M. ed. 1996, *Frege: Importance and Legacy*. Berlin, Walter de Gruyter.

Tappenden, J. 1995, Geometry and Generality in Frege's Philosophy of Arithmetic, *Synthese* 102, pp. 319-361.

Wilson, Margaret, Leibniz and Locke on "First Truths", *Journal of the History of Ideas* 28 (1967), pp. 347-366.

Part II

SENSE AND PROPOSITIONAL CONTENT

5

Sense and Objectivity in Frege's Logic

GILEAD BAR-ELLI

The essentials of Frege's revolutionary logic appeared in his *Begriffsschrift* (B, 1879). Important aspects of its philosophical basis, and its significance for the foundations of mathematics, appeared in *The Foundations of Mathematics* (FA, 1884). Six years later, at the beginning of the 1890s, Frege published three articles that mark significant changes in his conception: "Function and Concept" (FC, 1891), "On Sense and Reference" (SR, 1892) and "Concept and Object" (1892). Notable among these changes are: (a) The systematic distinction between the sense and the reference of expressions as two separate ingredients of their meaning. (b) The extension and generalization of the notion of function to include the conception of concepts and relations as functions to truth-values, and the corresponding conception of the two truth-values as objects.[1] These changes were immediately incorporated in the mature, authoritative exposition of his logic in his *magnum opus: Basic Laws of Arithmetic* (BL), whose first volume appeared in 1893.

What is the role of the notion of sense and of the distinction between sense and reference in Frege's *logic*? Is there a systematic connection be-

---

[1] The extension of the notion of a function was already a major theme in B (see B section 9). But there it was introduced as an expression and was perhaps flawed by a confusion of sign and thing signified, or expression and content expressed. Moreover, since Frege thought there in terms of a general undifferentiated notion of content, and he did not clearly distinguish a function from its values, essential features of his conception remained unclear. I shall not go into the details here.

tween the two points (a) and (b) mentioned above, so that their being incorporated together in Frege's mature logic is not accidental? These questions, I believe, are central to understanding Frege's mature conception.

In the sequel, after presenting the problem in a sharper way (1), I shall sketch what seems to me the general direction of an answer (2-3), and then add further clarifications of related issues (4-5). In three sentences the general direction is this: Logic, in its wide sense, is, for Frege, the science of justification and objectivity. These are correlative notions: the objective is what is justifiable, and justification requires objective standards. The role of the notion of sense in this enterprise is in establishing the objectivity of the basic truths of a domain (including logic itself), which is accomplished by presenting these truths as expressing features of the ways in which the objects of the domain are given to us. This appeal to objects and their modes of presentation gives a particular realistic turn to Frege's notion of objectivity: One face of it connects it to justification; another, to objects and their modes of being given to us.[2]

1 Two Characterizations of Sense

1.1 The Core Idea - Sense as a Mode of Being Given

Frege's notion of sense is usually presented as stemming from epistemological considerations, as carrying the "cognitive value" or informativeness of expressions and sentences. Various formulations of Frege's provide support for such a view, notably the famous paragraph at the beginning of SR, where Frege argues for the need to distinguish the sense from the reference of expressions. Apart from some general principles that govern these notions, the reference of a term is explained as what it denotes in its use in simple sentences, and what these sentences are about.[3] The sense of a term is introduced, on this conception, as the mode or way in which its reference is given to us. Thus "The morning star is the evening star" is true in that the two names have the same reference, and it is informative in that they have

---

[2] Sense, in Frege's philosophy, appears to belong to logic most clearly in definitions and in his theory of definition. I shall not go into these issues here. In its strict sense a definition for Frege is a stipulation of synonymy, as it stipulates identity of sense between definiendum and definiens. The definiendum in fact gets its meaning from the definiens through this stipulation. Clearly in such a conception the distinction between reference and some notion of sense is mandatory. Frege also recognized another, less strict notion of definition in which the definiendum is a term in current use, already endowed with meaning. Here again questions of adequacy and efficiency require appeal to some notion of sense. What the roles of these kinds of definition in Frege's logic are, whether these notions are the same, and whether they are the same as the ones explicated in the text are serious problems I shall not go into here.

[3] In these governing principles lies the great novelty of Frege's notion of reference; I shall not expand on it here. On the significance of this appeal to the notion of aboutness here, and for references, see chapter 7 of my book (1996).

or express different senses in which their "cognitive value" is contained; the sentence as a whole expresses the thought to the effect that these two senses belong to the same reference.[4]

As I said before, this is a prevalent conception of Frege's notion of sense, which finds its clearest formulation in Frege's own writings primarily in SR. Following the terminology I used in my book (p. 7) I call this notion of sense "the core idea" of sense. There is something "local" and lexical about this notion of sense: One begins with the senses of individual simple names, and moves on "from the bottom up" to more complicated ones. It is quite late in the article (32/62) that thoughts are presented as the senses of complete sentences (where presumably the notion of sense is taken as already understood). And nowhere in this article does there occur the crucial idea (central in other writings) that the sense of an expression is a constituent of a thought - the particular contribution the expression makes to expressing this thought.[5]

Being epistemically governed, this notion of sense is also individuated in epistemic terms. Frege often proposes or assumes that two senses are the same if and only if whenever one knows them one knows they are the same. Put in different terms, the criterion says that two expressions express the same sense if and only if it is impossible to understand them both, yet fail to know that they express the same sense.[6]

This account may be correct as far as it goes, but it does not go far enough. For Frege introduces and uses the notion of sense in his distinctly logical writings (e.g. FC, BL). One can naturally wonder about the role this notion of sense plays there, in Frege's logical doctrines, even when one grants the above account of its role in Frege's epistemology, and in his account of various features (such as cognitive value) of natural language sentences and expressions. Logic, as it is often conceived, is concerned with a clear and systematic presentation of deductions and proofs, and so it was

---

[4] Important ingredients of the core idea already appear earlier, though without the systematic terminology. See, for instance B, section 8; FA, section 62. Compare also my book 1996, p. 44, p. 54, p. 111.

[5] This article is unique among Frege's writings in being directly concerned solely with natural language. This is important because, on the one hand, it clearly shows that Frege intended to apply his notions of sense and reference to natural language sentences and expressions, while on the other, it may explain the particular way in which the introduction of the notion of sense here diverges from the way it is presented in later writings of a more logical orientation.

[6] See, for instance, "A Brief Survey...", PW p. 197. The principle is also assumed (though not stated) by Frege in T (65/25; cf. my book p. 70). It should be noted that there are other criteria, which Frege proposes and uses for sameness of senses and thoughts. See, for instance PW 140, letter to Husserl of 9 Dec. 1906, PMC 70. For a broader discussion cf. my book pp. 214-217.

generally conceived by Frege as well.[7] Sense, it may be claimed, does not belong here, even granted its importance in accounting for other, non-logical, features of sentences (in a natural language as well as a logical one).

To highlight the point it is quite typical that, although modern systems of logic derive their essentials from Frege's logic (the generalized function-argument conception, the conception of sentential logic as the logic of "truth functions", i.e. functions over truth-values, the basics of quantification theory, etc.), the most distinguished exception is Frege's notion of sense, which is hardly mentioned in most courses and texts of classical modern logic. Logicians do not seem to need this notion; many of them hardly know anything about it, and many of those who do, who tend to be more philosophically oriented, explicitly and doctrinairely reject it. All this may strengthen the suspicion that, in trying to incorporate the notion of sense into his logic, Frege was appealing to a different notion of sense.[8]

1.2 Sense as a Constituent of Thought

There is, indeed, another conception, or perhaps merely a different emphasis in the conception of sense, which is found mainly in Frege's later writings, and is dominant in his logical works. In this latter conception, thought is the primary notion, where senses are conceived as parts of thoughts (their "building blocks"). The sense of a (declarative) sentence is identified with the thought it expresses and the senses of its constituent expressions are presented as their contribution to that thought. This is the dominant conception of sense in Frege's later writings. It occurs as early as FC (13-14/29), but gets its conspicuous expression in the celebrated section 32 of BL:

> The names, whether simple or themselves composite, of which the name of a truth-value consists, contribute to the expression of a thought, and this contribution of the individual [component] is its sense.

---

[7] See for instance "Logic", PW p. 3, p. 4; "7 Key Sentences..." PW p. 175. This conception of logic is related to Frege's repeated claim that truth, as distinct from the recognition of truth, is the subject-matter of logic (PW 128/139; the beginning of T)

[8] With all its reliance on Frege's ideas, there are some respects in which modern logic took a course different from his, notably in its reliance on set theory and model theory. It may therefore appear that the role played by the notion of sense in Frege's logic is somewhat analogical to the role of the notion of a model in post-Tarskian logic. In some extensions of standard model theory in modal logic this idea has found explicit formulations, e.g. by Hintikka, who has explicitly suggested explicating Frege's notion of sense in terms of the extension of terms in various possible worlds. See e.g. his 1969, p. 105. I believe that this proposal is mistaken and misses some essential features of Frege's notion of sense (e.g. its particular perspectival cognitive character, and its intentionalistic nature (see my book 1996, ch. 1), but it may support the general point made above, that in Frege's logic, the notion of sense played a similar role to that played by model theoretic notions in later developments of logic.

Again, following the terminology I used in my book (p. 7-8), I shall refer to it as the thought-constituent notion of sense. This conception is obviously connected with the context-principle, and seems to be significantly different from the "local-lexical" conception of the "core idea". The difference is perhaps most conspicuous if one considers a thought (as many believe that Frege did) as a Platonic entity, existing in itself, independently of human minds (though perhaps, as Frege says in FA, not of The Mind), and being true or false independently of our cognitive limitations. This notion of thought has not so much to do with knowledge and modes of presentation, as with logic and logical relations: A thought is what is true or false, and what stands in logical relations of deducibility, contradiction and so forth, with other thoughts. Unlike the core idea, senses of sub-sentential expressions are not conceived of as modes of presentation of their references, carrying their "cognitive value", but as constituents of thoughts, constituents whose very being and individuation depends entirely on that of the thoughts containing them and their logical structure.

It is, moreover, difficult to see how sense can be conceived as mode of presentation when the notion of thought is regarded as the primary notion of sense and thus the basis of any other kind of sense. For it is difficult to see what the notion of the mode of presentation of a truth value could amount to, even apart from the grave difficulties in conceiving truth values, regarded as the references of sentences, as objects. As I argued in my book, Frege's notion of sense is primarily intentionalistic, and the idea of mode of presentation is vital to it. This idea is intuitively well understood (or at least relatively so) with regard to objects - primarily concrete "ordinary" objects, and with some refinements and adjustments, abstract objects; it begins, however, to creak and squeak when applied to concepts and functions; it seems completely ad hoc and unintelligible with regard to truth-values. It therefore appears that we are faced here with two unequivalent characterizations of sense, and one may wonder whether the primacy of thoughts and the conception of sense as thought-constituent can be naturally reconciled with the core idea of sense.

Looking back at our opening questions about the role of the notion of sense in Frege's logic, it appears now that the notion of sense relevant to logic is not the epistemic notion of the core idea (a mode of being given), but the later idea of a thought-constituent.[9] Logic, as mentioned before, is concerned with a clear and systematic exposition of inferences or in justifying and establishing truths on the basis of other truths. Whatever is relevant to this task is logic's concern. A thought is what is true or false, and in that sense thoughts form the subject matter of logic. Moreover, it is logic (including the study of the structures and properties of logical languages) that

---

[9] See the proviso about definitions in note 1.

determines what a thought is: A thought is that part of the content of a sentence, which is required for a clear and systematic exposition of the logical relations it can enter into, and, in particular, what is required for establishing and justifying the truth of a statement on the basis of other truths.[10]

Frege's repeated objection to the conception of logic as an abstract, purely formal calculus that can be interpreted in various models is a facet of his insistence on conceiving logical formulae as "full blooded" statements, expressing thoughts which are true or false.[11] This is an essential point in his conception of logic, and it is a point that places the notion of sense immediately into the very center of logic. Logic for Frege is concerned primarily with thoughts and it is what determines the parameters that make a thought what it is.[12]

These points about the difference between the core-idea and the thought-constituent conceptions of sense may appear to threaten the coherence of Frege's notion of sense. It is not clear, however, that they amount to more than a difference in emphasis. I have mentioned before that the difference is most conspicuous on a Platonic conception of thoughts (and senses). It may thus appear that the difference may be diminished if this Platonic conception is rejected, as it is arguable that it suggests a misleading picture of Frege's conception of thought, and that a thought, as well as the conception of the structure of a thought and the contribution its constituents make to it, are themselves epistemic notions, or epistemically constrained. This is the direction taken in my book, where the connection between these two faces of sense is explained along these lines (see, e.g. p. 15). Yet recovering the coherence of Frege's notion of sense in this way may be gained at the price of rendering it in its entirety irrelevant to logic. For it is doubtful whether such an epistemic notion can carry the burden of an objective conception of thought as what is true or false (under bivalence) and as what stands in logical relations, in the strong classical sense. It is also for this reason that the difference seems significant enough to deserve further attention, and that the relations between the two notions (or two aspects of the notion of sense) require careful study.

---

[10] This is central to both the "Logic" of the 1880s and to the later "Logic" of the 1890s (as well as many other writings), both written probably as parts of a general textbook on logic. See PW pp. 1-8; pp. 126-151. The notion of thought here stems from "conceptual content" of B, which is characterized in similar terms. (See B, section 3).

[11] See my article "Frege's Early Conception of Logic", Epistemologia VIII (1985), pp. 125-40.

[12] See Frege's PW 1979, pp. 197-8; compare also C. Diamond 1991, The Realistic Spirit, pp. 115-144, especially pp. 117-120.

2 Sense and Justification - The Coherence of Frege's Notion of Sense

The previous considerations seem to threaten to tear Frege's notion of sense apart, and to show that the notion of sense relevant to logic is the thought-constituent notion. This, I believe, is too hasty a conclusion. I shall try to show this by pointing out the role of the core idea in logic and in establishing the objectivity of logic. Being thus placed at the center of logic, the core idea is seen as correlative and complimentary to the thought-constituent conception of sense. With reference to our opening question about the role of the notion of sense in Frege's logic, we shall thus see that it is precisely its role in logic, conceived as the science of objectivity, which restores the coherence of the Fregean notion of sense.

The key to understanding this is the role of the notion of sense in establishing the objectivity of a domain of thoughts. The criterial sign of objectivity, for Frege, is justification or justifiability: something is objective insofar as it is justifiable or as statements about it are. The first of the three principles in the Introduction to FA is the demand to distinguish between the logical and the psychological, the objective and the subjective. These are parallel distinctions. It appears therefore that the objective is the logical. And logic, as Frege makes clear on numerous occasions, has to do with the justification of propositions. (See the Preface to B; FA section 3; PW p. 3; PW 147.) The main tenor of FA is to establish the objectivity (or "objective factuality", as Frege sometimes says) of arithmetic by clarifying the grounds or justification of arithmetical propositions. Logic, objectivity and justification form an inseparable triad for Frege. This, however, raises a question, for in its simple sense (and so also in Frege) what is objective is what is "out there" in the world, or what concerns objects that are out there in the world, and which are accessible and can be examined by different people, from different perspectives, etc. What, then, is the relationship between these two aspects of the objective: the logical aspect, on the one hand, and being concerned with and based on objects in the world, on the other? In trying to answer this, I believe, we must appeal to the third element of the triad - the notion of justification. What is objective is only what is justifiable or what is used in a justification; in short, what is in the justification-space. Logic is not only itself objective in this sense, but is constitutive of objectivity. It is what sets the standards for justification and objectivity, what constitutes the justification-space.

The main task Frege set up for himself was to establish the objectivity of various domains - particularly mathematics (arithmetic). For him this means presenting statements in this domain as justified or at least justifiable. Logic was the paradigm and primary means of such justification. Deductions and proofs are chains of justifications of some truths on the basis of others. In this sense, logic, being the paradigm of justification is also the heart of objectivity. It is not only a paradigm of objectivity, but it is what sets the standards of objectivity, and is thus constitutive of the very notion of objectivity. It is obvious that on this conception both logic and objectivity have to do mainly with the notion of sense as thought-constituent. The core-idea notion of sense seems to be out of the picture.

But, and this is the main point, there is another level or stage of justification and objectivity, which is not strictly deductive, but can be considered logical still in the wide sense. Logic in this wide sense is precisely the theory of justification or justifiability.[13] This other level is where we justify the basic truths of a domain not by proving them or deriving them from more fundamental truths (since there aren't any), but by showing them to be clear, justified, or evident by the way "their objects", the objects they are about, are given to us. One can even say that these basic truths are justified by the fact that they express (aspects of) the ways "their" objects are given us, or, in other words, by the modes of presentation or senses of these objects.

Frege's primary example of this was geometry. Geometrical truths (theorems) are objective in being justifiable. They are justified, through logical proofs, on the basis of other geometrical truths, and ultimately by the basic truths, or axioms of geometry. But what about these axioms themselves? Obviously, they cannot be derived logically from more basic truths. Should we say they are not justifiable, and therefore not objective? Certainly not. This would ruin the objectivity of the whole edifice built on the basis of these axioms(cf. FA section 26). It is here that this other form of justification is used. The axioms are justified on the basis of the ways their objects, the objects of geometry, are given to us: "Everything geometrical must be given originally in intuition" (FA, p. 75). The axioms, one may say, express at least some basic aspects of these modes of presentation of the geometrical objects.[14]

Frege sets himself the task of constructing something similar for arithmetic, thus establishing solid foundations for mathematics. The defects he found in arithmetic were not only that many arithmetical proofs were unclear or obviously faulty, but also that the whole science of arithmetic lacked an objective basis. To remedy the former fault it was necessary, according to Frege, to present arithmetical thoughts in a systematic logical language that would render their proofs transparent and detectable. That

---

[13] See, for instance, "Logic", PW p. 3; "17 Key Sentences..." ibid. 175. Cf. also my book 1996, pp. 40-46.

[14] Scholars have debated the question of whether this way of being given is basically Kantian spatial intuition, and whether Frege can be regarded as a Kantian in this respect. I shall not discuss this here. Cf. Dummett 1981, IF, pp. 463-470.

was obviously the task of logic, or of constructing a logical language. In principle this was accomplished by the logical language of B (1879). But the latter deficiency was no less severe, and called for no lesser a task: the task, namely, of presenting the objects of arithmetic, the objects the axioms are concerned with (namely, numbers), in such a way that the axioms themselves will be justified.

Frege's logicism - the program of presenting arithmetic as logic- was designed to solve both problems. Expressing arithmetical truths in the language of the *Begriffsschrift* enabled him to present their proofs completely and systematically. But it served a further and, in a way, more basic aim. Being convinced that there is no other way in which numbers can be construed that can justify their axioms, Frege thought that the only way to achieve this goal was to construe them as logical objects. This, together with a logical rendering of other arithmetical notions, would enable us to present and justify the arithmetical axioms as logical truths. Again, the crucial step here is the double move of regarding the axioms, the basic truths of arithmetic, as being about objects of a certain kind (numbers), and regarding the ways these objects are given us as justifying these axioms, thus establishing the objectivity of the whole edifice of arithmetic. This double move may explain Frege's persistent view that establishing the objectivity of arithmetic requires an explication of the nature of numbers and their way of being given to us. This was not just a sort of a Socratic wondering about essences; it was rather a requirement implied by the conception of objectivity under discussion, and by the task of establishing the objectivity of arithmetic. It is evident (as, e.g., the structure of FA makes manifest) that had Frege been satisfied with other ways of establishing the objectivity of arithmetic and explicating the nature of numbers, he would have seen no need and no point in reducing arithmetic to logic. But, of course, for most of his life Frege was convinced that no non-logical account was possible, and was thus "forced" into his logicistic project. Frege's logicism is, from this point of view, not only a reductivist program and a technical achievement, but also a philosophical discovery: it is the discovery that one can present the basic truths of arithmetic as being about objects whose mode of presentation to us as logical objects justifies these truths. Let me elaborate a bit.

3 Logical Objects - Frege's Fundamental Principle

The idea of logical objects is a notorious one. It was not part of the lore of logical tradition, which makes it even more puzzling why Frege held so firmly to it.[15] Moreover, the inconsistency of the fundamental axiom (V) in BL, which concerns logical objects, gave a fatal blow to Frege's "life-project", according to his own admission. Why then was he so persistent (some would say obsessed) about logical objects? I suggest that the answer is important for understanding not only Frege's conception of logic and mathematics, but also his conception of objectivity and sense, and their interrelationships. I offer a partial answer to this puzzle by suggesting two general points and a more specific one:

(a)　　　The idea that any truth or any meaningful statement must be about something, primarily about objects.[16]

(b)　　　The idea that the basic truths of a domain are objective in that they are justifiable, and that the justification of such truths or axioms can be attained in terms of the ways the objects they are about are given to us. (This is the main thesis argued for here).

There must of course be objects, in order for there to be ways in which they are given to us. Hence, these two principles imply that the objectivity of logic as a system of truths based on logical axioms rests on the existence of logical objects, whose ways of being given to us justify the axioms (even if only partially).

(c)　　　Now the specific point: The specific reduction of arithmetic to logic suggested by Frege required appeal to classes (in one version or another), and the immediate Fregean question was how these classes are given to us. Since this is conceived as a reduction to logic, then, if the above position is valid, these classes must be given to us as logical objects. Giving up appeal to how these objects (classes) are given to us as logical objects (their senses) means giving up an account of the objectivity of arithmetic and parts of logic. This was a price Frege was unwilling to pay, and it is hard to blame him for this.

---

[15] "Object-producing principles" were at the basis of Frege's philosophy as early as FA (1884). There Frege adopted a version of the "Hume-Principle", which says, roughly, that The-object-of-F is the same as The-object-of-G iff the concepts F and G are equinumerous (equipotent). George Boolos saw this as a principal reason for regarding Hume's principle as non-logical (see his 1990, pp. 261-77).

[16] Frege held this doctrine throughout his career. See e.g., the early "Dialogue with Punjer on Existence" (PW pp. 53-60), and the late "Numbers and Arithmetic", where he writes: "I, for my part, never had doubt that numerals must designate something in arithmetic, if such a discipline exists at all [...] We do after all make statements of number. In that case what are they used to make an assertion about?..." (PW p. 275). The *locus classicus* of this view is FA section 46, and ch. IV. For a detailed discussion of this point see ch. 7 of my book.

The last point involves some technical questions concerning the exact nature of the reduction involved and the set theory assumed. I shall not get into these issues here, but will confine myself to the essential general point: that on Frege's conception the objectivity of logic and its basic truths relies on there being logical objects and on the ways they are given to us. In order to see that, it is worthwhile to recall some features of the way in which logical objects are introduced (or discovered) in Frege's mature logical system. As early as 1891 (cf. FC, p. 9-10/26) Frege presented the basic idea of what was to become the fifth axiom of BL. He explains and defends a move from a general equivalence of the form $(x)(Fx \leftrightarrow Gx)$, what he calls there an "equality holding generally between values of functions", to an identity between objects - the "courses (or ranges) of values" of these concepts: $\hat{x}Fx = \hat{x}Gx$.

The move from the former to the latter - from the equivalence to the identity - is, according to Frege, irresistible and reliant on a fundamental and indemonstrable logical principle. It is this relationship that expresses the way the logical objects, the courses of values of functions (including extensions of concepts), are given to us. This then is the way in which we get to the logical objects - objects which are given to us by way of logic. Ignoring irrelevant subtleties, we may regard these objects, the courses of values, as classes. The above, then, is the move by which we get classes as logical objects with which the relevant part of logic - predicate logic - is concerned. They are given to us in a particular way which is expressed by that elementary move from general equivalence to identity. And it is this mode of being given that is purported to justify the relevant axiom (axiom V), which says roughly $\hat{x}Fx = \hat{x}Gx \leftrightarrow (x)(Fx \leftrightarrow Gx)$, as the axiom expresses an essential aspect of this mode.

Of course, I do not intend to defend here an axiom that has been proved inconsistent. This particular account of the way the logical objects are given to us has been proved a failure.[17] But this does not mean that the basic position on the relation between objectivity and the ways objects are given to us - a position from which this account emerged - is faulty. It is this position, in its Fregean version, that I am trying to explain. Even if Frege's particular account was a failure, it is important to understand an account of what it was intended to be. It may be relevant to recall that even when, towards the end of his life, Frege gave up the logicistic approach to arithmetic, he still kept unquestioned the view argued for here: that accounting for the objectivity of arithmetic requires an explication of the nature of arithmetical objects and how they are given to us, which he then suggested should be construed on the basis of geometry (cf. "Number and Arithmetic" (PW 275-7),

---

[17] Frege, as has been often noted, had reservations about the fifth axiom of BL right from the beginning, even before learning of the contradiction.

and "A New Attempt..." (PW 278-281)). Moreover, his qualms about axiom V of BL notwithstanding, he never questioned the very idea of logical objects and the need to appeal to them in accounting for the objectivity of logic. He kept talking of the "logical source of knowledge", which requires logical objects (ibid.) and there is no sign that he ever questioned his view that truth and falsity are logical objects.[18]

It may be instructive to consider a passage Frege wrote to Russell (after learning of the contradiction) on 28.7.1902:

> "I myself was long reluctant to recognize ranges of values and hence classes; but I saw no other possibility of placing arithmetic on a logical foundation. But the question is, How do we apprehend logical objects? And I have found no other answer to it than this, We apprehend them as extensions of concepts, or more generally, as ranges of values of functions" (PMC 140-1).

Classes or courses of values are not the only logical objects in Frege's system. There are also two other important logical objects - the two truth-values - the True and the False. These two, as we shall see, are obtained by a similar move from equivalence to identity, although in this case the original move, in SR, is not made by Frege explicitly. In SR truth-values are introduced as the references of sentences by a somewhat strange argument to the effect that if we are concerned with the references of proper names (or sub-sentential expressions), this cannot be because of the thought expressed by the sentence (for which they are irrelevant), but only for its truth-value, which must then be regarded as the reference of the sentence (33/63). Frege then proceeds to say in a uniquely uncritical move:

> "Every declarative sentence concerned with the reference of its words is therefore to be regarded as a proper name, and its reference, if it has one, is either the True or the False. These two objects are recognized, if only implicitly, by everybody who judges something to be true..." (ibid.)

Even if we are ready to accept this strange version of the slingshot argument - ascribing a reference to a sentence - Frege's further move of regarding this reference as an object and the sentence as its proper name might still appear singularly strange and unmotivated. But the idea is quite similar to the one we have seen above with regard to the introduction of value-ranges as objects: an irresistible move from equivalence to identity, from 'P iff Q' to 'p=q', (the capitals stand for sentences, combined into a complex sentence by a sentential operator, and the small letters stand for the

---

[18] In IF (1981) p. 464 Dummett writes that for the late Frege (in "Sources of Knowledge..." of 1924/5) "there are no objects given by logic alone". I don't think this is correct. Frege indeed denies there that sets are objects, and speaks of the dangerous ways in which language can mislead us to postulate objects where there are none. He even speculates that number-words are not names and do not designate objects. But he does not say that there are no logical objects.

appropriate names of truth values). Putting the point in a way more similar to Frege's principle, we might introduce a special operator '*' carrying propositions (or thoughts or the contents of statements, whatever they are) into objects. The transition would then be from 'P↔Q' to '*P = *Q'. We may accordingly formulate a principle, somewhat analogous to axiom V, which would on the one hand express, and on the other be justified by, this elementary logical transition: (*) *P = *Q ↔ (P↔Q). Again, this irresistible move from equivalence to identity expresses a feature of the way we get to these objects - logical objects that are given to us by way of logic.[19]

Here, within the domain of truth-functional logic the equivalence plays a somewhat similar role to that of the general equivalence in the predicate logic. Both express individuation conditions of the basic units of the logical domains concerned: truth and falsity here, functions and their range-values there. In both cases Frege assumed (once explicitly, once implicitly) an elementary and irresistible transition from the equivalence in question to identity between objects. This is the crucial step in which he introduced (or discovered) logical objects as the basis of the objectivity of logic.[20] These objects are the basis of the objectivity of logic in the sense that their modes of presentation, expressed by the elementary transitions involved, justify the basic truths of the said logical domains: "The truth of a logical law is immediately evident from itself, from the sense of its expression" (CP 405). This, according to Frege, is the only way in which such basic truths (axioms) can be justified, hence they form the basis of their objectivity. Senses, according to the core idea, are such modes of presentation, which means that they stand at the very basis of the objectivity of the logical axioms.[21]

---

[19] In my article, "Identity and the Formation of the Notion of Object", *Erkenntnis* 17 (1982), pp. 229-48, I proposed that the ontology of a theory is determined by the "identity stipulation", which identifies a general equivalence relation (indiscernibility defined over all the descriptive predicates of the language) with identity. I was not aware then of the affinity between this idea and the basic Fregean idea I am trying to present here.

[20] Frege calls axioms and basic logical truths "general" (e.g. FA section 3). This means, I suppose, that no particular objects (or functions) are referred to. It seems to me that this does not conflict with my emphasizing objects and their ways of being given as an epistemic ground of the axioms, for I am obviously talking about kinds of objects (truth-values, courses of values of functions) and not particular objects. For example, the propositional axiom a⊃(b⊃a) is, in Frege's mature conception, a generalization over truth-values. It does not refer to a particular truth-value or object. On the conception I propose here it expresses a feature of the ways truth-values are given to us, wherein its justification lies.

[21] The above formulations are quite general and should be qualified in various ways. One of the most important is this: It could be argued that the logical transition mentioned does not express the sense of, e.g., truth-values, for the sense of a truth-value is a particular thought, and the sense of, e.g., a class is certainly more complex than the said elementary logical transition, and contains an element that relates to the sense of the function determining that class. This is true when the sense of a particular truth-value or a particular class is concerned. I am discussing more generally the way in which truth-values and classes are given to us. A thought expresses the sense which "belongs" (as Frege says) to its truth-value, but this is *subordinate to*

4 Frege's Principle and Equivalence-Relations

The equivalence involved in Frege's fundamental principle is not exactly an equivalence-relation, but rather a propositional equivalence. Not just any definition in terms of equivalence relation discovers or presents objects in the sense in which logical objects are presented by Frege's principle. One might fix the meaning of identity between such things as spatial directions or income levels in terms of the appropriate equivalence relations. But these would not amount to "discovering" these objects and would not express the ways these "objects" are given to us, similarly to the way I described above with regard to logical objects. Some light may be shed on this if we compare the above with what might seem to be a similar move in FA. It must of course be remembered that in FA Frege held neither the systematic distinction between sense and reference, nor the doctrine of truth-values as the references of sentences. Moreover, the correlative doctrine of sentences as proper names of objects (the truth-values) seems to conflict with the emphatic conception in FA of sentences as being radically different from names, and of their having a unique and primary character.

In a famous section Frege prefaces to his proposed definition of number in FA (#64) he says that we can introduce directions (as objects) by stipulating that the directions of two lines are identical iff the lines are parallel $(D(a)=D(b) \leftrightarrow a//b)$. This again is a sort of transition from an equivalence to strict identity. Frege agrees with Kant that lines and parallelism are grounded in our (spatial) intuition, and the above principle expresses (at least an important aspect of) a way in which directions might be given to us as objects.

There is, however, a great difference between this example and the general point we made above. The equivalence we talked about in connection with axiom V and (*) is "propositional equivalence"; from a modern point of view, it is, on the face of it, not a relation at all, but is expressed by a truth-functional connective between sentences. The equivalence on the basis of which Frege introduces directions in FA, in contrast, is an ordinary equivalence-relation, which is a relation between objects.[22] The difference I have in mind may seem somewhat non-Fregean in spirit. For in *Be-*

---

the mode in which truth-values are given to us as objects in general. Similarly, a particular sense belongs to a class under the mode in which classes are given to us in general. The elementary transitions discussed are intended to express such general features of the mode of presentation of logical objects.

[22] The status of the general equivalence relation of "indescernibility" in the "identity stipulation" in my paper in note 18 above is more complicated. It may appear that it is an ordinary equivalence relation between objects. This however, is not exactly so. The indiscernibility relation is intentionally defined in terms of propositional equivalence with no presumption of an objectual construal of the semantics involved. The whole point of the "identity stipulation" proposed there is to fix the ontology of the language on the basis of a non-objectual basis.

griffsschrift Frege introduces "identity of content" for "judicable" (i.e. propositional) and non-judicable contents alike. But, besides a notorious confusion of use and mention in that early discussion, the distinction concerned (between propositions and objects) became to be of central importance for Frege in FA. The difference is again blurred by Frege's later view that equivalence (like other propositional operations) is a (first-order) relation of truth-values. I think, though, that the difference holds also for this late view, since even on this view, truth-values are very special objects, and there are reasons to believe that in his mature and late writings Frege continued to adhere to his context principle and the primacy of propositions proclaimed in FA. But I shall not go into this much debated point, for here I am concerned with FA, in which Frege had not yet held this view of truth-values as objects.[23]

The definition of directions in terms of the equivalence relation of parallelism, discussed in FA, is, therefore, not an instance of that transition from (propositional) equivalence to identity of which we spoke above. The problem with such definitions is not only that they are contextual - that what is defined is only the whole identity context of, e.g., $D(a)=D(b)$. It is also the (related) problem that they are definitional stipulations that fix the mode of presentation "vacuously", and do not express an independently existing mode of presentation of the objects concerned. The definition as a whole is therefore not a justifiable truth (though, as Frege himself remarked, it itself may justify a corresponding truth). This is part of what Frege means by saying that one can understand that a//b with no appeal to directions at all. With regard to truth-values, on the other hand, Frege asserts that "these objects are recognized, if only implicitly, by everybody who judges something to be true". The move from parallelism to identity of directions is not the sort of irresistible, fundamental transition in terms of which Frege describes his axiom V.

Directions are not (basic) objects on which the objectivity of geometry rests. Accounting for the way in which they are given to us is thus no part of an account of the objectivity of geometry. Directions *can* be introduced into geometry by the above principle. They *can* be also explicitly defined, on familiar lines, on the basis of the principle. But this is not necessary for the objectivity of geometry. What is required is a conception of the basic

---

[23] In a letter to Russell of 28.7.1902 Frege, mentioning his view in FA, explains the transition from equivalence-relation to identity as the general principle behind Russell's "definition by abstraction". He then remarks that the difficulties involved with this procedure of definition by abstraction are the same as those of "transforming the generality of an identity into an identity of ranges of values" (PMC, p. 141). The English translation here mistakenly put "not" into the sentence (probably a misprint), as if the difficulties concerned in the two cases are different. The original is: "Die Schwierigkeiten sind hierbei aber dieselben, wie bei der Umsetzung der Allgemeinheit einer Gleichheit in eine Werthverlaufsgleichheit" (p. 224). I thank the editors for pointing this out to me.

geometrical objects - lines and points. These are given to us in a particular way expressed (in part) by the geometrical axioms, thus forming a justification for the axioms themselves.[24] The logical case we discussed above is similar: Here we are looking for the basic objects whose modes of being given to us form the basis of the objectivity of the logical domain. What, then, is the point of the example about directions, which Frege discusses at such length?

In FA Frege did not pretend to have "discovered" that there are arithmetical objects, nor was this his aim. That numbers are objects is a fact he was convinced of prior to the logical analysis of their nature. If numbers in arithmetic were the analogues of lines and points in geometry, Frege would have ended up with a sort of Kantian conception of arithmetic, believing that the arithmetical axioms are *sui generis* and irreducible (like the axioms of geometry). But that, of course, was not his view. The task of defining the natural numbers (and the concept of a natural number) was designed to prevent this result. It was designed to show that the axioms are not *sui generis* in this manner. Hence, the numbers are the analogues of directions in geometry rather than of lines. As directions can be defined in terms of "basic" geometrical objects - lines, objects whose mode of being given justifies the axioms - so numbers can be defined in terms of "basic" logical objects - courses of values of functions, objects whose mode of being given to us justifies the basic truths of the domain.

5   Digging into the Self-Evident

In order to sharpen the edges here, I will compare some aspects of the above account with some recent alternatives. Fundamental logical principles (rules of inference as well as axioms) were considered self-evident by Frege. And this has been presented by many authors as their ultimate justification. There is no going beyond this point, according to this conception; this is the end point of the justification-game. Some people regard any attempt to step "beyond" this point as betraying a misunderstanding of Frege's conception of the "autonomy" of logic, the view that there is no "meta-logical perspective" (to use Ricketts' suggestive expression; see his 1986) from which the fundamental logical truths may be justified. It may seem that our previous account about the role of sense in justifying the basic truths of a domain (including logic) is opposed to that, as if we have

---

[24] Cf. Boolos 1990, p. 248. Boolos argues that the Fregean analogy between "the direction of l" and "the number of Fs" is misleading, because "we do not suspect that lines are made up of directions, that directions are some of the ingredients of lines". This is another way of saying what I argue in the text - that directions are not basic geometrical objects. But in contrast to Boolos, I believe that this substantiates Frege's analogy, as the point of these sections in FA is to show that numbers are not "basic" objects either - they are definable in terms of the logical objects. Hence the analogy does serve a point.

suggested an epistemological perspective (grasping the ways in which logical objects are given to us) precisely as such meta-logical perspective.

This may indeed be the case, if logic is narrowly construed as being concerned solely with deductions and proofs. On this narrow conception any attempt to view logical axioms as within the justification space, as being susceptible to any form of justification would amount to attempting a meta-logical perspective. I have argued, however, that Frege's conception of logic was broader: logic, on this broad conception, inheres in, and actually constitutes, the entire justification-space; it is concerned with whatever is relevant to justification. If this broad use of "logic" is adopted (in line, I believe, with Frege, as well as many other nineteenth-century logicians), and logic is construed as the science of justification and objectivity, then the theses of the autonomy of logic and the lack of meta-logical perspective are correct. But then the sense-oriented justification of the basic logical principles and an account of their objectivity are within the logical enterprise. It is not a step beyond logic.

Tyler Burge has rightly emphasized Frege's epistemological concerns in this connection (see Burge 1992, pp. 645-649). However, he characterizes the self-evidence of the basic logical truths in terms of understanding: "[Frege] did see [the basic logical truths] as a source for the justification of the belief in them by a *person who understood them"* (645, my emphasis - G.B). Burge then (rightly again) connects "understanding logical truth" with "understanding the nature of justification for our mathematical judgments" (646) and tries to explain this in terms of Frege's late conception of logic, in *Der Gedanke,* as the science of the laws of truth ("what is") and as the normative science of the laws of thought. The connection is couched in very general terms - the general notions of reason and understanding - and as such seems to me of limited explanatory value. In any case the line I suggest in the text is much more specific in its reliance on a fully fledged notion of sense as a mode of presentation, and on the two faces of objectivity - justification, on the one hand, and relation to objects, on the other.

Burge expands on these themes in his more recent paper of 1998. Frege proposed ways of justifying the basic truths of his logic in what Burge calls "justification through application" (Burge 1998, pp. 330-335). He rightly comments that these applications serve as partial, inductive "tests" of the logical system (1998, p. 332). With regard to the axioms he says that "the recognition of advantages seems to provide a prima facie, probabilistic justification [...] Such recognition may provide indirect grounds for believing that the axioms are indeed basic and indeed true. But the supposed self-evidence of the axioms is ideally the primary source of their justification" (334). The self-evidence of the axioms is not a subjective, or even an epistemical, conviction. It is an objective property concerning which we are fallible, as we may wrongly judge a proposition to be self-evident. We may be wrong either in ascribing self-evidence to a proposition that lacks it, or, inversely, in failing to recognize it where it inheres. And if a proposition is self-evident we come to recognize this by a thorough understanding of it (339).

Understanding a truth may come in various degrees and may involve various factors, including, e.g., the inferential relations it has within a system. But what I am suggesting here is that a thorough understanding of a basic truth must also include a feature of its justification (or grounding), which, in the case of a truth, consists in its expressing the ways in which its objects present themselves to us - their sense. Frege says that "the truth of a logical law is immediately evident from itself, from the sense of its expression" (CP 405). We should take "sense" here very seriously. Understanding a law is grasping its sense, the thought expressed by it; and a thorough understanding is a thorough grasping of the sense, which includes knowing the way it is built up by its constituent senses. These, in typical cases, include the modes of presentation of the objects of these thoughts. Thus recognizing the truth of an axiom and justifying a basic truth are grounded in grasping the senses of their constituents, the modes of presentation of their objects.

Burge points out that although, in some sense, Frege presents arguments for his axioms (e.g. in section 18 of BL), these arguments are neither semantic, nor justificatory. They are not semantic in that they don't mention symbols, and they are not couched in a semantic meta-language. They are not justificatory in that they do not provide a justification of the axiom on the basis of other, more basic axioms. How then should these explanations or arguments to be regarded?

They should be regarded, Burge claims, as explications or articulations of the meaning of the axioms, as expressing a proper understanding of them (1998, pp. 316-329). I basically agree with all that, but wish to emphasize a point that seems to me crucial. With regard to his first axiom, $a \supset (b \supset a)$ Frege argues, or explains, that "it could be false only if both a and b were the True while a were not the True. This is impossible. Therefore $a \supset (b \supset a)$" (BL, section 18). Comparing this to its "counterpart" passage in *Begriffsschrift*, Burge concludes that "The argument serves to articulate understanding of the thought content. It does so in a way that enables one to recognize that its truth is guaranteed by its content" (1998, p.317). This may be an apt description of the *Begriffsschrift* passage, but the BL one contains more. On the face of it, there does seem to be an argument there: Frege articulates what would be required for the axiom to be false, in a way that makes it manifest that this is impossible, and concludes that it must be true. Burge may be right that this is not a semantic argument, and that it does not prove the axiom on the basis of other truths. What then is the point of the argument? The argument, I suggest, couched in the object language, highlights features of the ways the objects concerned (the two truth-values) are given to us (ways constrained by the principles of the classical truth tables presumed here) as justifying the axiom, and laying its truth open to view. Frege does not merely appeal to the meaning of the axiom and to our understanding of it; he appeals to it in a particular way that makes manifest the way its objects are presented to us by appealing to the principles constraining this way.

The justification relation between senses and basic truths is not a foundational one. It is not that senses are prior to or more basic than logical principles. The principles express aspects of the senses of the fundamental objects of the domain, whereby they (or our beliefs in them) are justified.[25]

Justification is not construed here as what one might call a purely epistemic notion: It is not concerned only with the question of how a belief in the truth of a certain principle is justified, but also with the (ontological) question of what such a truth amounts to. On this Frege held a firmly realistic view according to which such truths are about objects and their properties and relations, and this, for him, was an essential feature of their truth. The justification I am talking about concerns modes of presentation of these objects and properties - their senses - in the fully fledged senses of these notions. I emphasize this in order to distinguish this position from others such as Peacocke's (1992), which seem to avoid such realistic commitments to objects and their modes of presentation. Peacocke presents a theory that connects what he regards as a Fregean notion of sense with justification. But, leaving aside for the moment the connection itself, it seems to me that the notion of sense alluded to is not the fully fledged Fregean notion of mode of presentation. What Peacocke presents is in fact a version of a Davidsonian conception which in this respect is clearly non-Fregean.

Peacocke's idea is that a system of "understanding conditions" or "possession conditions" for a certain expression (conditions accepted by anyone who understands the expression) determine a "semantic value" for that expression. In fact Peacocke assumes that, under certain requirements, it determines the semantic value uniquely. The semantic value may then justify principles including the expression, in the sense that, given the semantic values of the expressions involved, the principle may be shown to be correct (803; section 4). Now, Peacocke realizes that such semantic values are not Fregean senses - they have different modes of presentation and may be given to us in various ways. Peacocke assumes, however, that the main effect of Fregean sense can be accomplished by a theory of "canonical derivation", according to which, e.g., the truth conditions of a sentence may be

---

[25] P. Simons pointed out that Frege's note 16 to section 10 of BL, when read in light of FC, suggests that "the two sides of [Axiom] V express the same sense but in different ways" (Simons 1992, p. 765) The fact that Frege could think so fits the non-foundational character of his conception of justification alluded to in the text.

"canonically derived" from the semantic values of its constituent expressions. But such a theory, if can be worked out, would not actually be using Fregean senses. On the contrary, it is designed to bypass them, to show them to be dispensable. For Frege, in contrast, Fregean senses – modes of presentation of objects and functions – are indispensable in an account of the objectivity and justification of the basic truths of any domain, including logic.

References

Bar-Elli, G. 1996. *The Sense of Reference*, W. De Gruyter, Berlin and New York.

Bar-Elli, G. 1982. Identity and the Formation of the Notion of Object, *Erkenntnis 17*, 229-48.

Bar-Elli, G. 1985. Frege's Early Conception of Logic, *Epistemologia VIII*, pp. 125-40.

Boolos, G. 1990. *The Standard of Equality of Numbers*, reprinted in: *Frege's Philosophy of Mathematics*, ed. W. Demopoulos. Cambridge, Mass., 1995, pp. 234-254.

Burge, T. 1992. Frege on Knowing the Third Realm, *Mind 101:* 633-650.

Burge, T. 1998. Frege on Knowing the Foundations, *Mind 107:* 305-347.

Diamond, C. 1991. *The Realistic Spirit*, Cambridge, Ma.

Dummett, M. 1981. *The Interpretation of Frege's Philosophy*, Duckworth.

Frege, G. 1879 - B – *Begriffsschrift*, Halle, translated in *From Frege to Goedel*, ed. J. van Heijenoort, Harvard, 1967.

Frege, G. 1893 - BL – *Grundgesetze der Arithmetik* Part I. Jena. Translated by M. Furth, *Basic Laws of Arithmetic*. Berkley, 1964.

Frege, G. 1984 - CP – *Collected Papers on Mathematics, Logic, and Philosophy*, ed. McGuiness, Oxford, 1984.

Frege, G. 1884 - FA – *Die Grundlagen der Arithmetik,* Breslau. Translated by J. Austin, *The Foundations of Arithmetic*. Oxford, 1950.

Frege, G. 1891 - FC – *Funktion und Begriff*, Jena. pp. 1-31, translated by P. Geach, *Function and Concept*, in G&B, pp. 21-41.

Frege, G. 1952 - G&B – *Translations from the Philosophical Writings of Frege,* ed. P. Geach and M. Black. Oxford, 1952.

Frege, G. 1980 - PMC – *Philosophical and Mathematical Correspondance*, ed. By G. Gabriel et. al. Translated by H. Kaal, Chicago.

Frege, G. 1979 - PW – *Nachgelassene Schrifften*, 1969. Translated by P. Long and R. White: *Posthumous Writings*. Oxford, 1979.

Frege, G. 1892 - SR – Über Sinn und Bedeutung, *Zeitschrift für Philosophie und philosophische Kritik 100*: 25-50. Translated by M. Black in G&B.

Hintikka, J. 1969. *Models for Modalities*, Dordrecht.

Peacocke, C. 1992. Sense and Justification, *Mind 101*: 793-816.

Ricketts, T. 1986. Objectivity and Objecthood, in: *Frege Synthesized,* eds. Haaparanta and Hintikka, Reidel.

Simons, P. 1992. Why Is There So Little Sense In Grundgesetze?, *Mind 101:* 753-766.

6

Fregean Senses and the Semantics of Singular Terms

ALBERT NEWEN

The leading question of this article is: What does a proper name or an indexical contribute to the thought expressed by an utterance of a sentence containing that term, and what is the meaning of such terms? In the first part of this paper I will discuss in detail Frege's views on thoughts and singular terms. In the second part I will then outline a systematic theory of meaning for singular terms which is inspired by my reconstruction of Frege: the so-called vector theory of meaning.

Frege's philosophy of language is (at least) based on the following claims: (1) Semantics is a project of attaching the content (Fregean sense) of utterances and parts of utterances to sentences and parts of sentences as types: Frege describes one of his main discoveries as the distinction between the categories of sign (as a type of expression), sense, and reference.

(2) There is only *a single* logically relevant level for characterizing the content of sentences, i.e. the level of thoughts. I would like to show that Frege had severe problems with both claims while working out the details of his semantics. Concerning the second claim it is argued that Frege's epistemic criterion of identity and his logical criterion of identity are extensionally equivalent. This means that there is one level of classifying sentences which Frege calls the level of thoughts. Nevertheless, Frege introduces further, more fine-grained levels of classifying sentences which are logically relevant and not just psychologically important: the level of assertions and the level of definitions. Concerning the first claim it is shown that while

dealing with proper names and indexicals, Frege himself noticed that in order to describe the relation between a sentence and the thought expressed one has to distinguish different ways of understanding a sentence which is already part of natural language. This leads to a discussion of Frege's views on proper names and indexicals. On the basis of this reconstruction of Frege's philosophy of language a systematic theory of meaning for singular terms is developed which denies the dogma of standard semantics, according to which an unambiguous utterance (without any deficits, i.e. no missing words, demonstratives are accompanied with gestures if necessary etc.) expresses exactly one semantic content (one Fregean thought). I will argue that the question about the thought contribution of singular terms has to be distinguished from the question concerning the meaning of singular terms. Although Frege answered both questions by characterizing a relevant mode of presentation, it will be shown that the answer concerning the thought contribution only partly answers the question about the meaning of the term. The meaning of a singular term is a vector containing different possible contributions to the semantic content expressed by an utterance of the sentence containing that singular term. Which part of the vector contributes to constituting the semantic content of an utterance (a truth-condition) depends on the communicative situation. Therefore, there is no strict separation between the semantics and pragmatics of singular terms.

1   Characterizing Thoughts in Frege's Philosophy

1.1   General Features of Thoughts

Let me review the general features of thoughts according to Frege. Thoughts are the senses that are expressed by sentences. They are imperceptible, non-spacial, non-temporal entities. Nevertheless, they are objective entities (and not subjective entities such as ideas), i.e. they are "independent for their existence and nature from any person's thinking them or thinking about them"[1]. A person is related to thoughts by *grasping* them, while he/she is related to ideas, feelings, etc. by *having* them. Thoughts are either true or false if they can be expressed by using only terms which refer. Under this condition they always have a truth-value and it remains the same (relative to the actual world). Finally, thoughts are abstract objects with a special kind of reality, since there is no reciprocal action concerning thoughts (Thoughts, p. 29).

One central feature of thoughts is the compositionality of sense: Thoughts are composed of the senses of the meaningful parts of the relevant sentence. They can be analyzed in a sense expressed by an unsaturated expression and - if the unsaturated expression is a one-place predicate - a

---

[1] Burge 1992, p. 634.

sense expressed by the saturated expression, i.e. is a sense determining a concept and a sense determining an object.

> "And it is natural to suppose that, for logic in general, combination into a whole always comes about by saturation of something unsaturated." (Compound Thoughts, p. 56)

1.2 Thoughts and their Individuation

Frege explicitly says in a letter to Husserl that it is important to him to have a clear notion of thoughts since thoughts are the relevant entities when characterizing logic. Frege proposes the following criterion of identity in his letter:[2]

> ### *The logical criterion:*
> *Version 1a:*
>> Sentence A expresses the same thought as sentence B if the assumption that non-A and B entails a contradiction and if the assumption that A and non-B entails a contradiction as well, simply on the basis of logical evidence.

If we understand logical evidence such that it excludes any knowledge of identities that is not part of standard language competence we can transform it into an epistemic criterion. Although Frege only formulates the conditional version, it seems reasonable to ascribe to him the biconditional version of the criterion:

> *Version 1b :*
>> Sentence A expresses the same thought as sentence B if and only if A entails B and B entails A, simply on the basis of logical evidence (as characterized above), i.e. if they are equivalent sentences.[3]

How is this criterion related to the epistemic criterion Frege uses? According to Stuhlmann-Laeisz[4] a transformation into an epistemic criterion is possible if we presuppose the notion of an ideal subject. We can then formulate the following:

---

[2] Brief von Frege an Husserl, 9.12.1906 (in: Frege 1980).

[3] This criterion can be illustrated as follows: "A pair of sentences are equivalent if and only if the arguments that take one as premise and the other as conclusion are both valid. Validity of argument, in turn, is understood as the preservation of truth in passing from premises to conclusions, irrespective of the contributions to truth values by the nonlogical components." Salmon 1992, p. 741.

[4] Stuhlmann-Laeisz 1995, pp. 62-67.

The epistemic criterion:

Sentence A expresses the same thought as sentence B if and only if an ideal subject cannot believe that A is true and at the same time believe that B is false (and vice versa).

The ideal subject has to know all conditionals "if A then B" which are true only on the basis of logical evidence and standard language competence. Logical evidence does not include any knowledge of "informative" identities. An ideal subject only knows an identity if it is part of standard language competence. Such an ideal subject can also be called an ideal rational subject, because it cannot believe any contradiction if the contradiction can be discovered only on the basis of logical knowledge and standard language competence. To discover a classical Fregean "hidden contradiction" one needs additional world knowledge. One has to know that the entities referred to by the terms 'a' and 'b' are identical, e.g. one has to know that the morning star is the same as the evening star. If Charly lacks this knowledge, the following sentences can nevertheless all be true:

(1a) The morning star is identical with the evening star.

(And therefore: "The morning star is F" $\leftrightarrow$ "The evening star is F")

(1b) Charly believes that the morning star is a planet with a shorter period of revolution than the earth.

(1c) Charly believes that it is not the case that the evening star is a planet with a shorter period of revolution than the earth.[5]

Both the logical and the epistemic criterion allow for the same kind of examples of "contradictory", but still rational beliefs:

(2a) The G is F $\leftrightarrow$ The H is F.

(2b) A believes that the G is F.

(2c) A believes that it is not the case that the H is F.

According to Frege these groups of sentences are not incompatible because the sentences "The G is F" and "The H is F" express different thoughts although they fulfill condition 2a. The fact that they express different thoughts is determined by the epistemic (or as well by the logical) criterion of thought identity, i.e. if 2b and 2c are true and A understands

---

[5] To ascribe contradictory, but still rational beliefs it would be sufficient to have the following version of 1c: (1c*) Charly does not believe that the morning star is a planet with a shorter period of revolution than the earth. Since I would not like to discuss cases of agnosticism concerning an attitude here (which still makes 1c* true) I prefer the stronger version 1c.

"The G is F" and "The H is F" and A is a rational and competent speaker, then both implicationally equivalent sentences express different thoughts. How can both sentences express different thoughts although the G is identical with the H? Here Frege's well known solution is the distinction between sense and reference: "the G" and "the H" have the same reference but different sense. The sense of a definite description like "the morning star" is a mode of presentation of the reference object, i.e. the mode of presentation expressed by "the star which is the brightest in the morning sky". To present a principled solution for the compatibility of groups of sentences such as those presented above Frege has to take this strategy as a general solution for all kinds of singular terms. Although his proposal is intuitively anchored in our treatment of definite descriptions, it is not very plausible in the case of proper names and indexicals. Frege himself already noticed some of the difficulties while answering the following questions: What is the thought expressed by a sentence containing a proper name or an indexical? What is the sense expressed by a proper name or an indexical expression? Before I reconstruct Frege's claims and present a different systematic theory of meaning for singular terms, I would like to show that Frege - although he had a criterion for the identity of thoughts - introduces further levels of classifying sentences which are logically relevant. If those additional levels of classifying sentences were only psychologically relevant, then this would be irrelevant for Frege because his general project of characterizing meaning and logic is essentially antipsychologistic. But these additional levels are logically relevant. To argue for this I first roughly characterize Frege's antipsychologism.

1.3   Frege's Antipsychologism

Frege's antipsychologism concerning thoughts has two core aspects: First of all, Frege argues that thoughts are objective entities that exist independent of any mind. The second aspect of Frege's criticism of psychology is based on his aim to characterize only those features of language which are relevant to logic, these being the thoughts expressed by sentences. With a few examples he illustrates which aspects he counts as irrelevant to logic and not involved in thoughts expressed by sentences (Thoughts, p. 9):

(i) Thoughts do not involve intonation, the atmosphere or the mood of an expression, e.g. the difference that you have between a use of 'horse' or 'steed' or 'nag' or 'prad'.

(ii) Furthermore, words like 'still' in 'Alfred has still not arrived' that are used to give us hints do not express a part of the thought.

(iii) The difference between sentences which result from changing the verb from active to passive form and at the same time transforming the accusative into the subject is irrelevant for the classification of thoughts.

In general Frege claims that "all constituents of sentences not covered by the assertoric force do not belong to scientific exposition; but they are sometimes hard to avoid, even for one who sees the danger connected with them." (Thoughts, p. 9)

With 'scientific exposition' Frege means a description at the level of thoughts since science only deals with thoughts leaving aside all aspects of psychology and aesthetics. Having this rough characterization of those psychological aspects in mind which Frege would like to put aside, I would like to show that Frege introduces different levels of classifying sentences which are all logically relevant but which are distinct from the level of thoughts. While analyzing the specialities of language, Frege noticed that his level of thoughts is not enough to account for all logically relevant aspects of language.

2 Levels of Classifying Sentences in Frege's Philosophy

2.1 Thoughts and their Parts

We already mentioned that thoughts are composed of senses, and a standard simple thought, e.g. the one expressed by "Socrates is a philosopher" is composed of the sense expressed by the proper name "Socrates" and the sense expressed by the predicate "is a philosopher".

(I) The principle of compositionality has to be understood as follows:

The thought expressed by a sentence is determined by the senses of the expressions which constitute the sentence.

(II) An important observation in Frege's philosophy is that the same thought can be expressed by different sentences even if the thought components associated with the corresponding parts of the sentences are different.[6]

(2a) Socrates is a philosopher. $\sigma_2 (\sigma_1)$

(2b) Being a philosopher is a property of Socrates. $\sigma_4 (\sigma_3)$

The thought expressed by 2a is composed of and determined by the sense of "Socrates" (σ_1) and the sense of "is a philosopher" (σ_2), while the thought expressed by 2b is composed of and determined by the sense of "Being a philosopher" (σ_3) and the sense of "is a property of Socrates" (σ_4). The senses of the syntactically corresponding parts of the sentences σ_2 and σ_4 as well as σ_1 and σ_3 are different. It is also clear that σ_1 and σ_4 are different senses.[7] Nevertheless, 2a and 2b express the same thought. How is this possible according to Fregean compositionality?

---

[6] Kemmerling 1990, pp. 10-13.

[7] "Socrates" as used in 2a is a saturated expression and therefore the reference of the expression is an object, while the reference of "is a property of Socrates" is a concept. Since the ex-

(III) The analysis of a thought is not determined by the thought:

Frege only claims that the parts of the thought determine the thought but not that the thought determines its parts. Frege explicitly denies this direction of compositionality and he introduces the possibility of analyzing one thought in different ways.

> "This <possibility, A. N.> will be surprising only to somebody who fails to see that a thought can be split up in many ways, so that now one thing, now another, appears as subject or predicate. The thought itself does not yet determine what is to be regarded as the subject. If we say 'the subject of this judgement', we do not designate anything definite unless at the same time we indicate a definite kind of analysis;" (On Concept and Object, p. 49)

The thought expressed by one unambiguous (and nonindexical) sentence can be characterized in different ways. Since we have no direct access to thoughts but only via sentences, these ways can be e.g. characterized by different ways of analyzing one of the sentences expressing the thought: The sentence "Socrates is a philosopher" can be analyzed such that "Socrates" is the subject (as in 2a) or such that "Being a philosopher" is the subject of the sentence (as in 2b). Frege introduces the notion of assertion ("Aussage") to characterize the difference between 2a and 2b. They express the same thought, but they are different assertions for an assertion is the result of one way of analyzing a sentence and thereby analyzing the thought expressed by it. We can characterize this level by looking at one of Frege's examples where he illustrates that a thought has to be completed by an analysis to determine what the subject of the sentence is which the thought expresses, e.g. the thought expressed by "There is at least one square root of 4" can be characterized in many different ways. Here are four ways of expressing the same thought, in which different features relevant for distinguishing different ways of analyzing sentences are involved (On Concept and Object, p. 49-50):

(3a) "There is at least one square root of 4"

(3b) "The concept *square root of 4* is realized."

(3c) "There is something that has the property of giving the result 4 when multiplied by itself."

(3d) "The number 4 has the property that there is something of which it is the square."

---

pressions have different references and sense determines reference, the senses ($\sigma 1$) and ($\sigma 4$) must be different.

2.2 Analyzing the Logical Surface Structure: The Level of Assertions

If we compare 3a and 3b then according to Frege the analysis shows that we have different assertions because of the difference in logical structure. The structure of the Fregean reference of the sentences is the following:

3a: second order concept - first order concept

3b: object - first order concept[8]

3c: second order concept - first order concept

3d: object - first order concept

According to this structural analysis 3a and 3c, on the one hand, and 3b and 3d, on the other, are equivalent, i.e. each pair consists of sentences making the same assertion. The level of assertions can be described as follows: Two sentences are used to make the same assertion if and only if they express the same thought and have the same logical surface structure. The logical surface structure is determined by the reference of the expressions which are the result of analyzing a sentence into an unsaturated expression and the respective saturated expressions.

2.3 Analyzing the Concept-Structure: The Level of Definitions

Let us now compare 3a and 3c in more detail since both sentences have the same logical surface structure. To receive 3c from 3a we simply have to substitute a complex expression by its definition. Therefore we have definitionally equivalent sentences with the same logical structure:

(3a) "There is at least one square root of 4"

(3c) "There is (at least, A. N.) something that has the property of giving the result 4 when multiplied by itself."

A parallel example is discussed by Dummett, Bell and Bermúdez:[9]

(4a) 13 is prime.

(4b) 13 is greater than 1 and, for any number n, if n divides 13 then either n = 13 or n = 1.

---

[8] Here one may have a different reading if "being realized" is understood analogously to "there is", since "there is" denotes according to Frege a second order concept. Then 3b would have a different structure. But Frege explicitly makes clear that he uses the anyalsis given above. (On Concept and Object, p. 50)

[9] The discussion of the example is nicely summarized in Bermúdez 2001.

The relevant predicates are the following:

(4a*) ( ) is prime.

(4b*) ( ) is greater than 1 and, for any number n, if n divides ( ) then either
n = ( ) or n = 1.

Bell claims that 4a* and 4b* designate different concepts. But this is not consistent with Frege's explicit views on definitions:

> "We shall call the simple sign the definiendum, and the complex group of signs which it replaces the definiens. The definiendum acquires its sense only from the definiens. This sense is built up out of the sense of the parts of the definiens." (Frege, "Logic in Mathematics" 1914, in: Posthumous Writings, 208.)

Dummett accepts that 4a* and 4b* are synonymous but he claims that 4a and 4b express different thoughts. His argument is based on the following principle that Bermúdez calls *principle K:* If one sentence involves a sense (σ_1) that another sentence does not involve, then these sentences express different thoughts.[10]

We have already presented a Fregean counterexample to this claim:

(2a) Socrates is a philosopher. $\qquad\qquad\qquad\sigma_2\,(\sigma_1)$

(2b) Being a philosopher is a property of Socrates. $\qquad\sigma_4\,(\sigma_3)$

2a and 2b are examples parallel to the explicitly mentioned Fregean examples; they express the same thought, although they are not composed by the same senses. Therefore we cannot ascribe principle K to Frege. He accepts the following *principle of sense-constituency*:

Even if two sentences s1 and s2 express the same thought, they can have different sense constituents.

Furthermore, Frege explicitly makes claims that imply that 4a and 4b express the same thought:

> "We have to distinguish between a sentence and the thought it expresses. If the definiens occurs in the sentence and we replace it by the definiendum, this does not affect the thought at all. It is true we get a different sentence if we do this, but we do not get a different thought." (Frege, "Logic in Mathematics" 1914, in: Posthumous Writings, 208.)

---

[10] Dummett ascribes this principle to Frege. But it is only seemingly implied by the principle that one cannot grasp a thought expressed by a sentence without grasping the constituent senses expressed by the parts of the sentence. Since Frege notes different ways of analyzing sentences (and thereby thoughts), a difference in constituent senses need not entail a difference in thoughts expressed. This is noted by Bermúdez 2001; Kemmerling 1990 argues also against this principle.

According to this quotation, Frege holds the principle that definitionally equivalent sentences express the same thought:

> A sentence s1 and a sentence s2 express the same thought if they are definitionally equivalent, while two sentences s1 and s2 are definitionally equivalent if and only if s2 is the result of substituting all tokens of an expression in s1 by a definition of that expression (or vice versa).

This is compatible with principle K if we presuppose that definitionally equivalent sentences involve the same constituent senses. But we had to give up priniciple K for the reasons already mentioned. Therefore contrary to what Dummett claims, principle K cannot give us a reason for holding that 4a and 4b express different thoughts. Frege's principle of compositionality is misunderstood if it is interpreted as implying principle K. Frege accepts the following as a *sufficient condition for thought identity*, but he does not accept the corresponding necessary condition:

> If sentences s1 and s2 involve the same senses then they express the same thought.

And obviously he thereby accepts the converse (without accepting principle K):

> If sentences s1 and s2 express different thoughts then s1 involves at least one sense that s2 does not or s2 involves at least one sense that s1 does not.[11]

Furthermore, Frege accepts the following principle of sense-constituency:

> Even it two sentences s1 and s2 express the same thought and have the same logical surface structure, they can have different thought constituents.[12]

We have characterized two additional levels of classifying sentences according to Frege's remarks: The first is the level of sentences which express the same thought and have the same logical surface structure. I call this, according to Frege, the level of assertions. The second is the level of definitionally equivalent sentences where this criterion implies that those sentences are making the same assertion. I call this the level of definitions. Although both additional levels of classifying sentences are more fine-grained than the level of thoughts, the classifications are logically relevant:

---

[11] The 'or'-clause accounts for the possibility that s1 is simply a part of s2.

[12] 3b and 3d are two sentences which illustrate this principle, since they express the same thought and have the same logical surface structure, although they are not definitionally equivalent.

The level of assertions includes distinctions between e.g. first-order and second-order concepts which are obviously relevant to logic. Furthermore, we have the level of definitions which is logically relevant, because definitions play an important role in the systematic construction of a logical frame.[13]

3   The Sense Expressed by the Use of Proper Names

The second important point I wish to develop in this paper is the claim that we must distinguish different ways of understanding sentences to account for Frege's remarks on singular terms. According to Frege, communication has the following basic structure: The speaker grasps a thought which he expresses by uttering a sentence and the listener grasps the same thought by hearing the sentence.

Frege's Basic Model of Successful Communication:

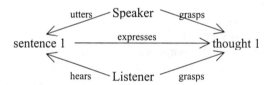

One presupposition of this basic model is that a sentence expresses exactly one thought, i.e. that the sentence has a determined relation to a thought. But Frege noticed that there are several aspects of natural language which do not allow for such a determined relation in the case of sentences containing proper names and indexicals. These aspects will be explained in the following by introducing different ways of understanding a sentence while using proper names and indexicals.

---

[13] There is a philosophically central way in which we can use two sentences which are neither equivalent at the level of definitions nor at the level of assertions, but which express the same thought. Such pairs of sentences are an important tool for realizing a project of sentence reduction with the aim of developing some kind of theory reduction. A Fregean example is the following pair. (A) There are just as many Fs as Gs. (B) The number of Fs is identical with the number of Gs. Both sentences express the same thought. But it is obvious that they have different logical surface structures, because A is an existence claim and B is an identity statement. Furthermore, the sentences are not definitionally equivalent, because definitional equivalence implies sameness of logical surface structure which is not the case. This example confirms not only that we have separated two additional levels of sentence classification which are more fine-grained than the level of thoughts, but also that examples like A and B are important for every programme of reduction for an interesting form of reduction is dependent on essentially different sentences expressing the same thought.

The paradigmatic example involving "Phosphorus" and "Hesperus" as two proper names denoting the planet Venus illustrates, firstly, that we need the level of senses to characterize the content of utterances, e.g. we have to distinguish different modes of presentation of one object, and, secondly, that the epistemic situation is an important aspect of thought identity. It is clear that if someone believes that Hesperus is not the same as Phosphorus, then the sentences "Hesperus is F" and "Phosphorus is F" express different thoughts.[14] What should Frege say if someone knows that Hesperus is identical with Phosphorus? For a person who has this knowledge the thoughts expressed can be the same although they need not be. If this person associates the same sense with the word "Phosphorus" as with the word "Hesperus", e.g. the sense expressed by "the star which is the lightest in the early evening sky", then both sentences express the same thought because the same sense constituents are involved in the thoughts expressed. It is possible for someone who knows that Phosphorus is identical with Hesperus to grasp this mode of presentation in combination with understanding the word "Phosphorus" even though this is not the sense usually associated with and used to introduce the word.[15]

The conclusion is that the sentences (6a) "Phosphorus is F" and (6b) "Hesperus is F" express different thoughts not absolutely but only relative to a specific understanding of the sentences, i.e. relative to a way of combining the words with senses. Ways of understanding a sentence are different ways of relating an expression with the relevant sense expressed. One feature of proper names and indexicals in natural language is that they can be related to many different senses depending on the epistemic situation of a subject. The linguistic meaning does not determine the sense grasped by such terms. In an ideal language Frege demands that each proper name express exactly one mode of presentation. But he admits that in natural language this is not the case and sometimes causes problems.

> "So we must really stipulate that for every proper name there shall be just one associated manner of presentation of the object so designated. It is often unimportant that this stipulation should be fulfilled, but not always." (Thoughts, p. 12)

Now I would like to discuss the problematic cases of sentences containing proper names or indexicals as presented by Frege in 'Thoughts'.

---

[14] The fact that this belief is false is irrelevant. If someone correctly believes that Jupiter is not the same as Saturn and uses the sentences "Jupiter is F" and "Saturn is F" then he/she expresses different thoughts because sense determines reference.

[15] In this example it is irrelevant that the belief is true. If someone falsely beliefs that Saturn is identical with Jupiter and uses the sentences "Jupiter is F" and "Saturn is F" then he/she may express the same thought (if the same mode of presentation is associated with the two proper names) or he/she may express different thoughts (if different modes of presentation are associated with the two proper names).

3.1 Frege's Example dealing with 'Dr. Gustav Lauben'

(7a) "I was wounded" uttered by Dr. Gustav Lauben
(7b) "Dr. Gustav Lauben was wounded" uttered by Leo Peter

In one passage of the article 'Thoughts' Frege asks whether utterance 7a and 7b express the same thought. The interesting point according to my reading is that we do not get an absolute answer but only an answer relative to a way of understanding the utterances.

> "Suppose that Rudolph Lingens was present when Dr. Lauben spoke and now hears what is related by Leo Peter. If the same thought was uttered by Dr. Lauben and Leo Peter, then Rudolph Lingens, who is fully master of the language and remembers what Dr. Lauben said in his presence, must now know at once from Leo Peter's report that he is speaking of the same thing. But knowledge of the language is a special thing when proper names are involved." (Thoughts, p.11)

This passage contains the following principle:

If two sentences s1 and s2 express the same thought, then a rational, attentive and a *fully* language-competent subject must know that s1 and s2 express the same thought, a fortiori that they are speaking of the same object.

Does Frege hold or deny this principle? I would like to argue that he holds this principle although he argues that the condition is usually not fulfilled when using proper names in natural language. The comment that knowledge of the language is a special thing where proper names are involved cannot be understood as a denial of this principle, but as accepting that normally people are not fully language-competent concerning proper names. This reading fits very well with the following passages. First Frege says that if the word 'Dr. Gustav Lauben' is understood by Leo Peter as well as by Rudolph Lingens such that it has the sense expressed by 'the only doctor living in a house known to both of them', then they associate the same thought with the sentence.

> "Now, if both Leo Peter and Rudolph Lingens mean by 'Dr. Gustav Lauben' the doctor who is the only doctor living in a house known to both of them, then they both understand the sentence 'Dr. Gustav Lauben was wounded' in the same way; they associate the same thought with it." (Thoughts, p.11)

This is an example of the standard Fregean case of successful communication:

Frege's Standard Model of Communication

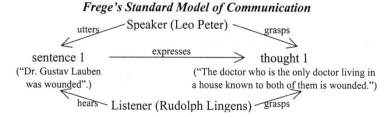

A central aspect concerning the relation between a sentence and the thought expressed by an utterance of it is the way the proper names and the indexicals used in the sentence are understood. Although Frege does not say this, we may add that 7a and 7b express the same thought if the singular terms 'I' and 'Dr. Gustav Lauben' are both understood in such a way that they express the same sense, whatever that sense may be. The only constraint that Frege has concerning the sense is that it determines the reference.

Now Frege's main aim in this paragraph is to figure out that, although 7a and 7b express (in modern terms) the same singular proposition, they can be understood such that they express different thoughts. This is possible in a special epistemic context in which someone, Rudolf Lingens, is only partially informed about the utterance context of 7a:

> "But it is possible that Rudolph Lingens does not know Dr. Lauben personally and does not know that it was Dr. Lauben who recently said 'I was wounded'. *In this case* Rudolph Lingens cannot know that the same affair is in question. I say, therefore, *in this case*: the thought which Leo Peter expresses is not the same as that which Dr. Lauben uttered." (Thoughts, p.11; My italics, A. N.)

Frege uses the phrase "in this case" twice to note the fact that the utterances 7a and 7b express different thoughts is not true absolutely but only true relative to a way of understanding, characterized by the epistemic context of a rational and language-competent subject.

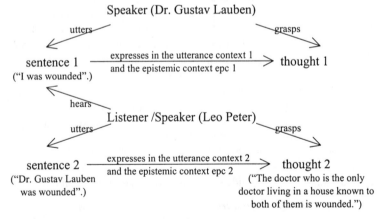

Although the sentences 1 and 2 can be characterized by the same singular proposition and only two distinct, but in this case extensionally equivalent singular terms are used, the utterances can express different thoughts. Here it is important that one of the singular terms is the indexical "I". But before we discuss the special problems of indexicality (e.g. which thought

is expressed by sentence 1?), we should have a look at further arguments
for the special role of proper names.

3.2   Nonstandard epistemic contexts: The example of *Herbert Garner*

The function of the next paragraph in 'Thoughts' is to illustrate the dependency of proper names on an epistemic context in extreme cases. Let us first
have a look at the setting of the example:

Herbert Garner's epistemic context (epc3): He believes that Dr. Gustav
Lauben is the (only) person who was born on 13 September 1875 in N. N.
He has no further information/beliefs about Dr. Gustav Lauben.

Leo Peter's epistemic context (epc4): He believes that Dr. Gustav
Lauben is the (only) person living in the house ABC. He has no further
information/beliefs about Dr. Gustav Lauben.[16]

Frege first argues that the utterance expressed by one person and understood by another person can express different thoughts relative to the different epistemic contexts of the two persons. He then additionally shows
that relative to the same epistemic context of one subject as speaker and
listener two utterances can express different thoughts even if the only difference between the two sentences uttered is that they contain two incomplete versions of the same proper name.

*Sophisticated examples of nonsuccessful communication on the basis of
an understanding of the sentences:*

(i) One utterance can express two different thoughts:

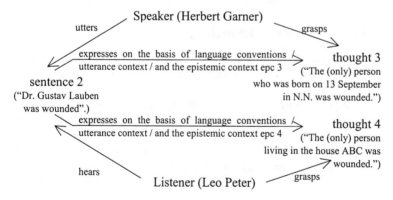

---

[16] It is sufficient to suppose that Leo Peter does not know that Dr. Gustav Lauben is the
(only) person who was born on 13 September 1875 in N. N. This is what Frege says in the text.
I choose a more radical epistemic context to stress the point.

Frege admits that one may argue that in such a case we no longer have any reason for saying that Herbert Garner and Leo Peter speak the same language. To prevent such criticism Frege constructs an extreme case in which the speaker and the listener is one subject using different versions of the same proper name without knowing that this is so.

(ii) Two utterances which can be characterized by the same singular proposition and furthermore use different incomplete versions (e.g. 'Dr. Lauben' and 'Gustav Lauben') of the same complete proper name ('Dr. Gustav Lauben') can express two different thoughts:

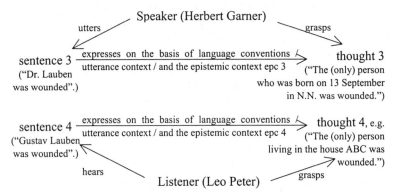

Frege claims that these utterances express different thoughts and he explicitly stresses that this difference in thought is dependent on the difference in epistemic context.

4 Indexicality and I-Thoughts

There are at least three problematic questions for Frege's philosophy of language concerning indexical utterances like "I am wounded" uttered by Dr. Gustav Lauben:[17]

(i) The problem of utterance completion: What is the Fregean proper name which completes the predicate 'is wounded' in Lauben's utterance to the expression of a thought?

(ii) The problem of content completion: Which Fregean sense completes the sense of the predicate 'is wounded' to yield the thought expressed by Lauben's utterance? Which thought does Dr.Gustav Lauben express by making his utterance?

(iii) The problem of successful communication: Which thought does Leo Peter grasp when he hears and adequately understands Lauben's utterance 'I was wounded'?

---

[17] Künne 1997, pp. 50-53.

Ad (i): Frege says that the thought is expressed not only by the mere wording but by an indexical sentence in combination with the circumstances. The relevant entity is the reference of the word "I" in the utterance context, i.e. Dr. Gustav Lauben. I argue - against an interpretation of Künne - that this can be adequately understood without presupposing hybrid proper names.

> "...[O]ften... the mere wording, which can be made permanent by writing or the gramophone, does not suffice for the expression of the thought... If a time-indication is conveyed by the present tense one must know when the sentence was uttered in order to grasp the thought correctly. Therefore the time of utterance is part of the expression of the thought."[18]

Frege is interpreted by Künne to introduce *hybrid proper names*. Each occurrence of a hybrid proper name consists of a token of 'I' and Dr. Gustav Lauben *in propria persona*: "The proper name used in Gustav's utterance of (1) is not the (type)-expression 'I', but the (type-) expression every occurrence of which contains an 'I'-token produced by Gustav and Gustav 'I'himself."[19]

In the text Frege uses the German phrase "der bloße Wortlaut". This is translated by "the mere wording". It is unambigiously used to talk about word-types. And Frege is extremely careful and consistent in using his words. In the same paragraph of 'Thoughts' the expression 'Wortlaut' is always used to talk about word-types. This is noted by Künne who corrects Geach's translation at one place.[20] Furthermore, if we read Frege very carefully in this passage, he only claims that the thought is not only expressed by the sentence-type, but by the sentence-type in combination with the circumstances while the relevant entity is the object which is the reference of the indexical expression. If we look at the sentence 'I am wounded' as uttered by G. Lauben then the thought is expressed by the unsaturated word type '( ) is wounded' and by the saturated word-type 'I' in combination with the speaker in the utterance context, i.e. Gustav Lauben *in propria persona*. If we would like to characterize the Fregean proper name as a hybrid proper name, then it consists of the word-type 'I' combined with its reference, Dr. Gustav Lauben. We can think of this expression as the word 'I' indexed by its reference in the utterance context. This is equivalent to thinking of the Fregean proper name simply as the token of 'I'. Therefore, it is sufficient to ascribe to Frege the position that while dealing with indexical sentences he became aware of the fact that he could not ascribe thoughts

---

[18] Thoughts, p. 10.

[19] Künne 1997, p. 51.

[20] Künne substitutes the word 'verbal expression' for the incorrect translation of 'Wortlaut' by 'utterance' in the phrase: "The same verbal expression ['Wortlaut'] containing the word 'I' in the mouths of different men will express different thoughts of which some may be true, others false."

to sentences but only to utterances. It is not an important part of Frege's view on indexicality that he seems to introduce hybrid proper names, since it is completely equivalent for all Fregean claims to distinguish types (the word 'I') and tokens (the utterances of the word 'I').[21]

Ad (ii): The thought expressed by the indexical utterance depends on the way of understanding the utterance.

We have already explained that 'I was wounded' uttered by Dr. Gustav Lauben and 'Dr. Gustav Lauben was wounded' uttered by Leo Peter do not express the same thought given the epistemic context of Rudolf Lingens who hears both utterances. But in the unpublished work "Logic" of 1897 Frege wrote that the sentence 'I am cold' uttered e.g. by Dr. Gustav Lauben could also be expressed by 'Dr. Gustav Lauben is cold'.

> "The word 'I' simply designates a different person in the mouths of different people. It is not necessary that the person who feels cold should himself give utterance to the thought that he feels cold. Another person can do this by using a name to designate the one who feels cold." (Logic, 1897, in: p. 134-135)

This remark seems to contradict the distinction made in the published paper 'Thoughts', which is why some people[22] tend to take this remark as an aberration in an unpublished manuscript. I would like to argue that Frege's remarks are consistent if we take into account that he distinguishes different ways of understanding sentences. 'I was wounded' uttered by Dr. Gustav Lauben is understood by Rudolf Lingens in so far he saw Lauben making the utterance, but does not know his name. Therefore, he does not know that the person named Dr. Gustav Lauben is the same as the speaker of the utterance containing 'I'. The thoughts he grasps are consequently different. The sentence 'I was wounded' uttered by Dr. Gustav Lauben is understood by Rudolph Lingens in so far it expresses the following thought: [he who is speaking to you at this moment was wounded]. How is it possible that the two sentences, which express different thoughts as understood by Rudolph Lingens, can express the same thought as Frege claims in his remarks of 1897?

This is possible relative to another epistemic background. If Rudolf Lingens heard the utterance 'I was wounded' made by Dr. Gustav Lauben and he knows or is informed about the fact that the speaker is Dr. Gustav

---

[21] In a discussion of Künne's paper Edward Harcourt shows that Künne's solution to the problem of utterance completion is insufficient, because it leads to redundancies concerning the determination of the reference. Harcourt suggests that the Fregean proper name that we are looking for is simply the token of 'I' characterized as a token of the word 'I' in combination with its reference in the context. In this paper I show that this is not only systematically more satisfying but is explicitly claimed by Frege if we read him very carefully. Harcourt 1993, pp. 301-312.

[22] Dummett 1981.

Lauben, then the utterance 'Dr. Gustav Lauben was wounded' can express the same thought, if in both cases the same mode of presentation is associated with the different singular terms 'I' and 'Dr. Gustav Lauben'.[23] This interpretation is confirmed by the following passage in 'Thoughts':

[7] "If someone wants to say today what he expressed yesterday using the word 'today', he will replace this word with 'yesterday'. Although the thought is the same its verbal expression must be different in order that the change of sense which would otherwise be effected by the differing times of utterance may be cancelled out. The case is the same with words like 'here' and 'there'."[24]

This remark shows that (1) "Today Carina is in Germany" uttered on the 1st of Jan. 2000 expresses the same thought as (2) "Yesterday Carina was in Germany" uttered on the 2nd of Jan. 2000. But the fact that these utterances express the same thought can only be accounted for by a subject that has correct nonindexical beliefs about the reference of the indexicals. These utterances can express the same thought only relative to a correct nonindexical background knowledge about the contexts. But nonindexical background knowledge is not guaranteed by language competence together with an understanding of the utterances. If Frege claims that the utterances containing temporal indexicals express the same thought, then he presupposes a correct nonindexical background knowledge of the relevant subject. If he claims that these utterances express different thoughts, then Frege presupposes that at least one of the utterances is understood on the basis of an indexical (or context-dependent) background knowledge or that at least one of the utterances is understood in such a way that the indexical expression is associated with the incorrect reference.

Proper names and indexicals are such that they can be combined with different modes of presentation depending on the epistemic context of the speaker/listener/thinker. The linguistic meaning of a proper name is not the sense expressed by the proper name nor does it determine the sense expressed by the name.[25] If we recall the examples where an utterance of 'Dr. Gustav Lauben was wounded' expressed the thought [The doctor, who is the only doctor living in a house known to both of them, was wounded], then this is clearly confirmed. Whatever one thinks about the linguistic meaning of proper names, the following seems to be generally acceptable: If one ascribes a linguistic meaning to the proper name 'Dr. Gustav Lauben' it is something like the metalinguistic description "the person named 'Dr. Gustav Lauben'". But this linguistic meaning is neither the sense nor does it determine the sense expressed in the situation mentioned

---

[23] Kemmerling 1996.

[24] Thoughts, p. 10.

[25] The difference between sense and linguistic meaning in Frege's philosophy of language was first worked out in Perry 1977.

above. Analogously, there is a difference between the linguistic meaning of an indexical and the sense expressed by a use of it. The linguistic meaning of 'I' can be characterized by the description "the speaker of the utterance". But the sense expressed may be characterized by a different description (when a public thought is expressed) or, in the case of expressing a so-called private thought, the sense of a use of 'I' is a nonidentificational EGO-mode of presentation.

4.1   The Privacy of I-Thoughts

"Now everyone is presented to himself in a special and primitive way, in which he is presented to no-one else. So, when Dr. Lauben has the thought that he was wounded, he will probably be basing it on this primitive way in which he is presented to himself. And only Dr. Lauben himself can grasp thoughts specified in this way. But now he may want to communicate with others. He cannot communicate a thought he alone can grasp. Therefore, if he now says 'I was wounded', he must use 'I' in a sense which can be grasped by others, perhaps in the sense of 'he who is speaking to you at this moment'; by doing this he makes the conditions accompanying his utterance serve towards the expression of a thought." (Thoughts, p. 12-13.)

In this paragraph Frege admits that the word 'I' uttered by one person, e.g. Dr. Gustav Lauben, can be associated with different senses. He distinguishes a private and a public sense although in principle he allows for more than one public sense. One public sense could be characterized by the description 'he who is speaking to you at this moment'; another public sense could be characterized by 'he who is waving his hand at this moment'. The private sense that can be associated with a use of 'I' can only be grasped by the speaker of the utterance. From a systematic point of view we can call this private sense the EGO-mode of presentation. It is simple (noncomplex), it is not based on any kind of identification (since it is immune to error through misidentification in Shoemaker's sense) and it is necessarily the case that if x is presented to y by the EGO-mode of presentation then x is identical with y.[26] The private thought that is associated with 'I am wounded' can be characterized by the EGO-mode of presentation realized by Lauben and the sense expressed by 'being wounded'. What exactly is the feature expressed by privacy? It is not the case that there is only one person with epistemic access to the private I-thought, because everyone can ascribe a private I-thought as Frege himself does while describing the situation:

"So, when Dr. Lauben has *the thought that he was wounded*, he will probably be basing it on this primitive way in which he is presented to himself." (Thoughts, p.13; My italics)

---

[26] Künne 1997, p. 55; Newen 1997, p. 118 ff.

But we may admit that ascribing is a different mode of epistemic access than grasping a thought. Ascribing a thought is grasping a thought about a thought. Private thoughts can be the object of an intersubjective thought. Analogously we *have* ideas and they are private but ideas can be the object of an intersubjective thought. Frege mentions the example that two doctors discuss the pain of a patient.[27] But *having* is the mode of epistemic access that is characteristic for ideas and *grasping* is the mode of epistemic access that is characteristic for thoughts, a fortiori for I-thoughts. According to Frege, each entity has a characteristic mode of epistemic access and we can use this feature to characterize privacy:

> An entity is private if only one person has epistemic access to it (in the mode that is characteristic for this entity).[28]

As is already noted in the recent literature, the objectivity of thoughts is not destroyed by the fact that some thoughts are private: Even if the thoughts are private, i.e. they can only be grasped by one person, they nevertheless are independent from a mind. They can only be grasped by one person but they need not be grasped and their truth (or falsity) is independent from being grasped.[29]

Ad (iii): With this background we are now able to answer the following question: Which thought does Leo Peter grasp when he hears and adequately understands Lauben's utterance 'I was wounded'? The thought understood by Leo Peter is dependent on his epistemic context. It may be characterized by 'he who is speaking to you at this moment was wounded' or by 'he who is waving his hand at this moment was wounded' or 'he whom I am addressing at this moment was wounded'. According to Frege's model of communication, the understanding is only adequate, i.e. communication is successful, if and only if the speaker and the listener grasp the same thought.[30] But this model is systematically inadequate: It can be shown that with indexical utterances a systematic difference in thoughts is necessary for an adequate understanding: If Tom and Charly are sitting on the grass and a ball is placed between them, then Tom can use the sentence 'This is a basketball' to express the thought 'The ball to my right is a basketball' and Charly adequately understands Tom if he grasps the thought 'The ball to my left is a basketball'. In the case of indexicals an adequate understanding demands that the listener grasp a mode of presentation which determines the same object as referred to by the speaker and which differs from the mode of presentation of the speaker only in those aspects which are relevant to account for the difference in perspective of speaker and lis-

---

[27] Thoughts, p. 23.

[28] This idea was developed in Lotter 1999, p. 390.

[29] Kemmerling 1996, p. 15; Künne 1997.

[30] Dummett 1981, p. 122; Künne 1997, p. 62

tener. A mode of presentation of the listener which fulfills these conditions is called contextually corresponding.

If we accept this - what seems to be undeniable - then we have to give up the Fregean dogma according to which communication is successful if and only if speaker and listener grasp the same thought. Then we do not have to claim, as Frege must, that private I-thoughts cannot be communicated. If Lauben has a private I-thought and wants to express this private thought by uttering 'I was wounded', then I can only understand him correctly (not using ascriptions) if I grasp the thought which I would express by "You were (resp. He was) wounded". Successful communication with indexical expressions is based on the fact that the speaker and the listener know that they are related to the same object with contextually corresponding modes of presentation. In combination with the word 'I' this is only possible if the listener relies on a different kind of relation to the same object (if he is not relying on the indirect relation based on ascriptions).

To summarize: Frege's philosophy is essentially based on the notion of thoughts. While dealing with natural language, Frege discovers that he additionally needs more fine-grained classifications of sentences. He introduces the classification of sentences at the level of assertions (the logical surface structure) and of definitions. These differences are explicitly not differences in thought content, but they are also not psychological differences. Frege discovers here aspects which are logically relevant, although he did not invent a framework to account for them. Furthermore, while investigating sentences containing proper names or indexicals, Frege noticed that natural language does not have a sentence-type semantics. To account for proper names and indexicals we have to distinguish different ways of understanding sentences. Some of the relevant features for determining the relation between a sentence and the thought expressed are the language conventions, the utterance context, and the epistemic situation of the relevant person. From a systematic point of view these aspects are not sufficient to construct an adequate semantics. In the following I argue that an adequate semantics of singular terms has to give up what I call the dogma of standard semantics.

5   Singular Terms and Theories of Semantic Content

5.1   The Contribution of Singular Terms to Thoughts according to Standard Semantics

Modern semantic positions can be split up into two groups: The Fregean accounts accept the constraint that the special cognitive role associated with a use of a singular term should be represented by the semantic content of the utterance containing the singular term. Therefore, they introduce some kind of mode of presentation as a part of the semantically expressed proposition. The Russellian accounts deny this constraint. They claim that the semantically expressed proposition is a singular proposition (including the object(s) and the property or relation). The special cognitive role associated with a use of a singular term is represented by the pragmatically conveyed content of the utterances. Both views share the following presupposition which one may call **the dogma of standard semantics**:

> An unambiguous utterance (without any deficits, i.e. no missing words, demonstratives are accompanied with gestures if necessary etc.) expresses exactly one semantic content (one thought according to semantics).

I would like to deny this dogma. Although Frege is usually treated as one of the founders of the dogma of standard semantics, a detailed investigation has shown that Frege maintains it only for ideal languages, not for natural languages. We saw that Frege implicitly denied this dogma in the discussion of first person thoughts: He distinguishes the thought one *thinks* from the thought one *communicates* while using a first person utterance even if there is only one unambiguous first person utterance. Furthermore, he introduced several levels of classifying sentences which are different from and more fine-grained than the classification of thoughts but which are nevertheless logically relevant. Since according to Frege everything that is relevant to characterize the logical structure of a sentence in natural language should be accounted for in semantics, he implicitly noticed that there is not one clear level of semantic content for an utterance in natural language.

Semantic theories are mainly based on three intuitions: While making an assertive utterance a speaker, firstly, makes a claim about the world; secondly, he transfers the information that a competent and rational speaker has while understanding the utterance without having any special world knowledge; thirdly, he informs others about his cognitive situation. To illustrate this: While using the utterance "I am hungry" I can inform about the state of affairs that Albert Newen is hungry or about the linguistically associated knowledge that the speaker of the utterance (whoever this may be) is hungry or about my special cognitive situation, i.e. I am disposed to eat.

(i) The meaning of a sentence should characterize the truth-condition relative to possible worlds. This leads to a linguistically driven Russellian semantics of direct reference.

(ii.) The meaning of a sentence should characterize the knowledge competent and rational speakers associate with a sentence independent of any contextual information. This leads to a word-type semantics as proposed e.g. by Kent Bach.

(iii) The meaning of a sentence should characterize the special cognitive situation of the speaker. This leads to a Fregean cognitive semantics.

All these three intuitions are strongly anchored and there is no absolute criterion for favoring one of them. While dealing with informative identity statements, a Fregean cognitive semantics seems to be adequate, but when dealing with modal arguments a Russellian semantics of direct reference seems to be the only acceptable view. Which intuition seems to be the correct one depends on the context and the communicative situation. Therefore, there is no one-one relation between an utterance and its semantic content. Depending on the context and the communicative situation, i.e. the intentions of the speaker and the interests of the hearer, one may change the focus to the kind of information that is *literally transferred* by an utterance. I would like to defend the following proposal: One can account for the three semantic intuitions in different communicative situations by distinguishing several ways of classifying utterances. The contribution of the singular term to the semantic content depends on the level of classifying utterances which is determined by the communicative situation. One model which accounts for these claims is a vector theory of meaning. Before developing the general idea of this theory of meaning, I wish to introduce several ways of classifying utterances.

5.2   Ways of Classifying Utterances

(a) I am f. (uttered by Mach)

(b) Mach is f.

(c) The speaker of the utterance is f. (The definite description is used attributively and the sentence is uttered by Mach)

(d) You are f. (adressed to Mach)

(e) He is f. (while pointing at Mach)

(f) The author of 'Die Analyse der Empfindungen' is f. (The definite description is used attributively)

We can classify these utterances

(i) **by their truth-conditions**, i.e. truth-conditions relative to possible worlds according to standard semantics:

(a), (b),(d) and (e) express the singular proposition <Mach; being f>

(c) expresses the proposition <the speaker of the utterance in the possible world w; being f>

(f) expresses the proposition <the author of 'Die Analyse der Empfindungen' in a possible world w; being f>

(ii) **by the linguistic knowledge** that is associated with an utterance by a competent speaker:

(a) and (c) are equivalent concerning the linguistic competence.

(iii) **by the cognitive role** the thought expressed plays, e.g. in motivating actions:

Relative to this standard all utterances express different thoughts.

An unambiguous utterance alone does not determine the content expressed. Which level of classifying utterances is the relevant one depends on the communicative situation. An utterance does not have just one semantic content but rather (at least) three kinds depending on the way of classifying the utterances.

5.3   The Vector Theory of Meaning of Singular Terms

The general idea of a vector theory of meaning is that we presuppose that a singular term can contribute different parts to the content of the whole sentence: either the object referred to or a description expressing the linguistic knowledge associated with the singular term or a mode of presentation of the object. All three possible contributions can be part of the semantic content expressed by an utterance containing the singular term. Which one is relevant depends on the utterance context and the communicative situation, i.e. the intentions of the speaker and the interests of the hearer. To symbolize this view we can introduce a vector which contains at least these three possible contributions. This vector is constructed on the basis of the utterance context and the epistemic background of a speaker/thinker. For singular terms used referentially the following elements are determined on the basis of those conditions: 1. the object referred to, 2. the linguistic meaning, and 3. the relevant mode of presentation.

Using a Fregean example, we can characterize the meaning of the singular term 'I' as used in the sentence 'I was wounded' uttered by Dr. Gustav Lauben by the following vector containing the three elements as possible contributions to the content expressed:

<Dr. Gustav Lauben; 'the speaker of the utterance'; EGO-mode of presentation>

The vector is constructed according to the convention that the first element is the object referred to, the second is the description expressing the linguistic meaning that a competent speaker associates with the singular term independent of any specific knowledge about the context, the third is a mode of presentation of the object.

The vector theory can also account for proper names. Using a Fregean example we can characterize the meaning of the singular term 'Dr. Gustav Lauben' as used in the utterance 'Dr. Gustav Lauben was wounded' by the following vector containing the three elements as possible contributions to the content expressed:

<Dr. Gustav Lauben; 'the person named *Dr. Gustav Lauben*'; 'the (only) person living in the house ABC' >

The first element of the vector is the person. The second element characterized by the description is the linguistic meaning which a competent speaker associates with the proper name independent of any specific knowledge about the context, the third element is a mode of presentation of the object which is expressed by the definite description and which is the relevant one according to the epistemic context.

One of the advantages of this theory of meaning is that it can easily account for empty names. Empty names have no reference but they are not without meaning. The meaning vector contains only two of the possible elements, because there is no reference, but it need not be empty: If the empty name is used in a conventionally established way, it has a linguistic meaning and if someone uses the name by associating a mode of presentation (i.e. by having a relevant epistemic background) the third element in the vector is also realized. Only the first component of the vector is empty.[31]

The vector theory of meaning has the further advantage that it integrates the standard views of semantics. On the basis of the vector, which is determined by an utterance context and an epistemic context, the communicative situation is the relevant factor for determining which component of the vector contributes to the content of the utterance. If the relevant component is chosen then the classical views of compositional semantics can do their job. The important difference regarding classical semantics is the denial of the dogma of standard semantics according to which an unambiguous utterance (without any deficits, i.e. no missing words, demonstratives are accompanied with gestures if necessary etc.) has exactly one semantic content. According to different criteria of adequacy for semantics, we can distinguish different levels of characterizing utterances which are equally relevant to semantics although at least some levels do involve aspects which are traditionally classified as pragmatics. Therefore, there is no strict separation between semantics and pragmatics. The core ideas of this systematic proposal is inspired by a careful interpretation of Frege, who was not only a pioneer in logic but also in the semantics of natural languages.

---

[31] More details are developed in Newen 1996.

References

Bach, K. 1987, *Thought and Reference*. Oxford: Clarendon Press.

Bermúdez, J. 2001, Frege on thoughts and their structure. *Philosophiegeschichte und logische Analyse / Logical Analysis and History of Philosophy*, Paderborn: mentis. Vol.4: 87-105.

Bell, D. 1987a, Thoughts. *Notre Dame Journal of Formal Logic* 28:36-50.

Bell, D. 1987b, The Art of Judgement. *Mind* 96:221-244.

Bell, D. 1996, The Formation of Concepts and the Structure of Thoughts. *Philosophy and Phenomenological Research* 56:583-596.

Black, M. and P. Geach., eds., 1960, *Translations from the philosophical writings of Gottlob Frege*. Oxford: Basil Blackwell.

Burge, T. 1992, Frege on Knowing the Third Realm. *Mind* 101:632-650.

Dummett, M. 1973, *Frege. Philosophy of Language*. London: Duckworth.

Dummett, M. 1981, *The Interpretation of Frege's Philosophy*, London: Duckworth.

Frege, G. 1959, *The Foundations of Arithmetic*. Austin J., trans., Oxford: Basil Blackwell.

Frege, G. 1960, Begriffsschrift. *Translations from the Philosophical Writings of Gottlob Frege*. Black, M. and P. Geach., eds. 1960.

Frege, G. 1960, Function and concept. *Translations from the Philosophical Writings of Gottlob Frege*. Black, M. and P. Geach., eds. 1960.

Frege, G. 1960, On concept and object. *Translations from the Philosophical Writings of Gottlob Frege*. Black, M. and P. Geach., eds. 1960.

Frege, G. 1960, On sense and reference. *Translations from the Philosophical Writings of Gottlob Frege*. Black, M. and P. Geach., eds. 1960.

Frege, G. 1977, *Logical Investigations*. Geach, P. and R. Stoothoff, eds. Oxford: Basil Blackwell.

Frege, G. 1977, Compound Thoughts. Frege, G. *Logical Investigations.*

Frege, G. 1977, Negation. Frege, G. *Logical Investigations.*

Frege, G. 1977, Thoughts. Frege, G. *Logical Investigations.*

Frege, G. 1979, *Posthumous Writings*, ed. by Hans Hermes, Friedrich Kambartel, Friedrich Kaulbach, Oxford: Blackwell.

Frege, G. 1980, *Gottlob Freges Briefwechsel*, ed. by Gottfried Gabriel, Friedrich Kambartel, Christian Thiel, Hamburg: Meiner Verlag.

Harcourt, E. 1993, Are Hybrid Proper Names the Solution to the Completion Problem, *Mind* 102: 301-313.

Kemmerling, A. 1990, Gedanken und ihre Teile. *Grazer philosophische Studien* 37: 1-30.

Kemmerling, A. 1996, Frege über den Sinn des Wortes „ich". *Grazer philosophische Studien* 51: 1-22.

Künne, W. 1992, Hybrid Proper Names. *Mind* 101: 721-731.

Künne, W.; Newen, A.; Anduschus, M. (eds.), 1997, *Direct Reference, Indexicality and Propositional Attitudes*, Stanford: CSLI.

Lotter, D. 1999, Private Gedanken und Subjektivität, Ein Beitrag zu Freges Philosophie des Geistes. *Philosophisches Jahrbuch* 106: 379-404.

Neale, S. 1990, *Descriptions*, Cambridge/Mass.: MIT Press.

Newen, A. 1994, How to Fix the Reference of 'that' in Demonstrative Utterances, in: ANALYOMEN 1. *Proceedings of the 1st Conference 'Perspectives in Analytical Philosophy'*, hrsg. v. Meggle, G. u. Wessels, U., Berlin: de Gruyter, 493-508.

Newen, A. 1996, *Kontext, Referenz und Bedeutung: Eine Bedeutungstheorie singulärer Terme*, Paderborn: Schöningh.

Newen, A. 1997, The Logic of Indexical Thoughts and the Metaphysics of the 'self', in: Künne, W.; Newen, A.; Anduschus, M. (eds.): *Direct Reference, Indexicality and Propositional Attitudes*, Stanford; CSLI publications, 105-131.

Newen, A. 1998, Reference and Reference Determination: The Interpretational Theory, *Lingua et Style*, in the special volume: *Reference, Thought and Context*, ed. by A. Voltolini , 33, 515-529.

Peacocke, C. 1992, Sense and Justification. *Mind* 101: 793-816.

Perry, 1977, Frege on Demonstratives. *Philosophical Review* 86: 474-497.

Perry, 1993, The Problem of Essential Indexicals, New York/ Oxford: Oxford University Press

Recanati, F. 1993, *Direct Reference. From Language to Thought*. Oxford: Blackwell.

Rheinwald, R. 1997, Paradoxien und die Vergegenständlichung von Begriffen - zu Freges Unterscheidung zwischen Begriff und Gegenstand. *Erkenntnis* 47: 7-35.

Salmon, N. 1992, On Content. *Mind* 101: 733-752.

Stuhlmann-Laeisz, R. 1995, *Gottlob Frege's >Logische Untersuchungen<. Darstellung und Interpretation,* Darmstadt: Wiss. Buchgesellschaft.

7

Frege on Identity, Cognitive Value, and Subject Matter

JOHN PERRY

1 Introduction

No paragraph has been more important for the philosophy of language in the twentieth century than the first paragraph of Frege's 1892 essay 'Über Sinn und Bedeutung'. He begins,

> Sameness [Gleichheit] gives rise to challenging questions which are not altogether easy to answer. Is it a relation? A relation between objects, or between names or signs of objects[1]

Frege continues by explaining what bothered him in the *Begriffsschrift*, and motivated his treatment of identity in that work.[2] He goes on to criticize that account. By the end of the paragraph, he has introduced his key concept of *sinn*, abandoning not only the *Begriffsschrift* account of identity, but also its basic semantical framework.

---

[1] Quotations from this paragraph use Black's translation (Frege 1960) of Frege 1892 with a couple of changes. The most important change is using 'real' for both 'eigentlich' and 'wirklich', which I do to emphasize my view that a fairly clear and robust concept of 'real knowledge' as opposed to knowledge about words and language plays a key role in Frege's argument. Black uses 'proper' for 'eigentlich' and 'actual' for 'wirklich'.

[2] Henceforth I simply assume that it is identity, in the sense in which if A and B are identical there is only one thing that both is A and is B, that is at issue. See Frege's footnote to the first sentence.

In the *Begriffsschrift* Frege's main semantic concept was *content [Inhalt]*. Already in the *Begriffsschrift*, he is struggling with this concept. In §3 he emphasizes that the content of sentences that have different subjects and predicates can be the same; the subject/predicate distinction pertains to language, and not to content. In §9 he emphasizes that the function/argument structure we take a sentence to have represents a certain point of view. 'Cato killed Cato' can be thought having 'to kill Cato' or 'to be killed by Cato' or 'to kill oneself' as the function

> For us the fact that there are various ways in which the same conceptual content can be regarded as a function of this or that argument has no importance so long as function and argument are completely determinate (Frege 1867: 23).

These remarks point to a concept of relatively unstructured contents. They are in line with the 'semantic holism' that some of Frege's remarks and ideas have inspired.

In §8, 'Identity of Content', however, a somewhat different view of content emerges. Individual signs that are parts of sentences have contents, and the combinations into which the signs enter express a relation among those contents --- except in the case of identity sentences. The things Frege says about content in §8, setting aside the exceptional case of identity, fit the following picture pretty well. Signs have contents, the things they stand for, among which are objects, functions, and relations. So the content of '2' is the number 2, the content of '+' is the function of addition, the content of '<' is the relation of smaller than, and so forth. The content of a complex will be determined by the contents of the parts, so the content of '2+3', namely 5, will be determined by the contents of '2', '3' and '+'. The content of '2+3 > 4' will be determined by the contents of its parts, viz., the numbers 5 and 4, and the relation of larger than. Given this picture, the content of a sentence, the sort of thing that could be judged true or false, could be represented and individuated by a suitably structured complex of the contents of its parts.

The remarks we noted earlier do not fit this picture of structured content very well. We saw that Frege emphasizes that sentences with different functions and relations can have the same content: '2+3 > 4 ' and ' 4 < 2+3 ', for example. The idea seems to be that contents are individuated by unstructured truth conditions, so that two quite different structures could correspond to the same content, and sentential contents cannot be seen as complexes of the contents of their parts. Even in §9, however, following the remark quoted above, Frege seems to retreat to a more structured view when what he calls *indeterminate* arguments or functions are involved:

...if the argument becomes *indeterminate*, as in the judgement 'You can take as argument of "being representable as the sum of four squares" an arbitrary positive integer, and the proposition will always be true', then the distinction between function and argument takes on a *substantive* [inhaltliche] significance. On the other hand, it may also be that the argument is determinate and the function indeterminate. In both cases, through the opposition between the *determinate* and the *indeterminate* or that between the *more* and the *less* determinate, the whole is decomposed into *function* and *argument* according to its content and not merely according to the point of view adopted. (Frege 1867: 23)

These two pictures of content are in tension in Frege's early thought, and suffer different fates in his later thought (See Weitzman 1989). For this discussion I am going to suppose that it is the structured contents, or perhaps the structured aspect of contents, that gave Frege a problem with identity in the *Begriffsschrift* , and led him to provide a solution there he later found unsatisfactory. I'll take the content of a statement $\phi(\alpha)$ to be or at least to be representable as, a complex consisting of the condition ϕ designates and the entity α designates. If α designates an object, the conceptual content of $\phi(\alpha)$ will be similar to what we now call a *singular proposition*. If it designated a concept, it would be similar to what we now call a general or qualitative proposition (See Kaplan, 1989).

At the beginning of §8 Frege says,

Identity of content differs from conditionality and negation in that it applies to names and not to contents. Whereas in other contexts signs are merely representatives of their content, so that every combination into which they enter expresses on a relation between their respective contents, they suddenly display their own selves when they are combined by means of the sign for identity of content; for it expresses the circumstance that two names have the same content (Frege 1867: 20-21).

In this passage Frege expresses an account of content corresponding to the picture above, and then amends this theory to handle the problem about identity, so that a complex consisting of names and the relation of co-designation, rather than one consisting of object(s) and the relation of identity, is signified. The key semantic concept of the amended theory was still content; the effect of the amendment was simply to give identity statements a different content than they would have had without it.

In using the term 'amended' I am suggesting that at some point Frege had a theory that didn't treat identity statements in a special way, then saw a problem, and amended that theory with special treatment of them that we find in the *Begriffsschrift*. Thus I am thinking of Frege's thought as falling into three periods, which I'll call '*Ur*- Frege', 'Early Frege' and 'Classical Frege'. Classical Frege is the Frege of 'Über Sinn und Bedeutung'. Early Frege' is the Frege of the *Begriffsschrift* . And 'Ur- Frege' is the Frege of the hypothetical original period, before he decided to treat identity statements differently than other statements in the *Begriffsschrift*.

Now for all I know Frege's *Begriffsschrift* theory never had any unamended form. In using the terms 'amendment', 'amended theory', 'unamended theory', and 'Ur- Frege' as I do, I am simply adopting a way of referring to the theory he actually gave us (the theory 'as amended') as one which *could* have resulted from amending a simpler theory (the 'unamended theory') which had no special treatment of identity. I am not claiming that there was some earlier draft of the *Begriffsschrift* without the special treatment of identity. I am pretending that, for some period of time, perhaps no more than a few minutes, Frege had settled on the main outlines of the *Begriffsschrift* theory of content, but hadn't yet seen the need, or what he took to be the need, for a special treatment of identity statements.

Classical Frege criticizes the *Begriffsschrift* theory, and introduces the concept of sinn and the distinction between sinn and bedeutung not only as an alternative to the *Begriffsschrift* way of handling the problem, but as a new semantical framework.[3] Sinn and bedeutung replace content in Frege's thinking; sinne are more fine-grained than contents, and bedeutungen are less fine-grained. Frege's level of bedeutung was the inspiration for the semantic values we now think of as extensions: objects, sets of objects, and truth-values. Extensions provide the standard interpretation of the predicate calculus, and, according to Quine constitute the only intelligible semantic values for a scientifically respectable language. Frege's level of sinn was the inspiration, at least in part, for much of the work on intensional logic, from Church and Carnap to Kripke and Kaplan.[4]

Thus the argument in the first paragraph is important, if for no other reason, because it records an important part of the motivation for Frege's theory of sinn and bedeutung. Some think that Frege's argument in this paragraph gave him a valid reason to abandon the content framework---especially the structured version of it---in favor of the sinn and bedeutung framework. This is a mistake. The considerations Frege raises in this paragraph, including his criticism of the *Begriffsschrift*, provide no reason whatsoever for abandoning structured content as his basic semantic concept.

On my view, Frege's considerations do provide reasons for seeing both the content provided by a sentence and the cognitive value of a sentence as relative concepts. The concept of 'real knowledge' is motivated the distinction between linguistic conventions that is presupposed in the use of lan-

---

[3] To avoid problems of translation, I use 'sinn' and 'bedeutung' as English words, with the plurals 'sinne' and 'bedeutungen'.

[4] See Church 1956, Carnap 1956, Kaplan 1989, Kripke 1963. In contrast Jaakko Hintikka's model for intensions was multiple reference rather than sinne (Hintikka 1969).

guage, and the knowledge about the things the linguistic items designate, which is what we use sentences to record, store and communicate information about. But what counts as presupposed knowledge of language, and what counts as real knowledge, is not fixed for all situations. Consider, for example, these two sentences

The biggest city in Nebraska = the biggest city in Nebraska.

The biggest city in Nebraska = the municipality larger than any other in Nebraska.

Both statements are reasonably thought of as guaranteed to be true by the conventions of English, and so analytic. But the conventions at issue are quite different. With the first sentence, knowledge of the convention that sentences of the form $A=A$ are true will suffice.[5] With the second sentence, knowledge of the meaning of the various words is also required. The different sorts of knowledge required to recognize the analyticity corresponds to different types and subsets of the conventions of English that account for the analyticity. The second sentence might be used to convey to a person the meaning of the word 'municipality'. One would be exploiting the person's knowledge of many of the conventions of English, in order to convey the information that that 'municipality' means about the same as 'city'.

I argue that if we appreciate the relativity of both the information contained in a sentence and the cognitive value of a sentence, Frege's considerations need not push us away from the view of structured content suggested in §8 of the *Begriffsschrift.*

So, in this paper, I provide an interpretation of Frege's opening paragraph, and then argue that (i) Classical Frege is correct that the *Begriffsschrift* account is flawed; (ii) However, the *Begriffsschrift without the amendment*, could deal successfully with the problem. Thus, whatever strong arguments there may be for abandoning the content framework in favor of the sinn and bedeutung framework, they are not to be found in Frege's treatment of the problem of informational identities in his opening paragraph.

---

[5] As a statement about natural language, this would need to be qualified in various ways, which I ignore.

2   Some Interpretive Tools

Propositions

I'll assume that any n-ary condition R and sequence $<e_1...e_n>$ of appropriate entities determine what I shall call a B-proposition, $P = B(R, e_1... e_n)$, which is true if and only if $<e_1...e_n>$ meet the condition R. I assume that conditions have parameters or argument roles that can be ordered so that we can talk about the ith argument role of the condition R. I assume that each parameter is suitable for either an object or a condition. If the ith parameter of R is suitable for an object I will say that P is *objectual* at its ith parameter. If it is suitable for a condition, I will say that P is *qualitative* at its ith parameter. A proposition that is qualitative at all of its parameters is a *general* proposition, one that is objectual at some parameter is *singular* proposition.

B-propositions are intended simply to enable us to model certain choices that Frege had within the framework of structured content, as conceived according to the above picture. Thus I assume only that the contents of simple statements something like B-propositions, according to one of the strands of Frege's thinking in the *Begriffsschrift*.

The Example

Frege gives rather similar examples of identity statements in the *Begriffsschrift* and in 'Über Sinn und Bedeutung'. Although he ends up with two different accounts in the two works, the examples in both force us to distinguish between a single geometrical point and two modes of presentation of that point. I want to use just one example to compare the two treatments, so I'll use the simpler and more familiar example from 'Über Sinn und Bedeutung'. It involves three lines, a, b, and c, that intersect at the same point. The informative identity statement is:

(1)   The point of intersection of a and b = the point of intersection of b and c.

For later reference, call the term on the left-hand side of (1) α, and the term on the right hand side β and call the point they both designate, 'Albert'. The uninformative identity statement is:

(2)   The point of intersection of a and b = the point of intersection of a and b.

Some Key Concepts

Frege's two treatments of identity are both motivated by a problem that involves the following concepts. All of these concepts are more or less explicit in 'Über Sinn und Bedeutung'.

The **subject matter** of a sentence. This is the objects (or conditions) designated by the terms in the sentence, and the condition designated by the condition word in the sentence. The condition is asserted of the objects for which the terms stand. Take for example the sentence 'α is inside a circle'. The subject matter is the point Albert, which is designated by α and the condition of being inside a circle.

The **epistemic value** [Erkenntniswert] of the sentence. As far as the cases discussed in the first paragraph, this means being a priori and analytic, or a posteriori and synthetic. $a=b$ is assumed to be an example of a synthetic sentence, while $a=a$ is a priori.

The **real knowledge** [eigentliche Erkenntnis, wirkliche Erkenntnis] expressed by the sentence. This determines the cognitive value of the sentence. It is not knowledge about signs, but knowledge *above and beyond that contained in the knowledge of the linguistic conventions*; hence, knowledge that can be conveyed by different languages.

I'll call a condition (a relation or property) an *identifying condition* if it is the sort of condition that at most one thing can meet. That is, an identifying condition is the sort of condition that we express with the definite article, for example 'x is the most influential German philosopher of the nineteenth century' or 'x is the point of intersection of a and b'. I use two special kinds of identifying conditions and the relation of co-instantiation among conditions to reconstruct Frege's argument. Where Fx and Gx are conditions there will be a qualitative proposition that there is something that co-instantiates them. I'll use CI for the relation of co-instantiation. So $B(CI; Fx, Gx)$ is the B-proposition that Fx and Gx are coninstantiated.

Modes of designation. I take a mode of designation to be a condition of being designated by a certain term, e.g., being the designatum of 'Gottlob Frege'. A mode of designation is hence a species of an identifying condition, a condition that only one thing may satisfy. Consider:

$B(CI; x$ is the designatum of 'Gottlob Frege', x was a logician)

This is the proposition whose condition is CI, the relation that holds between two conditions when some object instantiates both. The first condition is a mode of designation, a condition that will be satisfied by at most one thing, the thing that is designated by 'Gottlob Frege', namely, Frege. The second condition is the condition of having been a logician. This proposition is true, since there is one thing, the person Frege, that satisfies the mode of designation, and he also satisfies the second condition, of having been a logician.

Modes of presentation. A mode of presentation is also an identifying condition. But a mode of presentation has to do with satisfying a condition expressed by the words, not a condition relating directly to the words. It is one thing to be designated by the words 'the present Queen of England' and another thing to be the present Queen of England. The first condition is a mode of designation that Elizabeth II satisfies, the second a mode of presentation that she satisfies. It is one thing to be designated by the words 'the point of intersection of a and b' and another to be the point of intersection of a and b. The point we named 'Albert' satisfies both.

Thus if we consider a sentence like 'The point of intersection of a and b is inside of a circle' we can distinguish among three propositions that will have to be true for the sentence to be true.[6] First, there is $B(x$ is inside a circle, Albert), a singular proposition, the **subject matter proposition**. Then there is $B(CI; x$ is the object designated by α, x is inside a circle). This is a general proposition, the **modes of designation proposition**. Finally there is $B(CI; x$ is the point of intersection of a and b, x is inside a circle). This is a general proposition, the **modes of presentation proposition**.

The Problem

Let $A=B$ and $A=A$ be forms of statements, and $\alpha = \beta$ and $\alpha = \alpha$ are particular statements of those forms. Suppose that $\alpha = \beta$ is true, and that there are no internal connections of structure or dictionary meaning that insure that α and β designate the same thing. Now consider these six statements:

(A) (i) $\alpha = \beta$ is true; (ii) $\alpha = \beta$ is not a priori; (iii) $\alpha = \alpha$ is a priori

(B) A statement of the form $A=B$ asserts identity of the designata of A and B, that is, its subject matter proposition is B(Identity A,B).

---

[6] I assume that in order to be the object designated by 'the F' an object has to have the property designated by 'F'. In Donnellan's famous example, a speaker successfully uses the phrase 'the man drinking a martini' to point out a man who is drinking a glass of water with an olive (Donnellan 1966). He uses this as an example of a 'referential' as opposed to an 'attributive' use of a definite description. The points I am making don't hold for that kind of example, and I don't here discuss how to treat such cases. Donnellan's concept of 'referential' combines the feature of allowing inaccuracy, as in the martini case, and the feature of conveying a singular proposition. I do not need to assume that the description is used attributively, in the sense of expressing a general proposition as opposed to a singular one. It may be used referentially, in the sense of expressing a singular proposition about whoever is in fact the F. However, the object must be the F, as opposed to merely almost being the F, or being taken by speaker or listener to be the F, for the points I am making to apply.

(C) Hence, $\alpha = \alpha$ and $\alpha = \beta$ have the same subject matter proposition (from (Ai) and (B)).

(D) The real knowledge expressed by a sentence is its subject matter proposition.

(E) The real knowledge expressed by a sentence determines its cognitive value.

(F) Hence, $\alpha = \beta$ and $\alpha = \alpha$ have the same cognitive value (from (C), (D), and (E)).

But, clearly,

(G) $\alpha = \alpha$ and $\alpha = \beta$ have different cognitive values. (From (Aii) and (Aiii))

This is my reconstruction of the problem that bothered Frege. In the *Begriffsschrift*, he resolves it by giving up (B). In 'Über Sinn und Bedeutung he resolves it by giving up (D). I will argue that (D) and (E) both need modification.

3 Frege's *Begriffsschrift* Theory

Now let's return to the text. Frege asks, then, whether sameness, if it is a relation, is a relation between objects, or between names or signs of objects. He continues:

> In my *Begriffsschrift* I assumed the latter.

Let's take another look at relevant passage in his *Begriffsschrift* to remind ourselves what he actually said there.

> Identity of content differs from conditionality and negation in that it applies to names and not to contents. Whereas in other contexts signs are merely representatives of their content, so that every combination into which they enter expresses on a relation betweeen their respective contents, they suddenly display their own selves when they are combined by means of the sign for identity of content; for it expresses the circumstance that two names have the same content. Hence the introduction of a sign for identity of content necessarily produces a bifurcation in the meaning of all signs: they stand at times for their content, at times for themselves (Frege 1867: 20-21).

Almost seeming to anticipate the objection he will make in 'Über Sinn und Bedeutung', he goes on,

> At first we have the impression that what we are dealing with pertains merely to the *expression* and *not to the thought*... (Frege 1867: 21)

He rebuts this suggestion, as resting on the false premiss that

> ...we do not need different signs at all for the same content and hence no sign whatsoever for identity of content. (Frege 1867: 21)

To show that this is wrong-headed, Frege uses an example that is quite similar to, although as I mentioned, more complicated than, the one he was to use in 'Über Sinn und bedeutung'. For simplicity, I am pretending that he simply uses the later example in both places, so that informative identity statement is:

(1) The point of intersection of a and b = the point of intersection of b and c

We are calling the term on the left hand side of (1) α and the term on the right hand side β. Frege points out---in the *Begriffsschrift*!--- that α and β correspond to two ways of determining the content. He then says:

> To each of these ways of determining the point there corresponds a particular name. Hence the need for a sign of identity rests upon the following consideration: the same content can be completely determined in different ways; but that in a particular case *two ways of determining it* really yield the *same result* is the content of a *judgment* (Frege 1867: 21).

There is a certain tension in this account. There seem to be three possible $\boldsymbol{B}$-propositions one might want to associate with (1):

(3) $\boldsymbol{B}$(Identity; Albert, Albert)

This is a singular proposition about Albert, to the effect that it is identical with itself. This is the subject matter proposition on the unamended theory, that treats identity statements like everything else. Frege clearly doesn't want (3).

(4) $\boldsymbol{B}$(CI; α designates x, β designates x)

This proposition requires that the two modes of designation are co-instantiated. This is (roughly) Early Frege's candidate for the subject matter proposition.

(5) $\boldsymbol{B}$(CI; x is the point of intersection of a and b, x is the point of intersection of b and c)

This proposition requires that the two modes of presentation are coinstantiated. This is not the content according to Early Frege, although at the end of the passage I quoted above, it sounds as if it might be what he really wanted. At any rate, this is more or less the proposition that Classical Frege came to think was the 'real knowledge' conveyed by (1).

4 Frege's Reconstruction

So now to return to our main target, the first paragraph of 'Über Sinn und Bedeutung'. So far Frege has said, to repeat,

> Sameness gives rise to challenging questions which are not altogether easy to answer. Is it a relation? A relation between objects or between names or signs of objects? In my *Begriffsschrift* I assumed the latter.

He then goes on to give the reasons which 'seemed' to favor this:

> The reasons which seemed to favor this are the following: *a=a* and *a=b* are obviously statements of differing epistemic value [Erkenntniswert]; *a=a* holds *a priori* and, according to Kant is to be labelled analytic,while statements of the form *a=b* often contain very valuable extensions of our knowledge and cannot always be established *a priori*. The discovery that a new sun does not rise every morning, but always the same one, was one of the most fertile astronomical discoveries. Even today the identification of a small planet or a comet is not always a matter of course.

Frege presumably means to recall the considerations that found expression in the *Begriffsschrift* simply as, 'The same content can be fully determined in different ways.' In that work he called the object which a name designated the *content* of the name. As we saw, when he talked about 'two ways of determining' there, he seemed to have in mind not simply two modes of designation or two signs but two modes of presentation.

In 'Über Sinn und Bedeutung' Frege reconstructs the problem that bothered him in the *Begriffsschrift*, and still bothers him, in this way:

> Now if we were to regard sameness as a relation between that which the names '*a*' and '*b*' designate, it would seem that *a=b* could not differ from *a=a* (i.e. provided *a=b* is true). A relation would thereby be expressed of a thing to itself, and indeed one in which each thing stands to itself but to no other thing.

Above I explained the problem that bothered Frege in terms of (A) -- (G). Now I'll use that apparatus to explain Classical Frege's reconstruction of Early Frege. The appeal to (D) and (E) is implicit:

Stipulate, of some significant empirically discoverable identity sentence $\alpha=\beta$:

(Ai) $\alpha=\beta$ is true

It's obvious that:

(A ii) $\alpha=\beta$ is not a priori

(A iii) $\alpha=\alpha$ is a priori.

Assume:

(B) A statement of the form $A=B$ asserts identity of the designata of A and B, that is, its subject matter proposition is **B**(Identity; *A,B)*

Then:

(C) $\alpha=\alpha$ and $\alpha=\beta$ have the same subject matter proposition.

But, [given (D) and (E)], it follows:

(F) $\alpha = \beta$ and $\alpha = \alpha$ have the same cognitive value

But from (Aii) and (Aiii):

(G) $\alpha=\alpha$ and $\alpha=\beta$ have different cognitive values.

So our assumption must be wrong---we must reject (B).

This conclusion corresponds to only half of the position in the *Begriffsschrift*, the half that says that identity statements do *not* assert identity of the designata of their terms. Classical Frege provides an argument for the second half of Early Frege's position, that identity statements *do* assert co-designation of the terms, in the next passage:

> What is intended to be said by $a=b$ seems to be that the signs or names '*a*' and '*b*' designate the same thing, so that those signs themselves would be under discussion; a relation between them would be asserted.

For future reference, I want the reader to focus on Frege's thought here. He is reporting, accurately, that at the time of *Begriffsschrift* , he had noted that '*a=b*', unlike '*a=a*', carries the information that the signs '*a*' and '*b*' co-designate. This seems quite correct. Suppose I am puzzled, driving through the Basque Country, by the fact that the mileage signs always have Donastia and San Sebastian exactly the same distance away. Seems an odd coincidence. You tell me that 'Donastia is San Sebastian'. One thing I will learn, whatever else I may learn, is that 'Donastia' and 'San Sebastian' name the same city. Early Frege explained this by holding this bit of information is what you asserted. Classical Frege gives good reasons for thinking this is not what is asserted. But he does not give reasons for denying what Early Frege noticed, that this information is conveyed.

5   Frege's Critique of his Earlier View

At this point, the word 'But' signals the shift back to Classical Frege's own opinions:

> But this relation would hold between names or signs only insofar as they named or designated something. It would be mediated by the connection of each of the two signs with the same designated thing. But this is arbitrary. Nobody can be forbidden to use any arbitrarily producible event or object as a sign for something. In that $a=b$ would no longer refer to the subject matter, but only to its mode of designation; we would express no real knowledge by its means. But in many cases this is just what we want to do.

Here Classical Frege seems to be zeroing in on just the tension we noted in the *Begriffsschrift* discussion. Note that he is not directly rebutting the negative argument, the argument that sameness sentences do *not* express a relation between the objects designated by their terms.

The term 'real knowledge' ['eigentliche Erkenntnis'] bears considerable weight.

Recall our non-trivial identity:

(1):The point of intersection of a and b = the point of intersection of b and c.

We noted that in order for (1) to be true, three quite different propositions must be true. (3) is about Albert, the designatum of the terms flanking the identity sign; Albert must be identical with Albert. (4) is about the modes of designation, that they are coinstantiated. (5) is about modes of presentation, that they are coinstantiated.

Which of these three is the content of (1)? In the passage just quoted, Classical Frege provides a reason to favor the mode of presentations proposition (his choice) over the mode of designations proposition (Early Frege's choice). The reason is that the knowledge that is embodied in the modes of designations proposition is not *real* knowledge, but knowledge that a certain relation holds between signs.

As I interpret the next passage,

> If the sign 'a' is distinguished from the sign 'b' only as object (here, by means of its shape), not as sign (i.e. not by the manner in which it designates something), the cognitive value of $a=a$ becomes essentially equal to that of $a=b$, provided that $a=b$ is true.

Frege tries, not completely successfully, to provide a reason for favoring the modes of presentations proposition over the subject matter proposition, that Albert is Albert. The basic idea is that the real knowledge, which determines the cognitive value, is what we learn in addition to what is fixed by our knowledge of language; that is, what the truth of the sentence requires beyond what is required by the truth of the conventions of language. To consider signs 'only as objects' is to ignore the fact that the conventions of language connect the signs with modes of presentation, not directly with their designata. If we disregard this link between the signs and modes of presentation, and consider only the link between signs as differently shaped objects and their designata, then the conventions of language determine the truths of both sentences. Language assigns the terms '*a*' and '*b*' to the same object, and so '*a=b*', like '*a=a*', does not provide us with any information beyond the conventions of language.

This passage seems odd, because even if we ignore the manner in which signs designate, there is still a difference between '*a=a*' and '*a=b*'; the shapes that flank the identity sign are the same in the first case but are not the same in the second. The convention that different occurrences of the same shape designate the same thing would assure the truth of '*a=a*', but not of '*a=b*'. So what is Frege driving at? On my interpretation he is driving at the fact that if we ignore modes of presentation, our semantical rules will directly tie signs, considered simply as objects of various shapes, to their designata. In that case, and given that it is true, the truth of '*a=b*' will be determined by the semantical rules. And then its cognitive value will be the same as '*a=a*'---analytic and a priori. He is basically arguing against a view of reference or designation as unmediated by a mode of presentation, and hence, almost a century in advance, against some versions of the 'direct reference' theory.[7]

Classical Frege then seems to be eliminating possibilities to arrive at the right view, as follows:

(i) The mode of designations proposition is not analytic, and constitutes knowledge, but it is not *real* knowledge, but knowledge about signs. So, contrary to the *Begriffsschrift* , it won't do.

(ii) The subject-matter proposition isn't about language. But it is the same for both sentences. What's more, the point of view that leads to this choice seems to make the truth of both a matter of the conventions of language. So sentences of the forms $A=B$ and $A=A$ would have the same content, and both be a priori, if we were to make this choice for their content. So (contrary to the Ur-*Begriffsschrift*) it won't do.

---

[7] I say 'some versions' of direct reference theory, because the definition of 'direct reference' that Kaplan gives in Kaplan 1989, where the term is introduced into the literature, doesn't require that the mechanism of reference be unmediated. See Marti 1995 and Perry 1997.

(iii) Thus: the subject matter proposition doesn't give us *a posteriori* knowledge, the mode of designations proposition doesn't give us *real* knowledge, and that leaves the mode of presentations proposition:

A difference can arise only if the difference between the signs corresponds to a difference in the mode of presentation of that which is designated. Let *a*, *b*, *c* be the lines connecting the vertices of a triangle *with* the midpoints of the opposite sides. The point of intersection of *a* and *b* is then the same as the point of intersection of *b* and *c*. So we have different designations for the same point, and these names ('point of intersection of *a* and *b*', 'point of intersection of *b* and *c*') likewise indicate the mode of presentation; and hence the statement contains real [wirkliche] knowledge.

This passage makes a very similar point to the one we quoted from the *Begriffsschrift*. There he noted that we needed two signs to convey the knowledge that is involved in this sort of example, that two modes of presentation are of the same object. Here he twists the same point around: two names flanking an identity sign would not be cognitively different from one another, at least as far as real knowledge goes, unless they were associated with different modes of presentation.

6   Classical Frege's Position

In terms of (A)-(G), here is what I take to be Classical Frege's position. He accepts (A), (E) and (G):

(Ai) $\alpha=\beta$ is true; ii) $\alpha=\beta$ is not a priori; iii) $\alpha=\alpha$ is a priori

(E)   The real knowledge expressed by a sentence determines its cognitive value.

(G) $\alpha=\alpha$ and $\alpha=\beta$ have different cognitive values.

He rejects (D),

(D) The real knowledge expressed by a sentence is its subject matter proposition.

and replaces it with (D'):

(D')The real knowledge expressed by a sentence is its modes of presentation proposition.

And thus avoids (F) and the contradiction with (G):

(F) $\alpha = \beta$ and $\alpha = \alpha$ have the same cognitive value.

The concept of a subject matter proposition comes to a dead end in Frege's philosophy at this point. He retains the concept of the bedeutungen of the parts of a statement, and of a statement being about these bedeutungen, but the concept of a subject matter proposition, a complex that embodies the claim the statement makes about the bedeutungen of its terms, vanishes. In its place are only the truth-value, at the level of bedeutung, and the thought expressed by the statement, at the level of sinn. Thus (B) and (C),

> (B) A statement of the form $A=B$ asserts identity of the designata of A and B, that is, its subject matter proposition is B(Identity;A,B).

(C) $\alpha=\alpha$ and $\alpha=\beta$ have the same subject matter proposition

play no role in Frege's solution, but he also gives us no reason, in this paragraph, to reject them as false. They simply drop from sight, because the key concept in them, the subject matter proposition, has no role in Frege's semantics.

7 Back to Ur- Frege?

The solution to the problem of identity and epistemic significance that Frege provides in the first paragraph is completely compatible with the Ur-Frege account and the semantics of structured content. He has provided a reason for abandoning the *Begriffsschrift* treatment of identity sentences, but not for abandoning the *Begriffsschrift* account of content.

A semantically competent user of the relevant language who hears (1), believes the speaker, and has a clear view of the diagram, will learn *all three* of the propositions in question, the subject matter proposition, the mode of designations proposition, and the mode of presentations proposition. All three propositions must be true, if (1) is to be true; each of them is in that sense part of the truth conditions of (1). The mode of designations proposition must be true, if (1) is to be true, *given* that (1) is an English statement of the form $a=b$. The mode of presentations proposition must be true, *given* all of that *plus* the fact that 'the point of intersection of a and b' and 'the point of intersection of b and c' mean what they do. And the subject matter proposition must be true, *given* all of *that*, and adding the fact that Albert is the point of intersection of a and b and the point of intersection of b and c.

Note that credulous hearer who *wasn't* a fully competent speaker or who didn't hear the words clearly might learn the mode of designations proposition; this might help him to identify the words, or to learn their meanings. Someone who understood the language, but couldn't see the diagram and so couldn't identify Albert as the referent of the terms, might learn the mode of designations and the mode of presentations propositions, but not the subject matter proposition.

The Ur- Frege theory gives us all the semantics we need to distinguish the three propositions, and to account for the fact that all three must be true for (1) to be true.

What about the cognitive value of (1)? Frege's view that (1) is not analytic and a priori, but synthetic and a posteriori, in virtue of the different meanings of the terms, seems quite reasonable. That is to say that it is the truth conditions of a statement, fixing only the facts about meaning, and not those about reference, in which we are interested when we ask whether something is analytic or a priori.

But is that the right way to look at '$a=a$'? We don't have to look at the modes of presentation associated with the terms of this identity, to know that it was true. The meaning of '=' and the conventions (of a language as well-behaved as Frege wanted his *Begriffsschrift* to be) that terms name something and that the same terms name the same thing guarantee the truth, without taking into account the conventions that assign meaning to 'a'.

A reasonable way to look at it seems to be that a statement can be analytic in virtue of *various subsets* of the conventions of language that pertain to it. Analyticity is relative to which aspects of meaning are kept fixed. To return to the example I introduced earlier, two analytic statements can differ in as the following pair do: 'The biggest city in Nebraska is the biggest city in Nebraska' and 'The biggest city in Nebraska is the municipality larger than any other in Nebraska'. A person who knew English fairly well, but didn't know what 'municipality' meant, might know the first to be true in virtue of meaning but not the second. They are analytic in virtue of *different* conventions of language. It is this relativity that Frege needed in his ur-theory, in addition to structured content, to handle the problem of identity, rather than a special treatment of identity sentences, or the new semantical approach of 'Über Sinn und Bedeutung'.

I conclude that a theory of analyticity, and the informational value of statements, based on the Ur- Frege semantic apparatus of structured content, can support a theory that handles the examples Frege considers in the first paragraph of 'Über Sinn und Bedeutung', in line with the points he makes there. The considerations of the first paragraph of this famous essay provide no reason for abandoning the basic semantic approach of the *Begriffsschrift*, but only for abandoning the special treatment of identity statements contained therein.

References

Barwise, J and Perry, J. 2000. *Situations and Attitudes*. 2nd ed.. Stanford: CSLI Publications.

Carnap, R. 1956. *Meaning and Necessity*. 2nd ed.. Chicago: University of Chicago Press.

Church, A. 1956. *An Introduction to Mathematical Logic*. Princeton: Princeton University Press.

Donnellan, K. 1966. Reference and Definite Descriptions. *Philosophical Review* 75: 281-304.

Frege, G. 1949. On Sense and Nominatum. Translation of Frege, 1892 by Herbert Feigl. In *Readings in Philosophical Analysis*, ed. H. Feigl, H. and W. Sellars. New York: Appleton-Century-Crofts: 85-102.

Frege, G. 1960. On Sense and Reference. Translation of Frege 1892 by Max Black. In *Translations From the Philosophical Writings of Gottlob Frege*, edited and translated by P. Geach and M. Black. Oxford: Basil Blackwell: 56-78.

Frege, G. 1892. Über Sinn und Bedeutung. *Zeitschrift für Philosophische Kritik* NF 100: 25-30. Reprinted in Frege, G. 1962. *Funktion, Begriff, Bedeutung: Fünf logische Studien*, edited by Günther Patzig. Göttingen: Vandenhoeck & Ruprecht: 40-65.

Frege, G. 1879. *Begriffsschrift, eine der arithmetischen nachgebildete Formelsprache des reinen Denkens*. Halle.

Frege, G. 1967. *Begriffsschrift, a formula language, modeled upon that of arithmetic, for pure thought*. Translation of Frege 1879 by Stefan Bauer-Mengelberg. In *From Frege to Gödel: A Source Book in Mathematical Logic, 1879-1931*, edited by J. van Heijenoort. Cambridge: Harvard University Press: 1-82.

Hintikka, J. 1969. *Models for Modalities*. Dordrecht: D. Reidel.

Kaplan, David. 1989. Demonstratives *Themes From Kaplan*, J. Almog, J. Perry, and H. Wettstein, editors. New York: Oxford University Press: 481-563.

Kripke, S. 1963. Semantical Considerations on Modal Logic. In *Acta Philosophical Fennica*, Fasc. XVI: 83-94.

Marti, G. 1995. The Essence of Genuine Reference. *Journal of Philosophical Logic*, 24: 275-289.

Perry, J. 2000. *The Problem of the Essential Indexical and Other Essays, 2nd ed.* Stanford: CSLI Publications.

Perry, John. 1997. Indexicals and Demonstratives. In R. Hale and C. Wright (eds.) *Companion to the Philosophy of Language*. Oxford: Basil Blackwell.

Weitzman, L. 1989. *Propositional Identity and Structure in Frege*. Doctoral Dissertation, Stanford.

8

How to Kripke a Frege-Russell

ROSEMARIE RHEINWALD

In his paper *How to Russell a Frege-Church,* David Kaplan shows how one can start with Frege-Church and end up with Russell.[1] I am going to show how one can start with Frege-Church-Russell and end up with Kripke.

In *Naming and Necessity,* Saul Kripke criticizes Russell's theory of ordinary proper names which, he claims, is a description theory.[2] I will argue that this claim is mistaken. It rests on a confusion between ideal and ordinary language. My aim is to show that Russell's and Kripke's theory of ordinary proper names are essentially equivalent. Russell's theory of ordinary proper names is not a description theory but rather a theory of direct reference.

Kaplan has to add an additional component to Frege's philosophy of language - namely haecceitism - in order to get Russell's philosophy of language.[3] From Kaplan's and my claim it seems to follow that the crucial difference between Frege and Kripke is haecceitism. I will defend a modified version of this conclusion: The crucial difference between Frege and Kripke concerns the rigidity thesis.

---

[1] Kaplan 1975.

[2] Kripke 1980.

[3] Kaplan 1975, p. 726, says that he is concerned with metaphysics and not with epistemology. He characterizes Russell as holding a description theory of ordinary proper names at the *epistemological* level but being a haecceitist at the *metaphysical* level. It is not clear to me how he would characterize Russell's *philosophy of language* in the context of my discussion. I am concerned with Russell's philosophy of language which, to my mind, cannot be seperated from his epistemology and metaphysics.

1 Kaplan's Comparison of Frege's and Russell's Philosophies of Language

Let me start by summarizing the content of Kaplan's paper. Kaplan compares Frege's philosophy of language and Russell's philosophy of language from a very general standpoint. In this comparison, he neglects many small differences in detail and also some important differences. (For example, he neglects that Frege's concepts are not objects and that Russell's theory should be ramified.[4]) In order to compare the theories, he reconstructs and formalizes the theories on the basis of a possible worlds semantics. His formalization of Frege's semantics is a modification of Church's formalization.[5] Kaplan states the following three main differences between Frege and Russell.[6]

(1) They have different theories of definite descriptions and different analyses of intensional contexts. I suppose that these differences are well known and do not have to be laid out.[7]

(2) They have different ontologies of intensional entities. Frege's ontology consists of individuals, truth values and a hierarchy of senses and functions. Russell's ontology consists of individuals, propositions and propositional functions. Frege's senses of sentences can be identified with Russell's propositions. If one does so Russell's intensional ontology is a small part of Frege's intensional ontology. Frege's ontology of intensional entities is larger than Russell's since it contains not only propositions but also a hierarchy of senses. This larger intensional ontology seems to have advantages over Russell's ontology: It can be used to give a satisfactory analysis of certain[8] intensional verbs like "to seek". Frege can analyze sentences like "Schliemann sought the site of Troy" with the help of senses of

---

[4] Cf. Rheinwald 1997 for a discussion of Frege's distinction between objects and concepts. Cf. Rheinwald 1988, pp. 108-113, for a discussion of Russell's theory of types and a comparison of Russell's propositional functions and Frege's concepts.

[5] Church 1951 and 1973/ 1974 attempts to formalize Frege's semantics. There are several differences between Frege's and Church's semantics. In the context of my paper, to speak of "Frege-Church" or "Church" would be more adequate than to speak of "Frege". For example, Frege's sharp ontological distinction between objects and concepts (or functions) is not reflected in Church's system, since Church considers functions as objects. I follow Kaplan in neglecting these differences.

[6] Kaplan 1975, pp. 717-719.

[7] Cf., e.g., Linsky 1983 for a discussion of the two theories.

[8] Namely verbs which are completed by singular terms rather than sentential clauses. In order to be precise, one should speak of *occurrences* of intensional verbs, since intensional verbs can take different complements in different contexts.

singular terms. For Russell, there is no obvious way to eliminate the definite description from this sentence.

(3) They have different views about the structure of propositions. For Frege, a proposition is always composed of intensional entities - namely senses. For example, the proposition that Venus is a planet is composed of the sense of "Venus" and the sense of "is a planet". For Russell, there are singular propositions - i.e. propositions which have individuals as immediate constituents. For example, the singular proposition that Venus is a planet contains Venus as an immediate constituent.

Kaplan claims that only the last difference is crucial. In order to justify this claim, he shows that if one adds singular propositions to Frege's theory the resulting theory is essentially equivalent to Russell's theory. In more detail, he shows in a technical way that the addition of singular propositions to Frege's theory has the following two results.

1) One can reduce Frege's larger intensional ontology to Russell's intensional ontology of propositions and propositional functions. The leading idea of this reduction is roughly the following. Senses of singular terms are identified with senses of individual predicates. An individual predicate is a predicate which contains a uniqueness claim - like, e.g., "is a unique queen of England". Individual predicates denote individual attributes. Given the existence of singular propositions, individual attributes can be identified with functions from individuals to propositions - i.e. with Russell's propositional functions. For example, these identifications have the following result: The Fregean sense of the singular term "the morning star" is identified with the Russellian propositional function that x is a unique planet which is located at a certain position in the morning. An analogous identification can be made for senses of higher levels: Intensions of higher levels are reduced to propositional functions of higher levels.

2) One can give a translation of Frege's language into Russell's language. This translation preserves the meaning as well as the most important features of Frege's analysis of intensional contexts and approximates Russell's analysis of these contexts. Russell's analysis of definite descriptions as involving existence- and uniqueness-claims approximates Frege's analysis of definite descriptions on the level of their senses. Also the analysis of intensional verbs like "to seek" is the same in both languages. In the sentence "Schliemann sought the site of Troy", *to seek* is a relation between the individual Schliemann and the propositional function that x is a unique site of Troy.

What Kaplan has shown is the following. Frege only needs his large ontology of senses because he does not accept singular propositions. If one adds singular propositions to Frege's theory the resulting theory is similar to Russell's theory. One could express Kaplan's result with the following equation: *"Frege-Church + singular propositions = Russell"*. And this equation does not only hold with respect to ontology but also with respect to semantics.

Kaplan claims that the acceptance of singular propositions is equivalent to haecceitism. (I will criticize this claim later on.) Using this equivalence, he expresses his main thesis with the following equation: *"Frege-Church + Haecceitism = Russell"*.[9]

2 The Usual Account of Russell's Theory of Proper Names

In *Naming and Necessity*, Kripke defends a causal theory (or historical chain theory) of proper names. He claims that Frege and Russell are adherents of a description theory of proper names. He describes the so-called Frege-Russell theory of proper names as follows:[10] "Frege and Russell both thought [... that] a proper name, properly used, simply was a definite description abbreviated or disguised. Frege specifically said that such a description gave the sense of the name."

I think that with respect to Frege, Kripke's characterization can be defended, though I would not defend it. I am more sympathetic with Dummett's criticism of this characterization.[11] According to Dummett, the Fregean sense of a name can be given by a definite description but it does not have to be given in that way. For Dummett, the sense of a name should be identified with the criterion of identification of the object which is the reference of the name.

With respect to Russell, I believe that Kripke's characterization is not adequate. Kripke concedes two deviations from Russell in his characterization of Russell's view:[12] "First, we stipulate that 'names' shall be names as ordinary conceived, not Russell's 'logically proper names'; second, we regard descriptions, and their abbreviations, as having sense." The two deviations are not negligible. In the context of my discussion, especially the first deviation is problematic. I do not think Russell's view should be described as a description theory of proper names. In my view, this characterization - which is not only given by Kripke - is the result of a confusion between natural and ideal language.

---

[9] Kaplan 1975, p. 727.
[10] Kripke 1980, p. 27. Cf. also pp. 58-59.
[11] Cf. Dummett 1981.
[12] Kripke 1980, p. 27, fn. 4.

Russell's theory of proper names does not have many defenders. Usually this theory is described as follows. Ordinary proper names (like "Scott") are disguised definite descriptions. Ordinary proper names are replaced by definite descriptions (e.g. by "the author of Waverley") which are eliminated according to Russell's description theory. Sentences containing definite descriptions are turned into general sentences. Since, according to the description theory, definite descriptions have no reference, it follows that ordinary proper names have no reference. Ordinary proper names are not genuine proper names. Genuine proper names are called "logically proper names". The only logically proper names are demonstratives like "this" and "that" - and maybe the word "I". Logically proper names have a reference. They denote individuals with which we are acquainted. Such individuals are constituents of certain propositions - namely of singular propositions.

Philosophers like Kripke criticize Russell's alleged description theory of ordinary proper names. Adherents of a Fregean philosophy of language criticize Russell's theory of logically proper names because they think that individuals cannot be part of propositions. Defenders of a causal theory of names may hold that individuals can be parts of propositions but even they do not seem to be committed to this idea. Sainsbury[13] criticizes Russell for not having said what he - Russell - should have said. Sainsbury reinterprets Russell's theory as being a genuine reference theory of names and argues that Russell's epistemology - especially the doctrine of acquaintance - is responsible for Russell's error about what expressions are names. He tries to explain "how Russell came to adopt the erroneous view that most so-called 'names' are not names".[14] I think that all these criticisms are unjustified. They are directed against what I take to be an inadequate reconstruction of Russell's theory of proper names.

3 Russell on Proper Names

What is Russell's theory of proper names? - If one looks at Russell's papers on the subject - especially at *On Denoting* and *The Philosophy of Logical Atomism* - one can select many unclear and even obviously contradictory quotations.[15] It follows that there is no interpretation of Russell which is compatible with everything he says. But there can still be more and less adequate interpretations. My aim is to explain why there are contradictions

---

[13] Sainsbury 1979, pp. 57-94, esp. pp. 58-59.
[14] Sainsbury 1979, p. 59.
[15] Russell 1956a and 1956b. Cf. also Russell 1963.

in Russell's formulations and to give a coherent reconstruction of Russell's theory of ordinary proper names.

Russell's main aim in *On Denoting* is not to present a theory of proper names but a theory of definite descriptions. That makes it difficult to extract his view on ordinary proper names from this text. In the paper, two sorts of ordinary proper names occur. Proper names of the first sort are unproblematic ones - like "Scott", "George IV" and "Charles II". When Russell analyzes the sentence "George IV wished to know whether Scott was the author of *Waverley*" the name "Scott" is contrasted with the definite description "the author of *Waverley*". The name is considered as having a reference and is not treated as a disguised description. Unlike the definite description, the name "Scott" is not eliminated from the sentence. Proper names of the second sort are problematic ones - for example, mythological or fictional names like "Apollo" or "Hamlet". Only with respect to those names does Russell defend a description theory. Since the paradigm of an ordinary name certainly is an unproblematic and not a problematic one, Russell's theory of ordinary proper names in *On Denoting* is not a description theory.

In *The Philosophy of Logical Atomism* proper names are extensively treated. In this paper, Russell makes many remarks about ordinary proper names, but these remarks seem to be incoherent. For example, he seems to defend a description theory when he writes:

> "The names that we commonly use, like 'Socrates', are really abbreviations for descriptions [...]"[16]

> "We are not acquainted with Socrates, and therefore cannot name him. When we use the word 'Socrates', we are really using a description."[17]

> "The only words one does use as names in the logical sense are words like 'this' or 'that'."[18]

Contrary to these claims, he seems to make a distinction between names and descriptions when he writes:

> "[...] 'the author of *Waverley*' is not a name [...]"[19]

> "[...] a name is what a man is called [...]"[20]

> "When I say 'Scott is the author of *Waverley*' [...] the one is a name and the other a description."[21]

---

[16] Russell 1956b, p. 200.

[17] Russell 1956b, p. 201.

[18] Russell 1956b, p. 201.

[19] Russell 1956b, p. 244.

[20] Russell 1956b, p. 244.

At some places it sounds as if names can be *used* either as names or as descriptions:

> "When I say 'Scott is the author of *Waverley*' [...] the one is a name and the other a description. Or they may both be descriptions."[22]

> "[...] 'Scott' and 'Sir Walter' are being used as names and not as descriptions [...]".[23]

> "'Scott' taken as a name has a meaning all by itself. It stands for a certain person, and there it is."[24]

Since (according to the description theory) a description has no meaning all by itself and does not stand for an object (i.e., it has no reference), "Scott" taken as a name differs essentially from "Scott" taken as a description.[25]

4   Ordinary Language and Ideal Languages

In order to make sense of Russell's contradictory remarks and to reconstruct Russell's theory of ordinary proper names in a coherent way one has to distinguish and keep apart *ideal (or logically perfect) languages* and *ordinary (or natural) language.* Russell describes an ideal language as follows.[26]

> In a logically perfect language the words in a proposition would correspond one by one with the components of the corresponding fact, with the exception of such words as 'or', 'not', 'if', 'then', which have a different function. In a logically perfect language, there will be one word and no more for every simple object, and everything that is not simple will be expressed by a combination of words, by a combination derived, of course, from the words for the simple things that enter in, one word for each simple component. A language of that sort will be completely analytic, and will show at a glance the logical structure of the facts asserted or denied. The language which is set forth in *Principia Mathematica* is intended to be a language of that sort. It is a language which has only syntax and no vocabulary whatsoever. Barring the

---

[21] Russell 1956b, p. 247.

[22] Russell 1956b, p. 247.

[23] Russell 1956b, p. 246.

[24] Russell 1956b, p. 253.

[25] Russell's claim that proper names can be used either as names or as descriptions is (in certain respects) similar to Donnellan's claim that definite descriptions can be used either referentially or attributively. In the next section I will describe different points of view which result in different uses. The main difference between Russell's and Donellan's notion of use is that Donnellan's distinction between uses has nothing to do with different points of view.

[26] Russell 1956b, pp. 197-198.

omission of a vocabulary I maintain that it is quite a nice language. It aims at being that sort of language that, if you add a vocabulary, would be a logically perfect language. Actual languages are not logically perfect in this sense, and they cannot possibly be, if they are to serve the purposes of daily life.

Against criticism, Russell justifies his project of an ideal language:[27]

> Mr. Black objects strenuously to my suggestion of a philosophical language. I have never intended to urge seriously that such a language should be created, except in certain fields and for certain problems [... for example in mathematical logic and theoretical physics]. No doubt my suggestions as to how a philosophical language should be constructed embody my opinions to a considerable extend. But that does not prove that we ought, in our attempts at serious thinking, to be content with ordinary language, with its ambiguities and its abominable syntax. I remain convinced that obstinate addiction to ordinary language in our private thoughts is one of the main obstacles to progress in philosophy.

Russell's remarks about the relationship between ideal and ordinary language are not as clear as one might wish. What is worse is that he often confuses these different languages. This is responsible for his numerous contradictory remarks and makes it difficult to give a unique interpretation of his writings in the philosophy of language.[28] Russell's aim is to develop a theory for an *ideal language*. But his preoccupation with an ideal language is not an end in itself. An ideal has to be an idealization of something. An ideal language is an idealization *of the natural language* and can only be justified with recourse to the natural language. From a normative point of view, the structure of an ideal language can be used in order to improve the natural language. But even from a descriptive point of view, an ideal language can be conceived as an idealized picture of the natural language. It can help our analysis and improve our understanding of the natural language.[29]

Naturally, most of Russell's examples are taken from ordinary language but many of his theses in the philosophy of language only characterize an ideal language. Discrepancies and confusions arise when he uses examples from ordinary language in order to argue for a thesis which is - strictly

---

[27] Russell 1971, pp. 693-694.

[28] A further problem results from the fact that Russell does not make a strict distinction between *world* and *language*. Consequently he does not strictly distinguish between *use* and *mention*. There is a controversy about whether Russell just confuses use and mention (as, for example, Church claims) or whether the lack of this distinction is an integral part of Russell's philosophy of language at a certain time (as, for example, Cassin claims). I favor the second claim.

[29] Cf. Rheinwald 1988 for a defence of the relevance of Russell's ideal-language-solution of the semantical paradoxes for the natural language.

speaking - only valid for an ideal language but, as a matter of fact, does not hold for the natural language. I will argue that this is the case in Russell's discussion of proper names.

If one wants to reconstruct Russell's view one has to distinguish not only ordinary and ideal *language* but also *the point of view* from which one describes a language. Whereas an ideal language has only one adequate description - the description from an ideal point of view -, *ordinary language* can either be described from an *ideal* (or *strict*) or from an *ordinary point of view*. A description from an ideal point of view imposes strict standards, a description from an ordinary point of view imposes daily-life-standards. The standards determine what should be considered as being a proper name, as being an individual and as being a proposition.

In an *ideal language,* all proper names are logically proper names and denote individuals. Individuals are particulars with which we are acquainted. In the *natural language,* ordinary proper names - considered from an *ideal point of view* - are not logically proper names but disguised descriptions. Nevertheless, also in the natural language we have the distinction between ordinary proper names and definite descriptions. They function differently. From an *ordinary point of view,* ordinary proper names denote what we ordinary take to be individuals, whereas definite descriptions do not denote anything but have to be eliminated. Sentences whose singular terms are only proper names can stay as they are. Sentences containing definite descriptions have to be replaced by general sentences. This feature of ordinary language can be used in order to illustrate the corresponding feature of an ideal language.

5   Russell's Theory of Ordinary Proper Names

Let's consider Russell's thesis about proper names:

(P) Proper names denote individuals.

If one describes an ideal language this thesis reads:

(PI) Logically proper names denote individuals in a strict or logical sense.
(For example, the name "this" denotes a sense datum.)

If one describes the natural language from an ideal point of view the thesis (P) does not hold. Instead one gets the result:

(not-PO$_i$) Ordinary proper names do not denote anything.

If one describes the natural language from an ordinary standpoint the thesis (P) reads:

(PO$_o$) Ordinary proper names denote individuals in an ordinary sense. (For example, the name "Scott" denotes Scott.)

When Russell seems to defend a description theory of ordinary names - which is based on the thesis (not-PO$_i$) -, he describes the natural language from an ideal point of view. Actually he wants to illustrate the thesis (PI) by a counterexample. Instead of giving a counterexample from an ideal language - an ideal description - he gives the wrong sort of counterexample: a name from the ordinary language. When Russell contrasts ordinary names with descriptions, he describes the ordinary language from an ordinary point of view - as in thesis (PO$_o$). Even then he is not really interested in ordinary language but wants to illustrate the corresponding contrast in an ideal language.

If one is less interested in Russell's view about an ideal language but primarily in his view about the natural language, the version (PO$_o$) of thesis (P) characterizes this view. It follows that Russell's theory of ordinary proper names is not a description theory but rather what we now call a theory of direct reference. The usual characterization of Russell's theory of ordinary proper names as description theory - which is based on the thesis (not-PO$_i$) - confuses both languages. It is a characterization of the natural language from the standpoint of an ideal language.

I now want to discuss Russell's thesis concerning singular propositions. I call this thesis *"constituent thesis"*. It has two versions. The first version characterizes an ideal language.

(CI) Individuals in a logical sense are constituents of ideal propositions.

The second version characterizes the natural language from an ordinary point of view.[30]

(CO$_o$) Individuals in an ordinary sense are constituents of ordinary propositions.

What can it mean to say that an individual in the ordinary sense is a constituent of a proposition? For example, what can it mean to claim that Frege is a constituent of the proposition that Frege is a philosopher? The absurdity which many philosophers see in this claim derives from the idea that concrete objects in space and time - especially people - cannot be constitutive parts of something like a proposition. They probably think that propositions belong entirely to the mental and conceptual world and have

---

[30] If one describes the natural language from an ideal point of view one gets the result: (not-PO$_i$) Individuals in an ordinary sense are not constituents of ordinary propositions. (Only individuals in a logical sense are constituents of ordinary propositions.)

no connection to the physical world. Maybe they admit that Frege is not only a part of the world but also a part (i.e. an element) of the set of all philosophers, and even a part of the domain of a possible world, but how could Frege be a part of the *proposition* that Frege is a philosopher? I want to show that this question can be answered in a way which is not absurd.

6 Comparison of Russell's and Kripke's Theories of Proper Names

In what follows, I will argue that Russell's constituent thesis about ordinary propositions - interpreted and generalized in a certain way - is essentially equivalent to Kripke's thesis that proper names are rigid designators.

I would like to add a personal remark. Many years ago - reading Kaplan's paper *How to Russell a Frege-Church* - I got the idea that Russell's and Kripke's theses are equivalent. I was rather surprised because at the time when *Naming and Necessity* appeared - 1972 -, Russell's constituent thesis had been considered obscure whereas Kripke's book - according to Richard Rorty - had been found "shocking and liberating". I thought that these different evaluations were strange. Since then, for example, Peacocke,[31] Sainsbury,[32] and Kaplan[33] himself have claimed that certain versions of the rigidity thesis are similar to a theory of direct reference. This claim is not surprising anymore. Today, theories of direct reference are en vogue and the valuation of Russell's theory of logically proper names seems to have changed to some extent. But the valuation of his theory of ordinary proper names - to my knowledge - has not changed. I suggest a change of this valuation too.

In order to interpret the constituent thesis let's suppose we have a meaningful sentence which expresses a proposition. I assume that propositions are structured and have constitutive parts. The question "What are the *constitutive parts* of a proposition?" can be answered in a Fregean or in a Russellian way. The first answer is (a version of) Frege's principle of compositionality:

(i) The constitutive parts of the proposition which is expressed by a sentence, are the *meanings* of the relevant parts of the sentence.[34]

---

[31] Peacocke 1975.

[32] Sainsbury 1979, pp. 60-63.

[33] Kaplan 1989a, pp. 492-497, Kaplan 1989b, pp. 568-571.

[34] This answer presupposes that it is clear what are *the relevant parts of a sentence*. In general, this is a difficult question but I only make use of the unproblematic claim that a sentence with a proper name contains the proper name as relevant part.

The second answer is based on Russell's view of propositions:

(ii) The constitutive parts of the proposition which is expressed by a sentence, are those entities one has to *refer* to if one gives a complete analysis of the meaning of the sentence.[35]

In both interpretations of "constitutive parts", the attempt is made to transfer the picture of part and whole from sentences to propositions - i.e. from syntax to the realm of meanings. In the first interpretation of "parts", we only have to consider the parts of the sentence, in the second interpretation, we firstly have to analyze the proposition - the meaning of the sentence - in order to identify its parts. In the context of my discussion, it is not necessary to decide between these two interpretations of the constituent thesis. This is the case because I want to show that Russell's constituent thesis in both interpretations of "constitutive parts" is equivalent to Kripke's rigidity thesis.

In *Naming and Necessity*, Kripke defends the thesis that proper names are rigid designators. This means that a proper name denotes the same object in every possible world. (The more accurate formulation would contain the proviso that the object exists in that world. I will neglect this proviso.[36]) An adherent of the rigidity thesis can have two different views about the meaning of proper names. Either he claims that a proper name only has reference but no meaning at all, or he claims that a proper name has not only reference but also meaning. I think that the second claim is more plausible than the first because it is hard to explain why a part of a meaningful sentence should have reference but no meaning at all. (Kripke, too, seems not to be opposed to this claim.[37]) If one wants to claim that a proper name has meaning, the meaning of a (rigid) proper name can either be identified with a constant function from possible worlds to individuals or with the reference of the name. I propose to identify the meaning of a (rigid) proper name with its reference.[38]

---

[35] This answer presupposes that it is clear what *a complete analysis of the meaning of a sentence* amounts to. In this context, I only make use of the claim that in a complete analysis of the meaning of a sentence containing a (referring) proper name, one has to refer to the bearer of the name.

[36] For the difficulties connected with this proviso, see the section "How does rigid designation come in?" in Kaplan 1989b, pp. 569-571.

[37] Cf. Kripke 1980, p. 59, fn. 22.

[38] If one does not want to make that identification my argument has to be modified. I then have to argue that if a constant function is a constitutive part of a proposition it follows that also the (constant) value of the function is a constitutive part.

The identification of meaning and reference faces certain existence problems. Today, Scott does not exist anymore (in some sense of "exists") but we do not want to say that the name

That the rigidity thesis - together with the identification of meaning and reference[39] - implies the constituent thesis in both versions can be seen as follows. Let's suppose that sentences express propositions and that propositions have constitutive parts.[40] Consider a sentence s which has a proper name n as a part and expresses a proposition p.

I start with the first interpretation of "constitutive parts" in the constituent thesis. According to this interpretation, the proposition p consists of the meanings of the relevant parts of the sentence s. The name n is a relevant part of the sentence. From the rigidity thesis it follows that the name n denotes the same object o in every possible world. This uniquely determined object o is the meaning[41] of the name n and is a constitutive part of the proposition p in the sense of the first interpretation of the constituent thesis.

Let's consider the second interpretation of "constitutive parts". According to this interpretation, the proposition consists of those entities one has to refer to in a complete analysis of the meaning of the sentence. Given the rigidity thesis, it is to be expected that the object o has to be referred to in a complete analysis of the proposition p. It follows that the object o is a constitutive part of the proposition p in the sense of the second interpretation of the constituent thesis.

I now want to show that the constituent thesis (in both interpretations) implies the rigidity thesis. If one embraces the constituent thesis, it should not only hold for simple sentences like, for example, "Scott is a man" and "Scott is an author" but also for certain modalized versions of simple sentences like "It is necessary that Scott is a man" and "It is possible that Scott is not an author". If one would restrict the constituent thesis to extensional contexts it could not be considered as giving a general characterization of individuals and proper names in opposition to definite descriptions. The sentence "It is necessary that Scott is a man" can be analyzed as "In every possible world Scott is a man". According to the constituent thesis the indi-

---

"Scott" is meaningless. This problem can be solved in several ways. For example, one can use a notion of *existence* according to which Scott exists even today. Or one can adopt Sainsbury's interpretation of a realist theory "as the claim that one adequately specifies the meaning of a name '*a*' by saying that it stands for its bearer, *a*." Cf. Sainsbury 1979, p. 59.

[39] If one generalizes the rigidity thesis to include certain definite descriptions - for example referentially used descriptions or descriptions like "the sum of 2 and 2" and "the square root of 4", the identification of meaning and reference is less plausible. I do not want to claim that a generalized rigidity thesis implies a generalized constituent thesis.

[40] Without this presupposition, the implication does not hold. I take it that this presupposition is generally accepted in the context of my discussion.

[41] Without the rigidity thesis the meaning of a name would be a non-constant function from possible worlds to individuals. In that case one could not identify the meaning of the name with its reference.

vidual Scott is a constitutive part of the proposition that in every possible world Scott is a man. This can only be the case if the proper name "Scott" denotes the same object - namely Scott - in every possible world. This completes my argument for the conclusion that the constituent thesis and the rigidity thesis are equivalent. One can express the result of my discussion with the following equation: *Frege-Church* + *rigidity thesis* = *Russell* = *Kripke.*

7 Haecceitism

What is the relation between my claim that the constituent thesis is equivalent to the rigidity thesis and Kaplan's claim that the constituent thesis is equivalent to haecceitism? Kaplan characterizes haecceitism and anti-haecceitism as follows:[42]

> The doctrine that holds that it makes sense to ask - without reference to common attributes and behavior - whether *this* is the same individual in another possible world, that individuals can be extended in logical space (i.e., through possible worlds) in much the same way we commonly regard them as being extended in physical space and time, and that a common 'thisness' may underlie extreme dissimilarity or distinct thisness may underlie great resemblance, I call *Haecceitism*. [...] The opposite view, *Anti-Haecceitism*, holds that for entities of distinct possible worlds there is no notion of trans-world being.

Kaplan claims that Russell and Kripke are haecceitists, Frege and Church are anti-haecceitists.

I believe that this claim is correct but that Kaplan's characterizations are not adequate: 1) Kaplan's characterization of haecceitism is too weak. It cannot be taken literally - that it *makes sense* to ask the question of trans-world identity (without reference to common attributes). One has to add that this question sometimes has a positive answer, i.e., that there are cases of trans-world identity. 2) Kaplan's characterization of haecceitism is too strong. The use of the indexical "this" - for Kaplan a rigid designator - should be avoided, since the formulation of haecceitism should be neutral with respect to questions of rigid designation. 3) According to Kaplan's characterizations, haecceitism and anti-haecceitism are not opposite views. One can hold that there is a notion of trans-world being but that trans-world identifications must rely on common attributes. In that case, one fulfils neither Kaplan's characterization of haecceitism nor of anti-haecceitism.

---

[42] Kaplan 1975, pp. 722-723.

The two equivalence claims (between the constituent thesis and the rigidity thesis/ haecceitism) sound similar and are certainly connected. Still, I believe that they are different and have to be justified differently.

In the first place, I take haecceitism to be a purely metaphysical position, whereas the constituent and the rigidity thesis are better classified as belonging to the philosophy of language. That haecceitism is a purely metaphysical doctrine can be seen if one considers one of the following usual formulations: Every object has the individual essence of being identical with itself. Every object is necessarily identical with itself. Every object is in every possible world identical with itself.[43]

Secondly, Kaplan claims that the constituent thesis and haecceitism are equivalent, but he is only successful in showing that the constituent thesis implies haecceitism.[44] His argument for the converse implication is not convincing. In order to show that haecceitism implies the constituent thesis he wants to show that the negation of the constituent thesis implies the negation of haecceitism. That is, he wants to show that without singular propositions, there is no trans-world identity. His argument for this thesis reads:[45] "if we limit ourselves to general propositions, any [...] transworld identifications would require a special and independent justification." In my view, this argument only shows that without singular propositions, the justification of trans-world identifications cannot rely on them. It seems to me that haecceitism is compatible with speaking a language which contains only non-rigid singular terms (and consequently contains no singular propositions). Instead of the name "Scott" a language of this sort only contains (non-rigid) definite descriptions like "the author of Waverley". A haecceitist speaking that language could still say that every object is necessarily identical to itself, he only could not express individual instances of this general statement.

I do not believe that there is any convincing argument for the claim that haecceitism implies the constituent thesis. It seems to be possible to embrace the metaphysical position of haecceitism without having any specific view about the constituents of propositions.*

---

[43] More accurately: Every object is in every possible world in which it exists identical with itself. Cf. the corresponding proviso with respect to rigid designation. See fn. 36.

[44] Cf. Kaplan 1975, p. 724. Kaplan gives two arguments. First, he shows that the usual possible worlds analysis of singular propositions implies haecceitism. Second, he shows that the representation of possible worlds as sets of propositions together with the acceptance of singular propositions presuppose a notion of trans-world identity.

[45] Cf. Kaplan 1975, p. 724.

* I would like to thank Ernst-Wilhelm Krekeler and Matthias Paul for critical comments on earlier versions of this paper. I also thank Dean Moyar for correcting my English.

References

Church, A. 1951. A Formulation of the Logic of Sense and Denotation. In P. Henle, H.M. Kallen, S.K. Langer, eds. *Structure, Method, and Meaning - Essays in Honor of Henry M. Sheffer.* New York: The Liberal Arts Press, pp. 3-24.

Church, A. 1973/ 1974. Outline of a Revised Formulation of the Logic of Sense and Denotation. *Noûs* 7: 24-33 (part I)/ *Noûs* 8: 135-156 (part II).

Dummett, M. 1981. *Frege - Philosophy of Language.* Second edition. London: Duckworth.

Kaplan, D. 1975. How to Russell a Frege-Church. *The Journal of Philosophy* 72: 716-729.

Kaplan, D. 1989a. Demonstratives - An Essay on the Semantics, Logic, Metaphysics, and Epistemology of Demonstratives and Other Indexicals. In J. Almog, J. Perry, and H. Wettstein, eds. *Themes From Kaplan.* New York and Oxford: Oxford University Press, pp. 481-563.

Kaplan, D. 1989b. Afterthoughts. In J. Almog, J. Perry, and H. Wettstein, eds. *Themes From Kaplan.* New York and Oxford: Oxford University Press, pp. 565-614.

Kripke, S. 1980. *Naming and Necessity.* Revised and enlarged edition. Oxford: Basil Blackwell.

Linsky, L. 1983. *Oblique Contexts.* Chicago and London: The University of Chicago Press.

Peacocke, C. 1975. Proper Names, Reference and Rigid Designation. In S. Blackburn, ed. *Meaning, Reference and Necessity - New Studies in Semantics.* Cambridge: Cambridge University Press, pp. 109-132.

Rheinwald, R. 1988. *Semantische Paradoxien, Typentheorie und ideale Sprache - Studien zur Sprachphilosophie Bertrand Russells.* Berlin and New York: Walter de Gruyter.

Rheinwald, R. 1997. Paradoxien und die Vergegenständlichung von Begriffen - Zu Freges Unterscheidung zwischen Begriff und Gegenstand. *Erkenntnis* 47: 7-35.

Russell, B. 1956a. On Denoting. In B. Russell, *Logic and Knowledge*, ed. R.C. Marsh. London: George Allen & Unwin, pp. 41-56.

Russell, B. 1956b. The Philosophy of Logical Atomism. In B. Russell, *Logic and Knowledge*, ed. R.C. Marsh. London: George Allen & Unwin, pp. 177-281.

Russell, B. 1963. Knowledge by Acquaintance and Knowledge by Description. In B. Russell, *Mysticism and Logic.* London: George Allen & Unwin, pp. 152-167.

Russell, B. 1971. Reply to Criticisms. In P.A. Schilpp, ed. *The Philosophy of Bertrand Russell.* Fourth edition. La Salle: Open Court, pp. 681-741.

Sainsbury, R.M. 1979. *Russell.* London, Boston and Henley: Routledge & Kegan Paul.

9

Concepts and Their Modes of Presentation

Ulrich Nortmann

1 Concept Words: How to Talk about their Referents and Senses

As is well known among Frege's interpreters, Frege contends that expressions like "the concept *horse*" ("*der Begriff Pferd*") do not designate what they purport to designate; against appearances, we are told, they do not designate concepts, but objects. (I am using "object" in the narrow sense which corresponds to Frege's narrow use of "Gegenstand".) Frege is apparently driven to this view by his observation that expressions of the type in question are saturated (*gesättigt*), not in need of completion (not *ergänzungsbedürftig*); for this reason, he claims, what they refer to is not something incomplete either: not a function, and in particular not a concept. Underlying these considerations there seems to be a principle of exclusive designation which reads as follows:

(Excl) Anything in need of completion can only be designated by expressions which are themselves in need of completion (or unsaturated).

In fact, Frege says in "Ausführungen über Sinn und Bedeutung" (= ASB), p. 129:[1]

---

[1] The page number refers to Hermes, H., Kambartel, F., Kaulbach, F. (eds.), Gottlob Frege – Nachgelassene Schriften (= NS).

175

"The name of a function *always* carries at least one blank position for an argument ..."; "Ein Funktionsname führt *immer* leere Stellen (mindestens eine) für das Argument mit sich ..." (emphasis U. N.; translations into English here and in the sequel by U. N.).

It is an astonishing fact that Frege adopts without hesitation a principle as strong as (Excl). One would expect him to take into consideration at least a weaker alternative admitting both unsaturated and saturated expressions into the possible designators of functions:

(Incl)   A function is (capable of being) designated by at least *one* unsaturated expression. (In contrast, objects (*Gegenstände*) are the referents of saturated expressions only.)

Indeed one can ask, setting aside the case of an ideal language: why should matters be always so neat that we can tell from the appearance of an expression what sort of individual it refers to, in particular whether it refers to a function or to an object? If a function is something at all and not nothing,[2] who could prevent a party of speakers from showing their reverence to Gauß by baptizing a certain function "Carl-Friedrich", for instance, and from thereafter referring to the function by that name?

I know of no argument in Frege which would conclusively establish the advantage of (Excl) over (Incl). In "Über Begriff und Gegenstand" (= BG), p. 200, Frege observes that in

"es gibt mindestens eine Quadratwurzel aus 4",

the predicate is not interchangeable (not interchangeable *salva sensibilitate*, one would add) with the term "den Begriff *Quadratwurzel aus 4*".[3] He concludes (BG, p. 201) that the predicate and the term must differ in what he calls *Bedeutung*, i.e. in reference. In fact one would argue from Frege's standpoint that if there were no difference in reference, a replacement of the predicate by the term could not affect the truth of the original sentence, and

---

[2] Sometimes Frege gives the impression that he actually tends to downgrade functions, or concepts at least, to an ontological status in close vicinity to nothing. In a letter to Marty from August 29, 1882, he writes: "Der Begriff ist ungesättigt, indem er etwas fordert, was unter ihn falle; daher kann er nicht für sich allein bestehen" (Gabriel, G., Hermes, H., Kambartel, F., Thiel, C., Veraart, A. (eds.), Gottlob Frege – Wissenschaftlicher Briefwechsel (= BW), p. 164). One should not follow Frege thus far. If functions have a "standing" at all, they are full-fledged individuals standing on their own, irrespective of their being "unsaturated". No doubt you might feel qualms about admitting abstract individuals in general. But I do not hesitate to concede to any clearly defined function as much reality at least as to any of the natural numbers. Regarding ontological dignity, I can find nothing of relevance in the saturated-unsaturated-distinction.

[3] In Frege's view, "existence" cannot be sensibly applied to singular terms.

could therefore even less ruin the sense. If Frege were justified in drawing his conclusion, he would be justified in arguing that in general nothing can be signified by phrases which belong to different syntactical categories (since substitutions which do not preserve grammaticality will *a fortiori* fail to preserve *sensibilitas*), and that in particular saturated and unsaturated expressions cannot have the same reference. This would severely undermine (Incl). But Frege is wrong even given his own premises. He treats any true sentence as an expression which signifies the truth-value *true*; on the other hand, the very same object is taken to be signified by an element of a different syntactical category, namely by the term "the True" ("*das Wahre*"), although in natural language an illformed expression would result from substituting a (true) sentence for that term in the predication "the True is a truth-value", for instance. [4]

Departing from Frege, I shall base my ensuing considerations on the inclusive principle, thereby clearing the ground for talking in a comparatively unsophisticated way about the things I wish to talk about – for talking about concepts, e.g., by using expressions of the type "the concept F". There is still more to be gained: I wish it to be certain that in using expressions like

"the sense of the predicate '... is (an) F'",

I am really talking about senses of concept words (*Begriffsausdrücke*). There is some evidence that Frege would feel as unhappy about the use of such expressions as about that of "the concept *horse*". Following (Excl), those expressions would be taken to refer to non-functions, since they are saturated. On the other hand, there is good evidence that Frege views *functions* as the senses of predicates:

(Fasp)   Senses of concept words are always functions.[5]

In more detail, it would seem that in the case of the concept word

(Phil) "... is a philosopher",

for instance, the relevant function is a function which takes senses of names of individuals as arguments and maps them to thoughts, namely (as was already stated by H. Jackson in following A. Church, and endorsed by

---

[4] It is only in the regimented language of "Grundgesetze der Arithmetik" (= GGA) that sentences are interchangeable *salva congruitate* with names of the common type.

[5] Here and in the sequel, I use the term "concept word", and its German counterpart "*Begriffsausdruck*", exclusively for those designators of concepts which are incomplete or "predicative", as for instance designators of the form "... is an F". Concept-designators such as "the concept *horse*", "the first arithmetical concept which U. N. was taught" (which for me, having adopted (Incl) instead of (Excl) in opposition to Frege, do designate concepts) will not be called concept words or *Begriffsausdrücke*.

P. T. Geach)[6] to (in each case) the thought that is expressed by the sentence which is generated by filling the blank in (Phil) with the name which carries with it the sense that figures as argument.[7] *Pace* Dummett, it is in my view fairly clear that Frege holds (Fasp), and conceives of the functions in question along the Church-Jackson-Geach-line. If this is true, Frege would have to deny that the expression

"the sense of the predicate '... is (an) F'"

denotes the sense of the mentioned predicate since that sense is a function, whereas what the expression, being saturated, denotes is not a function. Frege's entanglement in "paradoxes" like that seems to me to be reason enough for trying to work with (Incl) instead of (Excl).

Advocates of the hypothesis that Frege holds (Fasp) are in a position to adduce a number of supporting passages from Frege, one among them consisting of a few lines in "Einleitung in die Logik" (= NS, p. 209). In those lines Frege at least has simple categorical predications in mind; we read about the thought expressed by that sort of sentence:

"... in this [scil. thought] we distinguish a complete part from an unsaturated one. The former corresponds to the proper name of which however it is not the referent but the sense. The unsaturated part of the thought is also conceived as a sense, namely the sense of that part of the sentence which we find in addition to the proper name",

"... in diesem [scil. Gedanken] unterscheiden wir einen abgeschlossenen Teil und einen ungesättigten. Jener entspricht dem Eigennamen, ist aber nicht dessen Bedeutung, sondern dessen Sinn. Auch den ungesättigten Teil des Gedankens fassen wir als einen Sinn auf, nämlich des ausser dem Eigennamen vorhandenen Teils des Satzes."

So the sense of a predicate counts as unsaturated, and one would like to conclude: therefore it is a function. According to the quoted passage, that function appears moreover to conform to Church's characterization of it. Frege seems to view the thought as capable of being broken up into the sense of the subject-expression and the sense of the predicate, and this sug-

---

[6] Cf. Church, A Formulation of the Logic of Sense and Denotation, p. 16.

[7] In his "Frege on Sense-Functions", p. 379 seq., Jackson explains: "In Frege's terms, Church proposes the following: Where F is a name of the function Φ, there exists a function Φ' determined by the rule that the value of Φ' for an argument μ is the sense of F(*a*), where the sense of *a* is μ. It remains to identify Φ' with the sense of F ..." (the passage is here cited from the reprint of Jackson's article in E. D. Klemke (ed.), Essays on Frege). The view in question is also given expression by M. Dummett (who rejects it, however) in referring to Geach's review of Dummett's "Frege – Philosophy of Language" (= FPL): "In his review of FPL, Geach defended the equation of the sense of a predicate with the function which carries the sense of a proper name into the thought expressed by the sentence that results from putting that proper name in the argument-place of the predicate from the criticism that I made of it on pp. 293–4 of FPL" (Dummett, The Interpretation of Frege's Philosophy (= IFP), p. 251).

gests a parallelism with what he claims for the level of reference:[8] that by analogy with the relations on the reference level, the thought is the value of the function corresponding to the predicate (as the predicate's sense), for the sense of the subject-expression taken as an argument. How else could a function and an object go together to form a new object, from a Fregean viewpoint, than by the function's being saturated by the given object?

Dummett, however, emphatically rejects the above conclusion, opposing to it the hypothesis that the unsaturatedness of the sense of predicates (indubitably stated by Frege in the cited passage) was an unsaturatedness differing in kind from the unsaturatedness of functions.[9] Frege nowhere makes such a distinction. So in itself Dummett's hypothesis is not very credible. It will deserve closer scrutiny only if Dummett can advance some argument to the effect that other distinctively Fregean theses require us to deny functional status to the senses of concept words. Later on (sect. 5) I shall discuss, and reject, two arguments of Dummett's to this effect.

2 Concepts: Their Role in Construing the Numbers

Had Frege stuck less whole-heartedly to (Excl) than he actually did, he would no doubt have been in a position to avoid many of the difficulties which plagued his talk not only about concepts, but plausibly about the senses of concept words too; but it is also true that if Frege had simply abandoned (Excl) that would have opened up interesting prospects in other fields of his philosophy. Let me explain.

Frege rejects relations of identity and difference (= non-identity) between concepts, or more generally between functions. It is plausible to conjecture that in these matters, a role is played by the observation that logical grammar requires proper names (in Frege's sense) on both sides of the equality sign.[10] But according to (Excl) such names cannot refer to functions, and so identity and difference are not expressible in the realm of functions; what admits no expression, one might add, is non-existent.

---

[8] According to "Über Sinn und Bedeutung", p. 35 seq., the truth value of a predication can on the one hand be decomposed into the respective referents of the subject and the predicate expressions; at the same time, that truth value counts as the value of the referent of the predicate for the referent of the subject taken as argument.

[9] Dummett, IFP, p. 270.

[10] Cf. ASB, NS p. 131. In his earlier lecture "Über formale Theorien der Arithmetik", however, Frege is willing to admit concepts into the realm of the countable at least. (Cf. p. 103 of Angelelli's edition.) Frege seems not to have been aware that counting presupposes the possibility of stating identity and difference.

Philosophers will be glad if they can manage to get so clear about what kind of things concepts or properties[11] are that it can thereby be settled what identity and difference of such entities consist in. Perhaps the task is extremely difficult to accomplish. As long as it is assumed, however, that concepts are something and not nothing (keeping the problem of their precise individuation for further investigation), it is so to speak obligatory to acknowledge the possibility of their enjoying relations of identity and difference (in keeping with Quine's famous slogan "no entity without identity"). Had Frege adopted a more critical attitude towards (Excl), he would perhaps have come to do so.

Maybe he had even noticed from the outset the possibility of construing natural numbers as *concepts*.[12] But with something like (Excl) in mind, Frege was forced to take the view that numbers are *not* concepts, since numbers can be designated by numerals, and numerals are saturated expressions. So there was no way for Frege to construe the number 2, for instance, as follows:

2 = the concept *concept which (precisely) two individuals fall under*,
= the property of being a property applying to just two individuals.[13]

One has of course to think here of the property of being a concept which two individuals fall under as being explained (following Frege's procedure in "Die Grundlagen der Arithmetik" (= GLA)) in terms of its being equinumerous to a particular fixed concept applying to just two things, as for instance to the property of being identical with 0 or with 1. In short: dropping (Excl) would have enabled Frege to consider the idea of construing the number 2 as the property of applying to two individuals, instead of construing it as the *extension* (*Umfang*) of that property – a line which fits even more smoothly with his doctrine that ascribing a number involves as-

---

[11] I make no distinction between concepts and properties. This is in accordance with Frege's view as it is given expression in BG, p. 201: "Ich nenne die Begriffe, unter die ein Gegenstand fällt, seine Eigenschaften ..."

[12] In actual fact, it was only towards the end of his lifetime that Frege began to seriously wonder whether numbers are not objects. Cf. his "Tagebucheintragungen über den Begriff der Zahl", NS, p. 282.

[13] In his treatise on "Die Grundlagen der Arithmetik", p. 80 fn., however, Frege seems to realize that this path was indeed open to him. Yet this impression is mistaken. The hypothesis that the earlier Frege seriously considered the possibility of construing numbers as concepts can only be credible for someone who is not aware of the fact that Frege was convinced (mistakenly from my point of view) that in using an expression like "the concept *concept which just two individuals fall under*" he was *not* referring to a concept. BG, p. 199, contains the due clarification: "Ich habe nur meine Meinung ausgesprochen, man könne in dem Ausdrucke 'die Anzahl, welche dem Begriff *F* zukommt, ist der Umfang des Begriffes *gleichzahlig dem Begriffe F*' die Worte 'Umfang des Begriffes' durch 'Begriff' ersetzen. Man beachte hierbei wohl, daß dies Wort dann mit dem bestimmten Artikel verbunden ist" – i.e. it refers to an object in Frege's opinion.

cribing a property to a concept ("dem Begriffe ... wird dadurch eine Eigen-schaft beigelegt", GLA, p. 59) than the line he actually took. Following the former line, Frege would have been able to manage without appealing to the notion of extension – a tactic which might well have appeared attractive to him when he wrote the GLA, because he seems at that stage to have felt somewhat uncomfortable about presupposing extensions without being able to provide an account of them.[14] Indeed towards the end of his life, Frege's suspicion of extensions was such that he sweepingly dismissed expressions of the type

"the extension of the concept F"

as illegitimate pseudo-names. [15]

Had Frege considered adopting the method of explaining natural num-bers which I have outlined, and had he in addition acknowledged the exis-tence of relations of identity among concepts, significant insights would have been within his reach. Let us take the number 2, for instance, as the property of being a concept applying to just two individuals; admitting identity among concepts, one can then form the concept

G   ... is identical with the property of applying to just one individual, or
      ... is identical with the property of applying to just two individuals.

There is no questioning that G applies to just two things (i.e. properties, in the present case).[16] Provided that all concept formation has been legiti-mate so far, we obtain as a consequence the relation

(Circ)   2 falls under G, and G falls under 2.

A concept which another concept falls under is assigned by Frege to a *higher* level than the subsumed concept.[17] Hence a circular relation such as (Circ), conflicting with the idea of linearity suggested by talk of higher and lower levels, could hardly have failed to arouse Frege's suspicion. Frege could have learnt from (Circ) that it is not quite harmless to assume that, given a predicate like "... is a concept applying to just two individuals", there is always a corresponding concept covering all of the things which the

---

[14] GLA, p. 80 fn.: "Ich setze voraus, daß man wisse, was der Umfang eines Begriffes sei."

[15] Cf. "Erkenntnisquellen der Mathematik und der mathematischen Naturwissenschaften", NS., pp. 288–9.

[16] It is obvious from the definition of G that at most two entities fall under G. Moreover, one thing is certain: whatever the precise way of individuating properties which is decided upon in the end, a property will count at any rate as different from another one if there is an item which has the first one but not the second. Since there surely are properties which are *einzahlig* (as one could express it in German), and *ipso facto* are not *zweizahlig*, *Einzahligkeit* and *Zweizahligkeit* are distinct properties, so that precisely two items fall under G.

[17] Cf. GLA, p. 65: "So kann man einen Begriff unter einen höhern, sozusagen unter einen Begriff zweiter Ordnung fallen lassen. "

predicate applies to; and that it is a good policy in contrast to impose upper limits to the effect that in order to count as existent, a concept must satisfy the requirement that from among the individuals which the corresponding predicate applies to it covers only those below a given upper limit. Observations like that might have prompted Frege to invent a real theory of types. In consequence, he might even have been led to the idea of restricting set comprehension in such a way as to prevent the system of "Die Grundgesetze der Arithmetik" from collapsing.

The strategy Frege actually adopted in GLA in construing the natural numbers was less likely to put him on the right track towards developing a type theory,[18] since, according to that strategy, the relation most similar to (Circ) is a relation which shows no manifest circularity:

> 2 (= the class of all concepts covering just two things) falls under H
> (let H here be the property of being identical with 1 or with 2),
> and H is an element of 2
> (not: H falls under 2).

3 Construing the Senses of Concept Designators

Present-day semantical theory has obvious roots in Frege's semantics; but it is largely shaped by more recent notions stemming from R. Carnap and D. Kaplan. A central notion is the semantical character associated with a linguistic expression. Context dependence and related matters are of no interest in the present paper; hence we may confine ourselves to what is got when characters are combined with contexts of utterance: that is, we may confine ourselves to Carnapian intensions. For the sake of simplicity, such intensions will be conceived as functions which take possible worlds (and not more complex indices) as arguments, according to Carnap's original ideas. The subject which I shall focus on in this section is:

> Assuming that we wish to bring Fregean semantics somewhat up to date along Carnapian lines (i.e. by adopting Carnapian intensions), while preserving several of its distinctive features, what will the consequences be for the senses of concept-designating expressions as they occur in utterances like "Aristotle is a philosopher?"

---

[18] Frege's procedure in GGA is somewhat different in that the cardinality operator is applied to names of courses-of-values in that later work. (Cf. GGA I, § 41.) This comes quite close to introducing the number 2, for instance, as the class of all two-membered sets. A derivation, on that base, of

"2 ∈ {1,2} ∈ class of all two-membered sets (= (?) 2)"

was again less likely than (Circ) to arouse Frege's suspicion, since he thought of no hierarchy of levels in the realm of *classes* (as opposed to concepts). He simply assigned all classes to a single level: the level of objects.

In describing my subject in this way I am taking a Fregean standpoint, in assuming that the concept word (Phil.) occurring in the mentioned sentence actually designates a concept: the concept *philosopher*. (On the basis of sect. 1 I take it that I really am talking about what I wish to talk about here in using the expression "the concept *philosopher*".) This is one of the distinctive features of Frege's semantical theory which I had in mind above as something to be preserved. It is well known that the Carnapian – as opposed to the Fregean – referent of a predicate is *not* a concept or property. Given a possible world, it is the class of things the predicate applies to (in the given world), instead.[19]

An "update" as envisaged above will not appear attractive to many readers, or will appear to them not to be an update at all, and moreover to miss Frege's intentions. I am thinking of readers who care for "subjective meanings", and wish to take seriously Frege's remarks about the individuation of thoughts. According to those remarks, any two sentences express the same thought if and only if they are equipollent in the sense that everybody who understands both and believes in the truth of one of them must also assess the other one to be true.[20] If on the other hand senses of sentences are conceived as Carnapian intensions, two sentences will already count as having the same sense if they are logically equivalent, no matter whether there are speakers who (failing to recognize the obtaining relation of logical equivalence) tend to attach different truth values to those sentences. Nevertheless I wish to start with a framework of intensions since this is the least complicated framework for which the construction I am going to describe works. Later on (sect. 4) it will be indicated how to spell out what is essentially the same construction within a more complicated framework which incorporates subjective concepts and the like.

Why try to integrate Carnapian intensions into Frege's semantics? One reason relates to Fregean senses. On the one hand, Frege's notion of the

---

[19] As in sect. 2, I make no distinction between concepts and properties. Frege favours a purely extensional treatment of concepts or properties, so that they are *very* closely related to classes: according to ASB, pp. 128/9, 133, it is a sufficient condition for two predicates to refer to the same property that they apply to the same individuals (in the actual world). I do not make my reflections conditional upon such an unusual understanding of properties; *readers may also think of properties in the usual intensional understanding throughout.* Even if a purely extensional treatment is assumed for the referents of concept words, so that the corresponding concepts in the intensional understanding offer themselves for the role of the senses of predicates, it should be clear that this (often proposed) solution to the problem of what to regard as the senses of predicates (cf. for instance F. v. Kutschera, Gottlob Frege – Eine Einführung in sein Werk (= EW), p. 80) has its difficulties: construed along Carnapian lines at least, concepts in the intensional understanding are functions which map possible worlds to classes; so they cannot be functions which map senses of names to thoughts – as the senses of predicates should do in a maximally Frege-style semantical theory (assuming that the pertinent interpretive hypotheses from sect. 1 are correct).

[20] Cf. Frege, "Kurze Übersicht meiner logischen Lehren" (= NS, pp. 213–218), p. 213/4.

sense of an expression is useful enough if we think of it as explained as the associated mode of presentation (*die Art des Gegebenseins*) of the referent of the expression. Explained in that way, the notion of sense suggests the helpful idea of a description of the referent (if there is one) which in the ideal case is so good that it provides a sort of blueprint enabling the understander to discover the referent so as to know it not merely by description, but also by acquaintance. (In less ideal cases, the mode of presentation of the referent of an expression will convey only more or less scanty information about the referent. Think of descriptions like "the man Socrates".[21]) On the other hand, though, it is not easy to get a grip on what Fregean modes of presentation are, insofar as it remains unclear where one should locate them in (for example) a set-theoretical universe, and what their precise criteria of identity are. In this respect, Carnapian intensions (as functions carrying possible worlds to extensions) are the more solid individuals.[22] Since they do not lack plausible interrelations with Fregean senses, the following recipe seems worth examining: take the Fregean senses of as many expressions as possible, and in particular, as far as is possible, the senses of concept-designating expressions, to be their Carnapian intensions.

Regarding concept-designators like

(Arco)   "the first arithmetical concept which N. was taught"

(which only the advocate of (Excl) views as *not* designating a concept), that move is very plausible. Someone who understands expression (Arco), and thereby has a grip on the special way in which (Arco) presents a concept (*if* it does so), is supplied with a sort of blueprint for finding that concept, however the state of the world may be, and for coming to know it under a more canonical description, like "the concept of natural number" (assuming he takes so much interest in the matter at all). The Carnapian intension of (Arco) would have to be an assignment of concepts to possible worlds, and would as such be closely related to the abovementioned blueprint, insofar as it displays the *effect*, so to speak, of making use of it. Hence it is a proper candidate for modeling the mode of presentation tied to (Arco), or even for being identified with that mode.

A more extensive accommodation, however, of Frege's semantics to the Carnapian framework appears to run into problems over concept-designators like

(Phil)   "... is a philosopher"

---

[21] I assume that "Socrates" is not synonymous with any description.

[22] As v. Kutschera puts it: "Es ist allerdings zu betonen, daß es bis heute keinen Ansatz zur Bestimmung von Bedeutungen [the word "Bedeutung" is here *not* used in the way Frege uses it] gibt, der sich an Exaktheit mit der Theorie der Intensionen messen könnte" (EW, p. 84).

as they occur in predications like "Aristotle is a philosopher". The difficulty is rather obvious. As we know, (Phil) refers, in Frege's view, to a concept. It seems impossible to let a Carnapian function from possible worlds to concepts play the role of the Fregean sense of (Phil). (On the basis of sect. 1, I take it again that, with the last five words of the last sentence, I really do talk about what it is my intention to talk about.) Remember the (presumptive) characteristic of Fregean semantics which has been dealt with in sect. 1 in connection with (Fasp). If we wish to preserve that characteristic, we will have to construe the Fregean sense of a (predicative) concept word as a function carrying senses of names to thoughts, instead of construing it along Carnapian lines as a function from possible worlds into concepts. (Senses of names are not possible worlds.)

Is this an indication that Dummett is right to dissuade us from interpreting Frege as having functions of the Church-Jackson-type in mind when speaking of the senses of concept words? I do not think so. In order to defend my opinion, let me first raise the following question:

What kind of very succinct description could be given of a Church-Jackson-function (assuming that the accommodation of Frege to Carnap has already been accomplished so far as to construe (i) senses of sentences as functions from possible worlds to truth values,[23] and (ii) senses of names, like "Aristotle", or of definite descriptions, like "Plato's most famous student", as functions from possible worlds to objects, i.e. to persons in the examples)?

In discussing this question, I shall take the predication

"Plato's most famous student is a philosopher" (for short: "F(a)")

as an example. Let α be the sense of the definite description "a" functioning as the grammatical subject in our sentence. α has been assumed, by (ii), to be a function from possible worlds to persons. Is there a natural way of assigning a thought (i.e., by assumption (i), a function from possible worlds to truth values) to that function α, by appealing to something more or less intimately related to the relevant predicate? The answer is "yes". One thing related to our predicate "F" is of course its Fregean referent, the concept F. According to Frege's notion of a concept, F maps objects to truth values. Hence, composing α with F would seem to yield a Carnapian thought:

$$\left[F \circ \alpha : \text{a possible world w} \overset{\alpha}{\mapsto} \text{the person } \alpha(w) \overset{F}{\mapsto} \text{the truth value } F(\alpha(w)). \right]$$

---

[23] Given a sentence s, the function in question is determined by the rule that it assign to a world w the truth value which s has in w.

(The scheme is bracketed because it will be replaced by a slightly different one in a moment.) We now have assigned to α a thought, namely the (result of the) composition of α with F; and we seem to have found a function which makes that assignment, for every appropriate function α, and which can be quite succinctly described as: *the composition (of ...) with F.*

Have we hereby arrived at the Church-Jackson-function associated with the predicate "F"? The answer is a provisional "yes." The proviso is occasioned by a slight complication. Frege views a (first-level) concept Φ as a function carrying objects on to truth values. Given an object a, $\Phi(a)$ is the True (*das Wahre*) if and only if a falls under Φ, that is (one would like to add), a falls under Φ *in the actual world.* For Frege, the addition would seem superfluous since he does not care about possible worlds other than the actual world. But as soon as the aim is to fit – so far as this is possible – Frege's semantics into a Carnapian frame, one cannot avoid possible worlds. As a consequence, one will have to construe concepts as functions of *two* arguments, one of them being a possible world: replace $\Phi(a)$ by $\Phi(a,w)$, and think of $\Phi(a,w)$ as being the True if and only if a falls under Φ in w.[24] Taking this modification into account, it is no longer fully adequate in the case of our example to talk about the composition of α with F; we must talk about the composition of α' with F, where α' is the function (closely related to α) which is determined by:

α': $w \mapsto (\alpha(w),w)$.

Moreover, it is no longer fully correct to say that F is the *Fregean* referent of "F" (crediting Frege with an extensional treatment of concepts); strictly speaking, F is the corresponding intensional (Carnapian) concept.[25] (A function Φ which maps pairs of objects and possible worlds to truth values can be identified with a function Φ^* mapping possible worlds to sets of objects: $a \in \Phi^*(w) \Leftrightarrow \Phi(a,w) = 1$.) Accordingly, the former too simple picture is to be replaced by:

$$F \circ \alpha': \quad \text{a possible world } w \overset{\alpha'}{\mapsto} \text{ the pair } (\alpha(w),w) \overset{F}{\mapsto} \text{ the truth value } F(\alpha(w),w).$$

---

[24] The original function Φ of one argument can then be regarded as the restriction of $\Phi(\ ,\ )$ to those argument-pairs whose second component is the actual world, in short: as the restriction of $\Phi(\ ,\ )$ to the actual world.

[25] Concerning the Fregean sense of a predicate, v. Kutschera conjectures: "Man wird nicht fehlgehen, wenn man diesen Sinn als jenen Begriff im normalen (inhaltslogischen) Sinn des Wortes auffaßt, den das Prädikat ausdrückt" (EW, p. 80). Since the intensional concept associated with the predicate "F" is a crucial ingredient in the composition with F which I am going to offer as the sense of "F", my proposal can so far be regarded as an elaboration of v. Kutschera's hypothesis in the direction of adjusting it to the Church-Jackson-account of the senses of predicates.

Given a possible world w, the result of composing α' with F for that world as an argument is the truth value F(α(w),w) – which is the True if and only if the object which the subject term "*a*" of our paradigm sentence refers to in w (i.e. α(w)) falls under F in w. Hence, F(α(w),w), or F ∘ α'(w), is just the truth value of the sentence "F(*a*)" in w, and so F ∘ α' is the (Carnapian) thought expressed by that sentence. (Cf. footnote 23.)

This shows that, if for the sake of simplicity the difference between α' and α is neglected, or the original approach modified by taking α' to be the sense of "*a*", *the composition (of such and such) with F* is in fact the Church-Jackson-function associated with the predicate "F", and can therefore be regarded as a good candidate for playing the role of the Fregean sense of that predicate – at least as far as the focus is on (Fasp) and the related matters as displayed at the end of sect. 1.[26] Readers who like to insist on the difference between α and α', and to reserve the role of the sense of expressions like "*a*" for functions of the α-type, may take *the composition*

---

[26] If intensional concepts (i.e.: functions which assign one of the truth values 1 or 0 to each pair consisting of an individual and a possible world) play the role of the referents of concept words, we have to swallow the (unwelcome?) consequence that concept words with the same reference always have the same sense. (But *not* the consequence: co-referential concept-designators in general have the same sense. Think of (Arco) and "the concept of natural number", of (Arco) and "...is a natural number".) This is obvious from the following relations: if F(i,w) = G(i,w) for all individuals i and possible worlds w, then (F ∘ α')(w) = (G ∘ α')(w) for all worlds w, and for all functions α'; so the composition of α' with F = the composition of α' with G, for all arguments α'. The consequence could be avoided by weakening the criterion of identity for concepts, for instance by requiring co-extensionality only in those worlds which conform to a certain selection of natural laws.

But maybe we ought to welcome the consequence at issue. Concept-designators like (Arco) serve to pick out a concept by characterizing it in a rather non-standard way (as compared with more canonical characterizations such as, for instance, "the concept (of) *natural number*"). So there is in the former case enough distance, as it were, to set up the concept itself and its special mode of presentation as two markedly distinct entities. In contrast, predicates (*Begriffs-ausdrücke*) seem not to pick out concepts in a similar vein, as was pointed out by Dummett: "... the role of predicates is not to pick out a concept – we still have no clear idea what doing that would be ..." (IFP, p. 244). Dummett tends to conclude that for that reason, it is a mistake to try to extend Frege's notion of the reference of an expression from the paradigm case of proper names to predicates. Yet we need not go as far as to dismiss concepts as the references of predicates. Given that with predicates there is no genuine picking out of concepts, and no obvious gap between something picked out and the way of its being picked out, there is still a more cautious reaction: just construe the sense of a predicate as being *very* tightly connected to its referent (assuming that there is one). This is what my proposal comes to. Something quite similar happens when genuine proper names, as opposed to definite descriptions, are treated as rigid designators and their senses construed as the corresponding Carnapian intensions. The sense of the name "Aristotle", e.g., will then be the function whose only value, for whatever possible world as argument, is the person signified; the very same function would have to be attached to any co-referential genuine name (if there is one at all) as its sense.

(of ... paired with id) with F^{27} as the proper candidate. The ensuing arguments will not be affected by this modification.

Our result seems to be quite satisfying. Remember that we started from the supposition that both expressions like (Arco), on the one hand, and expressions like (Phil) and "... is a natural number", on the other hand, designate concepts; should not the drastic difference in the grammatical roles which expressions of the two kinds play, and in the modes they present their respective referents be reflected in a difference of the associated senses? One should not therefore find fault with the fact that, on the present proposal, *different* kinds of functions are associated as senses with concept-designators of the two sorts: functions which carry possible worlds on to concepts in the first case, and functions which carry a specific kind of functions on to thoughts in the second case. In trying to accomodate Frege to Carnap, the critical case of concept-words, i.e. the case of predicative concept-designators, prevented us from overstretching the Carnapian scheme, and made us introduce a welcome distinction.

Our solution of the accommodation problem proves to be satisfying in a further respect. In general, the Fregean mode of presentation associated with an expression should somehow reflect what could be learned from an occurrence of that expression about its referent (if there is one). From an occurrence of (Arco), e.g., we learn quite a lot about the concept of natural number (provided that N.'s mathematical instruction did start with that concept), even though that lot certainly consists in rather incidental matters. From occurrences of "... is a natural number" and of (Phil), one can in contrast learn only very little about the concepts they designate (from a Fregean point of view). To take the case of (Phil), what one can learn is roughly the following (if the referent is taken to be the *intensional* concept associated with (Phil)): that the referent can be designated by (Phil), and that, in virtue of the occurrence of a blank within the expression, that referent is a function.[28] The *same* bit of information will be grasped by those who know the sense of the relevant concept-word as I proposed to construe it, or to be more precise, by those to whom the sense of "F" is known under the suc-

---

[27] The short form "id" refers to the identity-map (whose value for an argument – for a possible world, in the present case – is the respective argument itself. It is understood that $(\alpha,\text{id})(w) =_{\text{def.}} (\alpha(w),\text{id}(w))$, so that $(F \circ (\alpha,\text{id}))(w) = (F \circ \alpha')(w)$.

[28] If we chose to follow Carnap instead and construe the referent of (Phil) as the appropriate set of objects, the situation would of course be different. Assuming *that* referent, we can learn a lot from an occurence of (Phil): that the objects which the set contains as elements are precisely those individuals which are philosophers.

If it is supposed that the referents of concept words are concepts in the *extensional* understanding (what amounts to assimilating them to sets to a degree next to identifying them with sets), we can accordingly draw some additional information from an occurrence of (Phil): that the referent is the restriction (to the actual world) of the intensional concept associated with (Phil).

cinct description I offered: "the composition with F", or in the present case, "the composition with (the referent of) (Phil)".[29] For it is functions which can be composed (with other functions), and moreover the second phrase shows that the function in question can be referred to by (Phil). This correspondence is good evidence for the adequacy of our construal of Fregean senses.[30]

4 How to Include 'Subjective' Meanings

Let us briefly survey the items introduced in the preceding section. With a given predicate "F", I associated a full intensional concept: a function Φ^* which maps possible worlds to sets of individuals. A function of this sort could equivalently be conceived as a function which carries pairs of individuals and possible worlds on to truth values: the pair (i,w) is mapped to the number 1 (representing the True) if i is an element of $\Phi^*(w)$. In order to avoid confusion, I shall henceforth signify the intensional concept in the latter sense, associated with "F", by "F_i". The extensional concept associated with "F" is the function F_e which coincides with the restriction of F_i to those argument-pairs whose second component is the actual world. If it is true that Fregean concepts are extensional concepts, then F_e is the Fregean referent of "F". If they prefer for systematic reasons, readers may also think of F_i as the true referent of "F". I proposed to construe the sense of "F" as a function which is determined by F_i, namely as the function which operates by mapping an appropriate function α' (fit to play the role of the sense of a singular term) to the result $F_i \circ \alpha'$ of composing α' with F_i.

It was already mentioned that friends of subjective meanings, and of an extra fine individuation of propositions, will not be content with this proposal. But it seems to me to be not difficult to modify the proposal (while preserving the basic idea) so as to allay their uneasiness. Instead of focusing on F_i, we can associate (somewhat along Spohn's and Spohn's lines)[31] with our predicate "F" a function F_S, for every speaker S of the language under consideration, which has the same shape as F_i, but is interpreted as mapping a possible world w to the set of individuals to whom speaker S, furnished with all w-data he should like to base his belief upon, *believes* that the predicate "F" applies in w – or equivalently: as mapping a pair consisting of an individual and a possible world to the number 1 if and only if again S

---

[29] We have been using "(Phil)" as the name of an *expression*.

[30] If it is assumed again that the referent of (Phil) is a concept in the *extensional* understanding, the correspondence will persist. On that assumption, the sense in question will have to be characterized as: the composition with the result of extending the referent of (Phil) from (pairs of individuals and) the actual world to the associated intensional concept. From this characterization, we can again obtain the additional information that the referent of (Phil) is the restriction (to the actual world) of the relevant intensional concept.

[31] Cf. U. Haas-Spohn & W. Spohn, Concepts are Beliefs about Essences, this volume.

believes that "F" applies to the individual in that world. A function like that reflects, in a sense, the speaker's personal criterion for F-hood, and constitutes his subjective concept of F-hood. The analogous move can be made for other kinds of expressions, that is for singular terms and for sentences.

Frege certainly would not be content to leave the matter at that stage (involving nothing but a plurality of subjective concepts, subjective individual concepts, and subjective propositions). He seeks to attach to an expression a single item as *the* sense of the expression. As far as sentences are concerned, the attachment is subject to the constraint that not one and the same item be attached to different sentences as their common sense whenever there is a (sufficiently qualified) speaker who could understand these sentences, in a possible context of utterance, as differing in truth value. Given two predications "F(a)" and "G(a)", the constraint amounts to demanding that not one and the same item be attached to "F" and "G" as their shared sense whenever there is a speaker who does not understand "F" and "G" as applying to precisely the same stock of individuals (all over the possible worlds). Basically, there is only one way to meet this demand: let all of the subject-related functions F_S described above enter as factors into a single product, so to speak, that is: combine them, for each predicate "F", to form an n-tuple $\mathbf{F} = (F_{S1}, F_{S2}, \ldots, F_{Sn})$ (assuming a fixed enumeration of the totality of speakers of the underlying language).[32] Sequences like that are basically the only items at hand which can satisfy the requirement that $(F_{S1}, \ldots)$ be different from $(G_{S1}, \ldots)$ whenever there is *at least one* speaker S_j who could believe of an individual i (in a possible world) that "F" applies to i (in that world) while "G" does not, or vice versa. Let us assume that an analogous assignment of sequences of subject-related functions to expressions has been performed for singular terms and for sentences, and that the items assigned in these cases are taken to be the maximally Frege-style senses of the respective expressions. Then the counterpart of the (unbracketed) scheme in sect. 3 will look like the following:

$$\mathbf{F}$$

	α_{S1}'	the pair	F_{S1}	the truth value
a possible world $w^1 \mapsto$		$(\alpha_{S1}(w^1), w^1)$	$\mapsto$	$F_{S1}(\alpha_{S1}(w^1), w^1)$
$w^2 \mapsto$		$(\alpha_{S1}(w^2), w^2)$	$\mapsto$	$F_{S1}(\alpha_{S1}(w^2), w^2)$
$\vdots$		$\vdots$		

---

[32] The construction leaves out of consideration the question of how to demarcate the relevant "totality of speakers" in an actual application. It is probable that not really each and every individual will qualify as a "speaker".

$$w^m \overset{\alpha_{S1}{'}}{\longmapsto} (\alpha_{S1}(w^m),w^m) \overset{F_{S1}}{\longmapsto} F_{S1}(\alpha_{S1}(w^m),w^m)$$

$$*\qquad\qquad\qquad *$$

$$w^l \overset{\alpha_{S2}{'}}{\longmapsto} (\alpha_{S2}(w^l),w^l) \overset{F_{S2}}{\longmapsto} F_{S2}(\alpha_{S2}(w^l),w^l)$$

$$\vdots\qquad\qquad\qquad \vdots$$

$$*\qquad\qquad\qquad *$$

$$\vdots$$

$$w^m \overset{\alpha_{Sn}{'}}{\longmapsto} (\alpha_{Sn}(w^m),w^m) \overset{F_{Sn}}{\longmapsto} F_{Sn}(\alpha_{Sn}(w^m),w^m)$$

If we define the composition of n-tuples of functions (here: the composition of $\boldsymbol{\alpha} = (\alpha_{S1}{'}, \ldots ,\alpha_{Sn}{'})$ with $\mathbf{F}$) in the straightforward manner, namely componentwise, the result of the composition of $\boldsymbol{\alpha}$ with $\mathbf{F}$ will obviously be the n-tuple of subjective content-functions which has been associated with the predication "$F(a)$": speaker S_j believes that "$F(a)$" is true in world w^k if and only if S_j believes that, in w^k, "F" applies to the individual which S_j believes to be signified by "a" in w^k. This being so, we can again execute the construction described in sect. 3 and thus obtain a final candidate for playing the role of the Fregean sense of a predicate "F", a candidate which not only conforms to the Church-Jackson-Geach-account of the senses of predicates but should also please the adherents of an extra fine individuation of thoughts: take the sense of "F" to be the function which is the referent of "the composition of ... with $\mathbf{F}$".

The preceding considerations are intended to show that one can, in principle, transfer the construction which was my primary concern in sect. 3 to a framework which is suited to meet the demands of those who wish to take seriously Frege's criterion of identity for thoughts. My personal impression of that sort of framework, however, is that it's too complicated to be fruitful – as compared, e.g., with a framework of Carnapian intensions. Maybe Frege had better decided upon treating logical equivalence as being sufficient for two sentences to express the same sense, and been ready to introduce a certain amount of idealization in saying of a speaker who attaches different truth values to logically equivalent sentences that that speaker fails to fully grasp the sense of at least one of the sentences involved.

5 The Function Theory Reconsidered

A major part of the considerations in sections 3 and 4 depended on the supposition (i) that (Fasp) actually is in keeping with Frege's view, and (ii) that the functions attached to concept words as their senses actually operate as Church, Jackson and others (like Geach) think. I mentioned that Dummett is emphatically opposed to this combination of suppositions (which Geach calls "the function theory of the *Sinn* of predicates").[33] The more systematically oriented considerations of sect. 3 shed some light on this issue of interpretation. For the sake of simplicity, I prefer in fact to base my ensuing argument on those considerations of sect. 3, instead of referring to the far more complicated apparatus which was developed in sect. 4.

Dummett's arguments against the function theory are not easy to understand. I shall pick out a few sentences from FPL and IFP which seem central. Consider again a predication "F(a)".

> "Now the sense of the predicate does indeed determine, for any name whose sense is known, what thought is expressed by the sentence which results from filling the argument-place of the predicate with that name. But the sense of the predicate cannot be thought of as being given by means of the corresponding function, because if we did not already know what the sense of the predicate was, we could not know what was the thought which was the value of the function for the sense of some name as argument" (Dummett, FPL, p. 293).

The heart of the argument would seem to be this: In order to grasp a thought which is expressed by a sentence of the F(a)-type, e.g., we must at first grasp the sense of the predicate "F" (and that of the name or description "a", too), according to the intensional principle of compositionality. For that reason, the sense of the predicate cannot – according to Dummett as I understand him – be a Church-Jackson-function, since such a function is characterized (by Jackson, for instance) in a way which presupposes the thoughts figuring as values. In order to know the function one would therefore have to know the relevant thoughts in advance. If the function were the sense of the predicate, knowledge of that sense would *presuppose* knowledge of thoughts one can only know *after* having come to know the sense of the predicate – an epistemic absurdity.

Irrespective of its *prima facie* plausibility, the argument is a fallacy. Like anything else, you can know a function under a variety of more or less differing descriptions. It is not clear from the outset that *every* characterization of the Church-Jackson-function associated with a predicate "F" needs refer to thoughts. In fact, sect. 3 presented a characterization which did

---

[33] Cf. Geach, Critical Notice, p. 444.

without that: "the composition with F."[34] This shows that Dummett's criticism is not generally valid: there is at least one way of hardening a soft spot in Frege's semantical theory (the notion of sense), while preserving distinctively Fregean characteristics,[35] which leads to a version of that theory immune to Dummett's criticism.

In another passage (IFP, p. 252), Dummett imposes a condition of adequacy on any acceptable conception of the senses of unsaturated expressions. Given an atomic sentence, specifying the sense of the predicate along with the sense of the name occurring in the sentence must yield an *informative* specification of the sense of the sentence:

> "... an explanation of the sense of the proper name and of the sense of the predicate ought to yield an explanation of the sense of the sentence, that is, of the condition for the thought it expresses to be true ..."

The mere statement, e.g., that the sense of the given sentence is the value of the function which is the sense of the predicate for the sense of the subject term as an argument would then not count as an informative specification of the sense of the sentence in question, because it completely disregards that sentence's *truth conditions*.

Geach's understanding of the Fregean senses of concept words is wrong in Dummett's eyes because it fails to fulfil the above condition of adequacy. Yet we have seen that when the sense of the name "a" has been specified by adducing the function α (or the associated function α', to be more precise), and the sense of the predicate "F" has been specified as the function Γ which operates by composing an appropriate argument-function with F (or with F_i, to be more precise), the sense of "$F(a)$" can also be specified in a way which *is* informative in the sense of exposing truth conditions; the sense in question is the result $\Gamma(\alpha')$ of applying Γ to α', that is, the result of the composition of α' with F_i – which is nothing else but the thought that the actual world is a world w such that the predicate "F" applies in w to the individual $\alpha(w)$ designated by "a" in w (equivalently: the truth value $(\Gamma(\alpha'))$ (w) is the True).

Has Dummett himself finally come to have doubts about the impact of his attack against the function theory? There is some indication in Dum-

---

[34] This scheme stands for phrases like "the composition with the concept *philosopher*" of which it is understood that the occurring concept-designator refers to a concept in the familiar intensional (Carnapian) understanding.

[35] Not everything can be preserved. The Carnapian apparatus of intensions can be brought in only at the cost of neglecting Frege's demand that the senses of saturated expressions be saturated things (= objects), not functions. But this divergence affects no essentials. Among the essentials would certainly be Frege's solution of the problem of the unity of the proposition which draws on functions as glue. This solution does not necessarily require objects as the arguments and values of the gluing function; functions (as α' and $F \circ \alpha'$ in sect. 3) can also do the job of arguments and values.

mett's more recent book "Frege – Philosophy of Mathematics" that he has. Here we find an unexpected concession, relating to the complex predicate

"either Jupiter is larger than x and x is larger than Mars, or Mars is larger than x and x is larger than Jupiter"

(which can be regarded as expanding the more compressed "x is intermediate in size between Jupiter and Mars"):

> "... its sense may be seen as being given as a function carrying the sense of the name 'Neptune' on to the thought expressed by 'Either Jupiter is larger than Neptune and Neptune is larger than Mars, or Mars is larger than Neptune and Neptune is larger than Jupiter' [and so on with other names]" (op. cit., p. 40).

It would be a mistake, however, to conclude from the quoted lines that Dummett is now willing to fully subscribe to the previously dismissed function theory. The truth is rather that his concession is quite limited since it is conditional on a special feature of the predicate under consideration: as regards the completed sentences which result from filling the argument-places in our complex predicate with names, understanding does not require a prior understanding of the predicate itself; these sentences are truth-functionally composed of simpler predications, and it suffices to understand these simpler predications, along with the relevant sentential connectives, in order to understand the completed wholes. This shows that the present case is exceptional, in that a certain condition, which Dummett needs for the first of his abovementioned arguments to work, is not met. I mean the condition that the relevant thoughts (which figure as values according to the function theory) can be grasped only *after* the sense of the predicate involved has been grasped.

If I am asked the *systematic* question whether I prefer to stick to Carnap in letting sets of individuals play the role of the referents of concept words, or to return to Frege in assigning that role to concepts, I cannot but answer: I don't know. Anyhow the considerations in sect. 3 show that Dummett's criticism of the function theory of the sense of predicates is not sufficient to make us drop the *interpretive* hypothesis that Frege views the levels of reference (*Bedeutung*) and sense as being interrelated by a strict parallelism: the referent of a sentence "F(a)", its truth value, is the value of the function referred to by "F" for the referent of "a" taken as argument; in a similar way, the sense of "F(a)" is the value of the function attached to the predicate "F" as its sense for the sense of "a" taken as argument.

References

Angelelli, I. (ed.) 1967. *Gottlob Frege – Kleine Schriften.* Olms, Hildesheim.

Church, A. 1951. A Formulation of the Logic of Sense and Denotation, *Structure, Method, and Meaning – Essays in Honor of H. M. Sheffer,* eds. P. Henle, H. Kallen, S. Langer, pp. 3–24. The Liberal Arts, New York.

FPL: Dummett, M. 1973. *Frege – Philosophy of Language.* Duckworth, London.

IFP: Dummett, M. 1981. *The Interpretation of Frege's Philosophy.* Duckworth, London.

Dummett, M. 1991. *Frege – Philosophy of Mathematics.* Duckworth, London.

Frege, G. 1882. Brief an Marty, *WB*, 163–165.

GLA: Frege, G. 1884. *Die Grundlagen der Arithmetik – Eine logisch-mathematische Untersuchung über den Begriff der Zahl.* Koebner, Breslau.

Frege, G. 1885/6. Über formale Theorien der Arithmetik; *Sitzungsberichte d. Jenai-schen Ges. f. Medizin u. Naturwissenschaft f. d. Jahr 1885, Suppl. zur Jenai-schen Zeitschr. f. Naturwiss.* 19, N. F. 12, 94–104; repr. in *Gottlob Frege – Kleine Schriften,* ed. I. Angelelli, 103–111.

BG: Frege, G. 1892. Über Begriff und Gegenstand; *Vierteljahresschr. f. wiss. Phil.* 16, 192–205; repr. in *FBB*, 66–80.

Frege, G. 1892. Über Sinn und Bedeutung; *Zeitschr. f. Philos. und philos. Kritik NF* 100, 25–50; repr. in *FBB*, 40–65.

ASB: Frege, G. ca. 1893. Ausführungen über Sinn und Bedeutung; in *NS*, 128–136.

GGA: Frege, G. 1893–1903. *Grundgesetze der Arithmetik, begriffsschriftlich abge-leitet,* vols. I, II; Pohle, Jena.

Frege, G. 1906. Einleitung in die Logik; in *NS*, 201–212.

Frege, G. 1906. Kurze Übersicht meiner logischen Lehren; in *NS*, 213–218.

Frege, G. 1924. Tagebucheintragungen über den Begriff der Zahl; in *NS*, 282/3.

Frege, G. ca. 1924. Erkenntnisquellen der Mathematik und der mathematischen Naturwissenschaften; in *NS*, 286–294.

WB: Gabriel, G., Hermes, H., Kambartel, F., Thiel, C., Veraart, A. (eds.). 1976. *Gottlob Frege – Wissenschaftlicher Briefwechsel.* Meiner, Hamburg.

Geach, P. T. 1976. Critical Notice (Review of FPL), *Mind* 85, 436–449.

Haas-Spohn, U., Spohn, W. 2001. Concepts are Beliefs about Essences; *this volume,* 287–316.

NS: Hermes, H., Kambartel, F., Kaulbach, F. (eds.). ²1983. *Gottlob Frege – Nachge-lassene Schriften;* Meiner, Hamburg.

Jackson, H. 1962/63. Frege on Sense-Functions; *Analysis* 23, 84–87; repr. in *Essays on Frege,* ed. E. D. Klemke. Univ. of Illinois Press, Urbana 1968.

EW: v. Kutschera, F. 1989. *Gottlob Frege – Eine Einführung in sein Werk.* de Gruy-ter, Berlin.

FBB: Patzig, G. (ed.). ⁵1980. *Gottlob Frege – Funktion, Begriff, Bedeutung;* Vandenhoeck & Ruprecht, Göttingen.

10

Modes of Presentation: Perceptual vs. Deferential

FRANÇOIS RECANATI

1 Preliminaries

1.1. Two Dimensions of Content

The content of a representation (be it a concept, a thought, a word, or an utterance) is what it is a representation of. The content of my concept of tiger is the species *tiger*, the content of my concept of Cicero is Cicero. Similarly, I will assume that the content of my thought, or statement, that Cicero is a famous Roman orator is the state of affairs consisting of Cicero and the property of being a famous Roman orator.

But there is a complication. Suppose I heard of Tully in highschool, without ever realizing that Tully is Cicero. I believe that there are two persons, Cicero and Tully, who both were Roman orators. Consider my belief that Cicero was a Roman orator and my belief that Tully was a Roman orator. Do they have the same content? Yes, if the content of a representation is what it is a representation of. For (i) the only difference between the two beliefs is the fact that the concept of Cicero occurs in one while the concept of Tully occurs in the other, and (ii) both concepts are concepts of the same individual.

The problem with this answer is that there is another notion of content which seems equally legitimate. Arguably, two beliefs have different contents if their input-output connections are different. Suppose I believe that Cicero did, while Tully did not, denounce Catiline. Then, my belief that Cicero was a Roman orator will prompt the inference that a Roman orator denounced Catiline; not so with my belief that Tully was a Roman orator. This difference in inferential potential shows that the two beliefs somehow differ in content.

In the familiar terminology derived from Frege (1892), we can say that there are two dimensions of content: *what* is represented (the reference) and *how* it is represented (the 'mode of presentation'). In the Cicero/Tully case, the reference is the same, but the modes of presentation are different. The reference is what is relevant for evaluating a representation as correct or incorrect. In contrast, the mode of presentation — the way the reference is thought of — is relevant for explaining (and predicting) behaviour, including linguistic and mental behaviour.

1.2. Modes of Presentation as Mental Files

What are modes of presentation? How are they individuated? If concepts are construed as mental files, as I think they should be, it will be tempting to equate the mode of presentation with the information (or perhaps misinformation) contained in the file. Thus my Cicero-file and my Tully-file refer to the same individual, but contain different pieces of (mis)information concerning that individual: in contrast to my Tully-file, my Cicero-file contains something to the effect that he (the individual in question) denounced Catiline.

But this qualitative construal of modes of presentation is not ultimately satisfactory. The criterion for distinctness of modes of presentation, as stated by Stephen Schiffer after Frege, is:

(Frege's Constraint)

> If it is possible for a rational subject S to believe at the same time of a given object a both that it is F and that it is not F, then there are two distinct modes of presentation of a, m and m', such that S believes of a under m that it is F and under m' that it is not F.

Now for it to be *possible* to believe without irrationality that a is F and that it is not F, it is sufficient to have two distinct mental files for a, even if the two files contain the same information (e.g. that a was a Roman orator). It follows that modes of presentation are not to be identified with the informational content of the mental file, but rather with the mental file itself.

1.3.   Egocentric Files

One important type of case, much discussed in the recent literature on modes of presentation (e.g. Perry 1993), concerns indexical concepts like *here, now, this man, myself,* etc. What is it to think of an object under such a mode of presentation? What is it to think of myself as *myself,* and not, say, as *François Récanati*? What is it to think of a place as *here*? To think of a pen as *this pen*? Answer: these modes of presentation are 'egocentric files', that is, special files which serve as repository for information *gained in a certain way* — typically through perception. The 'self' file serves as repository for information gained in the first-person way (e.g. through proprioception); the 'here' file serves as repository for information gained about a place by virtue of occupying that place and being in a position to perceive what is going on there. Demonstrative files ('that man') also depend upon perception. In order to entertain a thought in which one of these modes of presentation occurs, one must be suitably related to the reference: one must be related to it so as to be able to gain information from it in the proper way.[1]

1.4.   Types and Tokens

The relational constraint I have just mentioned is a constraint on the context in which a certain type of mode of presentation can occur. This suggests the following, overall picture. There are mental symbols (types) which are very much like the words 'I', 'here', etc. They can be appropriately tokened only in a context which satisfies certain constraints (having to do with the subject's sensitivity to perceptual information from the object). When the constraints are satisfied, a reference is determined, and the symbol (token) counts as a genuine mode of presentation, that is, a mode of presentation *of* something. The symbols have therefore two sets of semantic properties: *qua* tokens (if the context is appropriate) they have a reference which they present in a certain way. *Qua* types, however, they have a 'character', a constant meaning which corresponds to the constraint itself and determines the way in which the reference, if any, is presented. That constant meaning can be described as a function from (appropriate) contexts to the referential contents assumed by the symbols in those contexts.[2]

---

[1] Of course one can have an *I*-thought (or an *here*-thought, or a *this*-thought) in the absence of any perception. (See Anscombe 1975: p. 58 for a description of such cases.) This shows that the relevant perceptual relation must be thought of in dispositional terms: thus understood, "the informational connection still obtains even if the subject's senses are not operating" (Evans 1982: p. 161n). For more on this issue, see Recanati 1993: pp. 120-2.

[2] In what follows I will use 'content' always in the sense of 'referential content' (as opposed to 'character').

2 Deference and Indexicality

2.1. Perception and Communication

All the ways of gaining information associated with egocentric files are perceptual ways of gaining information. But perception is not the only mode of acquisition of information: Communication is another. So the question I want to raise in this paper is this: Are there modes of presentation which depend on communication in the same way in which egocentric files depend on perception? My own answer to that question will be 'yes'. But many theorists would rather make a negative answer, and I will start by presenting an argument they might offer in support of their view.

The argument I have in mind goes roughly like this. There is an *asymmetry* between perception and communication. The latter is parasitic on the former, in the sense that whatever information is transmitted through communication must ultimately have been acquired through perception. The thought which occurs at the beginning of the communicational chain must therefore contain perception-based modes of presentation. What happens at the other end of the communicational chain? The recipient of the communicational act does not acquire the relevant information through perception.[3] Yet, arguably, he or she must be able to grasp the information thus transmitted, and that means that the information in question must be information she *might* have acquired through perception (even if, as a matter of fact, she acquired it through communication). In other words, the conceptual repertoire which communication exploits must be the same repertoire which we put to use in perception. This supports the claim that there are no modes of presentation which depend on communication in the same way in which egocentric files depend on perception.

As against this view I will suggest that there is a special, communication-based mode of presentation which plays quite a central role in our mental lives *precisely because* it enables us to go beyond our private conceptual repertoire. I will therefore reject the claim that the same conceptual repertoire is put to use in perception and communication.[4] But first, I want to spell out a consequence of the view I am going to oppose.

---

[3] Or at least, not directly. Hearing something on the radio, or from someone, certainly involves auditory perception, but *what* is perceived in such a case is the utterance which conveys the piece of information, rather than the fact stated by the utterance. To hear that John is presently in Paris is not to perceive that he is, but to be told that he is.

[4] An explicit rejection of that claim can be found in Sperber 1997.

2.2.   Deference as Metarepresentation

A woman goes to the doctor who tells her that she has arthritis. She believes what the doctor tells her. A number of representations are involved in this simple exchange. The doctor, after clinical examination, comes to entertain the thought: 'She has arthritis'. He expresses that thought by telling her: 'You have arthritis'. The woman then comes to believe something that might be expressed by the sentence: 'I have arthritis'.

It seems, at this stage, that the woman has acquired the belief that she has arthritis. But suppose, as Burge did in the famous article in which this example was introduced, that the woman has only a very vague, possibly mistaken notion of what arthritis is. Let us go even further: Suppose she has no idea what arthritis is — she lacks the concept altogether. Does she really come to believe that she has arthritis? Does she not, rather, come to believe that she has *some ailment called 'arthritis'*? This view seems more in line with the notion that whatever is actually communicated must be within the addresse's ken and could not exceed his or her conceptual repertoire.

On the suggested view, then, it is misleading to say that the woman comes to believe that she has arthritis as a result of the doctor's utterance. She does not actually believe that. Even if she goes about repeating 'I have arthritis', and that sentence expresses the proposition that she has arthritis, still that is not what she believes. What she believes would be more faithfully expressed by a metalinguistic sentence: 'I have an ailment called (by the doctor) *arthritis*' (Donnellan 1993). It follows that there is a divergence between the content of the utterance, which depends on social factors (viz. the conventions in force in the public language), and the content of the underlying mental representation. The mental representation is metalinguistic while the public representation is not.

2.3.   Another Approach to Deference

In contrast to that metalinguistic approach, the view I am going to put forward does not rest on a distinction between the content of the public utterance and the content of the underlying mental representation. On my view, one and the same proposition, namely the proposition that the woman has arthritis, is both the content of the woman's utterance and the content of her belief. (It is also, of course, the content of the doctor's utterance and the content of the doctor's belief.)

At this point a difficulty immediately arises. How could the woman believe she has arthritis? In order to believe that she has arthritis, she must entertain a mental representation whose content is the proposition that she has arthritis. Now such a representation must contain a constituent (a concept) whose content is arthritis, and we have granted that the woman does not possess the concept of arthritis!

That difficulty is not as dramatic as it seems. It is true that, if the woman is to believe that she has arthritis, she must entertain a mental representation whose content is the proposition that she has arthritis. It is true also that such a representation must contain a concept whose content is arthritis. But 'a concept whose content is arthritis' is *a* concept of arthritis, it is not *the* concept of arthritis — that concept which the woman lacks. When we say that the woman 'does not possess the concept of arthritis', we are not talking of any old concept whose content is arthritis: we are referring to a specific concept endowed not only with a certain reference (arthritis) *but also with a certain character*. The woman does not possess that concept, but she possesses another concept of arthritis. The concept of arthritis she possesses is a *deferential* concept, i.e. the sort of concept which people who use a public word without fully understanding it typically entertain. The difference between the woman's belief and the doctor's (or between the woman's belief and her utterance) is therefore not a difference at the content level but a difference in character or mode of presentation.

2.4.   The Deferential Operator

Qua types, indexical symbols have a character, a constant meaning which determines both their reference (in context) and the way the reference is presented. That constant meaning is a function from contexts to contents. My hypothesis is that there is, in the mental repertoire, a 'deferential operator' which enables us to construct deferential concepts with a semantics analogous to that of indexical concepts (Recanati 1997).

The deferential operator $R_x(\ )$ applies to (the mental representation of) a public symbol σ and yields a syntactically complex representation $R_x(\sigma)$ — a deferential concept — which has both a character and a content. The character of $R_x(\sigma)$ takes us from a context in which reference is made to a competent user x of σ, to a certain content, namely the content which σ has for x, given the character which x attaches to σ. What is special with the deferential concept $R_x(\sigma)$ is that its content is determined 'deferentially', via the content which another cognitive agent, somehow given in the context, attaches or would attach to σ in the context of utterance.

The deferential operator is the mental equivalent of quotation marks in written speech. It is metalinguistic in the sense that it involves a mention of the symbol σ and a tacit reference to its use by the cognitive agent x (which can be a community as well as an individual). But that metalinguistic aspect is located in the character of the deferential concept: the content of that concept is the same as the content of the symbol σ when used by x.

Take our 'arthritis' case. When the woman who does not know what arthritis is says 'I have arthritis', she does not entertain 'the' concept of arthritis, as the doctor does when he tells her 'you have arthritis'. They entertain different mental representations, involving different concepts. In the woman's belief a deferential concept occurs, namely: R_{doctor}(**arthritis**). But the content of that concept is the same as the content of the doctor's concept of arthritis — indeed the woman's deferential concept is parasitic on the doctor's concept and automatically inherits its referential content, by virtue of the mechanics of the deferential operator. That referential content — arthritis — is thought of metalinguistically as 'what the doctor calls *arthritis*', but the woman's thought is fundamentally about arthritis, not about the word 'arthritis'. If I am right, the difference between the doctor's concept of arthritis and the woman's is similar to that between 'I' and 'you' in their respective utterances 'You have arthritis' and 'I have arthritis': 'I' and 'you' refer to the woman under different modes of presentation. Similarly, the doctor's concept of arthritis and the woman's deferential concept R_{doctor}(**arthritis**) both refer to arthritis, under different modes of presentation.

2.5.   Deference as Social Indexicality

On the view I have sketched, deferential concepts are like indexical concepts, but instead of depending on perception they depend on communication. An indexical type of mode of presentation constrains the context of its tokenings: it demands that the subject who entertains the mode of presentation be directly related to the reference so as to be able to gain information from it in perception. Similarly there is a deferential type of mode of presentation which demands that the subject who entertains a mode of presentation of that type (a deferential concept) be indirectly related to the reference, via a chain of informants, so as to be able to gain information from it in communication.

3   Using Public Words in Thought

3.1.   Self-Conscious Deference vs Imperfect Mastery

Andrew Woodfield has put forward the following criticism of my view (Woodfield 2000). He accepts that there is a deferential operator which works in more or less the way I describe, but not my claim that it is at work in examples like the 'arthritis' example. The cases that support my view, according to Woodfield, are the cases in which we consciously use a word which we do not understand, in quotation marks as it were. In contrast to Donnellan, who holds that in such cases what is believed is a metalinguistic proposition, I hold that the content of the thought or utterance is the same as it would be if no quotation marks occurred and no deference took place: The metalinguistic component is located at the character level. Woodfield accepts all this. But my theory explains "a rather specialized range of phenomena", he holds. It was a mistake on my part to extend it to cases of imperfect mastery, like Burge's 'arthritis' example. Woodfield thus rejects my claim that "children, language-learners, and other imperfect understanders of picked up words normally bind such words inside deferential operators" (Woodfield 2000: 445).

Not only is there a phenomenological difference between self-conscious deference and imperfect mastery; there is, Woodfield points out, a good theoretical reason for not putting them in the same basket. Imperfect mastery is a matter of degree — one's mastery of a concept is more or less imperfect. In my original article on the topic, I myself insisted that deferentiality is a matter of degree: there is, I said, a continuum of cases between the deferential use of a symbol which we do not understand and its normal use, between full mastery of a concept and total lack of that concept. In between we find instances of partial mastery — as in Burge's original example. Now this raises a problem for my account, Woodfield says, because

> It seems impossible that there could be a *gradual* process of moving out of quasi-quotes. It's clearly not a process of bit-by-bit removal (like taking one's clothes off), nor it is a process of decay (like quotation-marks fading away on a page as the ink loses its colour). The learner starts off using mental symbols like R_x *('synecdoches')* and R_x *('kachna')* and ends up using completely distinct symbols like *synecdoches* and *duck*.[5] Prima facie, there has to be a saltation — a switch of symbol-*type* — at some point. (Woodfield 2000: 447).

I grant Woodfield both points: first, that there is a difference between self-conscious deference and imperfect mastery; second, that the gradual nature of imperfect mastery makes it hard, if not impossible, to account for the transition from imperfect to full mastery in terms of a switch of symbol-type. The problem for my account is that such a switch is precisely what adding or removing the deferential operator brings about.

3.2.   Deference By Default

Faced with those difficulties, we may allow for the following possibility. Whenever we mentally entertain a sentence containing a symbol we do not properly understand, the deferential mechanism operates *as if* we had used the deferential operator, that is, as if we had put that symbol within quotation marks and deferred to some authority for its interpretation. But we don't have to actually use the deferential operator — the deferential interpretation can be provided by default, simply because no direct interpretation for the symbol is available to the subject. On this account the difference between conscious deference and incomplete mastery is syntactic, not semantic. In ordinary cases of incomplete mastery, the deferential shift takes place without being syntactically articulated. Since that is so the continuum from incomplete to complete mastery no longer raises a problem.

---

[5] One of Woodfield's examples involves a non-Czech speaker looking at a menu written in Czech and uttering *For lunch I shall have 'kachna'*. 'Kachna' means *duck* in Czech, Woodfield tells us.

No saltation needs to be involved because the difference between normal and deferential use no longer lies at the level of the symbol-type. One and the same symbol-type is tokened in both cases. If that symbol is appropriately connected to some concept in the subject's repertoire, it expresses that concept and conveys its content. If the symbol is not appropriately connected to some concept in the subject's repertoire, the concept that is expressed is that which would be expressed by applying the deferential operator to that symbol. On this account, it is only to be expected that the process of connecting up a symbol with concepts in one's repertoire, hence the transition from deference to full mastery, will be gradual.

3.3. The Interpretation Principle

Though it is a step in the right direction, the foregoing account is not ultimately satisfactory, for it violates a principle which I put forward in my original paper, and which we can call the Interpretation Principle:

> It is hard to think of a symbol being mentally entertained without being 'interpreted' in some fashion or other... If a mental sentence is well-formed, it must possess a definite meaning — a character — even if it falls short of expressing a definite content. (Recanati 1997: 91, quoted in Woodfield 2000: 444)

If we accept this principle, as I do, then there is an incoherence in the revised account presented in the last section. We are to suppose that the subject entertains a mental sentence in which a symbol σ occurs. Whenever that symbol turns out to be uninterpreted by the subject's own lights, it receives a deferential interpretation by default. This violates the Interpretation Principle: for the so-called mental sentence will not be well-formed in the first place — it will *not* be a *mental* sentence — if it contains some uninterpreted symbol. Mental sentences must be constituted out of the right material — conceptual material. The symbols used in thought must be potential conveyors of content: they must be interpreted at least at the character level. That is what the Interpretation Principle requires. The role of the deferential operator was precisely to guarantee satisfaction of the Interpretation Principle. In the same way in which quotation marks can turn a non-word into a well-formed expression of English, the deferential operator can turn the uninterpreted symbol σ into a complex symbol $R_x(\sigma)$, which has a character and possibly a content.

On the revised account, the uninterpreted symbol σ will acquire a character when the deferential interpretation is provided by default. But this is too late: how will the uninterpreted symbol σ come to occur as a constituent in the subject's thought, unless it is already interpreted? This is a serious worry for anyone who accepts the Interpretation Principle.

3.4.   Words as Concepts

I suggest that we revise the revised account so as to satisfy the Interpretation Principle. Let us not say that the deferential interpretation is provided by default when an uninterpreted symbol occurs in thought. According to the Interpretation Principle, no uninterpreted symbol *ever* occurs in thought. Still, we want to capture the fact that sometimes, in our thinking, we use a public word which we do not understand. In line with the Interpretation Principle, we want the word in question to receive a deferential interpretation from the very start; and we do not want this interpretation to affect the identity of the symbol-type, as the use of the deferential operator would do. These are the desiderata.

I suggest the following account as a means of satisfying the desiderata. We must give up the Aristotelian view that words are labels associated with concepts. We must construe words themselves as concepts,[6] which we can associate with other concepts (e.g. recognitional concepts). Thus, when we acquire a public word, whose use we do not yet fully master, we automatically acquire a concept.[7] The concept in question is deferential: its content is determined via the users whom we get the word from (or via the commu-

---

[6] I am not suggesting that we should identify concepts with words. Obviously, there are many concepts to which no word corresponds. My point, rather, is that a sub-class of our concepts is constituted by public words which we imperfectly understand but which we are able to use in our thinking.

[7] See Millikan 1998, §6:

> It is... possible, indeed it is common, to have a substance concept entirely through the medium of language, that is, in the absence of any ability to recognize the substance in the flesh. For most of us, that is how we have a concept of Aristotle, of molybdenum, and, say, of African dormice. There, I just handed you a concept of African dormice, in case you had none before. Now you can think of them at night if you want to, wondering what they are like — on the assumption, of course, that you gathered from their name what sorts of questions you might reasonably ask about them... In many cases there is not much more to having a substance concept than having a word. To have a word is to have a handle on tracking a substance via manifestations of it produced in a particular langue community. Simply grasping the phonemic structure of a language and the rudiments of how to parse it enables one to help oneself to an embryo concept of every substance named in that language.

Similar remarks can be found in Kaplan's 'Afterthoughts':

> The notion that a referent can be carried by a name from early past to present suggests that the language itself carries meaning, and thus that we can *acquire* meanings through the instrument of language. This... provides the opportunity for an *instrumental* use of language to broaden the realm of what can be expressed and to broaden the horizons of thought itself. (...) Contrary to Russell, I think we succeed in thinking about things in the world not only through the mental residue of that which we ourselves experience, but also vicariously, through the symbolic resources that come to us through our language. It is the latter — *vocabulary power* — that gives us our apprehensive advantage over the nonlinguistic animals. My dog, being color-blind, cannot entertain the thought that I am wearing a red shirt. But my color-blind colleague can entertain even the thought that Aristotle wore a red shirt. (Kaplan 1989: p. 604)

nity in general). When we use a word we do not understand in our thinking, it is the deferential concept which occurs in our thought — hence the Interpretation Principle is satisfied. Again, the public word, insofar as we use it in thought, *is* the deferential concept, it does not have to be associated with a deferential or any other type of concept. In this account there no longer is a gap between the public word which occurs in thought and the deferential interpretation it receives: the deferential interpretation is a built-in feature of public words *qua* thought constituents.

What happens when (gradually) we come to understand the word in a non-deferential manner — when, for example, we get acquainted with what it applies to? We must not think of this process as the association of the word with a concept — an association which was lacking beforehand. Rather it is the association of two concepts: a deferential concept and another type of concept. This is the same sort of process which takes place when we recognize an object we have seen before: then a past-oriented demonstrative concept 'that object [which I saw the other day]' gets associated with a standard demonstrative concept based on current perception: 'that object [in front of me]'.[8] In such a re-identification situation typically the two concepts coalesce, are merged into a single recognitional concept, with a distinct character. (That arguably is a *third* concept, distinct from the first two as a child is from mother and father.) Similarly, when a deferential concept — for example, Putnam's concept of an elm — gets associated with a non-deferential concept (e.g. the demonstrative concept 'that type of tree'), and that association stabilizes, a new concept results, with a distinct character. How is the merging process to be properly described? I don't know, but I have no doubt that the merging process can be gradual, and that is all that matters for us.

3.5.   Conclusion

What is left of my original account? From a strictly semantic point of view, there is no significant difference between the original account and the account we arrive at. When in our thinking we use public words which we do not quite understand, our thoughts have deferential concepts as constituents. The character of these concepts is the same as the character of complex symbols built up with the help of the deferential operator. The character in question is metalinguistic, much as the character of indexicals is metalinguistic. Just as 'I' refers to the person who says 'I', 'arthritis', for the patient, refers to what the doctor calls 'arthritis'. But the content of the thought or utterance is metalinguistic in neither case: when she thinks 'I

---

[8] See Evans 1982: chapter 8 for illuminating remarks on this topic.

have arthritis', the patient entertains a thought which is about her (not about the word 'I') and about arthritis (not about the word 'arthritis').*

References

Anscombe, E. 1975. The First Person. *Mind and Language,* ed. S. Guttenplan, 45-65. Oxford: Clarendon Press.

Burge, T. 1979. Individualism and the Mental. *Midwest Studies in Philosophy* 4:73-121.

Donnellan, K. 1993. There is a Word for that Kind of Thing: an Investigation of Two Thought Experiments. *Philosophical Perspectives* 7:155-71.

Evans, G. 1982. *The Varieties of Reference*, ed. J. McDowell. Oxford: Clarendon Press.

Frege, G. 1892. On Sense and Reference. *Translations from the Philosophical Writings of Gottlob Frege*, by P. Geach & M. Black. 2nd ed., 56-78. Oxford: Clarendon Press, 1960.

Kaplan, D. 1989. Afterthoughts. *Themes from Kaplan*, eds. J. Almog, H. Wettstein and J. Perry, 565-614. New York: Oxford University Press.

Millikan, R. 1998. A Common Structure for Concepts of Individuals, Stuffs, and Real Kinds: More Mama, More Milk, and More Mouse. *Behavioral and Brain Sciences* 21:55-65.

Perry, J. 1993. *The Problem of the Essential Indexical and Other Essays*. New York: Oxford University Press.

Recanati, F. 1993. *Direct Reference: From Language to Thought*. Oxford: Blackwell.

Recanati, F. 1997. Can We Believe What We Do Not Understand? *Mind and Language* 12:84-100.

Schiffer, S. 1978. The Basis of Reference. *Erkenntnis* 13:171-206.

Sperber, D. 1997. Intuitive and Reflective Beliefs. *Mind and Language* 12:67-83.

Woodfield, A. 2000. Reference and Deference. *Mind and Language* 15:433-451.

---

* An ancestor of this paper, corresponding to the first two parts, was presented at the *Languages of the Brain* conference organized in Paris in March 1998 by the Mind/Brain/Behavior Interfaculty Initiative (Harvard University) and the Ipsen Foundation. It will be included in the Proceedings of that conference, to be published by Harvard University Press. The present paper, which I read at the Bonn conference, overlaps also with my 'Deferential Concepts: A Response to Woodfield' (*Mind and Language* vol. 15 n°4, September 2000). I am indebted to Steven Davis for helpful comments on an earlier draft.

Part III

EMPTY NAMES AND THE CONTEXT PRINCIPLE

11

Sense Without Reference

R. M. SAINSBURY

1 Introduction

Many people think that Frege allowed that expressions could have sense yet
lack reference. The question I wish to raise is how one could justify the
claim that a systematic description of natural language will make essential
use of such a view.

The project might be thought doubly unsuitable for a conference on
Frege. First, Frege himself probably had rather little interest in systematic
accounts of the semantics of natural languages. However, I take it to be
acceptable to see whether a thinker's ideas can be applied even to areas for
which they were not originally designed. Second, there is some interpreta-
tive doubt about whether Frege held that expressions genuinely having
sense, expressions capable of contributing to the expression of genuine
thoughts, could lack reference, or at any rate, whether he held it for long. I
am inclined to the view that he did hold it when he wrote "On Sense and
Reference", where he says of the definite description, "the least rapidly
convergent series", that it "has a sense but demonstrably lacks a reference".
However, by the time of the piece called "Logic", dated 1897 and published
only posthumously, he says that a sentence containing an expression lacking reference expresses at best a mock thought, a "Scheingedanke", and this
would seem to be something which is not a thought.[1] So I think that there is

---

[1] Despite Bell's contrary opinion (Bell, 1990), the soundings I have taken among native
speakers suggest that a Schein-F is something intended to seem an F even though it isn't an F.

a case to be made for saying that at least by that time he had abandoned the view that sense without reference was possible. I will not engage in this exegetical issue, relying on the clear statement in "On Sense and Reference" to justify labelling "Fregean" the doctrine that sense is possible without reference.

This paper argues for an affirmative answer to its question as applied to proper names, as this expression is commonly used nowadays: semantically simple singular terms.[2] I argue that one can justify using a description of natural language which is "Fregean" in just the following respect: it makes essential use of the possibility of empty proper names. In deference to Russell's view that "what does not name anything is not a name", I shall label any denial of this "Russellian". A full account would have at least three parts: (1) an attack on arguments for the Russellian view;[3] (2) a semantic theory which gives a recursive specification of meanings or truth conditions in a way that does not discriminate between empty and non-empty names; and (3) an account of the notion of a name-using practice which, likewise, is neutral between the case in which the practice involves an empty name and the case in which it involves a non-empty one.

The second task can be accomplished in more than one way. One could adopt the kind of descriptivist theory commonly (though controversially) associated with the historical Frege. On this view, a singular term is or abbreviates some kind of descriptive, effectively qualitative, condition, and its use in "primary occurrence" in a truth requires the unique satisfaction of this condition. However, there is no need for the relevant condition to be qualitative, in the way taken for granted in "descriptivist" theories. A theory neutral on this point, and which I shall take as my model in the present development of a Fregean position, has been provided by Tyler Burge (1974). In the semantics he develops, names are treated by axioms like

$$\forall x \text{ ("Hesperus" refers to } x \text{ iff } x = \text{Hesperus}).$$

Thanks to Max Kölbel for discussion. There are very useful discussions of Frege's position in Diamond 1991, especially "Frege against fuzz".

[2]As Jonathan Barnes pointed out to me, this is a rather inadequate characterization of the relevant class of expressions. Most westerners have forename and family name, and it is hard to see how this complexity (if that is what it is) is to be characterized. Are book titles names of books? These issues deserves closer scrutiny. A related issue is that I exclude demonstratives. While I certainly think that it is important to consider how the considerations of this paper relate to the use of demonstratives, I am unsure that the issues are logically connected. Both the view that the class of singular terms fractures into names and demonstratives, and the view that both are subsumed under a single category of singular terms, appears consistent with the main claim of this paper, viz. that there is a unified category of (empty and non-empty) proper names. Thanks to François Recanati and Ian Rumfitt for discussion.

[3]For which see Sainsbury 1999.

The setting is negative free logic: atoms with empty names are false, and universal and existential quantifier rules are modified. An axiom of the above form for an empty name like "Vulcan" is true, because the right hand side is false for each value of x, leading to the appropriate verdict that there is nothing to which "Vulcan" refers. One interesting feature of the theory, which I will carry through to my own discussion, is that the semantics associates names neither with an object nor with a description (in the usual qualitative sense of "description").[4]

Hostility to this kind of approach may come from a reluctance to consider alternatives to classical logic. The following is designed to disturb the reluctance. If one accepts a standard account of validity, according to which a valid argument is one such that, for each world at which the premises are true, so is the conclusion, one will reject the classical rule of universal instantiation, since, even though "Socrates" is (in fact) not empty, there are worlds at which "Everything is perishable" is true but "Socrates is perishable" is not (worlds at which Socrates does not exist).[5] Rejecting the classical rule of instantiation is at least a step towards a free logic.

By contrast to the Burge-style approach, Russellian orthodoxy starts with the idea that a name is to be associated with an object, so an axiom for "Hesperus" will be based on the idea that

the reference of "Hesperus" = Hesperus.

---

[4]Thus Bell (1990: p. 275), summarizing a sentence each from the Grundgesetze and the Grundlagen writes: "for Frege the sense of an expression is the condition that must be met by anything that is the reference of that expression. ... there can be a fully determinate, coherent, and intelligible condition which ... nothing fulfils".

The envisaged semantics also undermines any ultimate difference between reference and satisfaction. What we call reference is just satisfaction under a condition (like being Hesperus) capable of being satisfied by at most one thing.

Suppose the kind of haecceities invoked by the Burge-style theory I envisage turned out to be reducible to qualitative properties. Should one conclude that there is no difference between a Burge-style theory and a descriptive theory? The conclusion does not follow. I see a semantic theory as designed to state things which if known by speakers would explain their behaviour. But one might know something of the form "this has property F" without knowing anything of the form "this has property G" even if the property F is the property G. The space between a conventional descriptivist position and a Russellian one disappears only if conditions like being Hesperus really abbreviate qualitative conditions (as perhaps Russell himself thought). Thanks to David Sosa and Eric Loomis for discussion of this issue.

[5]The argument was mentioned to me (though not endorsed) by Yannis Stephanou. The case is only prima facie. Classical instantiation could be defended in a number of ways, including (as David Wiggins suggested) shifting to binary quantification, which would require the premise that Socrates is a thing; or, more simply and classically, by guiding one's formalization of the premise by the formulation "for all x, if x is a thing, then x is perishable".

Since, in the usual versions of such theories, the metalanguage does not contain primitive function symbols or a referential description operator, a formalized version would look more like:

(1) $\exists x$("Hesperus" refers to x and $\forall y$("Hesperus" refers to $y \rightarrow x=y$) and x = Hesperus).

I call such axioms "bearer-specifying" because they affirm that the name has a bearer and go on to identify it. They cannot truly be affirmed by the theorist if the object language name has no bearer. In the next section, I give some general considerations in favour of a Fregean semantics, a semantics which can supply true axioms for empty names.

2 Some General Fregean Considerations

Suppose one believes that one can get close to specifying the knowledge involved in understanding a sentence in terms of knowledge of what it would be for the sentence to be true.[6] What would be the corresponding thing to say about the knowledge involved in understanding a referring expression, say a name? A natural answer is that it is to know what it would be for the name to refer. This is not knowledge of what the name refers to, but rather knowledge of conditions under which it would refer, knowledge, that is, of how something would have to be in order to be what the name refers to. Just as one might make some progress in saying what it would be to understand "snow is white" in terms of knowing that the sentence is true iff snow is white, so one might make some progress in saying what it would be to understand "Hesperus" in terms of knowing that the name refers to something iff that thing is Hesperus. In short, if the meaning of a sentence is its truth condition, a cognate thought is that the meaning of a name is its reference condition; and this analogy is one general consideration in favour of a Fregean approach.

Suppose, however, that we start with the Russellian idea that a semantic theory should associate a name with an object. Running the analogy in the other direction would lead to the absurd suggestion that semantic theory should associate a sentence with a truth value. Current orthodoxy inexplicably associates sentences with conditions but names with objects. The only plausible way to restore the analogy is to associate names also with conditions rather than objects.

---

[6]I take it for granted that what it would be for "Hesperus is visible" to be true is not the same as what it would be for "Phosphorus is visible" to be true. This approach is, to put it optimistically, non-reductive: the distinction in question cannot be extracted merely from the nature of truth but must come from some "intensional" notion, in my opinion, following for example McDowell 1977 or Davies 1981, that of propositional attitudes.

A semantic theorist, as radical interpreter, must immerse himself in the language-using practices of his subjects. Vague as the notion of immersion may be, it is natural to suppose that some degree of it is sufficient for understanding. In that case, nothing else is necessary. So unless immersion in a practice covertly requires the existence of a referent if the practice involves a name, the Fregean view is imposed by the data of interpretation. The main part of this paper is devoted to trying to establish that it is not the case that the notion of a name-using practice requires names to have bearers.

We can give examples of how easily empty names can be introduced, whether as fiction, jest or through error, and point out that we feel a need to teach our children the "correct use" of various actual empty names ("Vulcan", "Santa Claus"), which implies that they are meaningful. We can insist that there is parity at the level of explaining behaviour. We can explain why many adults are excited by the thought of a trip to *Paris* in terms of their expectations that Paris is beautiful and has excellent restaurants, where the evidence for the relevant beliefs derives in part from the subjects' "Paris"-utterances. In just the same way, there is a prima facie case for saying that we can explain why children are excited at Christmas in terms of their expectations that *Santa* will bring them presents, where the evidence for the relevant beliefs derives in part from the children's "Santa"-utterances.

Cases in which the population under study is agnostic about, for example, whether there ever was such a person as Homer, or is divided on the question, are particularly striking. The Russellian theorist would need to resolve the issue. From his perspective, if "Homer" is empty, semantic theory has nothing to say about it: the activities relating to this mere sound do not constitute a name-using practice, and ordinary sentences containing it lack truth conditions. Yet it seems clear that semantic theory should be able to describe the relevant behaviour without risking falsification by the eventual discovery that the sceptics were right and there really is no such person as Homer.

We could not expect a semantic theorist to explore the historical origin of every name on the University's register to see if it is genuine or is, rather, like "Paul R. Zwier" (Larson and Segal 1995: 161); nor need he be an astronomer, which he would have to be to distinguish "Neptune" from "Vulcan"; nor a theologian, which he would have to be to determine which, if any, of his subjects' names for gods are empty; nor a chemist, which he would have to be to distinguish "phlogiston" and "ether" from "heat" and "air"; nor a literary theorist with sound views on the authorship of *Odyssey* and *Iliad*. To suppose otherwise is not merely implausible but potentially incoherent, for on a natural view the relevant investigations would take for granted that the names are intelligible, and would be guided by what that meaning is. This would underwrite the possibility of intelligible questions *whether* there is such a person as Paul R. Zwier, *where* Vulcan is supposed to be, if it exists, *what* phlogiston is meant to be like, and *who* Homer was, if anyone. The questions to be investigated are naturally expressed in a way that makes essential use of, and thus presupposes the intelligibility of, the names in question. Semantic theory is one thing, specialist knowledge of non-semantic fact another.

A preference for a Fregean over a Russellian theory can be motivated for non-empty names. It would seem possible that the users of such a name, say "*a*", which in fact refers to *a*, should fail to know that *a* exists, even if they have true beliefs to this effect. The failure of knowledge might derive from a deviant link in some causal chain, or from a serious lack of confidence (one can select an explanation to fit one's theory of knowledge). A Russellian semantic theorist, however, is required to make an explicit affirmation of the existence of *a*. Since the theorist should affirm only what he knows, he is required to have knowledge that outstrips that of the speakers whose knowledge he is trying to describe. Moreover, in attributing to the speakers implicit knowledge of the semantic theory, he is attributing to them knowledge which, by hypothesis, they lack. No such contradiction threatens Fregean theories.

One can view a semantic axiom as if it were a stipulation governing the use of an expression. One cannot stipulate things into existence, so a Russellian axiom affirming the existence of an entity to which a name refers could not count as an axiom of semantic theory. By contrast, one can stipulate an "at most one" condition, as a Fregean theory does (for example, as developed by Burge). For one can stipulate that a tie for victory is defeat: if there is a group containing more than one candidate for meeting an "at most" condition, like that of being Hesperus, and each candidate in this group is as good as any other in the group but is a better candidate than any of the candidates outside the group, then no candidate counts as meeting the condition.

The familiarity of many of these arguments has not made them persuasive,[7] especially to Russellians. I think that more persuasive considerations emerge from a look at the nature of name-using practices.

3 Name-using Practices

A necessary condition for the adequacy of an account of language is that it be able to provide an adequate description of its use, and this means in par-

---

[7] These considerations all have a prima facie character, for if there is a direct and decisive argument for the claim that a name must name, then this conclusion must somehow be accommodated in the methodology of semantic theorizing. Hence arguments against arguments for the view that every intelligible name must have a bearer (see Sainsbury 1999) are complementary to those offered here.

ticular that provision should be made for a distinction between the practice of using the name "Aristotle" for the philosopher and the practice of using it for the tycoon. This distinction will either figure explicitly in semantic axioms for names, or will at least supply guidance about how the theorist is to reach and understand such axioms. If there is no sense without reference, one can individuate by appealing to the referent, just as I did in setting up the problem. But once one grants sense without reference, this cannot in general be the right way to individuate (though its correctness in the cases in which it is correct ought to follow from a correct general condition).

The general answer I offer is that name-using practices are individuated by their source in acts of name-introduction, where such acts can associate the new name with at most one object. This last condition ensures as a consequence that practices of using non-empty names with different bearers are different practices (though the converse does not hold), and this meets the requirement at the end of the previous paragraph. This source-based approach has two main rivals: a referent-based approach, characteristic of Russellian and Kripkean theories; and an information-based approach, characteristic of description theories of names. I suspect that it is dissatisfaction with theories of the latter kind that have driven people towards object-based, Russellian or Kripkean, accounts of name-using practices. What this paper supplies is the sketch of an alternative to both informational and object-based accounts.

Spelling this out in full detail is quite hard, but, in defence of the Fregean approach, I shall suggest that the task is not made significantly easier by having referents in the story. Kripke (1972) sketched a picture of name-using practices which start with a baptism, and are propagated causally from that starting point. What I shall suggest is that we can arrive at a Fregean source-based account by using essentially the Kripkean picture, but without thinking of the originating events, the baptisms, as essentially relating to objects.

3.1   A Simple Model

A first rough shot at stating Kripke's picture might be:

> Two acts of using the name-type N belong to the same name-using practice iff there is an object x and a causal transmission relation R such that both acts are related to x by the ancestral of R.

The structure of his proposal is that there is an initiating event and a transmission relation. I say I can adjust the account of the initiating event and help myself to the same transmission relation.

For a Kripkean the transmission relation serves to put the recipient in epistemic contact with the referent, and this might make it seem that I cannot make use of the same transmission relation. But this is not so: this feature of the transmission relation results from the two Kripkean claims that transmission transmits knowledge of meaning, and that knowledge of the meaning of a name involves epistemic contact with its referent. It is only thanks to the second of these views that the transmission relation transmits knowledge of the referent. Once this is deleted, as it must be for a Fregean view, the transmission relation is neutral.

A Kripkean picture of an early part of a practice might be as follows:

Figure 1

The filled circle represents the baptism, the square represents the object, and the open circles represent two subsequent uses belonging to the practice, in virtue of being related to the baptism by the transmission relation.[8] Subsequent uses are related not only to the baptism but also to the baptised object. However, it is unclear that the relation to the object could do any work: so long as the baptism does invest the name with a meaning, we need only check whether subsequent uses are related appropriately to it in order to determine that they belong to the same name-using practice. The Kripkean referent thus appears to be idle in the account of the unity of a name-using practice, provided that distinct baptisms can be distinguished independently of which object, if any, is baptized.

The alternative I propose for a Fregean account adopts Kripkean ideas about transmission, while eliminating the object. This means that a "baptism" may be a baptism of nothing, which is verbally awkward but just registers the Fregean view that a name can be intelligibly introduced even if it names nothing.

Justifying the choice of this approach would require ruling out approaches based upon associated information, as would be implied by description theories of names. My reasons for ruling out such theories are of familiar kinds, which I will not rehearse directly here, though §3.2 and §3.3 reveal some inadequacies with description theories.

---

[8] The transmission relation is indicated by a solid line. The distinct relation which holds between a baptiser and the baptised object is shown by a broken line.

3.2 Duplicated Sources: Qualitatively the Same Information may Inform Different Practices

Even when name-using practices coincide in what information is invoked, they constitute different practices if they originate in different objects. Suppose there are two speakers, S1 and S2, each of whom knows just one of the twins, Jim and Tim, and each calls the one he knows Harry. S1's "Harry"-related information derives exclusively from Jim, S2's from Tim. Qualitatively, their information may be identical (both affirm "Harry is tall", "Harry is happy" etc.). But if they encounter one another, their apparently harmonious use of "Harry"-sentences provides merely an illusion of understanding: because their information derives from different sources, they are using the name in different ways (or, semantically, there are two different names with the same spelling). This result does not depend upon difference of object, for there is also difference of source: the "Harry"-uses of S1 and S2 lack a common source. The irrelevance of the object is made plain in the diagram (Figure 2).

Figure 2

One can imagine a structurally similar case for empty names. Two name-introducing rumours might coincide in information, but if they have different sources, I think we should rule that two names have been introduced and that there is a mere illusion of understanding when the distinct practices meet.

3.3   Information Involved in Distinguishing Practices?

Must we not appeal to associated information in distinguishing one who has authentically joined a practice from one who has tried but failed? Does not one who sincerely affirms "London is the capital of France" give one reason to suspect he does not understand "London"? Likewise, does not one who sincerely affirms "Santa Claus is a planet which affects the orbit of Mercury" give one reason to believe he does not understand "Santa Claus"?

In both cases, this is merely defeasible evidence of lack of mastery. In the one case it would be defeated by, for example, the discovery that while in other respects a normal user of "London", the speaker had been carried away by a dream about a new phase of British colonization. In the other case, it would be defeated by, for example, the discovery that while in other respects a normal user of "Santa Claus", the speaker had come to believe an Ovidian fantasy in which the sledge driver had offended the gods by excessive jingling, and in punishment had been transformed into a silent planet.

It may seem that although in the case of a non-empty name there is no information whose possession is required for understanding, this is not so for empty names. Precisely because there is no bearer, contact with which could be involved in what makes for understanding, surely there must be a body of information which plays a crucial role. This idea may be encouraged by the accidental fact that some empty names are associated with very little information ("Vulcan"), and others, though suffering no dearth of information, generally permit access to the full richness only to those who have passed through a narrow gateway of information ("Shylock"). These are not essential features of empty names. We could well imagine that the speculation about Vulcan was not rapidly quashed, but continued over several generations, the information being enriched by various myths, so that some later users are quite ignorant of the basis of the original postulation; so some competent users might rationally doubt that Vulcan was a planet. Likewise, it could be the case that a competent user of "Shylock" should be unaware of the Shakespearean origin, and suppose the name to refer to some nineteenth century miser. He would, of course, have needed to learn the name from a competent user, for example, a user well aware of the Shakespearean origin; but he might never have known, or have once known but forgotten, that Shylock was a fictional character. The hypothesis that he has just started up a new and non-Shakespearean fictitious use of a like-sounding name would be discredited by his having some recognizably Shakespearean line on such matters as who Shylock's daughter was and the kinds of contract into which he entered. One such line would be simple belief, but another would be recognition that others hold such beliefs, together with an account of their falsehood. ("That pound of flesh stuff was obviously just an anti-Semitic exaggeration of a normal, if exigent, business arrangement.")

Here is a story about how a name-introducing rumour might begin, which reveals the way in which information may diverge, and follows the simple model. An over-imaginative, or self-deceiving, or evil tongue, T_0, may start a rumour which is embellished by others. The rumour is that there's a dragon, Fiamma, who lives in the mountain just south of the village and whose preferred diet is human babies. You hear the rumour from T_1 and I hear it from T_2, each of whom heard it, on separate occasions, from T_0. You say that Fiamma is green, trusting to T_1's embellishment, and I say she is red, trusting to T_2's. By some standard, our Fiamma-related information has different origins; but there is a standard which rules that these different bodies of information have the same source, in T_0. This is the standard we need: it correctly represents us as disagreeing about Fiamma's colour. It rules as it does because, although the information that Fiamma is green is new to T_1, and the information that Fiamma is red is new to T_2, both these pieces of information were intended by their producers to link to Fiamma,[9] so the "ultimate" origin lies further back, with T_0. This is the source that is invoked by my proposal.

The view that no piece of information need be shared by all users in a practice has its analogue for empty names. Those who think that one can understand "Russell" without even knowing that its bearer is human will think that one can understand "Fiamma" without even knowing that its bearer is supposed to be a dragon: perhaps the rumour will develop, so that some say Fiamma is a gorgon, some say she prefers adults to babies, some that "she" is really a he, and some elders, wishing to reduce panic, claim she is vegetarian. These people disagree among themselves on the facts while agreeing on language, provided that their use of the name "Fiamma" has a common origin, and that each intends to speak of what the others speak of.

3.4 Fusion

Fusion of name-using practices provides a case in which an object of reference arguably dominates source in individuation.

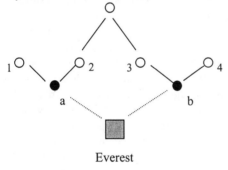

Everest

Figure 3

Suppose that one group of speakers (a) sees a mountain from the north side and calls it "Everest" and another group (b) sees it from the south side and calls it by a name which, coincidentally, sounds and is spelled the same. At first, the groups do not meet. But then the route through the range is dis-

---

[9]The context of this occurrence of "Fiamma" is intensional: one cannot infer the existence of Fiamma from the existence of this intention. Our need to use names we know to be non-referring in describing intentions and other attitudes makes a strong case for the Fregean approach.

covered. North-siders and south-siders talk to each other freely using "Everest". There is a strong intuition that what began as distinct name-using practices will eventually fuse. One way to describe this would be to say that at first there were two practices and then there was one. The object theory can account for this, as there is a single object; the source theory apparently cannot, for there are distinct sources.[10]

A similar structure can arise in the case of empty names, with a diagram just like Figure 3, save with the object omitted. Coincidentally, among both those who live on the north side and those who live on the south side of the mountain a rumour springs up about a dragon, Fiamma, who lives in the mountain above the village and whose preferred diet is human babies. At first, the groups do not meet. But then the route through the range is discovered. North-siders and south-siders talk to each other freely using "Fiamma". There is a strong intuition that what began as distinct name-using practices will eventually fuse. The object theory cannot account for any of this, as it cannot allow that there are any name-using practices in the story. But the story also presents problems for the source theory, as there are two sources but, on one account of fusion, a single practice.

I believe that in both cases, there is only an appearance of understanding in the initial encounters. For example, if (Figure 3) person 2 from the (a) practice meets person 3 from the (b) practice on the ridge, as contact is first established, it may seem as if they understand one another's "Everest"-utterances. If I am right to hold that this is only an illusion of understanding, the source theory at least gets the early history right.

Communication can transmit knowledge. Suppose person 2 expresses knowledge with the words "Avalanche yesterday Everest". Imagine that the first two words are not intelligible to 3, but that 2 explains them by signs and dumb-show. In connection with the third word, however, 3 indicates that he has no need for any explanation. Suppose that, before the utterance, 3 did not know that there was an avalanche on Everest yesterday. Suppose also, for reductio, that 3 understands what 2 said. Then, on any adequate account of knowledge by testimony, he ends up knowing that there was an avalanche on the north side of Everest on the previous day. However, it was just an accident that the sound 2 used for Everest coincided in its contribution to truth conditions with the similar sound as used by 3. Things could easily have been otherwise: the north-siders might easily have used "Everest" for the next mountain along. The method implicitly adopted by 3, homophonic translation, was not reliable. Knowledge is not acquired by unreliable methods. So 3 did not end up knowing that there had been an

---

[10]Another version, pointed out to me by Maite Ezcurdia, involves two scientists postulating the "same" object as unobserved cause of some phenomenon: distinct sources but, eventually, a single practice.

avalanche on Everest the previous day. The explanation is that 3 did not know what 2 said.

The source-based account thus gets the early part of the story right: at the beginning, there is at best an illusion of understanding. To do justice to this, the object-based account has to add some further condition. It is not enough for understanding that speaker and hearer derive their use of a name from a common object: in the present case, at least, it seems that they need to know that there is an object to which they both intend to refer. The object-based account thus needs some further condition, not contained merely in causal history, but most naturally to be found in the intentions, beliefs or knowledge of the speakers, in order to get the first part of the fusion story right; in order, that is, to allow that merely deriving the use of a name-type from a common object is not enough for the uses to belong to a single practice. The connection is that uses which belong to a single practice permit immediate and genuine understanding.

The difficulty for source-based accounts is to explain the fusion of distinct practices. A constraint upon a successful account is that it should respect the intuition that nothing more is needed for (a)-siders and (b)-siders to understand each other, and thus for their practices to fuse, than for them to know that they both use "Everest" for the same mountain. There are various options, among which I suggest we take seriously an analogue of what it is natural for object-based theories to say in order to explain the distinctness of the practices before fusion: in addition to the origin of uses we must also look to the intentions and beliefs by which they are governed. The most obvious suggestion for object-based theories is that there should be a single object about which participants in an exchange belonging to the same practice aim to speak. The analogue for source-based theories suitable for a Fregean is that participants in such an exchange must intend to speak of a single object. The idea is that the shift in the scope of the quantification over objects means that although, setting aside fiction, the users must believe there is something of which they both speak, the theorist describing this use need not.

This seems an entirely proper thing to say about the empty case. There is no object such that either community can know that "Fiamma" stands for it. On the other hand, we do have some inclination to represent the fused situation as one in which both north and south-siders intend to speak of the same dragon. Theorists can make sense of this without committing themselves to the existence of dragons. A sign of the presence of these coincident intentions is that north-siders view south-siders as well as north-siders as belonging to the community with whose practice they wish to accord and as potential suppliers of Fiamma-related information; they want to talk about whatever all these people, south-siders included, want to talk about. For south-siders, the position is analogous. In the absence of a dragon, the intentions cannot be realized. But they can be sustained by that fact that users have no evidence, or at least no decisive evidence, that there is more than one dragon (or less than one).

Returning to the "Everest" case: if, on the ridge, one party utters "Everest" while pointing to the mountain, and the other expresses agreement, mutual understanding is assured. On the present view, the explanation is that they come to appreciate that in using this word they are trying to speak of the same object. More happens: they come to know that there is an object concerning which both parties are trying to speak when using the word "Everest". But this additional knowledge, though relevant to whether the parties are so related that they can transmit non-semantic knowledge, is, I claim, not required for semantic knowledge. For the latter, it is enough to appreciate the coincidence of the intentions.

What can "coincidence of intention" amount to, if not to one of the following: both intentions involve the same object, or both involve the same content? The first option is unavailable to the Fregean theorist, for the coincidence must be possible even in the absence of an object. The second option threatens to be circular, if the coincidence in content is in part determined by an agreement about how a name is to be used. There is a third option. In the "Fiamma" case, each party thinks: what the other is trying to speak of in using "Fiamma" is just what I am trying to speak of when I use that name. This commits the speakers, but not the theorist, to belief in coincidence of object. Just this belief is what seems crucial in the "Everest" case. The difference is that in one case the belief is false, whereas in the other it constitutes knowledge. Given that a Fregean view is committed to typical serious uses of empty names being ones which involve false belief, it would not be surprising if false beliefs are among those that bind users together into a common name-using practice. These practices resemble other social practices in this respect: it is enough for the relevant people to believe that something is so for it to be so. In the present case, it is enough, in normal circumstances, for people to believe they are party to a common practice for this to be so.

Some of the problems for the source-based account arose from the supposition that after fusion has occurred there is just a single practice, rather than two fused practices. The very notion of *fusion* needs careful handling, since it can lead to contradiction. Suppose distinct things, x and y, fuse to z at point p. We are tempted to say that to fuse is not to cease to exist, so that x and y continue to exist beyond p. But then it may seem that both must be z, and we may be driven to the contradiction that $x \neq y$ and $x = z$ and $y = z$. There are two coherent descriptions: what we call z is really two things, though occupying a region into which just one thing of its kind will normally fit; or to fuse is to cease to exist. To apply this to a real example: Woodstock Road meets Banbury Road at St Giles, which carries on to Carfax. One option is to say that there are two roads which occupy a common space through St Giles: St Giles is both (a short stretch of) Banbury Road and (a short stretch) of Woodstock Road. Another option is to say that there are three roads: fusing is ceasing to exist. There seems to me no reason to think that every case of fusion must be treated in the same way. We are free to see how best to understand the fusion of name-using practices, and thus check on the consistency of the final picture with a source-based account.

On the first option, the fusion of the name-using practices means that there are two practices occupying the same "region", geographical and linguistic. Typical users in the post-fusion phase are masters of both, and their utterances are contributions to both. This is straightforwardly consistent with there being two sources. There is some oddness in speaking of two practices after fusion, when everything goes so smoothly; and some oddness in saying that a single speech-act involving a single occurrence of a name involves two (specially related) uses; but then there is some oddness in speaking of two roads occupying the same space. The oddness derives from this option about how to understand fusions, rather than from the source view as such. It would require one to say that the previously discussed coincidence of intentions is only necessary and not sufficient for a single practice, since such intentions can be common to two fused practices; indeed, such intentions partially constitute the fusing force.

On the second option, we should say that there are three name-using practices in north-side/south-side cases. The idea that a new practice is inaugurated by the meeting on the ridge is not wholly implausible. But it is very implausible that the previous practices cease to exist, and that stay-at-home south-siders, those who had had no contact, even indirect, with those who had encountered north-siders, have unwittingly embarked on a new practice. The old uses are adequately sustained by those who were not party to the historic meeting.[11] The best development of this position seems to be to imagine the three practices as overlapping for a while in space and time, with the newest practice gradually driving out both the old ones. If this option seems best, the source-based account can adapt to it by seeing the inauguration of the new practice as precisely that: a new source, from which subsequent uses derive. The gradual ousting of the old practices arises because best practice becomes that in which the participants aim to speak of whatever the wider community, their side as well as ours, aims to speak of.

In sum, any difficulties here spring from the notion of fusion; they are not special difficulties for the source-based mode of individuating name-using practices.

---

[11] The phenomenon of deference could causes change in a practice by, as it were, "action at a distance". If an expert to whom others defer changes his practice, their practice is automatically changed without their having any direct causal connection with the new usage. I can consistently stipulate that the example under discussion is not like this.

3.5 Confusions

A given utterance may be beholden, in ways normally suitable for making it part of a name-using practice, to two sources. In some of these multiple source cases, one may be at a loss (or in dispute) about how to individuate name-using practices. I learn the name "Harry" in the presence of Jim, but, without my realizing the shift, it's Tim I mostly meet thereafter. My original "Harry"-related information comes from Jim; but the majority of my "Harry"-related information comes from Tim. To whom do I refer when I use "Harry"? The options are: Jim, Tim, both, neither, there's no fact of the matter. To rephrase: should one count my possibly idiosyncratic name-using practice as one whose name refers to Jim, to Tim, to a Jim-Tim fusion, or to nothing? Or should one say there is no fact of the matter?

If the following diagram is appropriate to these cases, it may seem that object-based individuation is at no advantage compared to a source-based approach:

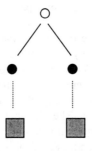

Figure 4

As there are as many sources as objects, it may seem that this case will be equally problematic for both approaches. However, the object-theorist is at an advantage when it comes to explaining the distinction between this case (*con*fusion) and fusion. The top part of Figure 4 corresponds to the top part of Figure 3, yet for Figure 3 I assumed that all theorists would wish to say that after fusion we had a fully coherent situation of mutual understanding: either a single practice, or two practices so fused as to resemble a single practice. Fusion can occur without confusion. It seems as if object-based theories can explain the difference: when two objects get into the story in this intermingled way, there is confusion; when practices relating to a single object mingle, there is fusion.

Fregean theorists will hold that confusion can occur even in the absence of an object, and so the object-based explanation just envisaged cannot be the full story. Suppose there are distinct and isolated "Fiamma"-using practices on each side of the mountain: they relate, as we feel inclined to say, to different dragons. Suppose a single intrepid trader finds a pass through the range and starts travelling back and forth. Should we say that his name-using practice belongs to the north-side practice? To the south-side practice? To both? To neither? Or that there is no fact of the matter? The same five options, and no reason of which I am aware to prefer one choice to another. So although I don't have much to say about these cases, or an explanation of what makes them differ from fusions, it does seem to me that at least the most obvious object-based explanations will not work.

3.6   Fission

Evans gives what he calls a simplified version of the "Madagascar" example, which I shall treat as a degenerate case of the fission of name-using practices:

> two babies are born, and their mothers bestow names upon them. A nurse inadvertently switches them and the error is never discovered. It will henceforth undeniably be the case that the man universally known as "Jack" is so called because a woman dubbed some other baby with the name. (1973: 11)

We could diagram a slight generalization of this story as follows:

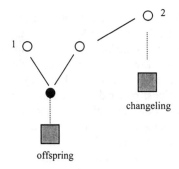

offspring

changeling

Figure 5

We envisage that some others (perhaps practical jokers on the nursing staff), represented by 1, continue to use "Jack" of the offspring, whereas the mother and various others, represented by 2, use it of the changeling, so that we have a case of fission. The mother's later uses count as uses of the name for the changeling, despite her link to her earlier practice. (In Evans's actual example, the first segment of the fission is not mentioned and perhaps does not occur: but we can see "bearer-shifting" as a degenerate case of fission.)

It indeed seems right to say that "Jack" refers to the man universally known as "Jack", in which case there is an apparent problem for a source-based account of the individuation of name-using practices: baptisms do not individuate name-using practices, for the baptismal use of "Jack" does not belong to the same practice as its subsequent use. After the switch, the mother started calling someone else's baby Jack, taking it to be her own. This use came to prevail. Unbeknownst to her, it inaugurated a new name-using practice, a distinct one from the short-lived practice inaugurated by a possibly more official baptismal ceremony. There are two names "Jack" in the story, just as there are (more than) two names "Aristotle".

Should a source-based theory count the mother's first use of "Jack" for the changeling baby as an unwitting baptism? This may seem to be inconsistent with the facts: she is surely making some kind of mistake when, on first confronting the little changeling, she utters "Jack is hungry", even if the child before her is hungry; she is certainly using the name intending to conform with her previous intentions; and she is in causal contact with her original baptism of her real child. As with fusion, it may seem more realistic to think of a gradual process, allowing that at first the mother is in error, but then at some indefinite later point, utterances of the kind just envisaged come to be true or false in virtue of how things are with the changeling rather than in virtue of how they are with her real offspring. It is not impossible to see how an object-based account might achieve this. But can a source-based account?

On her first encounter with the changeling, there is a radical failure in the mother's referential intentions. She is trying to conform her current use to her earlier use; but if an earlier use enabled her to refer to her child, a later use which does not enable this is hardly in conformity with that earlier use. We can account for the sense that the mother has made a mistake in terms of the failure of her intentions, rather than in terms of the failure of what the mother utters to be true (if the changeling is indeed hungry). What is gradual, I suggest, is not the inauguration of a new practice, but our appreciation of this. We need to be convinced that this is not just a one-off error but a systematic departure; and we could know this only after some reasonable lapse of time, during which she still takes the changeling for her own offspring. If this does not happen, we do not judge the case to be the inauguration of a new practice, and indeed it would not have been: rather, it would have been simply a mistake, and subsequent uses would have conformed to the original practice. (Or if the offspring and the changeling were frequently swapped, we would be in the "confusion" cases already discussed.) Thus whether or not something counts as the inauguration of a new practice depends in part on what the future holds; just as whether or not a poisoning is a killing. When we think that the new practice gets a hold gradually, we are confusing the metaphysics of the situation (if this is indeed a usage which is destined to become stable, then it is an inauguration of a new practice) with what we can know about it (the relevant knowledge is available only later).

This approach is supported by a comparison with empty names. To started the rumour about the dragon Fiamma by saying "In the mountains to the south of the village, there lives a dragon, Fiamma". Someone mishears this as "In the fountains near the mouth of the river, there lives a gorgon, Fiamma". Under the misapprehension, she continues what she takes to be the same tale, elaborating on how the gorgon likes to startle the villagers who come to bathe. Inadvertently, she has started a new rumour, and a new name-using practice. The name "Fiamma" has divided, or, if the original dragon-rumour dies out, we can say that the name has, as it were, switched bearers. The explanation seems to be that although the second user is trying to conform her use to that of the first, in this she radically fails; and this unifies the explanation of why we count her as starting a new rumour (about a new beast) with the explanation of why we count Jack's mother as having started a new name-using practice (about a new baby). In both cases, the event is an inauguration only if a practice descends from it; otherwise it is simply a mistaken attempt to continue an old practice.

4 Source a Disjunctive Property?

Since everyone agrees that, if a name is individuated purely syntactically, there are practices of using empty names and practices of using non-empty ones, the relevant notion of a source needs to mark out a non-disjunctive property of name-using practices. Yet I can imagine someone inspecting the concept of a source I have tried to develop and claiming that it is disjunctive.

I myself find it hard to engage with the objection, for I do not know what it is for a property (as opposed to a predicate) to be non-disjunctive in some absolute sense. What seems to me to matter is whether a property is treated disjunctively or not in some context. Thus the property of becoming a parent is treated disjunctively in English employment law: becoming a parent by becoming a mother is one thing, entitling the possessor to a decent period of paid leave; becoming a parent by becoming a father is another, entitling the possessor to a much shorter period of leave. On the other hand, in another context, effectively the same property is treated non-disjunctively by the English welfare benefits system. Being a single parent entitles you to the same benefits whether you are a single parent by being a single mother or whether you are a single parent by being a single father. So the question I can understand is whether semantic theory treats the notion of source as disjunctive or not.

What I have recommended in this paper is that it be treated as non-disjunctive. Practices using empty and non-empty names are individuated in the same way, in terms of their source. Semantic axioms will take the same form for both cases. They will not be discriminated within the theory, whose form, therefore, is restricted by these considerations (e.g. non-Meinongian model theory cannot in any straightforward way do justice to empty names). While I recognize that my reasons for making this suggestion may fall short of being conclusive, I do not think that a reasonable response is merely to claim, as if reporting on the upshot of a metaphysical inspection, that the relevant notion of source is disjunctive. What would need to be done would be to give theoretical reasons for treating it as such.[*]

References

Bell, David 1990. How 'Russellian' was Frege? *Mind* 99: 267–277.

Burge, Tyler 1974. Truth and singular terms. *Noûs* 8: 309–325.

Davies, Martin 1981. *Meaning, Quantification, Necessity: Themes in Philosophical Logic*. London: Routledge and Kegan Paul.

Diamond, Cora 1991. Frege against fuzz. In her *The Realistic Spirit: Wittgenstein, Philosophy and the Mind*, 145–77, Cambridge, Mass: The MIT Press.

Evans, Gareth 1973. The causal theory of names. *Proceedings of the Aristotelian Society: Supplementary Volume* 47: 187–208.

Evans, Gareth 1982. *The Varieties of Reference*. Oxford: Clarendon Press.

Frege, Gottlob 1979. *Posthumous Writings*. Oxford: Basil Blackwell.

Kripke, Saul 1972. Naming and Necessity. In Davidson, Donald and Gilbert Harman (eds.) *Semantics of Natural Language*, Dordrecht: Reidel.

Larson, Richard and Gabriel Segal 1995. *Knowledge of Meaning: an Introduction to Semantic Theory*. Cambridge, Mass: The MIT Press.

McDowell, John 1977. On the sense and reference of a proper name. *Mind* 86: 159–185. Reprinted in Moore, A.W. (ed.) *Meaning and Reference*, 111–136, Oxford: Oxford University Press (1993).

Russell, Bertrand 1919. *Introduction to Mathematical Philosophy*. London: George Allen and Unwin.

Sainsbury, R.M. 1999. Names, Fictional Names and 'Really'. *Proceedings of the Aristotelian Society, Supplementary Volume*, 99: 243–69.

[*] Thanks to the British Academy for contributing to my costs involved in travelling to the World Congress of Philosophy at Boston in 1998, where parts of this paper were presented; to audiences at the World Congress, at Philosophy Departments in the Universities of Lublin (the Catholic University), Texas (Austin), Mexico City (UNAM), Glasgow and St Andrews, and at the Frege Conference in Bonn in October 1998; and (in addition to those mentioned in other footnotes) to Stephen Barker, Herb Hochberg, Fraser McBride, Philip Percival, Sarah Sawyer, Yannis Stephanou and David Wiggins; and to Keith Hossack, who gave me very detailed and helpful comments on what would otherwise have been the final draft.

12

How Can '*a* exists' Be False?

EDGAR MORSCHER

1 True negative and false affirmative existentials – an old puzzle

Consider such true negative existential statements as 'A golden mountain does not exist', or 'A perpetuum mobile does not exist', or 'A round square does not exist'. Such statements have long puzzled those philosophers who adhere to the belief that to speak truly of something requires that that something exist; for otherwise, surely, nothing could be truly said of it.[1] But, then, a true negative existential statement seems to be a contradictio in adiecto. However, this conclusion is simply contrary to fact, since there are clear instances of true negative existentials – such as the very examples mentioned in the first sentence above. And if these statements are true, then the corresponding affirmative existentials (like 'A golden mountain exists', 'A perpetuum mobile exists', and 'A round square exists') must be false.

Some philosophers in the past have tried to settle the case of true negative existentials by applying an old doctrine about negative sentences in general. Its upshot is that a negative existential is not about the object whose existence it denies but rather about this existence itself. It is this existence which is denied in the sentence; the object's existence, however, exists even if the object itself does not. Such ideas should not distract us

---

[1] Or, as Frege puts it (in Frege 1892a: p. 33, English translation: p. 62): 'Whoever does not admit the name has a meaning can neither apply nor withhold the predicate'.

from our present problem, however. I therefore will stress in what follows the question of whether and how an affirmative existential sentence can be false rather than the question of whether and how a negative existential can be true.

2   The source of the troubles: NINO plus a constraint on it

The problem associated with false affirmative and true negative existentials just outlined originates from a widely held view about when and how a sentence gets a truth-value. According to this view, every declarative sentence is true or false depending on whether or not what it says is true or false *of* (applies or does not apply *to*) whatever it purports to be about. But if a sentence is about nothing, there is nothing for it to be true or false of and the sentence therefore lacks a truth-value: where there is no subject matter, there is no truth-value attaching to what is said about that purported subject matter.

This view reflects a very general principle of Fregean semantics, namely, that a reference gap in a sentence deprives the sentence of a truth-value. Taking – as Frege does – the truth-value to be the referent of a sentence, we can restate the principle even more generally: if an expression lacks a referent, then so does any complex expression of which it is a constituent; a hole in the reference pattern of a complex expression deprives it of a referent. Recently, this principle has been labelled 'NINO' by Scott Lehmann: No Input, No Output (Lehmann 1994: 310). It in turn is a consequence of the fundamental principle of semantics, the so-called principle of composition, which states that the referent of a complex expression is a function of the referents of its parts.

In this context, when we are talking about parts or constituents of a complex expression, we usually have certain qualifications in mind. For the purposes of later use of NINO we must make these qualifications explicit. First, in this context, by a constituent of an expression we usually mean a non-logical expression and not a logical one (like 'and', 'not', 'every', 'is' etc.). Second, we do not take all linguistic parts of a complex expression (like 'of', 'to' etc.) as constituents of it, but only such expressions which are in a certain sense *autonomous*. Third, even the autonomous constituents of a complex expression can be used in different ways such as in direct or indirect speech; with respect to NINO, however, we require that the expression in question be used within the complex expression neither in direct speech nor in indirect mood, but – as Frege puts it – in the *ordinary* or *customary* way.

We can now express NINO somewhat more precisely as follows:

NINO: If a non-logical expression e_1 occurs in the ordinary way as an autonomous constituent of an expression e_2 and e_1 lacks a referent, then e_2 too lacks a referent.

Its specification for sentences amounts to this:

NINO*: If a non-logical expression e occurs in the ordinary way as an autonomous constituent of a sentence s and e has no referent, then s has no truth-value.

That an expression e_1 occurs in the ordinary way as an autonomous constituent of an expression e_2, or within a sentence s, entails that e_1 is a member of the formation sequence of e_2 or s, respectively. A formation sequence for a complex expression of a language L is determined by the vocabulary and the formation rules of L. We therefore presuppose here that formation rules are available for every expression or sentence to which NINO is applied.

The troubles with false affirmative and true negative existentials, however, are not caused by NINO alone. They arise from NINO only in combination with a certain constraint which we sometimes have in mind when we are talking about the referent of an expression. In order for an expression to refer, obviously something must exist to which it refers. That an expression is referential therefore seems to mean that it refers to something existent – because otherwise (i.e., if nothing exists to which it refers) it is nonreferential. The adjective 'existent' appears to be redundant in this context, because – as one could argue – if the referent were not existent, there would be nothing to be referred to, i.e., there would be no referent at all. As soon as we allow nonexistent objects, however, the distinction becomes relevant: an expression can now be referential even without referring to an existent object, just because it refers to something nonexistent.

The constraint on NINO mentioned before can take two different forms: we can restrict NINO by denying plainly that there are nonexistent objects at all and claiming that all objects are existent, or by requiring of every referent of an expression that it exist (without thereby denying that there are nonexistent objects). In both cases I will speak for short of 'the constraint on NINO'.

The question raised in the introduction can now be stated more precisely: Given NINO plus the constraint on it, how can an affirmative existential sentence be false, or a negative existential sentence be true?

Clearly, to overcome the difficulties with false affirmative and true negative existentials occasioned by NINO plus the constraint on it, an existent referent for their subject terms, i.e. something existent for such sentences to be about, must be made available.

3   A classical solution to the puzzle

A *classical* solution to this puzzle was offered by Bernard Bolzano. According to his analysis, in an existential statement of the form 'An A exists' or 'A's exist' we do not attribute – contrary to appearances – a property (viz. existence) to A; rather, we attribute another property (viz. nonemptiness) to the idea-in-itself *of A* or (better) to the idea-in-itself expressed by the words which stand in place of the letter 'A'.[2]

For the sake of convenience, let us introduce the following notation: in analogy to the common practice of putting an expression within quotation marks when we speak about the expression itself, we will use brackets when we want to speak about an expression's sense. By '[A]' we therefore denote the sense of 'A' or whatever is expressed by 'A', e.g. – in Bolzano's case – an idea-in-itself. Our notational convention could therefore be stated as an identity scheme of the form

$$[A] = \text{the sense of } X,$$

where in the place of 'A' we have an arbitrary well-formed expression and in the place of 'X' we have any name of this expression.

Using this notation, Bolzano's view can be expressed in the following way: the property employed in existential statements of the form 'An A exists' is nonemptiness, and it is attributed not to A itself but to [A]. 'An A exists' means just that [A] is nonempty:

An A exists $\leftrightarrow$ [A] is not empty

This is Bolzano's analysis of existential statements. Ignoring the psychological overtones, Kant's analysis in *The One Possible Basis for a Demonstration of the Existence of God* coincides with Bolzano's.[3] Bolzano himself failed completely to notice this fundamental agreement with Kant, whereas Husserl saw it quite clearly (Husserl 1904: 104, note 1).

---

[2] Bolzano 1837, vol.II: pp. 52–54 (§137). In the present context I will ignore Bolzano's distinction between existential sentences and there-is-sentences. According to Bolzano there are objects which do not exist, e.g. numbers and propositions. For Bolzano 'to exist' means the same as or is at least coextensive with 'to be the cause of something'. If we do not take 'to exist' in this narrow metaphysical sense but in the general sense in which it is customarily used in logic, it coincides with Bolzano's usage of 'there is'. Bolzano's *nonexistent objects* exist and are existent in the usual sense of these words and are therefore not to be confused with the nonexistent objects as mentioned in discussing the constraint on NINO.

[3] Kant 1763, Reprint 1912: p. 72 (English translation: p. 57). I have compared Bolzano's and Kant's analyses in my dissertation (Morscher 1969: pp. 243–250, Morscher 1972: pp. 166–169), and in several subsequent articles (e.g. Morscher 1985/86).

Kant's and Bolzano's analysis of existential sentences provides more than just the truth-conditions for such sentences; it reveals also their basic logical structure. On the other hand, this analysis, on pain of circularity, is not a *definition* of 'existence' because Bolzano defines 'emptiness' explicitly in terms of 'existence':

[*A*] is empty :↔ it is not the case that there exists an *x* such that *x* is an object of [*A*]

4 Frege's solution to the puzzle

The Bolzano-Kant analysis of existential sentences concords with that of Frege. Indeed, they have a very important feature in common: according to Frege, in an existential sentence of the type 'An *A* exists' or '*A*'s exist' we state something not of *A* itself, but rather of a concept; we attribute a property not to *A*, but to a concept associated with *A*. As Frege puts it:

> I have called existence a property of a concept. How I mean this to be taken is best made clear by an example. In the sentence 'there is at least one square root of 4,' we are saying something, not about (say) the definite number 2, nor about –2, but about a concept, *square root of 4*; viz. that it is not empty.[4]

In later writings, Frege explains the same point by saying that an existential sentence states that a first-level concept falls *within* a second-level concept.[5]

5 What has Frege's solution in common with the classical solution?

To guarantee the existence of a subject for all existential sentences – including false affirmative and true negative existential sentences – neither Bolzano nor Frege takes *A* itself to be the subject of sentences of the form 'An *A* exists' or 'An *A* does not exist'. They rather take something else as the subject of such a sentence, something whose existence is moreover guaranteed from the outset and is completely independent of the existence of the *A*'s themselves. In Bolzano's case this is the idea-in-itself [*A*] and in Frege's case it is the corresponding concept. This is the way Bolzano and Frege acknowledge NINO in their analyses of existential sentences.

---

[4] Frege 1892b: p. 199 (English translation: pp. 48–49); cf. also e.g. Frege 1884: p. 65 (English translation: p. 65e), Frege 1969: p. 61, p. 74, pp. 116–117, p. 269 (English translation: p. 54, p. 67, p. 107, pp. 249–250).
[5] Frege 1903: p. 373, Frege 1969: p. 269 (English translation: pp. 249–250).

Nevertheless, it is inappropriate when Frege – and others following him – say that existence is a property of a concept. (Frege himself felt this inappropriateness and explained in the passage quoted above what he meant by his claim.) For it is not existence which we attribute to a concept in an existential sentence – the concept's existence is presupposed in such a sentence and guaranteed from the start; rather, it is another property, viz. nonemptiness, which we attribute to a concept in an existential sentence. Instead of saying that existence is a second-level property or a property of a concept, we should rather say: when we assert an existential sentence of the form 'An *A* exists' or '*A*'s exist' we do not attribute a property called 'existence' to *A*, but rather another property – viz. nonemptiness – to the corresponding concept. This concept itself, however, exists in any event, independently of whether or not an *A* exists.

6 How do Frege's and the classical solution differ from one another?

There are at least two points of disagreement between the classical and the Fregean account of existential sentences:

(i) Frege's analysis works only for 'existence' as applied to general names or concept-words which are *unsaturated* (i.e. incomplete or predicative),[6] and not as applied to singular names;

and

(ii) a Fregean concept is not the sense but the referent of a concept-word or predicate.[7]

According to Frege, therefore, (i) the subject matter of an existential sentence (i.e., what an existential sentence is about) must be incomplete or unsaturated (and, consequently, it cannot be an object – for objects, for Frege, are denoted by singular terms), and (ii) this subject matter must be the referent, not the sense, of a linguistic expression. Both claims stand in clear opposition to a classical solution à la Bolzano. It is a peculiar feature of Frege's theory of sense and reference that a concept is not the sense but the referent of a predicate. This feature distinguishes it from theories like

---

[6] Frege 1892b: p. 193, pp. 197–198, pp. 200–201 (English translation: p. 43, pp. 46–47, p. 50), Frege 1969: p. 99, p. 109, p. 129, p. 131, p. 192, p. 210, p. 212, p. 231, p. 246, p. 262 (English translation: p. 90, p. 99, pp. 119–120, p. 177, p. 193, p. 195, p. 214, p. 228, p. 243).

[7] Frege 1892b: p. 193, p. 198 (English translation: p. 43, p. 48), Frege 1969: p. 128, p. 135, p. 192, p. 210, p. 212, p. 246, p. 262 (English translation: p. 118, p. 124, p. 177, p. 193, p. 195, p. 228, p. 243).

those of Bolzano and Husserl. In a letter to Husserl, Frege uses a well-known scheme which makes this difference clear.[8]

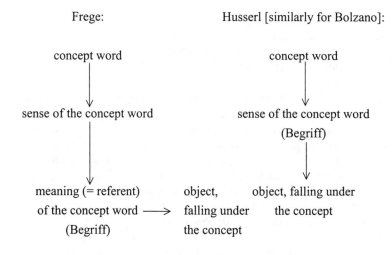

Frege versus the classical picture

Frege's solution has the benefit that it is solely a matter of the customary referents of a language as to which truth-value – i.e. which referent – an existential statement of the language has, and it does not depend on properties of the senses of any of the expressions used in this language. On the other hand, the classical solution has the benefit of being more general than Frege's because it also covers singular existential sentences, i.e. sentences of the form '*a* exists' where in the place of '*a*' we have a singular term (viz. a proper name or a definite description). How, then, are we to treat such singular existential sentences within a Fregean framework?

---

[8] Frege 1976: pp. 96–98 (English translation: p. 63). In the translation the ambiguity of 'Begriff', which is important for this comparison, disappears because the word 'Begriff' is translated first into 'concept' and then into 'sense'. I have therefore left the two occurrences of the word 'Begriff' here untranslated. Two further remarks are in order here: In this context, Frege is not concerned with the problem of existence, and he does not mention – either here or anywhere else – Bolzano's name.

7 Singular existential sentences within a Fregean framework

Let '*a* exists' be a simple singular existential sentence of everyday language containing a singular term (i.e. a proper name or a definite description) '*a*'. We usually take such a sentence to be true or false depending on whether '*a*' does or does not refer to an existent. If we follow Frege, the following dilemma arises:

(i) Subscribing to NINO, as Frege does, a reference gap in a sentence must deprive the sentence of its truth-value. Applying this principle directly to *everyday language,* sentences of the form '*a* exists' would turn out *truth-valueless* instead of false whenever nothing exists to which '*a*' refers.

(ii) To guarantee a truth-value to every sentence of a *scientific language*, for every singular term in that language something must exist to which it refers.[9] As soon as we apply this requirement unrestrictedly to such a language, however, all its simple singular existential sentences are in danger of turning not only into truths, but into *logical truths*.[10]

In this context the constraint on NINO mentioned in section 2 becomes relevant again, and we can easily be led astray if we ignore it. The following terminological distinction concerning the referents of singular terms should make quite clear whether or not we subscribe to the constraint on NINO: I will call a singular term 'referential' iff there is something (be it existent or nonexistent) to which it refers, and otherwise (i.e., iff there is nothing at all – not even a nonexistent object – to which it refers) 'irreferential' (or 'nonreferring'). If a singular term refers to something existent, I will call it a 'denoting singular term', and otherwise (i.e., iff it does not refer to an existent) 'nondenoting' or 'empty'. A nondenoting singular term therefore either does not refer to anything at all (i.e., it is irreferential), or it refers to a nonexistent object. As a result, a singular term can fall within one of three categories: (i) it does not refer to anything at all; (ii) it refers to a nonexistent object; (iii) it refers to an existent object. In the case of (i), it is irreferential, and in the case of (iii), it is denoting. A singular term is referential iff it falls within category (ii) or (iii), and it is nondenoting iff it falls within category (i) or (ii).

---

[9] Frege 1892a: p. 33, pp. 41–42 (English translation: p. 63, p. 70), Frege 1969: p. 135, pp. 193–194, p. 205, p. 210, p. 243 (English translation: p. 124, p. 178, p. 188, p. 194, p. 225).

[10] Even if an existent object is assigned to every singular term as its referent, not all simple affirmative singular existentials turn automatically into true or logically true sentences. According to a translation offered by Carnap (Carnap 1946: p. 37), an affirmative singular existential sentence can still turn out false while the corresponding negative existential turns out true because the referent of the singular term is identical with the arbitrarily chosen object a*.

8 Beyond Frege

It is often said that an everyday language sentence like '*a* exists' hides its logical structure, a structure that is revealed by translating the sentence into first order predicate logic with identity (PL1=). We therefore look for a formula of PL1= which is a translation of, or at least can represent, the sentence '*a* exists' and which is true under at least one interpretation, not true under every interpretation, false under at least one interpretation and hopefully true or false under every interpretation. The task therefore is to find an expression *e* which *says* that *a* exists and fulfils the following conditions thus satisfying NINO:

(1) *e* is well-formed in PL1=

(2) *e* is sometimes true (i.e. true under at least one interpretation)

(3) *e* is not always true (i.e. not true under every interpretation)

(4) *e* is sometimes false (i.e. false under at least one interpretation)

(5) *e* is always true or false (i.e. under every interpretation true or false)

These conditions on *e* obviously are not logically independent of one another – e.g., clause (3) follows from (4). The way they are presented here is simply for the purpose of separating the questions to be dealt with in a more or less natural order.

The task of finding an expression *e*, as described by the clauses (1)–(5), is of interest only if (i) we allow nondenoting singular terms to occur in our language and (ii) nevertheless attribute truth-values to all or at least to some sentences containing them. This means that we dispense either with NINO itself or at least with the constraint on NINO. With these conditions, however, the framework of Frege's semantics is left behind;[11] according to

---

[11] That Frege would reject our project from the start becomes quite clear in his 'Dialogue with Pünjer on Existence', where he raises, more or less explicitly, the question whether '*a* exists' can be false and gives a negative answer; cf. Frege 1969: p. 70, p. 73 (English translation: p. 62: 'Neither in "*A* is identical with itself" nor in "*A* exists" does one learn anything new about *A*. Neither statement can be denied. In either you can put what you like for *A*, and it still remains true'; pp. 65–66: 'If you want to assign a content to the verb "to be", so that the sentence "*A* is" is not pleonastic and self-evident, you will have to allow circumstances under which the negation of "*A* is" is possible; that is to say, that there are subjects of which being must be denied. But in that case the concept "being" will no longer be suitable for providing a general explanation of "there are" under which "there are *B*'s" means the same as "something that has being falls under the concept *B*"').

Frege, nondenoting terms and in particular nondenoting singular terms are allowed to occur only in everyday language and the language of poetry[12] – contrary to (i); and as soon as such a term occurs in the ordinary way in a sentence, this very sentence, be it atomic or complex, must lack a truth-value[13] – contrary to (ii).

The search for an expression of the sort described is therefore a non-Fregean task, at least non-Fregean *vis à vis* an account of reasoning in everyday (as opposed to scientific) language. Nevertheless, my aim is to solve this problem in the spirit of Frege.

9 Is there a formula of PL1= which *says* that *a* exists, and if so, which formula is it?

In current philosophical logic, most would offer – without a moment's hesitation – the formula '$\exists x(x = a)$' as expressing: *a* exists. At the outset of modern logic, this was far from clear to its founders – Frege, Russell and others. At many places in their writings, Frege and Russell claim that sentences of the form '*a* exists', where '*a*' stands for a genuine proper name, are not well-formed and therefore senseless. This is because 'exists' requires to be associated with an unsaturated expression like a concept-word (Frege), a propositional function (qua expression) (Russell) or a predicate to yield a sentence, whereas a proper name is itself already saturated and therefore not suited to saturate the expression 'exists'. Combinations of words like 'Julius Caesar exists' (or 'There is Julius Caesar'), 'Africa exists' (or 'There is Africa'), and '*a* exists' (where '*a*' is a genuine singular term) are – according to Frege and apparently Russell – not well-formed and therefore senseless, and there is no formula of PL1= which can be their counterpart.[14] Literally translated into PL1=, '*a* exists' would come out as '$\exists a$', which obviously is not a well-formed expression of PL1= as every student of logic knows. (In the thirties Rudolf Carnap still claimed in his famous paper 'The Elimination of Metaphysics Through Logical Analysis of Language' that this is the very reason why sentences like 'God exists' or Descartes' 'Cogito *ergo* sum' are mere nonsense; cf. Carnap 1931: 234, English translation: 74).

---

[12] Frege 1892a: p. 33 (English translation: p. 63), Frege 1969: pp. 133–134, pp. 141–142, pp. 193–194, p. 205, p. 211, p. 243, p. 250 (English translation: p. 122, pp. 129–130, pp. 178–179, pp. 188–189, p. 194, p. 225, p. 232).

[13] Frege 1892a: p. 32 (English translation: p. 62), Frege 1969: pp. 141–142, p. 211 (English translation: pp. 129–130, p. 194).

[14] Frege 1892b: pp. 200–201 (English translation: p. 50), Frege 1903: p. 373; Russell 1919: pp. 164–165; cf. also Whitehead & Russell 1910, vol.I: p. 175.

Frege, however, hastens to add that this does not hold for sentences like 'A man whose name is "Julius Caesar" exists' (or 'There is a man whose name is "Julius Caesar"') and 'Something [which is] called "Africa" exists' (or 'There is something [which is] called "Africa"'). His reason was as follows: we do not have here a proper name ('Julius Caesar' or 'Africa', respectively) alone, but rather a predicate or concept-word ('a man whose name is "Julius Caesar"' or 'something [which is] called "Africa"') of which the proper name 'Julius Caesar' or 'Africa', respectively – or, to be more accurate: a metalinguistic name of this proper name – is only a part. This predicate is capable, however, of saturating the word 'exists'.[15]

But does 'Something [which is] called "*a*" exists' *say* that *a* exists? Even if it did, it certainly is not a formula of PL1= as required by condition (1) in our list of conditions above, nor is its symbolic representation '$\lor o(o$ is called "*a*")' or '$\lor o($"*a*" refers to [denotes] $o)$'. At best this is a formula of the metalanguage of PL1=, but certainly not of PL1= itself.[16]

10 What's wrong with '$\exists x(x = a)$'?

As far as I know, Frege and Russell nowhere discussed whether '$\exists x(x = a)$' should be considered as the PL1= counterpart of the everyday language sentence '*a* exists'.[17] To my knowledge, Hintikka was the first who explicitly took '$\exists x(x = a)$' as the formal counterpart of '*a* exists'.[18] Does this formula *say* that *a* exists? Whatever the answer to that question, it is easier to decide whether '$\exists x(x = a)$' has the same truth-conditions as '*a* exists'. Ob-

---

[15] Frege 1892b: p. 200 (English translation: p. 50), Frege 1969: p. 119 (English translation: p. 109).

[16] Therefore, I used '*o*' (instead of '*x*') as an individual variable and '$\lor o$' (instead of '$\exists x$') as existential quantifier (as opposed to the corresponding symbols of PL1= itself) in order to indicate that these are not expressions of PL1= but of its metalanguage.

[17] It is very surprising that Frege did not offer some such reading of '*a* exists' given what he says in his 'Dialogue with Pünjer on Existence' where he states 'that instead of "exists" one can also say "is identical with itself"' (Frege 1969: pp. 69–70, English translation: p. 62). Also in other contexts – where existence is not under discussion – Frege uses examples of the kind 'no other than *a*' (i.e. ' = *a*'), like 'no other than Venus' and 'no other than Saturn'; cf. Frege 1892b: p. 294 (English translation: p. 44), Frege 1969: pp. 101–102 (English translation: pp. 92–93).

[18] See Hintikka 1959: pp. 133–134; cf. also Hintikka 1966: pp. 63–64 and pp. 70–71. But it was Lambert who showed first that Hintikka's proposal holds for any kind of free logic that contains Restricted Specification or its dual Restricted Particularization, Substitutivity of Identity and the formal counterpart of the principle that everything exists; cf. e.g. Lambert 1967. And later Meyer, Bencivenga and Lambert showed that an existence predicate was indefinable in at least positive free logic unless identity is present; cf. Meyer & Bencivenga & Lambert 1982.

viously, '$\exists x(x = a)$' *can be* true, i.e., it is true under some interpretations. Unfortunately, however, it is always true, i.e. true under all interpretations according to the *standard* semantics of PL1=. The formula in question therefore fulfils conditions (1) and (2), but not condition (3) of our list of requirements. In order to have a chance of fulfilling condition (3) we need a semantics deviating from standard semantics of PL1= – like that of free logic, a logic allowing singular terms that refer to no existent object. When we allow a nondenoting singular term (i.e. a singular term which does not refer to an existent object) in the place of 'a', '$\exists x(x = a)$' can turn out to be false if the existential quantifier '$\exists x$' has existential force. Therefore, there are interpretations under which '$\exists x(x = a)$' is false in this case. But this route leads to trouble *vis à vis* NINO – at least when we combine it with the constraint. Several solutions have been proposed by free logicians in order to avoid these problems.

11 Bas van Fraassen's solution

In his 1966 paper 'Singular Terms, Truth-Value Gaps, and Free Logic', Bas van Fraassen concludes that 'a exists' is appropriately expressed as '$\exists x(x = a)$'. It seems fair to suppose that by an *appropriate* expression of 'a exists' he meant a formula fulfilling all or at least some of our conditions (1)–(5). This is what he says: 'Given only this, it already follows that "t exists" is appropriately expressed as "$(\exists y)(y = t)$"' (van Fraassen 1966: 489).

Given only what? That 'we cannot plausibly reject that "$t = t'$" is false when t has a referent and t' does not' (van Fraassen 1966: 488), a principle he claims Karel Lambert convinced him of. (He also notes that 'this is only the least' of his debts to Karel Lambert.)

Certainly, if one agrees with van Fraassen's and Lambert's claim that '$b = a$' is false when 'b' has a referent and 'a' does not, then it is evident that van Fraassen's definiens has not only true but also false interpretations. Simply let 'a' be an irreferential singular term like 'Santa Claus' or 'the noncircular circle'; then '$b = a$' is false whatever referential term we choose for 'b', and therefore '$\neg\exists x(x = a)$' must be true. Given 'only' what van Fraassen takes to be obvious, it is clear that '$\exists x(x = a)$' is false under some interpretations and thus fulfils the important condition (4) in the list above. What van Fraassen takes to be obvious, however, constitutes a blatant violation of NINO.

But is it really the case that 'we cannot plausibly reject' the van Fraassen-Lambert principle? In an early paper, even exploiting van Fraassen's technique of supervaluations, Brian Skyrms *did* reject it, as we will see in a moment. But before we go into this we should make sure of the following: even if there are good reasons for rejecting the van Fraassen-Lambert position concerning the truth-value of identity sentences containing exactly one irreferential singular term, that would not amount automatically to rejecting also its consequence, i.e., that '*a* exists' is appropriately expressed as '$\exists x(x = a)$'. That '$\exists x(x = a)$' is logically equivalent to '*a* exists' or 'E!*a*' does not depend on the van Fraassen-Lambert principle to which van Fraassen appeals in its defence (cf. Lambert 1967).

12 The Skyrms solution

In his 1968 paper entitled 'Supervaluations: Identity, Existence, and Individual Concepts', Brian Skyrms argued that van Fraassen's decision for assigning or not assigning truth-values to identity sentences with irreferential singular terms is counterintuitive in many respects. He therefore concluded:

> Given *all* [my italics: E.M.] this, the question arises of how to say that *a* exists. '$(\exists x)(x = a)$' does not say it; for although it is true just when '*a* exists' is true, it is neuter when '*a* exists' is false (i.e., when '*a* does not exist' is true). The answer is that '"$(\exists x)(x = a)$" is true' says that *a* exists; for it is false to say that a sentence is true when it isn't. Thus, statements of existence involve a jump into the metalanguage (Skyrms 1968: 481).

Important as Skyrms' criticism of van Fraassen may be, his proposal to treat singular existence statements about a purported *object a* as '"$\exists x(x = a)$"' is true' is itself very counterintuitive. It certainly does not *say* that *a* exists; rather what it says is only that a certain sentence is true.

Having specified the task as looking for an expression *e* which is well-formed within PL1=, Skyrms' candidate '"$\exists x(x = a)$"' is true' fails because it is in the metalanguage of PL1=. If we were to allow *e* to be an expression of the metalanguage of PL1=, another expression would at least be closer to the meaning of '*a* exists', viz. 'There exists something called "*a*"' or 'There exists something denoted by "*a*"'. Recall that a similar proposal was made by Frege himself when he claimed that 'Julius Caesar exists' or 'Africa exists' is senseless whereas 'There exists a man whose name is "Julius Caesar"' or 'There exists something called "Africa"' is not.

13 Scott Lehmann's solution

Scott Lehmann recently has declared himself satisfied neither with van Fraassen's solution nor with that of Skyrms. According to him 'supervaluational semantics – promises more than it can deliver' (Lehmann 1994: 310). He tries to develop a 'Strict Fregean Free Logic' (SFFL) which allows of nonreferring singular terms (and is therefore a *free* logic), but also respects NINO (and therefore purports to be strictly Fregean). For what follows we have to keep in mind that in Lehmann's system identities are symbolized as $\ulcorner = st\urcorner$ and existentials as $\ulcorner\exists\upsilon F\urcorner$, and each term and formula is regarded as having the form $\ulcorner\phi\sigma_1...\sigma_k\urcorner$ (Lehmann 1994: 312), where in $\ulcorner\exists\upsilon F\urcorner$, $\phi = $ '$\exists$' and $\ulcorner\sigma_1...\sigma_k\urcorner = \sigma_1 = \ulcorner\upsilon F\urcorner$ (Lehmann 1994: 313). In Lehmann's SFFL, 'identities in which at least one term does not refer' do not get a truth-value. 'But existentials $\ulcorner\exists\upsilon F\urcorner$ always have a truth-value, since $\ulcorner\upsilon F\urcorner$ always describes a truth-valued function, albeit in some cases one whose domain is empty' (Lehmann 1994: 313). He therefore concludes:

> Since under interpretation and assignment, the input to an existential quantifier is always a truth-valued function (though perhaps one whose domain is empty), existentials always get a truth-value in SFFL; e.g., $\ulcorner\exists\upsilon R\upsilon t\urcorner$ is false if υ is empty or t does not refer. Since $\ulcorner\exists\upsilon = \upsilon t\urcorner$ is true iff t refers, $\ulcorner\exists\upsilon = \upsilon t\urcorner$ may be read as $\ulcorner t$ exists$\urcorner$ [note: 'Strictly, $\ulcorner r(t)$ exists$\urcorner$, where $r(t)$ is the reading of t'], taking υ to represent what there is (according to I) (Lehmann 1994: 327).

So Lehmann does offer a formula of PL1= as a reading for 'a exists'. This formula indeed has a truth-value under every interpretation, and is false under some interpretations. So it fulfils all of the conditions (1)–(5). Is this finally the solution to the initial puzzle? No, because Lehmann's solution itself violates NINO: every expression $\ulcorner\upsilon F\urcorner$ to which an existential quantifier is attached will get a value (viz. a truth-valued function) within his semantics. Here, F can be an arbitrary open formula or concept-word, as Frege calls it. In such an open formula F, a singular term can occur not only in a direct manner but also *customarily* or *in the ordinary way* as a constituent: 'a proper name can never be a predicative expression, though it can be part of one' (Frege 1892b: 200, English translation: 50).[19] But such an open formula F containing the singular term 'a', as e.g. '$x = a$', does not get a value according to either Frege, Lehmann, or NINO, if 'a' lacks a referent. Lehmann's semantics, however, assigns a value to $\ulcorner xF\urcorner$ and consequently to $\ulcorner\exists xF\urcorner$ even in this case – which violates NINO. Because Lehmann's semantics does not satisfy NINO, it does not deserve the name '*Strict* Fregean Free Logic'; it is at best a '*Weak* Fregean Free Logic'. Lehmann himself seems to have recognized this, because in a footnote he says: 'SFFL does not *completely* embody Frege's functional view of language' (Lehmann 1994: 335, note 6; *italics* by Lehmann himself).

---

[19] Cf. also Frege 1969: p. 209, English translation: p. 192: 'We may add to this the fact that in this [i.e. unsaturated] part of the sentence too there may occur proper names, where it does matter that they should have a meaning.' Frege gives many examples of such open formulas or concept-words which contain singular terms or proper names – e.g. 'no other than Venus' (Frege 1892b: p. 194, English translation: p. 44), 'no other than Saturn' (Frege 1969: p. 101, English translation: p. 92), or 'is smaller than 0' (Frege 1892a: p. 42, English translation: p.

14 A solution with nonexistent objects[20]

How can one guarantee a referent for every singular term without turning every singular existential sentence "automatically" into a truth and thereby into a logical truth? To raise the same question in a different way: how can one allow nondenoting singular terms and, nevertheless, assign a referent to all singular terms, including the nondenoting ones? The obvious answer is: by introducing nonexistent objects and allowing them to be assigned to singular terms. A singular term to which such a nonexistent object is assigned is referential, but it is still – according to our definition – a nondenoting singular term.

As soon as we adopt a semantics with an inner domain of existent objects and an outer domain of nonexistent objects, assign an element of our domain, i.e. an existent or nonexistent object, to every singular term of our language, we have reached our goal. As long as our quantifiers have existential import and '$\forall x$' and '$\exists x$' are read 'for every existent thing x' and 'for at least one existent thing x', respectively, the formula '$\exists x(x = a)$' fulfils all our requirements: (1) it is well-formed in PL1=, (2) true under at least one interpretation, (3) not true under every interpretation, (4) even false under some interpretations, and (5) under every interpretation true or false, thereby completely satisfying NINO. (The solution consists in merely giving up the constraint on NINO.) What else do we need?

The weakness of this solution is that it requires us to accept nonexistent objects. Why should we – merely for the purpose of being able to say appropriately of a certain object that it does or does not exist – accept or even be committed to nonexistent objects? Why, e.g., should an astronomer who wants to deny or affirm the existence of a certain planet be committed to the view that there are nonexistent objects? I think that it would be rather hard to explain this to a person with a minimal sense of reality.

15 The classical solution with *senses*

According to the classical view, all existential sentences, including singular ones, are about senses. In an existential sentence of the form 'An *A* exists' or '*a* exists', respectively, the general term standing in the place of '*A*' and the singular term standing in the place of '*a*', respectively, does not refer to

---

71), or 'is larger than Mars' (Frege 1969: p. 210, English translation: p. 193), or ' > 0' (Frege 1969: p. 212, English translation: p. 193).

[20] Due to my aversion to nonexistent objects, I had not included this solution in the original presentation of my paper at the Frege conference in Bonn. Wolfgang Spohn brought it up in the discussion of my paper.

its usual referent but takes as its referent what normally is its sense and states of it that it is nonempty. The classical view also fulfils all of our conditions, including NINO. A modern version of this solution – with its scope being restricted to singular existential sentences – was developed by Alonzo Church.[21]

But are senses any better than nonexistent objects? They are of a certain sort of abstract objects and are – if not nonexistent themselves – at least very close to nonexistent objects. Why should a scientist accept that he or she is talking about abstract semantic objects like senses when affirming or denying the existence of a certain object like a planet? Why should this be more reasonable than the acceptance of nonexistent objects in general?

The only argument in favour of the classical view might be that whoever uses a language has at least to accept the conceptual framework of this language and is ontologically committed to the existence of the entities which are part of this framework – including senses. One might doubt whether this argument can convince a hard-line realist. This ontological doubt parallels a methodological scruple: the only concern of science – not only in Frege's view – is truth, and the truth-value of a sentence, i.e. its referent, should depend only on the referents of its parts. A sentence of a language used in science, therefore, should – for this methodological reason at least – not be about senses or take senses to be the referents of some of its parts. In doing so, it evades the principle mentioned before.

Moreover, this solution has to face two additional problems:

(i) On this view, every existential sentence (or at least every singular existential sentence) is a sentence *about* a sense. What is usually taken to give the truth-conditions of an existential sentence in the metalanguage is now the very existential sentence itself.

(ii) It is therefore no longer clear that this *solution* really fulfils condition (1) which requires of our candidate that it be a well-formed formula of PL1=. Taking this solution seriously would mean that every formula of the form '$\exists x A$' or at least every formula of the form '$\exists x(x = a)$' hides the logical structure of the *real* existential sentences of which our existential formulas of PL1= are mere *disguises*.

---

[21] Church 1974: pp. 142–143 and p. 154 (note 10). In contrast to the classical view, Church does not use senses or intensions for the interpretation of the quantifiers. His axioms for elementary logic (propositional calculus plus quantification theory) are not intensional in character and can be used also within a standard extensional predicate logic. The existential quantifier and formulas constructed by means of it remain therefore untouched by Church's analysis; cf. Church 1974: p. 139.

16 Comparison and evaluation of the proposed solutions

I suppose it is clear already that my favourite solution is the classical one with senses. I am inclined to prefer this solution because it satisfies NINO completely, it does not require nonexistent objects and it does not turn existential sentences into sentences about items of a certain language.

But these reasons for preferring the classical solution with senses could be countered in different ways. In particular it could be objected that senses, after all, are – if not nonexistent objects by themselves – at least not much better off than these. We might question their ontological status and their identity criteria in the same way as we have criticized nonexistent objects. In answering this question I have to make clear that, when I speak of the classical solution with senses, I do not mean that the classical theory of senses along the lines provided by Bolzano is satisfactory. It is only the way he and others make use of senses for solving our puzzle which I admit, not the classical view of senses itself. The classical senses have to be replaced by whatever senses should correctly be taken to be – functions from possible worlds to sets of denotations or appropriate extensions or whatever we today take to be suitable. This, however, is another story.

Another objection could be[22] that even the solution with senses turns existential sentences into metalinguistic sentences about items of a certain language because – according to this view – they are sentences about the sense of a linguistic expression.

To this objection my answer is as follows: We can and usually do refer to senses via their linguistic expressions. It is usually the most convenient way to name a linguistic expression by using its quotation mark name – e.g. '*A*' – and to use this quotation mark name to name the sense of the respective expression – viz. 'the sense of the expression "*A*"'.[23] This, however, is not the only way of referring to senses. We can talk about senses even without reference to language.

In addition, we have to explain what it means for a general sense and for a singular sense (i.e. for the sense of a general term or predicate and for the sense of a singular term) to be empty: a general sense is empty iff the class it determines is empty, and a singular sense is empty iff it does not determine anything (or anything existent) at all.[24]

---

[22] This objection was brought up in the discussion of my paper during the Frege conference in Bonn by Gottfried Gabriel.

[23] As Frege does in Frege 1892a: p. 28 (English translation: p. 59).

[24] Rainer Stuhlmann-Laeisz pointed out during the Frege conference in Bonn that it is not the same thing for an object to *fall* under an individual concept or to *fall* under a general concept.

The main problem with this solution, however, remains that in accepting it, even if we may still apply a strictly regimented language, we certainly leave the area of a puritanical scientific language which allows only customary referents for their expressions.

As the second best solution I would take one which respects the puritanical feature of our scientific language but compromises with NINO by giving up NINO itself in its strict form and adheres only to a weaker version. This means that we require that the immediate parts or constituents of a sentence must have referents without requiring that also *all* of their parts must have referents;[25] for a sentence of the form '$\exists x(x = a)$' to have a truth-value, the weakened form of NINO requires that '$x = a$' has a referent, but this can be the case without 'a' having a referent (as NINO in its strict form would require).

By specifying what we take to be an autonomous constituent of a sentence we can get different versions of NINO thereby providing another solution of our puzzle.[26]

17 The moral to be drawn

The comparison and evaluation of the proposed solutions to our puzzle lead to a simple conclusion: we must give up or at least weaken one or other of our requirements. As soon as we try to fulfil all of them we get into conflict with certain ontological intuitions and/or methodological goals, rules or values. Whichever solution we choose we will have to pay a price, and it will depend in each case on the purpose we are pursuing which price we are willing to pay and which price it is reasonable to pay. In short, what is true for everyday life holds also for logic and semantics: nothing comes free.[*]

---

[25] In a similar way we could weaken NINO by restricting its scope to atomic sentences and thus exempting complex sentences.

[26] This solution was brought up by Tyler Burge at the Frege conference in Bonn. Lehmann's solution is in fact such a compromise but he does not defend this compromise by differentiating various versions of NINO.

[*] For his generous advice in writing this paper and for numerous valuable improvements to the present version I am deeply indebted to Karel Lambert. I would like to thank also Gary Bell, Johannes Brandl, Alexander Hieke, Otto Neumaier, Peter Simons and Barry Smith for their support in preparing the paper for publication.

References

Bolzano, B. 1837. *Wissenschaftslehre*. 4 vols. Sulzbach: Seidel. (2nd ed. Leipzig: Meiner, 1929–31; Reprint Aalen: Scientia, 1981. English translation by R. George as *Theory of Science*. Berkeley and Los Angeles: University of California Press, 1972; another translation, by B. Terrell, ed. J. Berg. Dordrecht and Boston: Reidel, 1973.)

Carnap, R. 1931. Überwindung der Metaphysik durch logische Analyse der Sprache. *Erkenntnis* 2: 219–41. (English translation by A. Pap as 'The Elimination of Metaphysics Through Logical Analysis of Language'. *Logical Positivism*, ed. A. J. Ayer, 60–81. New York: The Free Press, 1959.)

Carnap, R. 1947. *Meaning and Necessity. A Study in Semantics and Modal Logic*. Chicago: The University of Chicago Press. (2 nd ed. 1956, Reprint 1975.)

Church, A. 1974. Outline of a Revised Formulation of the Logic of Sense and Denotation (Part II). *Noûs* 8: 135–56.

Frege, G. 1884. *Die Grundlagen der Arithmetik. Eine logisch-mathematische Untersuchung über den Begriff der Zahl*. Breslau: Koebner. (Reprints Breslau: Marcus, 1934, Darmstadt: Wissenschaftliche Buchgesellschaft, 1961, Hildesheim: Olms, 1961, and Hamburg: Meiner, 1986. English translation by L. J. Austin as *The Foundations of Arithmetic. A logico-mathematical Enquiry into the Concept of Number*. Oxford: Blackwell, 1950; 2nd ed. 1953, Reprint 1989.)

Frege, G. 1892a. Über Sinn und Bedeutung. *Zeitschrift für Philosophie und philosophische Kritik* N.F. 100: 25–50. (Reprint in Frege 1967: 143–62. English translation in Frege 1952: 56–78.)

Frege, G. 1892b. Über Begriff und Gegenstand. *Vierteljahrsschrift für wissenschaftliche Philosophie* 16: 192–205. (Reprint in Frege 1967: 167–78. English translation in Frege 1952: 42–55.)

Frege, G. 1903. Über die Grundlagen der Geometrie II. *Jahresbericht der Deutschen Mathematiker-Vereinigung* 12: 368–75. (Reprint in Frege 1967: 267–72.)

Frege, G. 1952. *Translations from the Philosophical Writings of Gottlob Frege*, ed. P.Geach and M.Black. Oxford: Blackwell. (3rd ed. 1980, Reprint 1995.)

Frege, G. 1967. *Kleine Schriften*, ed. I. Angelelli. Darmstadt: Wissenschaftliche Buchgesellschaft.

Frege, G. 1969. *Nachgelassene Schriften und Wissenschaftlicher Briefwechsel*, vol. 1: *Nachgelassene Schriften*, ed. H. Hermes, F. Kambartel, F. Kaulbach. Hamburg: Meiner. (English translation by P.Long and R.White. Oxford: Blackwell, 1979.)

Frege, G. 1976. *Nachgelassene Schriften und Wissenschaftlicher Briefwechsel*, vol. 2: *Wissenschaftlicher Briefwechsel*, ed. G. Gabriel, H. Hermes, F. Kambartel, Ch. Thiel, A. Veraart. Hamburg: Meiner. (English translation by H. Kaal, ed. B. McGuinness. Oxford: Blackwell, 1980.)

Hintikka, J. 1959. Existential Presuppositions and Existential Commitments. *The Journal of Philosophy* 56: 125–37.

Hintikka, J. 1966. Studies in the Logic of Existence and Necessity. *The Monist* 50: 55–76.

Husserl, E. 1904. Bericht über deutsche Schriften zur Logik in den Jahren 1895–99. Fünfter Artikel. *Archiv für systematische Philosophie* 10: 101–25.

Kant, I. 1763. *Der einzig mögliche Beweisgrund zu einer Demonstration des Dasein Gottes.* Königsberg: Kanter. (Reprint in *Kant's gesammelte Schriften. Herausgegeben von der Königlich Preußischen Akademie der Wissenschaften,* vol. 2. Berlin: Reimer, 1912. English translation by G. Treash as *The One Possible Basis for a Demonstration of the Existence of God.* New York: Abaris, 1979.)

Lambert, K. 1967. Free Logic and the Concept of Existence. *Notre Dame Journal of Formal Logic* 8: 133–44.

Lehmann, S. 1994. Strict Fregean Free Logic. *Journal of Philosophical Logic* 23: 307–36.

Meyer, R., E. Bencivenga, and K. Lambert. 1982. The ineliminability of E! in Free Quantification Theory. *Journal of Philosophical Logic* 11: 229–31.

Morscher, E. 1969. *Das logische An-sich bei Bernard Bolzano.* Doctoral dissertation, University of Innsbruck. (Published: Salzburg and Munich: Pustet, 1973.)

Morscher, E. 1985/86. Was Existence Ever a Predicate? *Grazer philosophische Studien* 25/26: 269–84.

Russell, B. 1919. *Introduction to Mathematical Philosophy.* London: Allen and Unwin. (Reprint 1970.)

Skyrms, B. 1968. Supervaluations: Identity, Existence, and Individual Concepts. *The Journal of Philosophy* 65: 477–82.

van Fraassen, B.C. 1966. Singular Terms, Truth-Value Gaps, and Free Logic. *The Journal of Philosophy* 63: 481–95.

Whitehead, A.N. and B.Russell. 1910. *Principia Mathematica.* vol. 1. Cambridge: Cambridge University Press. (2nd ed. 1935, Reprint 1960.)

13

The Context-Principle

RAINER STUHLMANN-LAEISZ

1   Introduction

In his opus *The Foundations of Arithmetic* Frege states what is called his 'context-principle' in different formulations, e.g.:

(1)   [You must never] ask for the meaning of a word in isolation, but only in the context of a proposition (Nach der Bedeutung der Wörter muss im Satzzusammenhange, nicht in ihrer Vereinzelung gefragt werden. Introduction).

(2)   It is enough if the proposition as a whole has a sense; it is this that confers on its parts also their content (Es genügt, wenn der Satz als Ganzes einen Sinn hat; dadurch erhalten auch seine Theile ihren Inhalt. §60).

(3)   [I]t is only in the context of a proposition that words have any meaning (Nur im Zusammenhange eines Satzes bedeuten die Wörter etwas. §62).

(4)   We next laid down the fundamental principle that we must never try to define the meaning of a word in isolation, but only as it is used in the context of a proposition (Wir stellten nun den Grundsatz auf, dass die Bedeutung eines Wortes nicht vereinzelt, sondern im Zusammenhange eines Satzes zu erklären sei. §106).

These formulations are by no means all equivalent. Rather - as it has been shown in the literature - they give rise to substantially different principles. So I start my talk indicating some of these.

2 The variety of context principles

Obviously the formulations are not equivalent. For example, formulation (1) is compatible with the negation of (3), since it is well possible that a word has a meaning also in isolation, which one can grasp only within the context of a sentence. The negation of statement (3) is also compatible with (2), which guarantees the meaningfulness of sentence-parts provided that the sentence as a whole has a meaning not excluding, however, the meaningfulness of isolated words. Neither does formulation (2) exclude grasping a meaning in isolation, so (2) is compatible with the negation of (1) as well. Thus, since statement (1) might be read as being equivalent to statement (4), we have at least 3 principles expressed by the four formulations, which are non-equivalent in pairs.

Let us look for some labels to classify them (this also has partly been done in the literature).

Since formulations (1) and (4) - the candidates for an equivalence - tell us how to determine a meaning, how to grasp it or to get to know it, let us label them *epistemic*. And since (2) and (3) tell us conditions for there being a meaning, let us call them *ontic*. Thus we get *epistemic* and *ontic* interpretations of 'the' context-principle (which in fact is not one but many). - Another classification is given by the labels *sufficiency* and *necessity*: (2) makes the meaningfulness of a sentence as a whole sufficient for the meaningfulness of its parts. And since Frege also seems to allow that parts of sentences have a meaning, one can read (3) to the effect that it makes the meaningfulness of the whole sentence a necessary condition for the meaningfulness of its parts. Finally, if we import Frege's later distinction between sense and reference into the interpretation of his formulations in the earlier *Foundations*, for every principle under the labels established so far we get an interpretation concerning sense and another one concerning reference. Looking at matters from a systematic point of view, I want to make this import. - Thus we have three twofold divisions, which yield eight non-empty classes of context-principles. (I here use the plural, since it seems by no means evident to me, that there is one unique principle in every class.) It is obvious, how formulations (1)-(4) should be classified under the headings epistemic/ontic and sufficiency/necessity, and in each case we get an additional differentiation by applying the sense/reference distinction.

Since there is no explicit formulation of an ontic necessity principle concerning reference, let me construe one:

(5)   Only if a sentence as a whole has a reference (i.e. has a truth value), do all of its parts also have a reference.

Now, (5) is equivalent to:

(5')   If all of its parts have a reference, a sentence as a whole also has a reference (i.e. has a truth value).

Now, (5') is a formulation of the *compositional* principle for the reference of sentences. This shows how closely related this idea is to the contextual one. However, whereas Frege undoubtedly claims a principle like (5'), there is much controversy on the question, how seriously he takes the contextual idea, which is rather expressed by the converse of (5').

So far, this idea is not very strong yet, since all the principles within the eight classes allow syntactical units smaller than sentences to have a sense or a reference. However, if one reads, e.g., formulation (3) as prohibiting just that with respect to meaning one gets what I call *the strong contextual idea*. It again has its ontic/epistemic and its sense/reference versions. In what follows, I shall argue that Frege accepts this idea in special cases; but he rejects it in general.

3   Some evidence in favor of the contextual view

Let us recall from Frege's writings some evidence in favor of the hypothesis that he held the strong contextual idea in general or at least a weak version under the label *sufficiency* (as it is, e.g., expressed by formulation (2)). I call this hypothesis *the contextual view*.

There are, of course, the passages from the *Foundations* quoted above, which - taken in isolation - give strong evidence. Some evidence might also be seen in the following quote from §46:

> It should throw some light on the matter to consider number in the context of a judgment which brings out its basic use (Um Licht in die Sache zu bringen, wird es gut sein, die Zahl im Zusammenhange eines Urtheils zu betrachten, wo ihre ursprüngliche Anwendungsweise hervortritt.).

In what follows this passage, Frege gives examples for the ordinary usage of number words (not of numbers, as he literally puts it), which show that a statement of number says something about a concept. Others have inter alia pointed to passages from other works of Frege, e.g. from the essay *On the Foundations of Geometry II*:

> Well, let us recall that improper sentences individually do not express thoughts but they can be parts of a meaningful entity as a whole (Nun, erinnern wir uns, daß uneigentliche Sätze zwar einzeln keine Gedanken ausdrücken, daß sie aber Teile eines sinnvollen Ganzen sein können. *Über die Grundlagen der Geometrie II*, in: Kleine Schriften, p. 307).

From posthumous writings:

> Hence I do not start with concepts and use them to put together a thought or a judgment, rather I get the parts of a thought by splitting it up (Ich gehe also nicht von den Begriffen aus und setze aus ihnen den Gedanken oder das Urteil zusammen, sondern ich gewinne die Gedankenteile durch Zerfällung des Gedankens. *Aufzeichnungen für Ludwig Darmstaedter* (1919), in: Nachgelassene Schriften, p. 273).

> Therefore, in the *Begriffsschrift* one won´t find their terms [i.e. the terms for not further analyzable properties and relations] in isolation but always in compositions which are capable of expressing a judgeable content. I would like to compare this with the behaviour of atoms of which one assumes that they never occur in isolation but always in compounds, and they never leave the compound without forming a new one (Daher treten ihre Bezeichnungen [sc.: die Bezeichnungen von nicht weiter zerlegbaren Eigenschaften und Beziehungen] in der Begriffsschrift nie vereinzelt auf, sondern immer in Verbindungen, welche beurteilbare Inhalte ausdrücken. Ich möchte dies mit dem Verhalten der Atome vergleichen, von denen man annimmt, dass nie eins allein vorkommt, sondern nur in einer Verbindung mit andern, die es nur verlässt, um sofort in eine andere einzugehen. *Booles rechnende Logik und die Begriffsschrift*, in: Nachgelassene Schriften, p. 19).

In his *Basic Laws* (vol. II, §97) Frege writes:

> We can inquire about reference only if the signs are constituent parts of sentences expressing thoughts (Nach Bedeutungen kann nur gefragt werden, wo die Zeichen Bestandtheile von Sätzen sind, die Gedanken ausdrücken.).

However, it has also been said that these further passages give little evidence, if any at all. So let us stick to the four quotes above as the best evidence in favor of the contextual view.

4   Evidence against the contextual view

Let us now turn towards evidence against the contextual view. This evidence comes primarily from Frege's remarks concerning the task of definitions. Since to accept the contextual idea - either in the strong or in the weak sense - implies to accept contextual (especially: implicit) definitions, every Fregean objection against this type of definition goes against the contextual view as well.

That Frege rejected the idea of implicit definitions is evident from his objections to Hilbert's work on the Foundations of Geometry. As is well known, Hilbert thought to define, e.g., the concepts of point and straight line and the relation *between* by an axiomatic system - this being the context to yield the meanings of the terms. Towards this Frege objects:

> I demand that by a definition of the point one can judge, whether an arbitrary object, e.g. my pocket-watch, is a point or not (Ich verlange von einer Definition des Punktes, daß danach müsse beurteilt werden können, ob ein beliebiger Gegenstand, z. B. meine Taschenuhr, ein Punkt sei. *Über die Grundlagen der Geometrie I*, in: Kleine Schriften, p. 291).

Likewise in the case of a relation:

> If a relation has been correctly defined, then the definition together with sufficient knowledge of given objects must make it decidable, whether these objects stand in that relation (Wenn eine Beziehung richtig definiert ist, so muß diese Definition zusammen mit hinlänglicher Kenntnis gegebener Gegenstände genügen zu entscheiden, ob diese Gegenstände in der definierten Beziehung zueinander stehen. ibid., p. 292).

Implicit or contextual definitions do obviously not meet these two requirements concerning the definitions of predicates. Thus here we have strong evidence against the contextual view.

Further objections come from vol. II of the *Basic Laws*. Here Frege states two 'Principles of Defining', the second of which forbids defining a word by defining 'an expression in which it occurs' ('einen Ausdruck [...], in dem es vorkommt', §66). This passage almost literally contradicts formulation (4) from the *Foundations*.

Of particular interest under Frege's objections against contextual definitions is, however, a passage from the *Foundations* themselves. Here Frege discusses and rejects definitions of the numbers zero and one, although these meet exactly the consequences of his statement (3) above. Let us look at this in detail.

Frege says in §62:

> [O]ur problem becomes this: To define the sense of a proposition in which a number word occurs (Es wird also darauf ankommen, den Sinn eines Satzes zu erklären, in dem ein Zahlwort vorkommt.).

Well, this task is perfectly fulfilled by the following definition of the number zero:

(Def$_0$)   The number 0 applies to a concept, if whatever object a may be, the proposition universally holds, that a does not fall under that concept.

As the definiendum we here have the sentence 'The number 0 applies to a concept'. This sentence contains the number word 'zero', and its sense is given by the definiens. - Even more so: If one, e.g. by syntactical devices, restricts the use of the number term 'zero' to sentences of the form '0 applies to F', where 'F' stands for a concept name, then (Def$_0$) yields a rule, by which every well formed sentence containing the number term '0' can be transformed into and thus can be replaced by a sentence which does not contain the term. Thus (Def$_0$) is a perfect contextual definition. B. Russell would call it a 'definition in use' of the 'incomplete symbol' '0'. - All the same, Frege says in §56:

> It is only an illusion that we have defined 0 [...]; in reality we have only fixed the sense of the phrases 'the number 0 belongs to' [and dto. for number 1] (Es ist nur Schein, dass wir die 0 [...] erklärt haben; in Wahrheit haben wir nur den Sinn der Redensarten 'die Zahl 0 kommt zu' [ebenso für die Zahl 1] festgestellt.).

But where is the problem since - according to the contextual idea - this is precisely what should have been done? Well, in §56 Frege sees at least two problems posed by the criticized contextual definition. Since these problems turn out to be three, I shall handle them as three:

(a) The 'Julius-Caesar-problem' (cf. M. Dummett, 1981, pp. 402, 410-412; and 1991, pp. 156-162, 209-214):
Contextual definitions of numbers in the style of (Def$_0$) have as the definiendum a sentence of the form 'τ applies to F' where 'τ' stands for a number term (and 'F' for a concept name). The definiens gives sense to these sentences (usually by recursion to the predecessor of number τ). However, as Frege rightly says:

> [W]e can never [...] decide by means of our definitions whether any concept has the number *Julius Caesar* belonging to it, or whether that same familiar conqueror of Gaul is a number or is not ([W]ir können [...] durch unsere Definitionen nie entscheiden, ob einem Begriffe die Zahl *Julius Caesar* zukomme, ob dieser bekannte Eroberer Galliens eine Zahl ist oder nicht. §56).

A special case of this problem is, of course, that by (Def$_0$) we cannot decide, whether the identity statement '0 = Julius Caesar' is true or false.

(b) The uniqueness-problem:
The suggested definition does not justify the use of the definite description

'*the* number, which applies to the concept F', since it yields no means at all to prove the identity statement $a = b$ from the two premises *number a applies to F* and *number b applies to F.*

(c) The recognition-problem:
Even if the uniqueness-problem would have been solved, i.e. even if one would have established the existence of some operation or function, which associates with each concept F the number applying to F, in other words: *the number of F*, this would not eo ipso yield a method for deciding, whether *the number of F = the number of G*, if F is a concept different from G. A fortiori, the suggested contextual definition does not yield such means, since it does not allow, e.g., 'to pick out the 0 and the 1 here as self-subsistent objects that can be recognized as the same again' ('[E]s ist nicht erlaubt, hierin die 0, die 1 als selbständige, wiedererkennbare Gegenstände zu unterscheiden.' §56).

These three problems yield the reason, why Frege rejects the suggested contextual definitions. Two of them, i.e. the uniqueness- and the recognition-problem, are treated by Frege in §56 as if they were one. The reason might be that these two problems turn the whole story of the contextual idea into a new direction, namely the direction towards an account of numbers as self-subsistent objects.

5   Origin of the contextual idea within the *Foundations*

Before attempting to solve these problems, let us recall, how Frege came to hold the contextual idea when working on his *Foundations*. After stating - in accordance with the received view of arithmetic - that numbers are self sustained entities, he discusses the objection that one cannot form any idea or imagination of a number as an object. However, he rightly says, this is no reason for denying meaning to number words. (The name 'Earth' has a meaning, of course, even though it is hard, if not impossible, to have an imaginative picture of the respective object.) To regard that as a reason after all is rather a consequence of asking for the meaning of words in isolation, as Frege indicates. Here we have a source for the contextual idea: It is to ensure meanings for terms (here: number terms), with which we do not associate an imaginative picture.[1]

---

[1] Nevertheless does the idea play the role rather of a didactic or psychological advice than that of a systematic principle. Frege warns not to conclude the meaninglessness of a word from its content being inconceivable:

But even if we could imagine numbers, the image could not be the respective number itself, since the image is subjective and private, whereas the number itself is an objective entity, which 'is exactly the same for everyone who deals with it' ('genau dieselbe für jeden [ist], der sich mit ihr beschäftigt', §61). This objectivity, however, causes another false belief: If numbers are objective, they have to be located in space, 'but where is the number 4?' ('aber wo ist die Zahl 4?', §61). This belief is false, since objectivity 'has nothing to do with being spatial. Not every objective [entity] has a place' ('dies hat mit Räumlichkeit nichts zu schaffen. Nicht jeder objective Gegenstand hat einen Ort', §61). The objectivity of an entity X rather consists in two traits of X: (i) Its *being* one and the same entity in different occurrences, (ii) its being *recognizable* as one and the same entity in different occurrences.

> If we are to use the symbol *a* to signify an object, we must have a criterion for deciding in all cases whether *b* is the same as *a* (Wenn uns das Zeichen a einen Gegenstand bezeichnen soll, so müssen wir ein Kennzeichen haben, welches überall entscheidet, ob b dasselbe sei wie a. §62).

> And that is enough to give us a class of propositions which must have a sense, namely those which express our recognition of a number as the same again (Damit ist uns eine Gattung von Sätzen gegeben, die einen Sinn haben müssen, der Sätze, welche ein Wiedererkennen ausdrücken. §62).

Here Frege lets the cat out of the bag of context-principles: He needs an identity criterion for numbers in order to ensure their objective status without making them spatial entities. And since identity criteria can be construed as special contextual definitions of the form *the Φ is the same as the*

> That we can form no idea of its content is therefore no reason for denying all meaning to a word (Es ist also die Unvorstellbarkeit des Inhaltes eines Wortes kein Grund, ihm jede Bedeutung abzusprechen. §60).

One is in danger of this miss, if one asks for the isolated meaning, e.g., of a number term:

> We are indeed only imposed on by the opposite view [i.e. the view, that inconceivableness of content implies meaninglessness] because we will, when asking for the meaning of a word, consider it in isolation, which leads us to accept an idea as the meaning. (Der Schein des Gegentheils [also der Schein, dass ein Wort keine Bedeutung hat, wenn sein Inhalt nicht vorstellbar ist] entsteht wohl dadurch, dass wir die Wörter vereinzelt betrachten und nach ihrer Bedeutung fragen, für welche wir dann eine Vorstellung nehmen. §60).

Hence someone, who – as against the contextual idea – holds the position that the term '0' either has a meaning in isolation or does not have any meaning at all, *might* get into trouble if he looks for that meaning, but he *will not* if, e.g., he does know the definition '0 = Ø', where Ø is the empty set regarded as a von Neumann ordinal. Thus, by no means does his position *imply* that '0' has no meaning.

Ψ, iff C (where C is some suitable condition), he propagates the contextual idea.

6 Solution of the recognition- and the uniqueness-problem

As we have seen, Frege rejects the contextual definitions of numbers in §55, since they pose the Julius-Caesar-problem, the uniqueness-problem and the recognition-problem. Let us now consider, whether these problems can be solved by a contextual definition in the form of an identity criterion for numbers. In order to argue that, I shall make some remarks concerning the method of abstraction, by which Frege introduces numbers.

When we introduce entities by abstraction, they are not given to us and we have no (Russellian) acquaintance with them. What is given to us and what we are acquainted with, are objects of another sort, which in some sense represent the entities to be introduced. E.g.: If we want to introduce logical forms we have as representatives sentences of a formal language, and if we are to introduce styles as, say, objects of art history, we have works of art as representing them. Now Frege wants to introduce numbers, and these are given to us by concepts.

The task of the abstraction process is to introduce the new abstract entities - here: numbers - as self-subsistent objects. This requires a criterion which decides for any *two* representatives, whether they give the same and hence one or different and hence two entities, i.e.: the process requires an identity criterion. Therefore, if the representatives are concepts, we are looking for a binary relation $C(x,y)$ to the effect that: *the number of F = the number of G iff C(F,G)*. This statement is an explicit definition of number equality as well as a contextual definition of numbers. A simple argument then shows, that $C(x,y)$ has to be an equivalence relation. Frege takes for C equinumerousity between concepts.

Thus, by now he has concepts as representatives of numbers and an equivalence relation which might yield a definition for number equations, i.e. statements of the form: *the number of F = the number of G*. Is it possible to solve by these means the three problems posed by the contextual definitions mentioned above? The answer is 'no' for the following reason:

The abstraction process presupposes, that two conditions are fulfilled: (a) The first one requires, that with every representative *there is* associated at least one abstract entity of the new sort. This is an existence condition. (Frege seems so deeply convinced of this condition's being fulfilled, that he

- as far as I can see - does not state it explicitly.) (b) The second condition requires, that with every representative there is associated *at most* one abstract entity of the new kind. This is an uniqueness condition, and its fulfillment is guaranteed, once the uniqueness-problem just mentioned has been solved. - As long as the fulfillment of these two conditions has not been ensured, there is no solution to the three problems. How then can this be done? Well, in elementary set theory, one can easily prove a theorem to the effect that the two conditions are fulfilled. Here it is:

(Abstra)   Let A be a class and $\sim$ some equivalence relation on A. Then there is some function f, defined on A, to the effect that for any $x, y \in A$: $f(x) = f(y)$ iff $x{\sim}y$.

(Abstra) is proved, e.g., by taking as $f(x)$ the class of all objects in A, which are equivalent to x. - For the rest of my talk I shall assume that Frege had in mind a theorem like (Abstra) - at least for special abstraction processes like the introduction of numbers or courses of values (or perhaps directions).

Now, on the basis of (Abstra), the presupposed existence and uniqueness conditions for abstraction processes in general are fulfilled. The consequence for the introduction of numbers is evident: As soon as one has the equivalence relation of equinumerousity on the class of concepts, one has by (Abstra) a function, call it *the number of ...,* which fulfills the contextual identity criterion *the number of F = the number of G iff F is equinumerous to G.* Hence, the recognition-problem has got a solution, and so has the uniqueness-problem.

Thus, with (Abstra) at hand, the contextual definition of numbers by the equality definition solves the recognition-problem, which the contextual definition from §55 has posed. Hence the former is superior to the latter. This explains why Frege accepts contextual definitions of numbers, if the contexts are equations, whereas he rejects those of other types.

Now we can even state a context-principle, which underlies Frege's considerations; it concerns sense as well as reference. Here it is:

(Cont)   Sentences of the form *the f of x is the same as the f of y* (where f is an abstraction function yielded by theorem (Abstra)) have a sense and a reference (truth value) as a whole, but the contained terms *the f of ...* do not have a sense or a reference in isolation.

This is an ontic claim, which has an obvious epistemic analogon.

7   The Julius-Caesar-problem and the value of the contextual definition

But what about the Julius-Caesar-problem? Has it been solved, too? The answer is 'no'. Frege himself points to this, when he in the *Foundations* illustrates the method of abstraction with the definition of directions in geometry. The definition of the respective equality gives no means to determine the truth value of the identity statement *England = the direction of the Earth's axis* (cf. §66). The reason is, as Frege rightly tells us, that the definition of direction equality does not say, what a direction is: 'What we lack is the concept of direction' ('Es fehlt uns der Begriff der Richtung', §66), hence we cannot decide whether England is a direction at all. (The same holds for the concept of a number and the person Julius Caesar.) Moreover, not only can we not determine the truth value of the said identity statement, but in a certain sense, this value has not been determined at all by the given equality definition. But is that compatible with the alleged solution of the uniqueness-problem? Unfortunately, it is, as we learn in §10 of the *Basic Laws*. Let me argue this more systematically.

The uniqueness-problem has been solved in the following sense: As soon as one has fixed an equivalence relation on the class of representatives (concepts or straight lines) one can choose a function f (the number of ..., the direction of ...), whose existence is guaranteed by (Abstra). And with this function f at hand, one can be sure that with each representative x there is associated a unique object *the f of x* (f(x)); otherwise f would not be what it is, i.e. a function. Here you have the solution of the uniqueness-problem.

However, (Abstra) does not tell you what would even be wrong to tell, namely, that there is a unique function f associated with the respective equivalence relation. Rather, as can be shown by the 'permutation argument' (cf. Dummett, 1981, pp. 402-403, 421-424; and 1991, p. 211) or by other means, there are many such functions, which can even have different value-ranges, which may or may not contain Julius Caesar or England. We state this by the following *Indeterminateness Theorem:*

(Indet)   Under the premises of (Abstra), there are functions f_1 and f_2, which both fulfill (Abstra) and in addition the respective conditions:
(JC)   There is an x in A, such that $f_1(x) =$ Julius Caesar.
(NonJC) For every x in A: $f_2(x) \neq$ Julius Caesar.

Thus, the uniqueness-problem remains unsolved in the sense that the function f itself has not been uniquely determined. The problem persists as Julius-Caesar-problem. This diminishes the value of the equality definition. But things turn even worse, since within the *Foundations* we *prima facie* do have a solution of the problem, which seems to make the equality definition superfluous. As is well known, Frege in fact offers an explicit definition of number (I abbreviate):

(Def$_{numb}$) The number of a concept F is the extension of the concept *equinumerous to F.*

By this definition, Frege chooses from the variety of functions yielded by theorem (Abstra) that one, which associates with a representative (a concept) its equivalence class under the respective relation. Thus numbers are construed as classes of concepts, and since Julius Caesar is not a class of concepts, every statement of the form: *the number of F = Julius Caesar* is false; the problem seems to have been solved. - Moreover: The said definition *implies* the identity criterion for numbers, thus we need not stipulate this identity any more by a definition. This definition seems to be superfluous. Can we save it? Yes, we can by discussing the following question: Why does Frege stick to the contextual definition even after he stated the explicit definition mentioned above, as he does in §106 of the *Foundations*? Well, the said solution of the Julius-Caesar-problem presupposes the idea of the extension of a given concept. To be sure, Frege uses the idea, but he is uneasy about it. He says in a note on the explicit definition: 'I assume that it is known what the extension of a concept is' ('Ich setze voraus, dass man wisse, was der Umfang eines Begriffes sei', §69), but he does not say a word which could answer just this question. And in §107 he says with respect to the same definition:

> In this definition the sense of the expression 'extension of the concept' is assumed to be known. This way of getting over the difficulty [i.e.: the Julius-Caesar-problem] cannot be expected to meet with universal approval, and many will prefer other methods of removing the doubt in question. I attach no decisive importance even to bringing in the extensions of concepts at all (Hierbei setzten wir den Sinn des Ausdrucks 'Umfang des Begriffs' als bekannt voraus. Diese Weise, die Schwierigkeit [s.c.: das Julius-Caesar-Problem] zu überwinden, wird wohl nicht überall Beifall finden, und Manche werden vorziehen, jenes Bedenken in andrer Weise zu beseitigen. Ich lege auch auf die Heranziehung des Umfangs eines Begriffs kein entscheidendes Gewicht.).

There are substantial reasons for Frege's hesitation regarding the employment of concept extensions here, since they form a special kind of

courses of values, as we know from the *Basic Laws*; and before we introduce and come to know concept extensions, we have to introduce courses
of values. But these are - like numbers - abstract entities, which confront us
with the same problems as do numbers; in particular, we need an identity
criterion. - The representatives of courses of values are functions, thus we
need an equivalence relation between functions Φ and Ψ. Frege defines the
needed relation in §3 of the *Basic Laws* by the definiens:

(Eqfunc)   The functions $\Phi(\xi)$ and $\Psi(\xi)$ always have the same value for the
same argument.
(In modern notation: $\forall \xi\, (\Phi(\xi) = \Psi(\xi))$.)

And again presupposing a theorem like (Abstra), he says for Φ and Ψ,
which bear the said relation: 'The function $\Phi(\xi)$ has the same *course of values* as the function $\Psi(\xi)$' (§3).
Here we are in the same situation as we were with the identity criterion
for numbers: For no function Φ has it been determined, whether Julius Caesar is the course of values of Φ or not.
How would the explicit definition read, which prima facie solved the
problem in the case of numbers?
The answer is:

(Defcv)   The course of values of a function Φ is the extension of the concept *is a function Ψ, which has for every argument the same
value as Φ.*

But if we now look at the definition of concept-extensions, we run into
a circle:

(Defext)   The extension of a concept Φ is the course of values of Φ.

Thus, there is no way out of the Julius-Caesar-problem.
This, however, increases again the value of the contextual definition of
numbers by definition of equality. Though not solving the Julius-Caesar-
problem, it nevertheless makes us come as close to its solution as is possible. Of course, an ideal solution would - in the number case - determine the
truth value of any identity statement of the form 'the number of F = τ'
(where τ is any singular term). Instead, we have to be content with the second best solution comprising only those cases, where τ is a number term.
For these cases, however, the described contextual definition of numbers
determines the truth value, and since there is no explicit definition available

to do this we are in need of the contextual one. Therefore, Frege accepts it. But he does so only in the case of abstract objects and only for the said purpose. He accepts the contextual idea as a need in a particular methodological situation. But in general Frege rejects the idea, and in no case does he accept it as a virtue.

References

Dummett, M. 1981. *The interpretation of Frege's philosophy*. London: Duckworth.

Dummett, M. 1991. *Frege. Philosophy of Mathematics*. London: Duckworth.

Frege, G. 1959. *The Foundations of Arithmetic. A logico-mathematical enquiry into the concept of number*, transl. by J. L. Austin, 2nd ed. Oxford: Blackwell.

Frege, G. 1962. *Grundgesetze der Arithmetik. Begriffsschriftlich abgeleitet*, vol. I (1893) and vol. II (1903). 2nd ed. Hildesheim: Olms.

Frege, G. 1969. *Nachgelassene Schriften*, ed. H. Hermes, F. Kambartel, F. Kaulbach. Hamburg: Meiner.

Frege, G. 1986. *Die Grundlagen der Arithmetik. Eine logisch mathematische Untersuchung über den Begriff der Zahl,* ed. Ch. Thiel. Hamburg: Meiner.

Frege, G. 1990. *Über die Grundlagen der Geometrie I-III*, in: Kleine Schriften, ed. I. Angelelli, 2nd ed. Hildesheim [et al.]: Olms.

Geach, P./Black, M. (ed.). 1960. *Translations from the Philosophical Writings of Gottlob Frege.* 2nd ed. Oxford: Blackwell.

Part IV

CONCEPTS

14

Constituents of Concepts: Bolzano vs. Frege

WOLFGANG KÜNNE

In section 1 of this paper I shall point out that in one respect the grandfather of analytical philosophy was more conservative than its great-grandfather: Frege at least partially endorsed the Canon of Reciprocity which was a prominent ingredient of the post–Cartesian logical tradition, Bolzano rejected it completely. In section 2 I shall try to defend one part of this bipartite principle. In section 3 I shall try to show that this line of defence is open to Frege. This claim is based on a reconsideration of Frege's notion of the marks *(Merkmale)* of a concept, – a notion which is generally treated rather cavalierly in the literature on Frege. In section 4 I shall present a problem which Bolzano and Frege share because they both think of complex senses in part-whole terms. Finally, in part 5, I shall briefly celebrate what I deem to be Bolzano's victorious attack on the other part of the Canon of Reciprocity.

1   A Traditional Principle under Attack

If the adjective 'one' denoted a property of objects then it would denote a property instantiated by every object whatsoever. In his *Grundlagen der Arithmetik* (Gl) Frege offers an 'argument from vacuous contrast' for the contention that such a predicate would be entirely devoid of content:[1]

---

[1] In his 'Dialog mit Pünjer über Existenz' he calls such concepts 'pseudo-concepts (Quasi-begriffe)' (Frege 1969, p. 71).

(F1) It would be incomprehensible why we should still ascribe it [the alleged property of being one] expressly to a thing at all. It is only in virtue of the possibility of something not being wise that it makes sense to say 'Solon is wise'. The content of a concept diminishes as its extension increases; if its extension becomes all-embracing, its content must vanish altogether (Gl 40).

This argument is rather weak. To be sure, a predicate which applies to every object cannot be used to distinguish one object from another. But does lack of a discriminating function amount to senselessness? Frege himself, in the course of the very same book, implicitly denies that the significance of a predicate depends on its discriminatory power, for he acknowledges without further ado that being an object *(Gegenstand)* and being self-identical are properties (Gl 57, 87).[2] If they are, then surely they are exemplified by each and every object, and there is not even the possibility of an object not exemplifying them. Nevertheless, a remark to the effect that such-and-such is identical with itself, may not lack remarkableness: It may serve the function of making a formal point against Hegelians, for example.

Frege makes an analogous, and equally implausible, claim about second-order concepts when he says:

(F2) [I]t is possible that no object falls under [a certain concept]. If this were never the case then one could never deny existence, and *thereby* the affirmation of existence would also lose its content (Gl 62, my italics).

But doesn't every concept have the property of being either empty or not empty? Does Frege really want to condemn his own (rather dubious) claim that *every* concept is sharply delimited as devoid of content?

Let us now focus on the penultimate sentence of our first quotation: 'The content of a concept diminishes as its extension increases'. Here Frege endorses one prong of the two-pronged Canon of Reciprocity which was part of the post-Cartesian logical lore. Consider an example: The extension of the concept *triangle* contains more than just rectangular triangles, but its content is poorer than that of the concept *rectangular triangle*, since it lacks one of the conceptual building-blocks of the latter, the component *rectangular*. Inversely, the extension of the concept *rectangular triangle* contains less than all triangles, but its content is richer than that of the concept *triangle*. The *Canon of Reciprocity* (CR) generalizes such observations. Here is Kant's formulation of the CR:[3]

---

[2] As to self-identity cp. Kenny 1995, p. 67.

[3] *"Inhalt und Umfang eines Begriffs stehen gegen einander in umgekehrtem Verhältnisse. Je mehr nämlich ein Begriff unter sich enthält, desto weniger enthält er in sich und umgekehrt"* (Kant 1800, p. 148). Bolzano's contention in WL I, p. 294, 570, repeated by many authors, that (CR) is to be found already in the Logic of Port Royal is not tenable (Schmauks 1985, p. 14f.). An early (if not the earliest) formulation of (CR) is given in Wolff 1713, p. 138.

(CR) Content and extension of a concept stand in an inverse relation. The more objects fall under a concept, the fewer conceptual components are contained within the concept, and vice versa.

Bolzano attacks the CR in § 120 of his monumental *Wissenschaftslehre* (WL).[4] Here is a sketch of his argument. Bolzano first points out that the expression 'inverse relation' is not to be taken in its strict mathematical sense (so that, for example, the extension would be halved if the number of constituents of a concept would be doubled). He then goes on to formulate the CR in a more appropriate way. Using the sign '$<<$' in the sense of 'is a proper part of' and abbreviating 'the content of' and 'the extension of' by 'Cnt ( )' and 'Ext ( )' respectively, we can render Bolzano's clarification of the two-pronged CR thus:[5]

For all concepts x, y:

(CR^1) if Cnt (x) $<<$ Cnt (y), then Ext (y) $<<$ Ext (x), and

(CR^2) if Ext (x) $<<$ Ext (y), then Cnt (y) $<<$ Cnt (x).

Bolzano now tries to refute both principles by presenting examples which fulfill the antecedent matrix but not the consequent matrix.[6] (I replace some of his examples by structurally similar ones which are easier to treat.) Since Frege explicitly endorses only the second prong of the CR, let us focus on Bolzano's criticism of CR^2 . (At the end of this paper I shall return to the first prong.) Consider the following pairs of concepts:

(1) *understands German;* *understands German or Czech*

(2) *woman;* *relative of a woman.*

In both cases the extension of the first concept is a proper part of the extension of the second concept, but, contrary to CR^2, or so Bolzano contends, it is the *first* concept which is a component of the *second* – and not the other way round.[7]

Elsewhere in his WL the following pair of concepts is Bolzano's favourite evidence for the contention that the extension of a concept x can be

---

[4] Bolzano quotes (CR) in WL I, p. 292.

[5] (CR^1) *"Jede Vorstellung, die einen größeren Inhalt als eine andere hat (so nämlich, daß sie aus dieser und noch gewissen anderen Theilen zusammengesetzt ist), hat einen kleineren Umfang als diese, (so nämlich, daß ihr Umfang ein Theil ist vom Umfang dieser).*

(CR^2) *Und umgekehrt jede Vorstellung, die einen kleineren Umfang hat als eine andere (so nämlich, daß ihr Umfang ein Theil ist vom Umfange dieser), hat einen größeren Inhalt als diese (so nämlich, daß ihr Inhalt aus dieser und noch gewissen anderen Theilen zusammengesetzt ist)"* (WL I, p. 568 f.)

[6] WL I, p. 569; cp. Hoensbroech 1931 and Schmauks 1985.

[7] Cp. the mathematical examples in WL I, p. 399 f. (note).

a proper part of the extension of concept y even if y is not a proper part of the content of x:[8]

(3)   *actual*;   *possible*.

Each actual object is a possible object, but not every possible object is an actual one. Yet the concept *actual* does not contain the concept *possible* as a proper part. As to the putative explanation to be found in Leibniz and Wolff: 'The actuality of a thing is the completion of its possibility *(Actualitas sive existentia est complementum possibilitatis, Die Wirklichkeit oder das Daseyn eines Dinges ist die Erfüllung seiner Möglichkeit)*',[9] Bolzano presumes that 'hardly anyone will consider this as a proper dissection of this concept [sc. of the concept *actual*] into its parts' (WL II 66). The actual is a species of the genus of the possible, but the concept of *this* genus is *not* a component of the concept of that species. Hence

(B1) Not every species-concept contains that of its genus as a part (WL [1837] II 87).

One can transform the sentence-matrix 'Vixens are foxes which are ____' into a true sentence by inserting an expression ('female') which is not co-extensive with 'vixen', but one cannot do so with 'Actual objects are possible objects which are ____'. (Nowadays philosophers tend to call concepts of the latter kind (following W.E. Johnson) 'determinates' with respect to certain 'determinables'. The most prominent examples are colour-terms: We cannot transform 'Red objects are coloured objects which are ____' into a truth by inserting an expression which differs in extension from 'red'.[10])

As a matter of fact, Bolzano here abandons a position which he himself had taken in his early programmatic booklet 'Contributions to a more well-founded presentation of mathematics' (1810):[11]

(B2) Not every concept which is suboordinated to a more general concept is thereby prevented from being simple, for only a concept which can be dissected is no longer simple. But for a dissection one must specify at least

---

[8] WL I p. 291, p. 293, p. 295, p. 550 f.

[9] Wolff 1730 § 174 (German translation: Gottsched 1983, I: p. 211); Leibniz 1695, § 3: "l'acte ou le complement de la possibilité." This explication was critised by Kant in Kant 1763, I, 1, § 3. Cp. Zimmermann 1849, p. 26.

[10] Johnson 1921-1924, p. 174 f.; and Prior 1949.

[11] "*Nicht jeder Begriff, der einen allgemeinern über sich hat, hört darum auf, ein einfacher zu seyn. Ein Begriff hört nähmlich nur dann erst auf, ein einfacher zu seyn, wenn er zerlegbar ist. Zu einer Zerlegung aber gehört die Angabe von wenigstens zwey Bestandtheilen, die jeder für sich gedenkbar sind. Nun betrachten wir zwar den allgemeineren Begriff wirklich als einen Bestandtheil von jenem engeren, welcher ihm untergeordnet ist; aber es könnte wohl seyn, daß sich zu diesem ersten Bestandtheile (genus proximum) kein zweyter (differentia specifica) auffinden ließe, d.h. daß das, was zu dem allgemeinern Begriffe hinzukommen muß, damit der engere daraus hervor gehe, nicht für sich selbst darstellbar wäre.*" (Bolzano 1810, p. 47).

two components each of which is thinkable by itself. Now we take the more general concept really to be a component of the more narrow concept which is subordinated to it; but sometimes we may not be able to discover in addition to the first component *(genus proximum)* a second one *(differentia specifica)*, i.e. it may be the case that that which has to be added to the more general concept in order to obtain the narrower one cannot be represented by itself.

Let us first ignore the reference to thinking and representing in this passage. Then the view would be that the concept *possible*, for example, is a part of the concept *actual* although the latter lacks any further part.[12] But does this really make sense? In order to sharpen the question let me invoke the mereological two-place predicate 'x and y are disjunct $(x \mid y)$':[13]

(Df. Disj)

$x \mid y$ iff $(x \neq y \ \& \ \neg x \ll y \ \& \ \neg y \ll x \ \& \ \neg (\exists z)(z \ll x \ \& \ z \ll y))$.

So our question is, How can a concept be a (proper) part of another concept if the latter has no supplementary part which is disjunct from the former? Such an assumption would clearly run counter to the mereological principle of supplementation which belongs to the hard core of our understanding of the part-whole relation:[14]

(Suppl) If $x \ll y$ then $(\exists z)(z \ll y \ \& \ z \mid x)$.

Or did Bolzano in his early treatise work with an epistemic conception of simplicity? Then the view expressed in (B2) would be that a simple concept which is subordinated to a more general concept *has* indeed two constituents, but only one of them (the more general concept) can be *thought or represented by itself.* Whatever the second clause may mean, such an epistemic conception of simplicity is entirely alien to the position Bolzano takes in the 'Theory of Science'.

In playing off example (3) against (CR^2) Bolzano does not take possibility to be a modal property of propositions. Rather he considers it, like actuality *(Wirklichkeit,* i.e. causal efficiency, *Wirksamkeit)* as a property of non-propositional objects like the proverbial golden mountains. But he then goes on to define the first-level predicate 'possible' in terms of the modal predicate (WL II 230): 'Object A is possible' means the same as 'That A is actual is possible'. Hence, by Bolzano's lights, the concept *actual* is a constituent of the concept *possible.*[15]

---

[12] This is a position which Brentano was to take towards the end of the century: Brentano 1985, pp. 151-152, cp. 11, 53.

[13] This is the definition of 'discrete' in Chisholm 1976, p. 152, and it is logically equivalent with the definition of 'disjoint' in Simons 1987, p. 28, p. 188.

[14] In Simons 1987, p. 28, (Suppl) is called 'Weak Supplementation Principle'.

[15] Cp. Bolzano 1995, p. 343. As to the next steps in Bolzano's theory of the modalities cp. Morscher 1974, pp. 87-92 and Casari 1989.

2 A Line of Defence

One can defend CR^2 against Bolzano's criticism if one assumes that its proponents have a different conception of content. Bolzano himself saw this clearly (WL I 282 f., 570 f.). The authors of the *Logic of Port Royal*, for example, understand 'content' in such a way that the following condition (I shall call it the *Port Royal Constraint*, PRC for short) is satisfied:[16]

(PRC)
$(\forall x, y)\ (Cnt\ (y) \ll Cnt\ (x) \rightarrow \mathbf{N}\ (\forall z)(z \text{ falls under } x \rightarrow z \text{ falls under } y))$

According to the PRC a concept y is part of the content of a more complex concept x only if an object has to fall under the simpler concept y if it is to fall under the more complex concept x. If this constraint is accepted then CR^2 is no longer falsified by examples (1) and (2). Surely one does not have to understand German in order to fall under the concept *understands German or Czech*, and it is equally obvious that one does not have to be a woman if one is to fall under the concept *relative of a woman*.

One should resist the temptation to strengthen the PRC into a biconditional, for then the content of any concept would be so complex that one could not have *one* concept expressible in English in one's conceptual repertoire without having *all* of them. Take the concept *rectangular triangle:* If the biconditional strengthening of the PRC were correct one would have to say that every universal concept like *object, identical with itself* and *female if a vixen* is part of the content of the concept *rectangular triangle*, and that this content includes *all* concepts which are expressed by substitution-instances of the predicate schemata 'rectangular or P' and 'not both P and not-P'. But surely one can have the concept *rectangular triangle* without having, e.g., the concept *hypocritical* or the concept *baroque*.

Bolzano's conception of 'content' is very different, and it is intuitively near at hand. The sense of the expression 'understands German' is a component of the sense of the expression 'understands German or Czech'. Now the sense of the former expression is the concept *understands German*, and the sense of the latter expression is the concept *understands German or Czech*. The content of a complex concept is the collection (*Inbegriff*) of all its conceptual components. (According to this stipulation, the content of

---

[16] When the distinction between *compréhension, comprehensio* and *étendue, extensio* is introduced in part I, chpt. vi of Arnauld & Nicole 1662, this constraint does not yet come to light, but it is manifest in part II, chpt. xvii: 'When I say that a rectangle is a parallelogram I ascribe to the rectangle whatever is contained in the idea of a parallelogram. If any part of this idea did not apply to the rectangle the whole idea would not apply to it eiter.' No rectangle has the property of being a side, hence, according to Arnauld & Nicole, the idea of a side is *not* part of the idea of a parallelogram; but as this idea is that of a quadrangle with pairwise parallel sides, the idea of a side *is* a constituent of its Bolzano-content.

dull father of a bright son is the same as that of *bright father of a dull son*.) So the concept *understands German* is a component of the content of the concept *understands German or Czech*. Similarly the concept *finger* is, according to Bolzano's conception of content, a component of the content of the concept *finger-exercise*. But of course, this pair does not satisfy the PRC, since no finger-exercise is a finger. —

The same defence-strategy can be used to defuse part of Bolzano's highly illuminating criticism of Kant's explanation of the notion of analyticity. This explanation, Bolzano complains, 'does not fully meet the requirements of logical strictness':[17]

(B3) [Kant] asserts that in analytic judgements the predicate is contained (in a hidden manner) in the subject, or that the predicate does not lie outside the subject, or that it is a constituent of the subject [...]. These are in part only figurative modes of speech which do not analyse the concept to be expli-cated, in part expressions which permit an interpretation which covers too much. Everything stated here [...] can be said of propositions which no-body will want to call analytic, for instance

[S] *The father of Alexander, King of Macedonia, was King of Macedonia.*

(WL II 87 f.)

Bolzano's cute example exhibits a weakness in the way Kant formu-lates his account of analyticity: As it stands his formulation really does jus-tify the characterization of [S] as analytic, which is surely undesirable for Kant. After all, the expression 'King of Macedonia' is a significant compo-nent of the longer expression 'father of Alexander, King of Macedonia'. Hence the sense of the shorter expression is a component of the sense of the longer one. Thus it really suggests itself to say with Bolzano that the con-cept *King of Macedonia* is an ingredient of the concept *father of Alexander, King of Macedonia*. But presumably Kant would take the predicate-concept to be 'contained' in the subject-concept only if nothing can fall under the subject-concept without falling under the predicate-concept. And if he thus accepts the PRC, this part of Bolzano's criticism misfires. A person does not have to be King of Macedonia if he is to fall under the concept *father of Alexander, King of Macedonia*. So under this proviso Kant is no longer open to refutation *via* example [S].

---

[17] [Kants Erklärung scheint mir] *"der logischen Strenge nicht ganz zu entsprechen... Sagt man..., daß in den analytischen Urtheilen das Prädicat in dem Subjecte (verdeckter Weise) enthalten sey, oder nicht außerhalb desselben liege, oder schon als Bestandtheil darin vorkomme;...: so sind dieses theils bloß bildliche Redensarten, die den zu erklärenden Begriff nicht zerlegen, theils Ausdrücke, die eine zu weite Auslegung zulassen. Denn auch von Sätzen, die Niemand für analytische ausgeben wird, z.B.: Der Vater Alexanders, des Königs von Ma-cedonien, war König von Macedonien,... läßt sich Alles, was hier gesagt wird, behaupten."*

3   What are Marks *(Merkmale)* of a Concept?

The Fregean counterpart to the two-place predicate '(concept) y *is a proper part of the content of* (concept) x' in the CR is, I contend, 'y *is a mark of* x'. When explaining his notion of marks Frege again and again uses mereological terms. In 1884 he introduces the notion by saying that some concepts are such that marks 'compose *(zusammensetzen)*' them (Gl 64). And in the early decades of the 20th century he writes:

(F3ᵃ)   Most concepts are composed of parts which are themselves concepts *(zusammengesetzt aus Teilbegriffen),* its marks [...]. I compare the marks of a concept to the stones of which a house consists.[18]

(F3ᵇ)   Marks of a concept are concepts which are logical parts *(logische Teile)* of it.[19]

(F3ᶜ)   We see here a concept [....] composed of parts which are themselves concepts *(zusammengesetzt aus Teilbegriffen)* [....]. We call the latter 'marks of the complex concept'.[20]

It is both natural and correct, I think, to take marks, as characterised in mereological terms, to be components of certain complex senses. Thus not only in Gl but also (somewhat surprisingly) in his post-1891 writings Frege sometimes means by 'concept' the *sense* of a (monadic) predicate – rather than its reference. (Otherwise we would have to hold Frege to the mistaken doctrine, passingly suggested in *'Über Sinn und Bedeutung'*, but explicitly repudiated later,[21] that the referent of the part is part of the referent of the whole.) David Bell, too, understands Frege in the charitable way I suggest: 'For Frege a characteristic mark M of a concept C is a concept which is a component part of C, in the sense that M would be revealed by an analysis of C'.[22] Surely what gets analysed in an analysis is a sense. 'So,' Bell continues, 'the concept *unmarried* is a characteristic mark of the concept *bachelor*'. I couldn't agree more, but there is a problem here: Analysis reveals also the sense of the prefix 'un-' and that of 'married' as component parts of the concept *bachelor*. Are they also marks of this concept? The answer is, No, and as was to be expected Bell is clearly aware of this, for he goes on to say: 'And as Frege points out, the component characteristics of a [first-level] concept are properties of any object which falls under it: any-

---

[18] Frege 1976, p. 151.

[19] Frege 1903, p. 373.

[20] Frege 1969, p. 247.

[21] Cp. the beginning of his first Begriffsschrift II Lecture of 1913 (publ. in History and Philosophy of Logic 17 (1996), 20); and Frege 1969, p. 275.

[22] Bell 1982, p. 458.

thing which falls under the concept *bachelor* has the property of being un-married.' David Wiggins concurs: 'A mark of the concept F is a property that anything has if it falls under F'.[23] Now this is correct as far as it goes, but it doesn't go far enough. It is also true that anything which falls under the concept *bachelor* has the property of being longer than 10 inches, but there could be bachelors which are tinier than that, I suppose. Even if all creatures with a heart have kidneys (as Quine wants us to believe) the prop-erty of having kidneys is hardly a mark of the concept *has a heart*. What Frege himself actually says is stronger than what Bell and Wiggins suggest:

(F4a)   If we say: 'A square is an equilateral rectangle,' we define the con-cept *square* by specifying what properties something *must* have in order to fall under this concept. I call these properties 'marks' of the concept.[24]

(F4b)   A mark of a concept is a property an object *must* have if it is to fall under the concept.[25]

So there can be no doubt that Frege accepts what I called the Port Royal Constraint, and thus he does not fall victim to Bolzano's criticism of CR^2.

The notion of a mark was introduced in a book in which Frege did not yet draw a clear distinction between sense and reference. Hence it is not surprising that certain tensions arise when he continues to use it in his post-1891 writings. If we take a certain mark M to be a component of the sense of a certain non-empty first-level monadic predicate P, is it then true that M is a *property* which every object has to which P applies? That depends on how we individuate properties. If we identify them with senses of monadic predicates it is true. But if, following Frege, we identify them rather with the referents of such predicates, then mark M is (not identical with, but rather) a *mode of presentation of a property* which every object, P is true of, instantiates.

Kutschera tries to capture Frege's conception of a mark by saying: 'A mark of a first-level concept F is a first-level concept G for which the sen-tence "For all x, if Fx then Gx" is analytically true'.[26] The restriction to first-level concepts is an improvement over Frege's own formulation (and clearly in the spirit of his theory), and since modal notions play no official role in Frege's philosophical language the replacement of necessity by ana-lyticity may be a good idea, too. But there remains an ambiguity which is present in Frege's own formulations as well. Surely the condition for being a mark is to be taken as necessary, but is it also supposed to be *sufficient*? Is *every* property an object must have if it is to fall under a given first-level concept a mark of this concept? Is *every* first-level concept G for which the

---

[23] Wiggins 1998, p. 142; cp. Wiggins 1996, p. 269.
[24] Frege 1893, p. xiv, second italics mine, cp. Frege 1893, p. 3.
[25] Frege 1903, p. 373, my italics.
[26] Kutschera 1989, p. 100.

sentence "For all x, if Fx then Gx" is analytically true a mark of the first-level concept F?

My objections against strengthening the PRC into a biconditional apply here again. If we substitute for 'G' any predicate of the form 'not both H and not-H' then "For all x, if Fx then Gx" will become analytically true whatever 'F' may be. But then the content of any concept would be so rich that nobody could have *one* concept expressible in English without having *all* of them. But surely one can have the concept *bachelor* without having the concept *equator*, say. When elucidating Frege's conception of a mark we should not lose sight of his mereological characterisations of this notion.[27] It is also worthwhile to inspect Frege's examples closely. I have compiled a list which may well be complete:

(a)	concept:	*rectangular triangle*	(1884: 64)
	marks:	*rectangular, triangle*	
(b)	concept:	*positive whole number less than 10*	(1892: 202)
	marks:	*positive number, whole number, less than 10*	
(c)	concept:	*square (equilateral rectangle)*	(1893: xiv)
	marks:	*equilateral, rectangle*	
(d)	concept:	*black silken cloth*	(1893: xiv;
	marks:	*black, silken, cloth*	1900: in 1976, 150 f.)
(e)	concept:	*positive square root of 4*	(1903: 373)
	marks:	*positive, square root of 4*	
(f)	concept:	*positive cubic number*	(1914: in 1969, 247)
	marks:	*positive, cubic number*	
(g)	concept:	*blue silken ribbon*	(1919: 1976, 154)
	marks:	*blue, silken, ribbon*	

[27] Anthony Kenny is obviously acutely aware of them, for he even proposes to translate *'Merkmal'* as 'component (of a concept)' (Kenny 1995, p. 217).

The most striking feature of this list is that the analysis of the concept into its marks is always shallow and always conjunctive. Nobody who grasps the concept in question can fail to know that it is a concept of objects which have property A *and* property B (*and* ...). The examples strongly suggest the following explanation:

(Df. **Mark**)   x is a mark of y iff (x is a concept & y is a concept & x is a conjunctively connected part of y)

---

where x is a conjunctively connected part of y just in case y is the sense of a (predicate definable as a) conjunctive predicate and x is the sense of one of the conjuncts.

All examples from (a) to (g) are equally pertinent both to Frege's early criticism of Boole and Schröder[28] and to his more famous criticism of Kant in § 88 of Gl. Let me recall the latter passage:

(F5) [Kant] seems to think of a concept as determined by co-ordinate marks *(beigeordnete Merkmale)*; but this is one of the least fruitful methods of concept-formation. Anyone who surveys the definitions given above will scarcely find one of this kind. The same holds of the truly fruitful definitions of mathematics, for example that of the continuity of a function. In these we do not have a sequence of co-ordinate marks, but a more intimate – I should like to say, more organic – combination of determinations. The distinction can be made intuitive by means of a geometrical picture. If one represents the concepts (or their extensions) by regions of a plane, what corresponds to a concept defined by co-ordinate marks is the region common to all the regions representing those marks; it is enclosed by segments of their peripheries. In giving such a definition, therefore, it is a matter – to speak pictorially – of using already given lines in a new way to delimit a region.** Nothing essentially new emerges from this. The more fruitful determinations of concepts draw boundary lines which were not previously given at all. What we shall be able to infer from them cannot be predicted in advance; we are not simply taking out of the chest what we had put into it (Gl 100 f.).

Unfortunately Frege adds to this a footnote I find very confusing:

**) The case is similar when the marks are connected by 'or'.

To be sure, the cases when two concepts A and B are conjunctively connected and when they are disjunctively connected *are* similar in the relevant respect. Adopting the geometrical pictures of Frege's early paper 'Booles rechnende Logik und die Begriffschrift' (NS 37) we can represent the conjunctive (1) and the disjunctive (2) cases thus:

---

[28] 'Booles rechnende Logik und die Begriffsschrift', Frege 1969, pp. 9-52, esp. pp. 37-39.

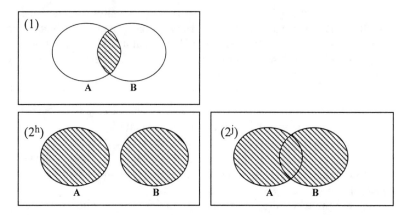

What is confusing is that Frege makes this point by using the notion of a mark in both cases. For if we go by this footnote then he might just as well have given the following examples to elucidate his notion of a mark:

(h) concept: *sibling (brother or sister)*
     marks (?): *brother, sister.*

(j) concept: *understands German or Czech*
     marks (?): *understands German, understands Czech.*

But then, of course, Bolzano's criticism of the second prong of the CR does apply to Frege with full force. However, the idea of disjunctively connected marks is plainly incompatible with Frege's endorsement of the Port Royal Constraint: Obviously one does not have to be a sister in order to fall under the concept *sibling*. If we make the ominous footnote a proper part of Frege's account of what a mark is then this account is simply inconsistent. I propose that we forget the footnote. After all, it is written only in small letters...

4   The Repetition Problem

Both Bolzano and Frege think of complex senses in mereological terms.[29] For this very reason they share a problem I call the *Repetition Problem*. Consider the complex expression-token

(T2)   *married son of a married mother.*

which contains two tokens of the (unequivocal) type-word "married". Surely the sense of T2 differs from that of

---

[29] As far as Frege is concerned, I entirely agree here with Michael Dummett as against Geach and against Baker-Hacker: Dummett 1981, pp. 265-270; Dummett 1991, p. 190 f.

(T1)   *son of a married mother.*

Hence one is tempted to say (and Bolzano often yields to this kind of temptation[30]): The sense of token (T1) contains the sense of 'married' only once, whereas the sense of (T2) contains it twice. But is this really a sensible thing to say? Can a whole contain one and the same part twice over? Or is the sense of 'married' a type of which there can be more than one occurrence within a complex sense? But then, how can these alleged occurrences be distinguished from one another? The first 'married'-*inscription* in (T2) is at another place than the second, but parts of senses do not occupy positions in space (or time). Or consider propositions expressed by doubly negated sentences. One is tempted to say that they contain the concept of negation twice, and Bolzano yields to this temptation when he says that this concept is 'capable of being combined with itself *(einer Verbindung mit sich selbst fähig)*' (WL I 355). But does this make sense? Bolzano soon came to recognize the Repetition Problem.[31] In a notebook we find the following entry:[32]

(B4) December 8, 1835. [...] Within the concept Figure With Equal Sides And Unequal Angles the concept Equal surely occurs twice.[...] [But:] One and the same Idea can only occur once *ex principio identitatis indiscernibilium.* There cannot be many completely equal Ideas etc., because they would be indistinguishable (BGA: 2 A 12/2, 148 f.).

A collection *(Inbegriff)*, Bolzano says, is 'something which has compositeness *(etwas, das Zusammengesetztheit hat)*' (WL I 393 f). Hence complex concepts (as well as propositions) are collections. Can a collection ever contain one and the same part twice? Series *(Reihen)* are a special kind of collections, and they might seem to give us a reason to answer this question affirmatively. After all, the series designated by '1^0, 1^1, 1^2, 1^3,...' does seem to contain one and the same element fairly often. No, it doesn't (Bolzano contends), because the parts of this collection are the *concepts* [1^0], [1^1], [1^2], [1^3],..., which certainly differ from each other (WL I 404). In his

---

[30] Cp. WL I, p. 309 ff, p. 355; III, p. 16.

[31] Without realizing that Bolzano himself was clearly aware of the Repetition Problem, Peter Simons re-discovered it: Simons 1987, p. 402. More recently: F. Krickel 1995, pp. 259-263.

[32] *"So kommt z.B. der Begriff der Gleichheit in dem Begriffe eines Rhombus, als einer Figur von gleichen Seiten, aber ungleichen Winkeln, gewiß 2mal vor.* [...] [Aber:] *Eine und dieselbe Vorstellung kann nur einmal sein ex principio* [identitatis] *indiscernibili*[um]. *Es kann nicht mehrere gleiche Vorstellungen geben, weil sie durch nichts zu unterscheiden wären"* (Bolzano 1978, p. 148 f. I have corrected here a bit of dog Latin imposed by the Gesamtausgabe on Bolzano.) Cp. also: WL III, p. 16: *"Unläugbar ist es, daß eine und eben dieselbe objective Vorstellung in manchem Satze zu wiederholten Malen erscheine. So kommt in dem Satze: Jedes gleichseitige Dreieck ist auch gleichwinklig, der Begriff der Gleichheit [...] zweimal vor"*; or WL I, p. 309 ff.

'Introduction to the Theory of Magnitudes' he states quite unambiguously:[33]

(B5) Obviously it is impossible that an object should be combined with itself to form a collection, i.e. a new object different from the one we started with *(Es ist offenbar unmöglich, daß irgendein Ding mit sich selbst zu einem Inbegriffe, d. h. zu einem neuen von ihm verschiedenen Gegenstande vereiniget werde).*

But then, how is the Repetition Problem for concepts like the one expressed by T2 and for propositions expressed by doubly negated sentences to be solved? Bolzano does not offer a solution.

Did Frege also recognize the problem? In his 1923 paper on 'Compound Thoughts' he wrote:[34]

(F6) Let us now consider cases where a thought is compounded with itself *(mit sich selbst gefügt)* rather than with some other thought.

Propositions expressed by sentences of the form 'p & p' form one class of examples. Frege goes on to say that the thought that p & p is the same as the thought that p. If this is right then in such a case the repetition occurs only on he level of thought-expressions. Bolzano would certainly protest: In the proposition expressed by 'Snow is white, and snow is white' the concept of conjunction appears which is entirely absent from the proposition expressed by 'Snow is white'. But this is a story for another occasion.[35] There is another passage which shows that Frege did recognize the Repetition Problem. In his 1919 essay 'Negation' he says about the sense of the expression 'the negation of the negation of (...)':[36]

(F7) Here we are presented with a singular case; we have something – the negation of ...– amalgamated with itself *(mit sich selbst verschmilzt).* Here, of course, metaphors derived from the corporeal realm fail us; for a body cannot be amalgamated with itself so that the result is something different from it *(so daß etwas von ihm selbst Verschiedenes entsteht).*

Frege seems to think that the Repetition Problem arises from the fact that the part-whole terminology is literally appropriate only when applied to corporeal entities (Vern 156). But he never goes on to propose a literally appropriate terminology.

If we were to take complex senses to be *sequences* of simple(r) senses,[37] this problem would be solved. But if one seeks a solution within Bolzano's own conceptual framework this proposal does not give us what

---

[33] Bolzano 1975, p. 105.

[34] Frege 1923, p. 49.

[35] Cp. Künne 1997, Sect. 6.

[36] Frege 1919, p. 157.

[37] Thus Jan Berg in his article on Bolzano in the *Cambridge Dictionary of Philosophy* (Berg 1997, p. 80): "A proposition in Bolzano's sense is a preexistent sequence of ideas-as-such *(Vorstellungen an sich)*", and Berg 1992, p. 73 f.

we want. Sequences are sets (in the modern sense). It is very doubtful, to put it mildly, that Bolzano has the modern conception of a set, so it is at least as doubtful that he thinks of complex senses as sets. And as for Frege, he surely does not conceive complex senses as sets either.

Can we solve the Repetition Problem by retreating to sign(-tokens)? A first suggestion might be: Sense x occurs n-times in sense y iff a sign(-token) cannot express y without containing n constituents expressing x. But this is not correct (as Michael Dummett pointed out in his reply to a paper of mine[38]): An inscription of the sentence 'Socrates was wise, and so was Salomo' contains only one inscription of 'wise', but the proposition expressed needs the sense of 'wise' twice. Or consider an inscription of *'gleichseitig und –winklig'*: It contains only one inscription of *'gleich'*, but the concept expressed, Dummett would say, needs the sense of *'gleich'* twice. The trouble arises because of our (stylistically praiseworthy) eagerness to avoid repetition. But then, an inscription of the sentence 'Socrates was wise, and so was Salomo' has the same sense as an inscription of the sentence 'Socrates was wise, and Salomo was wise', and an inscription of *'gleichseitig und –winklig'* can also be given a less lazy paraphrase. Dummett has another example which shows that the phenomenon is not dependent on the occurrence of proforms of laziness: 'Cato killed himself' needs the sense of 'Cato' twice. Actually, how often a sense S is required for the sense of a complex expression E may be linguistically even more hidden: S may be required more than once even if E contains *no* part expressing (nothing but) S: Thus an inscription of the phrase 'a bachelor's father' contains no 'male'-inscription but the sense of 'male' is a component of the senses of both nouns, hence the concept expressed by the phrase needs it twice.

So an improved version of the suggested solution might run like this: Sense x occurs n-times in sense y iff y can be expressed by a sign(-token) only if that token *either* itself contains n constituents expressing x *or* it can be paraphrased *salvo sensu* by a token which contains n constituents expressing x.

---

[38] Dummett 1997, p. 245.

5   The First Prong of the Canon

Let us return once more to the Canon of Reciprocity as clarified by Bolzano:

For all concepts x, y:
$(\mathbf{CR^1})$ if Cnt (x) $\ll$ Cnt (y),   then Ext (y) $\ll$ Ext (x),   and
$(\mathbf{CR^2})$ if Ext (x) $\ll$ Ext (y),   then Cnt (y) $\ll$ Cnt (x).

Since Frege explicitly endorses only the second prong of the CR, I have focussed on Bolzano's criticism of CR^2. It's time now to have a look at Bolzano's powerful attack on CR^1. Let me first explain the weapon used in this attack. Bolzano classifies certain concepts as abundant *(überfüllt oder überfließend)*.[39]

(Df. **Abd**)   A concept x is abundant iff there is a concept y such that
     (a) the content of x differs from that of y only insofar as y contains at least one constituent less (often) than x, and
     (b) x has the same extension as y (WL I 309 ff.).[40]

Let us first consider two individual concepts as examples: The concept *Bolzano's male father* is abundant, and the concept *Bolzano's father* is its economical counterpart. The concept *the author of the 'Phaedo' and the 'Symposium'* is abundant, and the concept *the author of the 'Symposium'* is (one of) its economical counterparts. One could distinguish the former case from the latter by saying that in the former case *(Bolzano's male father)* the concept is *intensionally* abundant: It is impossible that something falls under the economical concept without falling under its abundant counterpart.[41] Leibniz seems to mean by 'notions superflues' intensionally abundant concepts.[42] Now consider the following pairs of general concepts:

(4)   *chain-smoker;*   *chain-smoker who endangers his/her health*

(5)   *equilateral triangle;*   *equilateral triangle which is equiangular.*

---

[39] WL I, p. 164. Ultimately the terminology goes back to ancient rhetorics. In Quintilian πλεονασμος is defined as *abundans super necessitatem oratio*. Quintilian 1972-1975,IX p. 3, p. 46, cp. VIII p. 3, p. 53 f.
[40] WL III, p. 408 ff., IV p. 117 ff., p. 222 f.
[41] Dähnhardt 1992, p. 30 ff.
[42] Leibniz 1703-1705, II 30, § 4.

The second concepts in (4) and (5) are abundant. In both cases the first concept is a proper part of the content of the second, but, contrary to CR[1], the extension of the second is by no means a proper part of the extension of the first: Both concepts have the *same* extension. Now the more complex concept in (5) is intensionally abundant. Hence in this case the Port Royal Constraint *is* satisfied: Nothing can fall under the more complex concept without falling under the simpler one.

Example (5) shows that the intensional abundancy of a concept is not always self-evident. Frege could not deny that in (5) we have *two* concepts (predicative senses), for surely one can believe that something falls under the first concept without believing that it falls under the second: It is a geometrical discovery that they have the same extension. The next example makes this feature even more vivid:

(6)   *even number greater than 2;*   *even number greater than 2 which is the sum of two prime numbers.*

The second concept in (6) is intensionally abundant if it is abundant at all. It is abundant if Goldbach's Conjecture is true, but it is still an open question whether that conjecture really is true.

So Bolzano is right when he contends that CR[1] is refuted by examples like (5) even if we adopt the Port Royal Constraint. Is this an objection against Frege? No, for as far as I can see, Frege never declared his allegiance to the first prong of the CR. Let me finish on this irenic note.[*]

References

Arnauld A. and P. Nicole 1662. *Logique ou l'Art de Penser* [1]1662, lat.: *Logica sive ars cogitandi* 1704.

Bell, D. 1982. *Review of The Metaphysics of Gottlob Frege* by E.H.W. Kluge. *Mind* 91: 457 - 459.

Berg, J. 1992. *Ontology Without Ultrafilters*. St. Augustin: Academia.

Berg, J. 1997. Bolzano. *Cambridge Dictionary of Philosophy*, ed. by R. Audi: 80.

Bolzano, B. 1810. *Beyträge zu einer begründeteren Darstellung der Mathematik*. Darmstadt: Wissenschaftliche Buchgesellschaft 1974.

Bolzano, B. 1837. *Wissenschaftslehre*, 4 vol.s. Aalen: Scientia 1981.

Bolzano, B. 1975. *Einleitung zur Größenlehre*. In *Gesamtausgabe*, Vol. 2 A 7. Stuttgart-Bad Cannstatt: Frommann-Holzboog.

Bolzano, B. 1978. *Vermischte philosophische und physikalische Schriften 1832 - 1848, 2.Teil*. In *Gesamtausgabe*, Vol. 2 A 12/ 2. Stuttgart-Bad Cannstatt: Frommann-Holzboog.

---

[*] Many thanks to Jonathan Barnes, David Bell, Tyler Burge, Edgar Morscher, Benjamin Schnieder, Peter Simons and David Wiggins for helpful comments.

Bolzano, B. 1995. *Lehrbuch der Religionswissenschaft, Erster Teil, §§ 86 - 177.* In *Gesamtausgabe,* Vol. 2 A 7. Stuttgart-Bad Cannstatt: Frommann-Holzboog.

Brentano, F. 1985. *Kategorienlehre,* ed. A. Kastil. Hamburg: Felix Meiner.

Casari, E. 1989. Remarks on Bolzano's Modalities. *Atti del Convegno Internazionale di Storia della Logica,* ed. G. Corsi. Bologna.

Chisholm, R.M. 1976. *Person and Object.* London: George Allen and Unwin.

Dähnhardt, S. 1992. *Wahrheit und Satz an sich.* Pfaffenweiler: Centaurus.

Dummett, M. 1981. *The Interpretation of Frege's Philosophy.* London: Duckworth.

Dummett, M. 1991. *Frege and Other Philosophers.* Oxford: Clarendon Press.

Dummett, M. 1997. Comments on Wolfgang Künne's Paper. *Bolzano and Analytical Philosophy,* eds. W. Künne, M. Siebel, and M. Textor (= Grazer Philosophische Studien 53), 241-248.

Frege, G. 1884. *Grundlagen der Arithmetik.* Hamburg: Felix Meiner 1986.

Frege, G. 1892. Über Begriff und Gegenstand. *Funktion, Begriff, Bedeutung,* G. Frege, ed. G. Patzig. Göttingen: Vandenhoeck & Ruprecht, 1962.

Frege, G. 1893. *Grundgesetze der Arithmetik,* Vol. I. Hildesheim: Georg Olms 1966.

Frege, G. 1903. Über die Grundlagen der Geometrie, Part II. *Kleinere Schriften,* G. Frege, ed. I. Angelelli. Darmstadt: Wissenschaftliche Buchgesellschaft 1967.

Frege, G. 1913. *Begriffsschrift II* Lecture of 1913 publ. in *History and Philosophy of Logic* 17 (1996).

Frege, G. 1919. Die Verneinung. *Logische Untersuchungen,* G. Frege, ed. G. Patzig. Göttingen: Vandenhoeck & Ruprecht, 1966.

Frege, G. 1923. Gedankengefüge. *Logische Untersuchungen,* G. Frege, ed. G. Patzig. Göttingen: Vandenhoeck & Ruprecht, 1966.

Frege, G. 1969. *Nachgelassene Schriften,* Bd. 1, ed. H. Hermes, F. Kambartel and F. Kaulbach. Hamburg: Felix Meiner.

Frege, G. 1976. *Wissenschaftlicher Briefwechsel,* ed. G. Gabriel et al. Hamburg: Felix Meiner.

Gottsched, J.G. 1983. *Erste Gründe der gesamten Weltweisheit* (^{7}1762), 2 vol.s. Hildesheim: Georg Olms.

Hoensbroech, F. G. 1931. Beziehungen zwischen Inhalt und Umfang von Begriffen. *Erkenntnis* 2.

Johnson, W. E. 1921-1924. *Logic* 3 vol.s. Cambridge: Cambridge University Press.

Kant, I. 1763. Der einzig mögliche Beweisgrund zu einer Demonstration des Daseyns Gottes. *Werke,* I. Kant, ed. W. Weischedel, Vol. 1, Darmstadt: Wissenschaftliche Buchgesellschaft 1963.

Kant, I. 1800. *Logik. Ein Handbuch zu Vorlesungen,* ed. Jäsche. *Werke,* I. Kant, ed. W. Weischedel, Vol. 5, Darmstadt: Wissenschaftliche Buchgesellschaft 1963.

Kenny, A. 1995. *Frege.* London: Penguin Books.

Krickel, F. 1995. *Teil und Inbegriff.* St. Augustin: Academia

Künne,W. 1997. Propositions in Bolzano and Frege. *Bolzano and Analytical Philosophy*, eds. W. Künne, M. Siebel, and M. Textor (= Grazer Philosophische Studien 53). 203-240.

Kutschera, F. v. 1989. *Gottlob Frege*. Berlin - N.Y.: de Gruyter

Leibniz, G.W. 1695. Système nouveau de la nature et de la communication des substances. In G.W. Leibniz, Die philosophischen Schriften von G.W. Leibniz, ed. C.I. Gerhardt, 7 Bde., Berlin-Halle 1875-1890, Hildesheim: Georg Olms 1978.

Leibniz, G.W. 1703-1705. Nouveaux essais sur l' entendement humain. *Die philosophischen Schriften von G.W. Leibniz*, ed. C.I. Gerhardt, 7 Bde., Berlin-Halle 1875-1890, Hildesheim: Georg Olms 1978.

Morscher, E. 1974. *'Philosophische Logik' bei Bernard Bolzano*. In Bolzano als Logiker (= Sitzungsberichte der Österreichischen Akademie der Wissenschaften, Philos-.hist. Klasse, 293. Bd., 5. Abh.), Wien: Verlag der Österreichischen Akademie der Wissenschaften, 77-105.

Prior, A.N.1949. Determinables, Determinates, and Determinants (I & II). *Mind* 58: 1-20, 178-194.

Quintilianus, M.F. 1972-1975. *Institutionis Oratoriae Libri XII - Ausbildung des Redners*, ed H. Rahn, Darmstadt: Wissenschaftliche Buchgesellschaft.

Schmauks, D. 1985. *Der Kanon vom umgekehrten Verhältnis zwischen Extension und Intension*. Unpublished MA thesis, Salzburg.

Simons, P. 1987. *Parts*. Oxford: Clarendon Press.

Simons, P. 1987. *Bolzano, Tarski, and the Limits of Logic*. Philosophia Naturalis 24: 378-405.

Wiggins, D. 1996. Reply to Wilfrid Hodges. *Identity, Truth, and Value*, eds. S. Lovibond & St. Williams, Oxford: Blackwell.

Wiggins, D. 1998. *Needs, Values, Truth*. Oxford: Clarendon Press.

Wolff, Ch. 1713. *Vernünfftige Gedanken von den Kräfften des menschlichen Verstandes [...]*, Deutsche Logik (1713, [14]1754). In Ch. Wolff, Gesammelte Werke, ed. J. École u.a., Bd. I / 1, Hildesheim: Georg Olms 1962.

Wolff, Ch. 1730. *Philosophia prima sive Ontologia* (1730, [2]1736). In Ch. Wolff, Gesammelte Werke, ed. J. École u.a., Bd. II / 3, Hildesheim: Georg Olms 1962.

Zimmermann, R. 1849. *Leibniz und Herbart. Eine Vergleichung ihrer Monadologien*. Wien: Wilhelm Braumüller.

15

Concepts are Beliefs about Essences

ULRIKE HAAS-SPOHN, WOLFGANG SPOHN

1 Introduction

Putnam (1975) and Burge (1979) have made a convincing case that neither meanings nor beliefs are in the head. Most philosophers, it seems, have accepted their argument. Putnam explained that a subject's grasp of an expression's meaning is often insufficient to fix its reference, and that she needs help from her natural and social environment. Burge explained that having a belief, even in the de dicto sense, is really a relational property that may change merely when the implicit relatum, the linguistic community, changes.

To accept this, however, one does not necessarily need to accept all the anti-individualistic consequences Burge has drawn from these insights. On the contrary, these consequences have met much more reluctance. Many share the view, we do as well, that there must be something in the head, not only a brain, but also a mind, indeed a mind with internal or intrinsic representational or semantic properties. This view was also supported by arguments mainly concerning, on the one hand, psychological explanation and the causation of individual behavior, and on the other, self-knowledge. Of course, these arguments have been disputed, but the dispute has not shattered our prejudice.[1] Here, we would simply like to presuppose the correctness of this view without any further comments.

---

[1] We had and have good company: Loar 1986, Fodor 1987, ch. 2 (though ch. 4 apparently got the upper hand in the end – cf. Fodor 1994), Perry 1988, Block 1991, Lewis 1994, Chom-

Thus, all those sharing the prejudice set out to characterize what's in the head, i.e., so-called narrow contents. Now, narrow contents are rather expressed by, or associated with, whole sentences. But sentences are composed of parts, basically a singular and a general term, and hence narrow contents seem to be composed in the same way. We reserve here the term "concept" for those entities which a subject expresses by, or internally associates with, singular and general terms (and maybe other expressions as well). Having a concept is hence *defined* to be an internal, non-relational property. In the absence of a generally agreed usage of the term "concept", this stipulation is certainly legitimate and it is often made. The terms "narrow content" and "concept" thus stand essentially for the same thing; the only difference, which we do not strictly observe, though, lies in the associated kinds of expressions.

For internalists like us the existence of concepts and narrow contents is thus beyond doubt. The question is rather a constructive one: how precisely should one conceive of them? This is, as the title indicates, the topic of our paper. However, the offers so far are rather more problematic than impressive. We shall refer to two major options in the following.

First, the dominant view concerning the mind-body problem has been, and perhaps still is, functionalism. Functionalism is the view that internal mental states are functional states, i.e., to be individuated by the place they occupy within a large functional net spanned between perceptual input and behavioral output. Insofar as mental states have narrow content, their content is also characterized in a functional way. This gave rise to the program of so-called conceptual or functional role semantics which may thus be conceived as an attempt to establish internalism.[2]

Second, one may build upon the epistemological reinterpretation of Kaplan's character theory, which was not fully endorsed by Kaplan (1977), but acquired prominence through Fodor (1987, ch. 2), though it is first recognizable in Stalnaker (1978)[3] and Perry (1977). According to the character theory, semantics has to recursively specify a character for each expression, assigning to it its extension relative to a context (of utterance) and an index (or point of evaluation). And, according to the epistemological reinterpreta-

---

sky 1995, Chalmers to appear, and others. Moreover, most of cognitive science certainly sees itself as an individualistic enterprise.

[2] Cf., e.g., Field 1977 and Block 1986. Functional role semantics is not necessarily individualistic, though. It is ambiguous between short-arm and long-arm functional roles; cf. Harman 1987.

[3] Stalnaker is certainly not an internalist, as his (1989) and (1990) clearly show. However, his (1978) may well be interpreted as making more internalist sense of the character theory as Kaplan did.

tion, the diagonal of the character of an expression represents the cognitive significance of, or the concept associated with, this expression.[4]

Here we shall pursue only the second approach via the epistemologically reinterpreted character theory. Our main reason is that functional role semantics failed to give a clear and precise theory of how concepts and narrow contents build up in a recursive way. By contrast, the character theory has a clearly specified formal structure which is easily connected with linguistic semantics; in particular, characters combine recursively in much the same way as intensions do in intensional semantics. Prima facie, these formal virtues are an overwhelming reason for our choice (although we are well aware that formal structure alone does not determine its interpretation).

However, there are difficulties with the character theory as well. If one considers their interpretational questions, two serious problems emerge, as Schiffer (1990) and Block (1991) have forcefully made clear. The first problem is that the character theory seems to be either inadequate or superfluous. Schiffer argues that the character theory cannot avoid having recourse to functional roles or states. But then it seems to be only a detour, since one could have explained narrow contents rather by directly appealing to functional roles. We call this Schiffer's problem. The second problem, set up by Block, is that the character theory can apparently take only one of two inadequate forms. Either it must specify narrow contents by reference to linguistic expressions themselves, i.e., fall prey to syntacticism. Or, it must specify narrow contents in a profoundly holistic way, i.e., fall prey to an unacceptable degree of holism. We call this Block's dilemma.

Thus it seems that the character theory, whatever its formal virtues, cannot get off of the ground unless it offers some good response to these challenges. This is, more specifically, the task we want to address here. We tackle it in four sections: section 2 explains the epistemologically interpreted character theory and its problems in more detail, section 3 presents the solution we want to propose, section 4 explains it in a bit more detail, and section 5 argues that this solution indeed avoids Block's dilemma as well as Schiffer's problem.

2 The Problems Specified

We cannot go on after this rough and general introduction without referring to some specific statement of the epistemologically reinterpreted character theory. Let us therefore briefly look at the treatment it receives in Haas-Spohn (1995), where it is dealt with in book length. We shall see that her

---

[4] Perhaps one should also mention the very dense account of Lewis 1986, sect. 1.4, which is related to all three approaches mentioned, but not identical with any of them; to consider it seriously would, however, require a separate discussion.

account is also susceptible to the two problems just mentioned, but this will pave the way for improvement.

What is a character? A character is a function assigning to each possible context of utterance (context for short) an intension, which is, in turn, a function from points of evaluation (indices for short) to extensions. Equivalently, the character of an expression is a function assigning to each context and index the extension the expression has at this context and index. The characters of complex expressions build up recursively in the way familiar from intensional semantics.

We take a possible context c to be just a centered world, i.e. a triple $\langle s_c, t_c, w_c \rangle$ such that the subject s_c exists at time t_c in the world w_c and may (but need not) utter the relevant expression. A possible index i consists of all items which may be shifted by operators of the given language. Here, it will suffice to put only a possible world w_i into the index i.[5]

Sentences, in particular, are true or false at contexts and indices, according to their character. This entails a notion of truth at a context simpliciter. A sentence is true at the context c if and only if it is true at c and the index which consists of the context world w_c itself. The function assigning to each context the truth value the sentence has at the context is called the diagonal of the sentence.[6] Similarly, we may define the diagonals of other expressions. Note that this definition works only on the condition that for each item of indices there is a corresponding item of contexts, and note that our definitions meet this condition.

Now we can say what the epistemological reinterpretation of the character theory is supposed to be. Basically, it just consists in considering possible contexts at the same time as possible doxastic alternatives of some subject. Thus, what a subject believes is that she is in one of the contexts of a certain set of possible contexts. And if a subject believes a sentence to be true, she believes that she is in a context in which the sentence is true; that is, the sentence's diagonal is a superset of the set of the subject's doxastic alternatives.[7] All this agrees well with the characterization of contexts as centered worlds since centered worlds are known to be needed for the representations of beliefs de se and de nunc.[8]

Now, to be a bit more specific, consider a certain natural language L like English and some referring expression α of L; one best imagines α to be a name like "Aristotle" or a one-place predicate like "water", "table", or

---

[5] Cf. also Lewis 1980.

[6] Diagonals are called primary intensions by Chalmers 2001. His secondary intensions are what we call simply intensions.

[7] Here, and elsewhere, we do not distinguish between a set and its characteristic function.

[8] Cf. Lewis 1979 or Haas-Spohn 1995, sect. 2.2-3. But see Spohn 1997, sect. 9 and 10 for arguments that doxastic alternatives need a variable assignment as a further component.

"red".[9] Then Haas-Spohn (1995, pp. 99, 136, 150) explained the (*objective*) *character* of α in L in the following way:

> $\|\alpha\|_L (c,i)$ = the object or the set of objects at the index i which is the same or of the same kind, i.e., has the same essential properties as the object or the objects from which the usage of α in the language L originates in the context c.[10]

The crucial term is here "the usage of α in L". In the context c, it stands for the whole communicative pattern in c associated in L with the expression α. However, what is essential to this pattern are not all of its ramifications it actually has in the context, but only the methods of identifying or recognizing the reference of α which are available to the community speaking L. These methods may be those of Putnam's experts for gold as opposed to the laymen, or those of Evans' producers of a name who are acquainted with its bearer as opposed to the consumers of the name[11], or indeed those of almost everybody in the case of chairs and tables, in which nobody has privileged knowledge. Thus, such usages are in principle well described in the relevant literature.

Two points are important about such usages as conceived by Haas-Spohn (1995). First, the expression α itself is not essential to its usage; the very same usage may be associated with another expression as well. This entails, in particular, that different languages may have the same usage of different expressions; this is crucial for their translatability.[12]

Secondly, the extension, the object or objects from which the usage originates, is also not essential to the usage; in different contexts or context worlds different objects may fit the same usage. In our world, H_2O fits the usage of "water". But for all we know, or knew 250 years ago, it may as well have been XYZ from which our usage of "water" originates. Likewise, in the actual context world our usage of "Aristotle" originates from the actual Aristotle. But there may be another context world in which somebody else had the same career as our Aristotle and has triggered the same usage of "Aristotle". In this way, then, the extension of α may vary with the context; and thus Kaplan's strategy of explaining the informativity of identity

---

[9] We shall not address definite and indefinite descriptions and all kinds of indexicals and demonstratives since they involve a number of further problems which we better avoid.

[10] Obviously, the "i.e." is only justified if the essential properties are necessary and sufficient for individuating the object or the kind. This may be false. But at least it seems true that they are necessary and that nothing else (except the pure thisness) achieves the individuation. So we may ignore the point in the following.

[11] Cf. Putnam 1975, pp. 235ff. and Evans 1982, ch. 11.

[12] In fact it is often the other way around. Translation *merges* the usages of different languages and thus *makes* them identical; cf. Haas-Spohn 1997, sect. 3. This is an insight which seems to put the indeterminacy of translation and related issues into a very different light.

sentences between overt indexicals[13] may be carried over to hidden indexicals like "water" or "Hesperos". Hence, Haas-Spohn (1995) intends that a usage is something which may properly be called a communal concept which is internal to the relevant language community and does not change by merely changing the community's environment.[14]

The above explanation of the character of α in L is still incomplete since we have not yet specified its domain. Concerning indices, we may assume that all indices or possible worlds belong to its domain. Concerning contexts, however, the explanation presupposes that the very usage of α in the language L exists in the context; otherwise, the character of α in L is undefined simply because there is no origin of the usage if there is no usage.[15] Thus, if we understand a language to be the collection of all the usages of its terms, the recursive explanation of the characters of its expressions works only for those contexts in which the language exists.

So, what is, finally, the *diagonal* of the expression α in the language L? It is the function which is defined for all contexts in which the usage of α in L exists and which assigns to each context the extension α has there according to its usage. This indicates the heavy burden the notion of a usage has to carry, and, in view of this, the explanations given may well seem insufficient. We shall return to this point.

For the moment, however, we have to attend to another crucial point. Since usages are communal concepts which, as explained, summarize not what each individual knows, but what everybody together knows about the relevant extensions, they are unsuited for describing concepts and narrow contents, which are intended here to be internal to a given subject; the subject need not fully know about usages or communal concepts. This was indeed the basic point of Burge (1979): that a subject may have an incomplete or false linguistic understanding and still be amenable to de dicto belief ascriptions. So, how do we get down to the level of individual subjects?

A natural idea, indeed the one Haas-Spohn (1995) pursued, is the following. We repeat it here because it makes Block's dilemma very perspicuous. If a subject's knowledge of her own language may be incomplete, and indeed severely incomplete without clear lower boundary, then, it seems, we have to completely abstract away from such knowledge and to add it

---

[13] Cf. Kaplan 1977 who explains in sect. XVII how "this = that" may be informative and refrains in sect. XXII to generalize the method to "Hesperos = Phosphoros" because he considers names to be absolute. According to the above explanation, however, names are *hidden* indexicals.

[14] Anti-individualists will find this notion of a usage to be question-begging, whereas we attempt here to provide individualistic foundations to such communal concepts.

[15] The counterfactual question what the origin would have been if the usage had existed does not generally make good sense.

again for each subject according to her individual measure.[16] But what survives such abstraction? It seems the only thing we can hold fixed is the knowledge of the grammar, i.e. of the (purely morphologically conceived) words and their ways of composition. Thus we end up with what Haas-Spohn (1995, sect. 3.9) defines as *formal characters* which belong to a grammar G, the syntactic skeleton of a natural language:

$\|\alpha\|^{G}(c,i)$ = the object or the set of objects at the index i which is the same or of the same kind, i.e. has the same essential properties as the object or the objects from which the usage of α in the context language l_c originates – which is the language of s_c at t_c in w_c and has the grammar G.

In continuation of the parallel, the domain of a formal character consists first of all indices and second of all contexts in which the subject of the context speaks a language with the expression α or, indeed, with the whole grammar G. From this, *formal diagonals* are again easily derived.

Formal diagonals describe the minimal semantic knowledge accompanying the syntactic knowledge of the grammar. In order to know the formal diagonal of the expression α, one merely needs to know the triviality that α refers to whatever it is used for in one's language.

Thus, formal diagonals have at least some features desired by the internalist. Insofar as knowledge of grammar is internal, knowledge of formal diagonals is internal as well. Moreover, there is no problem of intersubjectivity since all subjects mastering the grammar G thereby master the same formal diagonals. However, if we identify concepts with formal diagonals, we clearly fall prey to syntacticism, one horn of Block's dilemma, since the words themselves, and only the words, are essential to concepts so understood. This is an understanding which is intuitively both too narrow and too wide at the same time. It is too narrow because it entails that speakers of different grammars must ipso facto have different concepts. And it is much too wide because any two persons associating whatever they want with the same word ipso facto have the same concept. By moving to formal characters, we have therefore lost the two virtues usages or communal concepts seemed to preserve.

This is no surprise because we have so far realized only the first part of our strategy, the step of maximal abstraction. However, a subject has beliefs about usages in her language just as beliefs about any other empirical matter, and only these beliefs add substance to the formal diagonals. Hence, we have to take the second step and enrich the picture by the subject's individ-

---

[16] This strategy and the quantification over possible languages it involves goes back to Stalnaker 1978. Thus, the formal characters to be defined immediately are our way of capturing the idea behind Stalnaker's propositional concepts.

ual beliefs. Our first attempt to do so will turn out to be too coarse; but without it one cannot understand the later refinements.

For the representation of beliefs, we propose following the standard line formalized in doxastic logic. There, a subject's doxastic state is simply represented as a set of so-called doxastic alternatives, her *belief set*, and each proposition which is a superset of the belief set is then believed in that state. This representation has well-known problems: it neglects the fact that beliefs come in degrees; it cannot account for mathematical, but at best for empirical beliefs; it seems to presuppose logical omniscience since it assumes propositions to be believed regardless of how they are expressed; and so on. However, rival accounts are beset with other and no less grave problems. We therefore stick to this representation.[17]

In order to understand it properly, however, one needs to get clearer about what a doxastic alternative is supposed to be. We already said that it is simply a possible context $c = \langle s_c, t_c, w_c \rangle$. But what precisely does it mean that c is a doxastic alternative of a given subject s at a given time t in the world w? The usual explanation is that it means that all the beliefs of s at t in w do not exclude that s_c is s itself, t_c the present time t, and w_c the actual world w. This explanation is certainly correct, but not very helpful because it inherits all the ambiguities of the notion of belief of which it makes essential use. In particular, it leaves unclear whether or not a doxastic alternative can be understood in an individualistic way. The following explanation (cf. also Haas-Spohn 1995, p. 34) is more explicit:

> $c = \langle s_c, t_c, w_c \rangle$ is a doxastic alternative of s at t in w iff the following holds: suppose that s would fully investigate the world w_c – where this includes that it may take the perspective of every individual in w_c during its entire existence (so far it has a perspective at all), that it may learn all the languages there are in w_c, that it may subject each part of the world w_c to any investigations and experiments it can think of, etc. – and suppose further that s would make its most considerate judgment about w_c after this investigation; then the assumption that it is now s_c at t_c in w_c is compatible with the doxastic state of s at t in w. More briefly, $c = \langle s_c, t_c, w_c \rangle$ is a doxastic alternative of s at t in w iff s' maximally experienced and considerate judgment about $\langle s_c, t_c, w_c \rangle$ is just an extension and not a revision of s' doxastic state at t in w.

---

[17] Spohn 1997, sect. 5, distinguishes two large families of representations of belief, the computational and the semantic ones, each of which has their characteristic problems, and he argues that from the perspective of a rationality theory of belief semantic representations have primacy – which we join here.

The counterfactual suppositions in this explanation are impossible to satisfy in various respects. However, the explanation is not thereby rendered incomprehensible; it just drives common counterfactuals to the extreme, as philosophers are prone to do. The explanation conforms to the common idea of characterizing a belief state (or any kind of partial assignment) by the set of all its maximal extensions. What it adds to this idea is a fuller description of what is involved in such a maximal extension: neither a maximally consistent set of sentences of a given language, nor a totality of facts with facts being individuated from some external point of view, nor just a possible world in the sense of a maximally inclusive object, but rather our normal ways of belief formation using experience and judgment which are maximally expanded with respect to such a possible world.

It is philosophically highly important to have a clear picture of what is involved in such a maximal extension.[18] Let us point out three consequences for the moment.

First, the above explanation of doxastic alternatives does not entail that the subject has to be able to express her belief set in her own language. Some context may not qualify as a doxastic alternative simply because it does not feel or look like the actual world in some inexpressible way. Second, the explanation leaves entirely open how the subject's belief set (and its supersets) relates to our external belief ascriptions couched in our language. This is a question full of incompletely understood intricacies which we may, and are well advised to, leave aside. Third, this is most important for the rest of the paper, *to have a given belief set is an internal, non-relational property* according to our explanation. The fact that the context c is, or is not, a doxastic alternative of s at t in w clearly does not depend at all on anything in w outside s at t; it merely depends on s' internal disposition at t in w. In any case, we find it obvious that s' belief set as characterized above is entirely unaffected by exchanging all H_2O by XYZ, or exchanging s' linguistic community by a slightly different one which can change, in some other sense, s' water and arthritis beliefs into twater and tharthritis beliefs.

This characterization of a subject's beliefs will be used throughout this paper. The present purpose, however, is only a limited one; namely, to carry out the above idea of abstracting away usages as they actually are and to substantiate the formal diagonals thus obtained by the subject's beliefs about these usages. This raises the problem of distinguishing her beliefs

---

[18] Christopher Peacocke pointed out to us that a lot of idealization is involved in what the subject's judgment would be under such counterfactual circumstances (perhaps it has only headache then and no judgment any more) and that the standards of idealization are not easily explained, maybe only in a circular way. Cf., e.g., the analogous critical discussion of the dispositional analysis of meaning in Kripke 1982, pp. 22-37. This is a legitimate worry which, however, we cannot further address here.

about the usages of her linguistic community from all her other beliefs. Since the problem appeared unsolvable[19], Haas-Spohn (1995, pp. 58f.) mentioned the possibility of restricting the domain of formal diagonals not to some selected beliefs, but to all beliefs, i.e. to the belief set of the subject. This has the desired effect that the subject's terms do not apply to any arbitrary objects so-called in the various contexts, but only to objects conforming to the subject's beliefs. In this way, the substance we have lost by introducing formal characters has returned to a subjectively relativized extent.[20]

Since formal diagonals, as well as belief sets, are internal, the restricted formal diagonals are internal as well. In this respect, they could qualify as concepts in the sense intended here. However, we are obviously stuck now with the other horn of Block's dilemma. If a subject's concepts are formal diagonals restricted to her belief set, any change in her beliefs changes her concepts; this is indeed an extremely holistic conception of concepts. Likewise, since any two subjects are almost guaranteed to have different concepts, communication and psychological generalizations seem like a mystery. Moreover, we have not gotten rid of the flaw that subjects having acquired different grammars are bound to have different concepts. All this seems unacceptable.

These considerations may suffice as a concrete exemplification of how Block's dilemma arises for a theory of internal concepts. So far, we have apparently avoided Schiffer's problem, since individualistic functional roles nowhere entered the picture, but we did so only by doing very badly on Block's dilemma. White (1982) has already anticipated a way out of that dilemma. His framework is quite similar to the one presented so far.[21] The domain of the partial characters he defines consists of what he calls contexts of acquisition, which are pairs of a possible world and some functional state the subject acquires in the world. In order to avoid the emptiness of syntacticism, White restricts the domain of the partial character of a given expression to equivalent contexts of acquisition having one and the same functional state as a component, and, by associating a separate functional state with each expression, White has prima facie avoided holism. However, these very sketchy remarks already show that it is the functional states which are doing the work here, and that the possible escape from Block's dilemma immediately leads into Schiffer's problem.

---

[19] See, however, footnote 30.

[20] Similarly, the propositional concepts of Stalnaker 1978 are not defined for all contexts whatsoever, but only within the context set consisting of the common presuppositions.

[21] For more detailed comparative remarks see Haas-Spohn 1995, pp. 141f.

3   How to Define Concepts: A Proposal

Should we give up, hence, trying to explain concepts and narrow contents via the epistemologically reinterpreted character theory? No; we have not yet tried hard enough. So far, we have considered only two extreme options: the minimal option that the concept a subject associates with an expression contains only the trivial belief that the concept refers to whatever the word is used for, and the maximal option that the concept contains all beliefs of the subject, in particular all the beliefs the subject has about the reference of the concept. This leaves open a huge range of middle courses which deserves inquiry.

Block (1991, p. 40) develops a nice picture by distinguishing between the lexicon entry and the encyclopedia entry of an expression. The encyclopedia entry of an expression corresponds to our maximal option; intuitively, however, it is rather the lexicon entry which corresponds to the associated concept. So, this is what we seek to characterize.[22] There seem to be two basic ideas, with ramifications, for driving a middle course towards an adequate notion of concepts.

One idea is to appeal to communal standards, e.g., to define a concept as containing just the social minimum of beliefs about its reference which is required for being recognized as a partner in communication. This is Putnam's idea of a stereotype. One may doubt whether such social standards of semantic competence exist in a salient way; but if they do, they certainly provide a useful notion for some purposes.

However, this idea seems to be the wrong one for our present purposes. If concepts are explained with reference to communal standards, then all competent speakers in the group automatically have the same concepts. This seems unwelcome for individualistic psychology, which should presumably allow for more conceptual variation across subjects. There is a further decisive objection which will be explained later on because it applies to other proposals as well.

The other basic idea, which appears sufficiently individualistic, is to appeal to the subject's recognitional capacities, i.e., to define a subject's concept of an object or a property as consisting of those features on the basis of which the subject recognizes the object or instantiations of the property. What this means, however, depends crucially on what one takes here recognition to mean.

---

[22] The task reminds of the task of explicating the analytic/synthetic distinction which is confronted with the objections so forcefully initiated by Quine; indeed, Block's despair of drawing his distinction in a more precise way may be seen as a late effect of Quine's negative conclusion. However, this conclusion is still contested; moreover, the two tasks are not identical. So we should not be discouraged by these objections.

There is room for interpretation since the strictest and simplest understanding of recognition does not work at all. The strictest understanding would be to say that a subject is able to recognize an object if and only if, under all possible circumstances, it is always and only the object itself which the subject takes to be the object. This is much too strict because we are hardly ever able to recognize objects in this sense; there are always circumstances under which we mistake the best known objects and even ourselves. Recall also how absurdly narrow Russell's acquaintance relation turned out to be. The same holds, mutatis mutandis, for the recognition of properties. Recognition therefore needs to be understood in a much weaker way. There are various options from which varying notions of a concept result.

Our recognitional capacities may first be seen in our normal means of recognition which work, according to our familiarity, fairly reliably in the circumstances we usually encounter. Something like this presumably comes closest to our intuitive notion of a recognitional capacity. However, it is utterly vague and entails that a recognitional capacity may be something very varied. For instance, I[23] may identify my son on the basis of my belief that he is somewhere in the crowd before me and that nobody else in the crowd is likely to wear the same kind of satchel. The example shows that my normal means of recognition use a lot of specific knowledge that varies from situation to situation. By contrast, concepts are intuitively something more stable or invariant. It would certainly be strange to say that the fact that he has that kind of satchel belongs to my concept of my son.[24]

There seem to be two ways of gaining more specificity here. One way is to narrow down a subject's means of recognizing an object or an instantiation of a property to the way the object or the instantiation looks to the subject under various circumstances. This line leads to what are called the subject's perceptual concepts. The other way is to raise a subject's recognitional means from those she normally applies to the best and most considered means which she usually cannot, or does not care to, apply.

So far, the available options are very sketchy. But there is an argument which tells at even this sketchy stage which direction to pursue more thoroughly. The argument is this:

---

[23] There is a kind of pragmatic contradiction in writing a joint paper on subjective concepts, since the authors cannot use the stylistic device of taking themselves as an example. So we decided to use "I" in examples, and the reader is free to choose which of the authors he takes to be speaking.

[24] This is the first time that we slipped into talking of the concept of an object (or a property) instead of the concept associated with a given term – certainly a convenient, but also very dangerous slip, since it imports the de re/de dicto ambiguity and its proliferating consequences. Throughout, however, "the concept of a" is to mean the very same as the more clumsy phrase "the concept associated with 'a'", though we are perfectly aware, of course, that the two phrases should be distinguished.

Clearly, we want our beliefs to be closely connected with our concepts since the contents of our beliefs should recursively build up from the concepts involved. For instance, in the primitive case of predication, we would like to characterize the content of a belief such as that a is F in the form of a truth condition, i.e., as something like the function from contexts to truth values given as follows:

A subject's belief that a is F is *subjectively true* in a context c if everything and at least something that conforms to the subject's concept of a in c also conforms to the subject's concept of F in c.

The strange term "subjectively true" indicates that some explanation is still missing. For the moment, however, we may ignore this and take the adverb "subjectively" as redundant. We shall return to the point at the end of the next section.

Moreover, one may stumble at the quantifier "everything and at least something". This is an attempt to do justice to the fact that there may be no or several objects in a single context c which conform to the subject's concept associated with the name "a". The attempt is certainly plausible. Finer analysis would show, however, that we here run into similar problems as does the counterpart theory of Lewis (1968) with non-identity-like counterpart relations. The corresponding proposal has there proven to be insufficient, and more complicated solutions are required.[25] But we need not dwell on this point; our attempt will do for the rest of the paper.

The crucial point about the truth condition is that it seems to yield inadequate results when it is based on anything other than the subject's best and most considered means for recognizing a. For instance, if the subject's concept of a would consist in some communal stereotype of a, the subject could possibly believe that a does not satisfy its stereotype or that many things different from a satisfy this stereotype, and then the above truth condition assigns truth or falsity to the belief that a is F in contexts in which the subject would intuitively not count it as, respectively, true or false. The same holds in the case where the subject's concept of a consists of the criteria normally used to recognize a. Again, it seems possible that the subject knows or believes in a given situation that a does not currently have the features normally used for recognizing a, or that things different from a satisfy the criteria normally used for recognizing a, and then the above and the intuitive truth condition for the subject's belief that a is F diverge again. The only way to avoid this discrepancy seems to be basing the subject's concept of a on her best means for recognizing a, as we have proposed. The same holds, mutatis mutandis, for the property F.[26]

---

[25] See Hazen 1979 and Kupffer 1999, ch. 3 and 4.

[26] It should be observed that this proposal nicely parallels with how Haas-Spohn 1995 understands the usage of a name "a" or a predicate "F" in a given language L. We noted above

One may fear, though, that the best recognitional means available to a subject with respect to an object a or a property F come close to what Block called an encyclopedia entry. Should the subject not optimally use *all* her beliefs concerning a or F for recognizing a or an F? The answer is decidedly no. There are, for sure, many possible contexts in which the subject would recognize something as a, though it there lacks many properties the subject believes a to have. The subject has her ways, whatever they are, of distinguishing contexts which contain a, but with other than the believed properties, from contexts which do not contain a at all. This is a crucial assertion, without which the rest of the paper would not make any sense.

The following explanation captures this subjective distinction, or the subject's best recognitional means, or indeed the subject's concepts in a more explicit way:

> Let α be a name or a one-place predicate and $@ = \langle s,t,w \rangle$ the actual context (which may be any context). Then the *concept* $\beta_@(\alpha)$ which s associates with α at t in w is the function which assigns to each possible context $c = \langle s_c, t_c, w_c \rangle$ the set of objects in w_c which, according to s' judgment at t in w, might be the object, or instantiate the property, denoted by α in $@$.
>
> Or to spell out the phrase "according to s' judgment" in analogy to the above explanation of doxastic alternatives: $x \in \beta_@(\alpha)(c)$, or x is a *doxastic counterpart* in c of what α denotes in $@$, iff the following holds: suppose that s would fully investigate the world w_c – where this includes that it may take the perspective of every individual in w_c during its entire existence (so far it has a perspective at all), that it may learn all the languages there are in w_c, that it may subject each part of the world w_c to any investigations and experiments it can think, etc. – and suppose further that s would make its most considerate judgment about w_c including x after this investigation; then the assumption that x is the object, or instantiates the property, denoted by α in $@$ is compatible with s' judgment at t in w about what is denoted by α in $@$.

This may look imperspicuous to some and trivial to others. But its meaning and power will unfold in the following explanations and arguments.

---

that she follows the literature which tends to base such usages or communal concepts on the best judgmental standards available to the community of L. Hence it seems appropriate to do likewise in the individual case.

4   Explanations

The final section will argue that this notion of a concept indeed helps the internalist against Schiffer's problem and Block's dilemma. This section is devoted to three kinds of explanations: some remarks about the features concepts have according to our definition; an explanation that the title of this paper is indeed appropriate; and a clarification of the relation of this definition to the proposals discussed in section 2. So, let us first explain five more or less expected and instructive features of concepts which are entailed by our definition.

(1) Concepts are usually not egocentric. By this we mean that, usually, things can conform to one's concept associated with α in a context c without there being anything in c which could be oneself. Hence, insofar as modes of presentation and acquaintance relations have usually been thought to be egocentric, they are not concepts in the above sense.

(2) To which extent is the look, sound, or feel of things important for their conforming to one's concepts? It depends. Often it is conditionally important. Consider my concept of my son. Clearly, there could be many possible things in possible contexts which look perfectly like my son without possibly being my son according to my concept of him. Conversely, however, something could hardly be my son according to my concept without looking very much like him. Hardly! Of course, my son could look very different from his present look, not only actually, but also according to my concept of him. But if I encounter, in a possible context c, such a differently looking object, it could only be my son if there is something in the context c explaining why that object started or emerged to deviate from my son's look which is so well known to me. In this sense, the look of my son (the sound of his voice, etc.) is a conditional part of my concept of him. In a similar way, the look of species, substances, and also individual things is a conditional part of my concepts of them; for instance, no doxastic counterpart of the black ball-pen in my drawer could be red during its entire existence. But there are other cases as well. It seems, for instance, that the look of things is not essential for their conforming to the concept I associate with the word "table"; what is essential is only what is done with the things in the relevant context. If there are culturalized beings in the context which use a given object only for sitting down *at* it, then that object counts as a table according to my concept, even if it never looks like a table. Conversely, if something looks like a table, but is only used as something else, say, for sitting *on* it, then my concept does not count it as a table, but, say, as a seat.

(3) To which extent does the place of objects enter into one's concepts of them? Again, it is very often conditionally important. According to my

concept of him, my son could be (almost) anywhere in the universe. However, the context must then provide some plausible story of how he got there. Any object, however intrinsically similar to my son, could not be my son if it is far away from Earth, or Germany for that matter, during its entire existence. The same holds for many concepts of many other objects; after all, most objects we know are on the surface of Earth. The same may even hold for predicates. One may think, for instance, that a species which develops somewhere else in the universe, but, as it happens, interbreeds with our tigers, does still not consist of tigers. If so, one's concept of tigers includes their emergence on Earth.

Hence, very many of our concepts are, so to speak, geocentric. This entails the question what my concept of Earth may be. It seems to be quite poor. According to my concept, at least, the history of and on Earth so richly known to me is highly contingent to Earth; almost any planet of comparable size, age, and composition revolving around a sun of comparable size, age, and composition in the Milky Way could be Earth. And, of course, my concept of the Milky Way is even poorer, since it contains hardly more than the Milky Way being some spiral galaxy.

(4) Their causal origin is essential to many objects. This is also reflected in our concepts of them. For instance, nothing which is not procreated by us could be our son, and since I also believe so, my concepts of myself and my spouse enter into my concept of our son. The same holds with respect to ourselves and our parents. Of course, my concepts of our ancestors soon get very dim; still, all of them are part of my concept of my son. In fact, my son could not exist without history being pretty much as it is. Thus, a lot I believe about history enters into my concept of my son. This makes for a perhaps unexpected richness of that concept. In the same vein, my concept of things is quite poor when I know very little about their causal preconditions, as is the case, for instance, with Earth. In fact, what we just said about the conceptual role of location presumably reduces to the present point about causal origin. Our son could not be born outside Germany or Earth, unless we, or our parents, etc., travelled. The same holds, mutatis mutandis, for tigers and other kinds if their causal origin is essential for them.

(5) Do concepts involve social relations, are they mutually connected by communication? Yes, of course; there is a clear relation between the concept I associate with a certain expression and the concepts others associate with that expression, a relation which Putnam (1975) has described as division of linguistic labor. Consider my concept of an elm, to take one of Putnam's examples. Elms might exist without mankind; in such a context, the extension of my concept of an elm would alternatively contain elms, beeches, and, maybe, other deciduous trees, since I, by myself, cannot distinguish elms from beeches and, maybe, other trees. This may entail that my

perceptual concept of an elm is the same as that of a beech, but it does not entail sameness of the two concepts in our sense. On the contrary, since I believe elms and beeches to constitute different kinds, and since I am allowed to identify the various kinds of trees in that context, my concept of an elm has any one of these kinds as extension in this context, and my concept of a beech any other kind, though I do not know which.[27]

In other contexts there is an even clearer difference in the extensions of the two concepts, namely in contexts in which there is a linguistic community which generally resembles my actual community as I know it and which I observe during my full investigation of these contexts applying the term "elm" only to certain trees and not to others (to which I might have been inclined to apply it as well). Then there are two possible cases. Either these applications of the term "elm" contradict my concept of an elm so flatly – say, the community applies it to coniferous trees – that I conclude that this could not be my linguistic community after all and that its judgment cannot help mine in this matter. In this case, my judgment is as bad and the extension of my concept of an elm as wide as before. Or the linguistic community in the context behaves like mine in every relevant respect, and in particular with respect to the term "elm", so that I conclude that this community could be mine and that I may trust its judgment. In such a context, the extension of my concept of an elm is as narrow as the usage of the community and certainly different from the extension of my concept of a beech (though, of course, it would be compatible with my concept of an elm that this counterfactual community applies "elm" only to beeches).

In this way, the division of linguistic labor is reflected in subjective concepts. This entails in particular that referential and deferential aspects are often inextricably mixed in subjective concepts. The simple reason is that subjects often trust the judgment of their fellows more than their own. Of course, the degree to which semantic deference enters into subjective concepts may vary considerably. For instance, my concept of an Indian deity, say, or of multiple sclerosis, is so poor, that I would follow almost any opinion if it presents itself as a consistent opinion of our experts. In such cases, the deferential component of concepts is overwhelming. By contrast, I may be convinced that I know more or less as well as all others what tables are. In such cases, my own most considerate judgment is hardly helped by others, and the deferential component of my concept of tables largely vanishes. However, it seems that it never vanishes completely in concepts associated with linguistic concepts; it seems present even in the

---

[27] This idea of alternative extensions in one and the same context is not mentioned in our above definition of concepts, because it entails additional complications. But it seems required in order to overcome the difficulties referred to in footnote 25.

concept associated with the predicate "*x* looks red to me" in the phenomenal reading.[28]

Let us next explain the appropriateness of the title of our paper. Our aim was, we said, to drive a middle course between the minimal and maximal option, both of which we found to be inadequate. So, which beliefs are contained in the concept a subject associates with the expression α if they are more than that α has an extension and less than all beliefs about that extension? Our title gives a simple and informative answer which runs as follows.

G is an essential property of *a* if and only if it is metaphysically or ontologically necessary that *a* is *G*, i.e., if nothing which is not *G* could be (identical with) *a*. For instance, being human or having the parents our son has are essential properties of our son. This is the common definition; it is full of niceties, which we better skip over, however. We can extend it to a relation between properties. *G* is essential for *F* if and only if it is metaphysically necessary that every *F* is *G*. For instance, being unmarried is essential for being a bachelor (though it is not essential for bachelors, for no bachelor is essentially a bachelor), or consisting of hydrogen and oxygen is essential for being water.

Now, one may express our definition of concepts also in the following way. The concept a subject associates with "*a*" is the conjunction of all concepts *G*, or the strongest *G*, such that the subject believes that *G* is essential for *a*. Similarly, the concept a subject associates with "*F*" is the conjunction of all concepts *G*, or the strongest *G*, such that the subject believes that *G* is essential for *F*.

When one compares this with the original definition, it is rather obvious that this is an equivalent characterization. Indeed, it is trivial in view of the fact that being identical with *a* is the strongest essential property of *a*, and being *F* is the strongest property essential for being *F*. The characterization would become more interesting if we were to introduce restrictions on the metaphysical side, for instance, by excluding identity from genuine properties and relations; or on the epistemological side, for instance, by postulating that all concepts are ultimately qualitative in some suitable sense. We would in fact be prepared to make such restrictions, but it would take us too long to go into this issue.

Let us rather briefly check whether this characterization agrees with the five features of concepts just noted. What we said about the fact that beliefs about causal origin often are part of concepts fits perfectly, of course. We also stated that the look of objects or kinds often enters into our concepts of them. But, as a rule, looks are certainly inessential. However, we qualified

---

[28] This point is made already by Austin 1962 (see his magenta example on p. 113). Cf. also Spohn 1997a and 1997/98. sect. 5.

our statement. Often, the look of an object or of a kind displays its essence provided that it is allowed to unfold its normal look; and it is only this complex concept which is part of the concept of an object or a kind. Finally, what about the deferential component of concepts? What others believe about an object or a kind is certainly not essential to it. Sure, but to the extent we trust others, we believe what they believe, and if we take the experts' beliefs about essences as trustworthy and they believe essences to be such and such, we also believe these essences to be such and such. So, the present characterization agrees well with the earlier observations.

Viewed in this way, is our proposal for defining concepts not a familiar one? We are not aware of this.[29] The only current place where we found it mentioned is in Block (1995, sect. 4) where he attributes the view to two lines in Fodor (1987), discusses it on one page, and dismisses it right away. The paper is about one example, namely the concept a teen associates with the word "grug" which denotes beer in his assumed dialect. The teen knows very little about grug; he knows, e.g., that it comes in six-packs. Block simply assumes that this belief is part of the teen's concept of grug, and he is certainly right to claim that it is not essential to grug to come in six-packs. But Block has a different notion of concepts here. His notion seems to be the one we have already mentioned, namely that concepts are something like normal means of recognition, and the teen's poor means of recognizing grug refer to its packing. However, we have already argued that this is not the best notion of a concept, and indeed we would flatly deny that the belief that grug comes in six-packs is part of the teen's concept of grug. So, as we say, there does not seem to be much discussion of the line of thought we are proposing here.

Let us finally explain how the present definition of concepts relates to the two kinds of diagonals in section 2. In a way, this is for our own records, but it also illuminates our definition in some important respects.

Recall that the objective diagonal of an expression α in a given language L was the function which is defined for all contexts in which the usage of α in L exists and which assigns to each such context the extension α has in that context. In particular, it assigns to the actual context the actual extension of α in the familiar sense. The formal diagonal of α as part of a grammar G did the very same. The only difference was that the formal di-

---

[29] Of course, our view of concepts may be related to a rich body of traditional conceptions, e.g., to medieval realism towards universals. Our point is only that the view does not play a role in the current vigorous discussion on concepts. It is perhaps significant that the Encyclopedia of Philosophy from 1967 says that concepts provide "a sort of passkey through the labyrinths represented by the theory of meaning, the theory of thinking, and *the theory of being*" (vol. 2, p.177 – our emphasis), whereas the Routledge Encyclopedia of Philosophy from 1998 shifts to the characterization that concepts lie "at the intersecton of semantics and philosophy of mind" (vol. 2, p.505). It is interesting, though, that similar ideas are discussed in psychology; see Gelman et al. 1994.

agonal has a larger domain consisting of all contexts in which the grammar G exists which might be realized in different languages. The specific language having the grammar G and spoken in the context was implicitly fixed by the subject of the context.

By contrast, concepts as defined above are functions defined for any contexts whatsoever (though most of them will be so alien that we find hardly anything in them conforming to our concepts). The all-important question is therefore: do they agree with diagonals on their common domain? And the crucial answer is: conditionally yes!

Imagine that the subject having the concept associated with α may investigate a context in which her actual language L exists with its very usage of α. Then we may expect that the subject judges that the context's linguistic community might indeed be her own, at least as far as the usage of α is concerned, that the community as a whole is more competent than she herself with respect to α, and that she should therefore follow the community's final judgment. In this way, semantic deference enforces an agreement between the extensions of the subjective concept and the public usage. This expectation may be wrong, however. The subject may also find the usage of α in L, as compared with her concept of α, so strange that she (falsely) concludes that this is not her actual linguistic community, rather than concluding that she is the victim of a severe misconception. Only then may the subject's judgment about α or α's deviate from that of the community. Semantic deference is thus an important ground for the subject's agreement with the community.

Note, however, that the extension of the subject's concept and the experts' concept may agree even in a context in which the subject does not defer to the experts or in which none of them exists at all. The context may be kind, so to speak; the subject may believe that her concept refers to a single natural kind, though she knows very little about that kind and the experts may know very much. But suppose the context provides only one natural kind which conforms to the little the subject knows about it. Then, only this kind is in the extension of the subject's concept, just as in the extension of the much better informed communal concept. And again the two agree.

Let us illustrate this with the two standard examples "water" and "arthritis". The actual extension of the concept Oscar presently associates with "water" consists of all H_2O and nothing else, even if Oscar knows nothing about chemistry. The primary reason for this is that Oscar believes water to be a natural kind amply instantiated in his environment and that there is no natural kind in the actual world which he would confuse with water in his maximally informed and considerate judgment. For the same reason, the actual extension of the concept which Oscar's ancestor associates with "water" 250 years ago also consists only of H_2O. Semantic deference becomes relevant in a context in which there are two kinds of liquid which Oscar by himself might take for water. If he finds there a linguistic community which might be his own and which acknowledges only one liquid to be water, then his subjective concept has only this liquid as extension in this context. If he finds there a community which is as indiscriminate as he is, then both liquids constitute alternative extensions of his concept in this context. And the same is true, if he finds that there are two trustworthy communities, as in Putnam's twin earth story, to which he might defer, and which refer, however, to different liquids. All this shows that there is, on the one hand, a lot of agreement in the extensions of various subjective and communal concepts at different times, and that, on the other hand, the differences among all these concepts show in suitable counterfactual contexts.

What about the actual extension of the concept Fritz associates with "arthritis"? This case is more delicate. If Fritz' belief that arthritis is an ailment which may occur in the thigh is conditional on the agreement of his community, then he will also defer to his actual community which denies this, and the extension of his subjective concept will congrue with that of the communal concept. If Fritz' belief about the essence of arthritis is unconditional, then he will not acknowledge the actual community to be his community, and his judgment will be unassisted. In this case, the subjective and the communal concept may diverge. But it may also be the case that, after fully investigating the actual world, his judgment is that arthritis occurs only in the joints because the investigation shows that there is a natural kind of appropriate ailments in the joints, but none which extends to thighs.

If we return to comparing our definitions of diagonals and concepts, a further important difference emerges. Concerning objective diagonals in L, we said that the extension of α consists of the object(s) with the same essential properties as the object(s) from which the usage of α in L *originates*. This is a clear heritage of the causal theory of reference on which Haas-Spohn (1995) relies; and therefore the usage of α in L had to exist in the context c in order for α's extension being defined in c. By contrast, the extension of α in c according to a subjective concept consists of the object(s) in c *conforming* to the concept. There, the causal aspect has disappeared and with it the restriction of the concept's domain. But how then can the two functions, the objective diagonal and the subjective concept, agree within their common domain?

The question does not really concern subjective concepts. It rather points to a tension in our notion of a usage. On the one hand, a usage has, we said, an extension only where it exists and has causes. On the other hand, we said that a usage is something like a communal concept internal to the community, and then objects in any world should be able to conform to the usage. The tension hides a confusion of metaphysical and epistemological matters. Metaphysically, it is inessential to most objects or kinds of objects that they are actually conceived of, i.e. that they cause an intelligent species to form specific concepts. We also believe this. So, if a (communal or subjective) concept assembles beliefs about the essence of its reference, such a causing does not belong to it. Within an epistemological perspective, however, the belief in such a causing is an a priori companion of the concept; any community (or subject) which acquires a concept associated with some term thereby acquires the belief that the concept and the term refer to the object(s) in confrontation with which the concept was acquired. This is so at least to the extent in which a causal theory of reference applies. Hence, insofar as the concept or the usage exists in a context, its extension is described by our objective diagonals in the same way as by our definition in this section.[30]

Similar remarks apply to the comparison of formal diagonals with the concepts of a subject s. Again, the two functions agree for those contexts in which the subject s_c of the context speaks a language with the grammar G (otherwise the context would not be in the domain of the formal diagonal) and in which the community speaking that language in that context could be s' community as far as s believes (so that s can defer judgment to the community). And the causal ingredients in the formal diagonal give an a priori condition on the extension within this common domain, and thus do not constrain the extension as specified by the concept. What about the fact that the formal diagonal of α essentially involves the expression α itself, whereas the concept associated with α does not? Again, this does not create a difference within the common domain, since it is a further a priori condition on the concept associated with α that it is associated with α.[31]

---

[30] This does not seem to agree with Putnam's Twin Earth stories. Suppose the English and the Twin English community exist in the same world and associate the same internal communal concept with "water", as Putnam suggests. Everybody agrees that the concept has different extensions in the two communities, namely, respectively, H_2O and XYZ. But we seem to have to say that both extensions consist of all H_2O *and* all XYZ since both, H_2O and XYZ, conform to this concept. This is not so, however. According to the concept, its extension in this world consists *either* of all H_2O *or* of all XYZ. We don't know of which; if our extension is H_2O, theirs is XYZ, and vice versa. The decision is made by the context which, by being a centered world, says which community is in the center.

[31] A further thought which we owe to Manfred Kupffer: In section 2, when restricting formal characters and their diagonals to the subject's belief set, we have, it may have appeared, given up too soon on distinguishing the subject's beliefs about her linguistic community and its meanings from her other beliefs. We may conceive of a doxastic alternative c in a richer way, consisting not only of an indiviudal s_c, a time t_c, and a world w_c, but, given s_c has the language l_c at t_c in w_c, also of the objective character function $\|.\|_{l_c}$. A subject's belief set then consists only of doxastic alternatives thus enriched (because she believes to have a language), and only of those enriched by a character function which might be, for all she believes, the character function of her own language. In this way, we may explicitly distinguish the subject's beliefs about the meanings of her language, and we could explain the subject's concepts by

All this enables us, at last, to explain what is subjective about our above truth condition of a subject's belief recursively built up from the concepts involved. In contexts in which the subject can defer her judgment to the surrounding community, there is nothing subjective about the truth condition. To that extent, the truth condition is intersubjective and indeed objective (since the relevant contexts may be fully investigated, with no space for error left), i.e. to that extent the subject's belief that a is F is subjectively true if and only if the sentence "a is F" of her language is true. The difference shows in other contexts without an appropriate community. There, the poverty of a subject's concepts and a large divergence from the concepts of her community may come to the fore. Hence, there is a difference in subjective and objective truth conditions, as it should be, but not a critical one.

5   Individualism Rescued?

To what extent does the proposal explained in the previous sections promote the individualist's project? Four points are worth discussing.

(1) Our proposal provides something of a definition at all; this is more than what one usually finds in the literature. It does so mainly because it firmly rests on the epistemologically reinterpreted character theory, which has by far the best formal grip on these matters. This theory also provides concepts and narrow contents with a recursive structure essentially[32] following the recursive structure of the expressions with which they are associated. No negligible advantages.

(2) Again, the crucial point is, of course, that concepts are individualistic according to our definition in the same way as belief sets are individualistic according to our definition; to have a concept is an internal, nonrelational property. Which function from contexts to extensions a subject associates with an expression depends solely on its internal cognitive state, does not presuppose the existence of anything outside the subject, and does in no way change when the environment of the subject changes without affecting her internal state. For instance, Oscar, Twin Oscar, and the (appropriate) Swamp Man would display precisely the same dispositions; they would respond in our huge counterfactual test in precisely the same way, and hence they have precisely the same concepts. Of course, agreement will

---

restricting the formal character and its diagonal not to the subject's belief set, but only to the larger set of doxastic alternatives enriched by a suitable character function.

There is no conflict, though. Our previous considerations rather imply that concepts thus explained (= the diagonals of the larger set of enriched doxastic alternatives) agree with concepts in our sense on their common domain; the difference is only that concepts in our sense have, desirably, a wider domain. However, the agreement supports our case; it is nice to see that this different line of thought arrives essentially at the same result.

[32] See the qualification giving rise to footnote 25.

usually be at most partial; the Frenchmen may associate with "Londres" the same concept as I associate with "London", while our concepts diverge elsewhere.

Defining concepts and contents in a narrow way is one thing; describing them is another. We have to build a theory of how concepts combine to contents, how contents become attitudinized, how perception acts upon the attitudes, how the attitudes result in action, and so on. By doing this we say how this huge array of counterfactuality integrates into factuality; conversely, this makes this array accessible from the facts we observe on the street and in the lab. Of course, theory is vastly underdetermined by the data, here as everywhere. We have not said a word about how this theory goes and which ways of describing all these internal entities go along with it. But this would clearly be a different task, one which does not impair the internality of its starting point.

On the contrary, spelling out this theory would fully display the strategy of individualism, which consists of defining the momentary states (i.e. state types) of subjects in such a way that they are connected with past and future only through causal laws. By contrast, externalists take such connections to be part of the identity conditions of these states, by defining them either as being caused in a specific manner, as does the causal-information theoretic account of Dretske (1981), or as dispositions or attitudes analytically tied to their manifestations or intentional objects – a false understanding of (most) dispositions, as Spohn (1997b) argues. Even the functionalist is externalistically biased insofar as he defines a mental state by its functional role, by its place in a causal net extending from past to future. In our account, however, the narrow mental states of a subject are not defined by their causal ancestry, but rather as dispositions which are only causally related to their actual manifestations. It is only the envisaged rich theory which conjectures the functional role of these states; that role is not definitionally fixed to begin with. These remarks show at the same time that our proposal has not led us into Schiffer's problem; our proposal is so far independent of functionalist conceptions.

(3) The next question, then, is how we fare with respect to Block's dilemma. Here, it is clear that we have perfectly avoided the syntacticist horn of that dilemma. Which expression a subject associates with a concept is fully contingent and does in no way add to the identity of the concept. This entails in particular that members of different linguistic communities may nevertheless have the same concepts. Of course, the deferential component of a subject's concept makes reference to her own linguistic community, and this distinguishes concepts in unconnected languages. However, translation has the effect of merging the experts of the communities and thus of merging their usages or communal concepts, and thereby differences of subjective concepts due to deference vanish as well.

(4) Whether we are equally successful with respect to the holistic horn of Block's dilemma is less clear. This is the final point, to be discussed at more length. We shall not attempt to clear up the term "holism"; there seems little agreement on its precise meaning. However, it is very clear that concepts as we have explained them are thoroughly interconnected. It would be extremely important to study the architectonics of concepts in detail – though this is nothing we can achieve here. We see no reason, though, to expect the conceptual connections to be unidirectional, i.e. that there is a set of basic concepts from which all the other concepts are defined step by step, as Carnap (1928), for instance, has tried to establish in an exemplary way. Rather, all kinds of circular dependencies among concepts are to be expected. Concepts will certainly turn out to be holistic.

The essential reason for this holism is that, in the first place, ontology is holistic. There is rich ontological dependence among objects and properties; we mentioned the example that many objects and maybe even properties ontologically depend on Earth, i.e., could not exist or be instantiated, if Earth would not exist. Hence, if essences are thoroughly intertwined, beliefs about them, i.e. concepts, will be intertwined as well.

However, if we follow Block's and Fodor's definition of holism, concepts as we have explained them are not holistic. Block (1991) says "that narrow content is holistic if there is no principled difference between one's 'dictionary' entry for a word, and one's 'encyclopedia entry'" (p. 40). But the whole point of this paper was to propose such a principled difference! The lexicon entry for a word contains only one's beliefs about the essence of its reference, whereas the encyclopedia entry contains all other beliefs about the reference as well.

The case is similar with Fodor (1987). What he says about holism does not exactly fit our present discussion. He there defines that "meaning holism is the idea that the identity – specifically the intentional content – of a propositional attitude is determined by the *totality* of its epistemic liaisons" (p.56). This does not exactly fit, first because Fodor addresses only the narrow content of propositional attitudes and not that of subsentential expressions, and second because the term "epistemic liaisons" refers to confirmatory or justificatory relations between propositions – something we have not touched at all. If, however, we straighten out the definition by taking the epistemic liaisons of a word to consist in the beliefs in which it occurs, we are back at Block's definition.

Let us look, hence, at what Fodor (1987) dubs the Ur-argument for meaning holism which runs as follows: "Step 1: Argue that at least some of the epistemic liaisons of a belief determine its intentional content. Step 2: Run a 'slippery slope' argument to show that there is no principled way of deciding *which* of the epistemic liaisons of a belief determine its intentional content. So either none does or they all do. Step 3: Conclude that they all do" (p. 60).

Fodor goes on to discuss three versions of the Ur-argument and tries to argue that in all three of them step 1 has erroneously been taken for granted. Given the above straightening out we have no quarrel with step 1, however. Rather, step 2 is faulty. There may be vagueness or indeterminateness in the beliefs about essences or perhaps even in the essences themselves. But there is no slippery slope.

However, it is not important whether or not concepts should be called holistic according to our definition; holism as such is not bad. The question is rather whether or not the unacceptable consequences for which holism is blamed in this area are avoided by our definition. Let us look at four such consequences.

A first bad consequence of holism appeared to be that belief change ipso facto meant conceptual change. This, however, is not so at all with our proposal. Take my concept of my son, again. I acquire new beliefs about him all day long and forget many old ones. But, according to our explanation, my concept of him has in no way changed in the last few years; all the beliefs I have acquired or forgotten concerned contingent matters and did not add to, or subtract from, my beliefs about his essence. The same holds, say, for my concept of tables. Almost every day I learn something about tables, for instance, at which places tablehood is instantiated. But my concept of tables is fixed since long ago.

A second bad consequence seemed to be that holism renders impossible intrapersonal and interpersonal psychological generalizations. This is an objection we never understood. Each individual constellation may be unique, but this does not prevent it from being subsumable under general laws. It was always clear that, strictly speaking, there is only one application for Newton's theory of gravitation, namely the whole universe. But this did not deprive it of its lawful character. Block (1991, p. 41) makes similar remarks to the effect that there is not really an objection here.

A third bad consequence of holism was said to be that it makes communication miraculous because the concepts of different subjects are almost guaranteed to differ, preventing them from understanding each other. There are several remarks to be made about this point.

To begin with, we are not sure whether subjects need to have the same concepts in order to understand each other. It rather seems to be sufficient to know which matter the others talk about, i.e. to which objects and properties they refer. As long as this is secured, it does not do much harm when we have a different grasp of the objects and properties referred to; communication may also serve to assimilate the differing grasps. In this perspective, sameness of concepts is required only insofar concepts are constitutive for ontology. This may indeed be a relevant aspect in abstract realms, but we do not think it has much relevance in everyday matters.

Still, it would be good to know the extent to which we have the same concepts according to our proposal. The answer is a mixed one. Take my son again. I know his grandparents, others don't. So, our earlier remarks imply that there are diverging concepts of him. Take Bill Clinton, by contrast. Most of us know him just from TV. Certainly, we have looked at TV at different times, and hence, we believe different things about him. But there is no reason to assume that our concepts of him differ in any way; we believe quite the same about Clinton's essence. Take tables. Again, there is no reason why our concepts of tables should differ despite our differing beliefs about tables. If we compare the functions from contexts to extensions which we associate with the word "table", our guess would be that the variance keeps well within the range of vagueness of that word. Take elms, finally. Presumably, many of us are still roughly in the poor state Putnam describes. But some of us may have been ashamed of this, and thus have informed themselves. Their concept of an elm, then, differs from that of the rest. Hence, there is neither a guarantee nor an impossibility of agreement in concepts.

However, one should observe that there is considerable conditional agreement. We argued in the previous section that subjective concepts and objective diagonals agree on their common domain (if the relevant condition is satisfied). Since this holds for all subjects, we find the same conditional harmony among their concepts.

These remarks do not add up to a satisfactory discussion of the question how communication is possible on the basis of concepts as beliefs about essences. But we may tentatively conclude that there is no clear evidence at all that a serious objection will be forthcoming here.

The fourth and final bad consequence of holism seems to be what Fodor (1987, p. 102) calls the disjunction problem, which is the problem of how error is possible – which it must clearly be – according to one's theory of meaning, content, or concepts. This problem arises in particular for the causal-information theoretic account of Dretske (1981), and in this way it is treated by Fodor (1987 and 1990, ch. 3 and 4). However, the problem of error also plagues holistic accounts. Suppose Fodor's Ur-argument, quoted above, is sound. Then all the epistemic liaisons of a content which I believe, i.e. hold to be true, would be constitutive of that content. Now suppose I change these epistemic liaisons. Could this result in a different balance of reason for that content and even in a different judgment, e.g., that this content is really false? No, because it would be a new content which I would judge false; the old content would cease to exist. That is, the old content can exist only as held true. Similarly, if a concept is an encyclopedia entry in Block's sense. I believe all parts of that encyclopedia entry to be true. Now, for some reason, I want to change my mind and to discard some parts. Because they have proven wrong? No, we cannot put it this way. If I change my encyclopedia, I change my concepts, and my beliefs change content. So, again, I can put together my concepts only to form contents with a fixed truth assignment; all contents would be conceptual truths or falsehoods. These would be fatal consequences indeed.[33] Of course, I often err even by my own lights, and any adequate theory must be able to account for this.

It should be clear, however, from our comments on the first possible objection that our proposal has none of these absurd consequences and enables us to change our mind without changing our concepts. In particular, our explanation of concepts and our subjective truth condition for beliefs clearly allow us to have beliefs which are false by our own lights; our most considerate judgment may well falsify our actual judgment. There is no error problem for our account.

So, to sum up: have we escaped the holistic horn of Block's dilemma? Our discussion does perhaps not firmly establish a positive answer, but it shows, we think, that the prospects for our proposal are bright – all the more so as it was clear that the syntacticist horn of the dilemma was definitely avoided and that there was no danger of stumbling into Schiffer's problem.[*]

References

Austin, J.L. 1962. *Sense and Sensibilia*. Oxford: Clarendon Press.

Block, N. 1986. Advertisement for a Semantics for Psychology. *Midwest Studies in Philosophy, vol. X, Studies in the Philosophy of Mind*, ed. P.A. French, T.E. Uehling jr., H.K. Wettstein, 615-678. Minneapolis: University of Minnesota Press.

Block, N. 1991. What Narrow Content is Not. *Meaning in Mind. Fodor and His Critics*, ed. B. Loewer, G. Rey, 33-64. Oxford: Blackwell.

Block, N. 1995. Ruritania Revisited. *Philosophical Issues, vol. 6*, ed. E. Villanueva, 171-187. Atascadero: Ridgeview.

Burge, T. 1979. Individualism and the Mental. *Midwest Studies in Philosophy, Vol. IV: Metaphysics*, ed. P.A. French, T.E. Uehling jr., H.K. Wettstein, 73-121. Minneapolis: University of Minnesota Press.

Carnap, R. 1928. *Der logische Aufbau der Welt*. Hamburg: Meiner.

Chalmers, D. to appear. The Components of Content. *Mind* : to appear.

Chomsky, N. 1995. Language and Nature. *Mind* 104: 1-61.

---

[33] In fact, this issue was first raised in relation to the account of the meaning of theoretical terms in Kuhn 1970, pp. 111ff. and 198ff., and, for instance, Feyerabend 1965.

[*]We gratefully acknowledge that work on this paper has been supported by the Deutsche Forschungsgemeinschaft, Grant No. Schr 275/12-1.

Dretske, F. 1981. *Knowledge and the Flow of Information*. Oxford: Blackwell.

Evans, G. 1982. *The Varieties of Reference*. Oxford: Clarendon Press.

Feyerabend, P. 1965. Problems of Empiricism. *Beyond the Edge of Certainty*, ed. R.G. Colodny, 145-260. Englewood Cliffs: Prentice-Hall.

Field, H. 1977. Logic, Meaning, and Conceptual Role. *Journal of Philosophy* 74: 379-409.

Fodor, J.A. 1987. *Psychosemantics. The Problem of Meaning in the Philosophy of Mind*. Cambridge, Mass.: MIT Press.

Fodor, J.A. 1990. *A Theory of Content and Other Essays*. Cambridge, Mass.: MIT Press.

Fodor, J.A. 1994. *The Elm and the Expert*. Cambridge, Mass.: MIT Press.

Gelman, S.A., J.D. Coley, G.M. Gottfried 1994. Essentialist Beliefs in Children: The Acquisition of Concepts and Theories. *Mapping the Mind*, ed. L.A. Hirschfeld, S.A. Gelman, 341-365. Cambridge: Cambridge University Press.

Haas-Spohn, U. 1995. *Versteckte Indexikalität und subjektive Bedeutung*. Berlin: Akademie-Verlag.

Haas-Spohn, U. 1997. The Context Dependency of Natural Kind Terms. *Direct Reference, Indexicality and Propositional Attitudes*, ed. W. Künne, A. Newen, M. Anduschus , 333-349. Stanford: CSLI Publications.

Harman, G. 1987. (Nonsolipsistic) Conceptual Role Semantics. *New Directions in Semantics*, ed. E. LePore , 55-81. London: Academic Press.

Hazen, A. 1979. Counterpart-Theoretic Semantics for Modal Logic. *Journal of Philosophy* 76: 319-338.

Kaplan, D. 1977. Demonstratives. An Essay on the Semantics, Logic, Metaphysics, and Epistemology of Demonstratives and Other Indexicals. *Themes from Kaplan*, ed. J. Almog, J. Perry, and H.K. Wettstein, 481-563. Oxford: Oxford University Press, 1989.

Kripke, S.A. 1982. *Wittgenstein on Rules and Private Language*. Oxford: Blackwell.

Kupffer, M. 1999. *Counterparts and Qualities*. Dissertation, University of Konstanz.

Kuhn, T.S. 1970. *The Structure of Scientific Revolutions*. Chicago: University Press, 2nd ed.

Lewis, D. 1968. Counterpart Theory and Quantified Modal Logic. *Journal of Philosophy* 65: 113-126.

Lewis, D. 1979. Attitudes *de dicto* and *de se*. *Philosophical Review* 88: 513-543.

Lewis, D. 1980, Index, Context, and Content. *Philosophy and Grammar*, ed. S. Kanger, S. Öhman, 79-100. Dordrecht: Reidel.

Lewis, D. 1986. *On the Plurality of Worlds*. Oxford: Blackwell.

Lewis, D. 1994. Reduction of Mind. *A Companion to the Philosophy of Mind*, ed. S. Guttenplan, 412-431. Oxford: Blackwell.

Loar, B. 1986. Social Content and Psychological Content. *Contents of Thought*, ed. R. Grimm, D. Merrill, 99-110. Tucson: University of Arizona Press.

Perry, J. 1977. Frege on Demonstratives. *Philosophical Review* 86: 474-497.

Perry, J. 1988. Cognitive Significance and New Theories of Reference. *Noûs* 22: 1-18.

Putnam, H. 1975. The Meaning of 'Meaning'. *Philosophical Papers, Vol. 2: Mind, Language and Reality*, 215-271. Cambridge: Cambridge University Press.

Schiffer, S. 1990. Fodor's Character. *Information, Semantics, and Epistemology*, ed. E. Villanueva, 77-101. Oxford: Blackwell.

Spohn, W. 1997. Über die Gegenstände des Glaubens. *Analyomen 2. Proceedings of the 2nd Conference "Perspectives in Analytical Philosophy". Vol. I: Logic, Epistemology, Philosophy of Science*, ed. G. Meggle, 291-321. Berlin: de Gruyter.

Spohn, W. 1997a. The Character of Color Predicates: A Materialist View. *Direct Reference, Indexicality and Propositional Attitudes*, ed. W. Künne, A. Newen, M. Anduschus, 351-379. Stanford: CSLI Publications.

Spohn, W. 1997. Begründungen a priori – oder: ein frischer Blick auf Dispositionsprädikate. *Das weite Spektrum der Analytischen Philosophie. Festschrift für Franz von Kutschera*, ed. W. Lenzen, 323-345. Berlin: de Gruyter.

Spohn, W. 1997/98. How to Understand the Foundations of Empirical Belief in a Coherentist Way. *Proceedings of the Aristotelian Society, New Series* 98: 23-40.

Stalnaker, R.C. 1978. Assertion. *Syntax and Semantics, Vol. 9: Pragmatics*, ed. P. Cole, 315-332. New York: Academic Press.

Stalnaker, R.C. 1989. On What's in the Head. *Philosophical Perspectives 3, Philosophy of Mind and Action Theory*, 287-316.

Stalnaker, R.C. 1990. Narrow Content. *Propositional Attitudes. The Role of Content in Logic, Language, and Mind*, ed. C.A. Anderson, J. Owens, 131-145. Stanford: CSLI Publications.

White, S.L. 1982. Partial Character and the Language of Thought. *Pacific Philosophical Quarterly* 63: 347-365.

Part V

SETS, TRUTH AND LOGIC

16

Concepts of a Set

FRANZ VON KUTSCHERA

How can Frege's concept of set be reformed in a philosophically satisfactory way? That is still a live question. In a short paper it cannot be dealt with adequately, of course. I can just give a brief sketch of an answer. I lead up to it by two steps: the classical Fregean concept of set, and then George Boolos' iterative concept. Although my discussion will be mainly philosophical, I cannot leave out formal details altogether, since it is only by translation into a formal system that a notion becomes precise in this field.

1 The classical concept

The classical concept of a set is that of an extension of a concept. Frege points out the differences between sets in this sense (*Begriffsumfänge*) and collections, aggregates or wholes in his letter to Bertrand Russell of 28.7.1902[1] and his *Grundgesetze*, vol.II p.150. His main points are (a) that talk of an empty collection makes no sense, and (b) that being a constituent (or part) of something is a transitive relation, while being an element of something (belonging to the extension of a concept, being an instance of a concept) is not.

The axioms of comprehension and of extensionality are direct consequences of this classical conception. First, *every (one-place, 1st order) concept has an extension.* The axiom of comprehension

---

[1] *BW*, p. 222f.

C: $\exists x \forall y(y \varepsilon x \equiv A[y])$

is not quite the same principle. It only says that each concept *expressed by a predicate* has an extension.

Second, *sets that have exactly the same elements are identical.* If we envisage only sets as objects this is expressed by the axiom of extensionality

E: $\forall z(z \varepsilon x \equiv z \varepsilon y) \supset x=y$.

C and E together form a complete set of axioms of classical, or as hindsight puts it: naive set theory.

When I said that the two axioms arise immediately from the concept of a set as the extension of a concept, this is not quite right, however. The axioms are formulated in a language with only one universe of discourse, the class of all sets[2], in contradistinction to systems of type theory, e.g. Furthermore, it is tacitly presupposed that sets are given independently of our thoughts and are not intellectual constructions. This corresponds to a realistic or Platonistic conception of sets. This, indeed, was Frege's position[3], as it was that of Georg Cantor[4] and Kurt Gödel. Gödel writes:

> Classes and concepts may ... be conceived as real objects ... existing independently of our definitions and constructions. ... It seems to me that the assumption of such objects is quite as legitimate as the assumption of physical bodies and there is quite as much reason to believe in their existence. They are in the same sense necessary to obtain a satisfactory theory of mathematics as physical bodies are necessary to obtain a satisfactory theory of sense perceptions ...[5]

It is this realism that, together with the classical notion of a set as the extension of a concept, leads straight into the paradoxes. Realism takes the universe of all sets as given, and then there is no reason whatsoever not to assume the existence also of the universal set and no objection to the power set axiom, and therefore no way out of Cantors paradox.

---

[2] Against Russells suggestions (cf. his letter of 8.8.1902 in *BW*, p. 226) Frege insisted that sets are objects, and that there is no natural basis for a distinction of sorts or levels of objects as there is in the realm of concepts. (Cf. Freges answer to Russells' letter of 23.9.1902 in *BW*, p. 227f.) - In the *Grundlagen der Arithmetik* Frege still thought that, instead of extensions of concepts, one could simply use the concepts themselves (cf. Frege 1884, p. 80, footnote), but he gave up this idea later on.

[3] Cf. Kutschera 1989, 10.2.

[4] Cantors concept of a set was not, it seems, very clear-cut. For an interpretation cf. I. Jané 1995, e.g.

[5] Gödel 1944, p. 137.

2 The Iterative Concept of Set

2.1 Intuitive Approach

As George Boolos emphasized in his paper *The iterative concept of set* (1971), any satisfactory system of set theory has to be based on an intuitively convincing notion of set which is translated into formal language by the axioms of the system. Classical set theory, as we have seen, satisfies this condition - with the exception that, on the intuitive level, realism is at odds with the set concept: If sets are extensions of concepts then realism as to sets implies realism as to concepts. But concepts are normally thought of as constructions of the human mind. Concepts are something we form, not something we find out there. Conceptualism is the proper attitude to concepts, therefore, not realism. If you want to hold on to realism with respect to sets you have to loosen the connection between sets and concepts, therefore, as in axiomatic set theory with its weakening of the axiom of comprehension.

How sets are to be conceived of if they are seen as extensions of concepts, and concepts, in turn, are seen as constructions of the mind, I will sketch in the next section. Here I shall first briefly describe Boolos' notion of set as a first step in the right direction. His notion is essentially conceptualistic. Sets are not given but formed. The formation starts with a class, V_0, of given individuals (non-sets). In pure set theory this class will be empty, but for a heuristic exposition suppose there are individuals. Now in a first step we can form collections of objects from V_0. These collections are now taken as new objects, thereby enlarging V_0 to V_1. Every possible collection of elements of V_0, then, is an element of V_1. Since a collection is uniquely determined by its elements, we have to accept the axiom E of extensionality (which in view of the individuals, has to be modified so that two *sets* are identical, if they have exactly the same elements.)

If $P(X)$ is the power set of X, we have then

a) $V_1 = V_0 \cup P(V_0)$.

As long as V_1 is our universe of discourse, V_1 is no set, but as we may say, only a *class*.

This step may be repeated, so that we generally have

b) $V_{n+1} = V_0 \cup P(V_n)$.

If the V_n are defined in this way for all natural numbers n, i.e. for all finite ordinals, we can, in a next step, form the class V_ω as the union of all the V_n's - ω being the smallest transfinite ordinal. We therefore set

c) $V_\omega = \bigcup_{\alpha < \omega} V_\alpha$.

Thus in V_ω as our universe of discourse we obtain no new objects. New objects come up only if we move on from V_ω to $V_{\omega+1}$, and so on. Let $\alpha,\beta,\gamma,...$ be ordinals, and λ, λ',... limit numbers, i.e. ordinals that have no immediate predecessor. Let us further assume now that V_0 is empty. Then we have

$$V_{\alpha+1} = P(V_\alpha) \text{ and } V_\lambda = \bigcup_{\alpha<\lambda} V_\alpha.$$

The result is a cumulative hierarchy characterized by the theorems

$$\alpha=\beta \supset V_\alpha \subseteq V_\beta$$

$$\alpha<\beta \supset V_\alpha \in V_\beta$$

$$V_\alpha \in V_\beta \vee V_\beta \in V_\alpha \vee V_\alpha = V_\beta \ (\in \text{ is connex on the set S of the } V_\alpha)$$

$$x \in V_\alpha \supset x \subseteq V_\alpha \ (\in \text{ is transitive on S}).$$

2.2 The General Notion of an Iterative Construction of Sets

From the hierarchy of the classes V_α we obtain a hierarchy of all sets in V. If $O(x)$, the *order* of set x, is the smallest ordinal α such that $x \varepsilon V_\alpha$, then we have $x \varepsilon y \supset O(x) < O(y)$. We further obtain that all sets in V are *grounded*. Groundedness is defined by

$$G(x) := \forall y(x \varepsilon y \supset \exists z(z \varepsilon y \wedge z \cap y = \varnothing)).$$

The definiens states that there is no infinite sequence $x_1, x_2, ...$ with $x_{n+1} \varepsilon x_n$.

Conversely, for each iterative notion of sets in the general sense that sets are constructed step by step, where every step presupposes the existence of the objects already constructed, there has to be an irreflexive and transitive relation $x<y$ obtaining if the construction of y presupposes the existence of x. This relation has to be grounded, i.e. there may not be an infinite sequence $x_1, x_2,...$ such that $x_{n+1} < x_n$. There must, then, be initial objects that do not presuppose other objects, and starting from them we can assign every set x an order $O(x)$ as the smallest ordinal greater than all numbers $O(y)$ for $y<x$. Then we can again define a hierarchy of cumulative classes $V_\alpha = \{x: O(x) \leq \alpha\}$. In the collective notion of set as a special iterative conception we have $x<y$ iff $x \varepsilon y$ or $\exists z(x \varepsilon z \wedge z \varepsilon y)$ or ..., i.e. iff $x \varepsilon^{>0} y$. $\varepsilon^{>0}$ is grounded iff $\forall x(x \varepsilon V \supset G(x))$ holds.

2.3 The Formal System Σ of Axiomatic Set Theory

Since ordinal numbers are introduced only in set theory, we cannot already use them in the axioms of such a theory. The preceeding considerations, therefore, have only a heuristic function. I can describe the axiomatic system only very briefly here, but as the whole point of Boolos' paper is that

Zermelo-Fraenkel set theory (**ZFF**, to be exact) turns out to be a translation of his iterative-collective concept, I cannot just leave the axiomatics aside.

Let **S** be our set-theoretical language. I shall use a free logic here for which sets are the existing classes - objects, in fact, if we envisage no individuals. As will come out, only elements exist, so the system is akin to v.Neumann-Bernays-Gödel set theory, but here we quantify only over sets, and while the language of NBG-set theory is (in effect) a 2nd-order predicate logic, ours is a 1st-order one. We introduce a constant V such that $x\varepsilon V$ is our existence predicate. Then we have $\forall x A[x] \wedge y\varepsilon V \supset A[y]$, and a predicate logical rule $A \wedge x\varepsilon V \supset B[x] \vdash A \supset \forall x B[x]$. The abstraction principle

M1: $s\varepsilon\lambda x A[x] \equiv s\varepsilon V \wedge A[s]$

is our first axiom. We further have

M2: $s\varepsilon t \supset s\varepsilon V$ - elements are sets (they exist)

M3: $\forall x(x\varepsilon s \equiv x\varepsilon t) \supset s=t$ - extensionality.

To determine a hierarchical order on V without referring to ordinals we follow an idea of Dana Scott in (1974) and introduce a constant S. $x\varepsilon S$, intuitively, means that x is one of the V_α. The properties of the S-sets are determined by

M4: $\forall x(x\varepsilon S \supset \forall y(y\varepsilon x \equiv \exists z(z\varepsilon S \wedge z\varepsilon x \wedge (y\varepsilon z \vee y\subseteq z))))$ - axiom of cumulation.

It corresponds to $V_\alpha = \bigcup_{\beta<\alpha}V_\beta \cup \bigcup_{\beta<\alpha}P(V_\beta)$. The axiom of restriction

M5: $t\varepsilon V \equiv \exists x(x\varepsilon S \wedge t\subseteq x)$

says that every set is an element (or equivalently: a subset) of an S-set.

Up to M5 the axioms are direct consequences of the collective notion of set. M1 to M5 do not imply the existence of sets. Our existence axioms are to be

M6: $\emptyset\varepsilon S$

M7: $\forall x \exists y(y\varepsilon S \wedge x\subseteq y \wedge \forall x_1...x_n (x_1\varepsilon y \wedge...\wedge x_n\varepsilon y \supset (A^y [x_1,...,x_n] \equiv A[x_1,...,x_n])))$.

Here $x_1,...,x_n$ are to be the only free variables in $A[x_1,...,x_n]$, and $A^y[x_1,...,x_n]$ is obtained from that predicate by restricting all quantifiers to the set y, i.e. by replacing $\exists z \cdots$, $\forall z \cdots$ and $\lambda z \cdots$ by $\exists z(z\varepsilon y \wedge \cdots)$, $\forall z(z\varepsilon y \supset \cdots)$ and $\lambda z(z\varepsilon y \wedge \cdots)$, respectively. Therefore M7, Scott's axiom of reflection, implies that for every sentence A and every S-set x there is a S-set y with $x\subseteq y$, i.e. a partial universe in which A holds iff A holds in the whole universe V. And for each term s without free variables and each xεS there is a yεS with x$\subseteq$y, such that s, restricted to y, i.e. s^y, designates the same class as s$\cap$y in the whole universe. M7 is not a consequence of the conception of classes as iterative collections. That alone does not imply which S-sets there are, i.e. how far in the hierarchy of the V_α-universes one should go. M7 is a very powerful existence axiom, but further existence axioms may be added. The axioms M1 to M7 form the system Σ.

3 Sets as Extensions of Predicates

3.1 The Basic Idea

To justify the stepwise, iterative construction of sets we have to conceive of collections as the result of an activity of collecting. Now, I don't think that such an activity or its results are well defined unless we characterize collections by concepts. We can turn Frege's arguments against sets as aggregates or wholes against sets as collections, and therefore I think it intuitively much more convincing to return to something like Frege's definition of classes as extensions of concepts. What we have to change about his notion are just two points, I think: First, we have to eliminate the realism and take concepts as something we form. Second, we should speak of the extension of predicates instead of speaking of the extension of concepts. I have stated my reasons for the second recommendation elsewhere.[6] They arise, briefly, from a pragmatic theory of language combined with the old Platonic idea that thinking (to a large extent, at least) is a kind of silent speaking.[7] It is surely plausible to think of concepts as wedded to predicates. This view, moreover, is the only natural basis for deriving rules for the formation of concepts, and finally the restriction to concepts expressible by predicates is already made in the classical axiom of comprehension.

This approach results in a different theory of sets that is related to **ZFF**, roughly (and somewhat enigmatically) speaking, as a cumulative Ramified Type Theory to a cumulative Simple Type Theory.

3.2 Heuristics

As in section 2.1 I shall first describe the system intuitively. Let L_0 now be a class of individuals - in pure set theory it will again be empty. While in the collective theory of sets the class $V_{\alpha+1}$ was simply $P(V_\alpha)$ - or, for $V_0 \neq \varnothing$, $V_0 \cup P(V_\alpha)$ - we can adopt into $L_{\alpha+1}$ only sets definable from predicates of **S** defined on L_α. If A[x] is a predicate of **S** defined on L_α, we cannot say that the term s=λxA[x] designates an object of $L_{\alpha+1}$, since with the step from L_α to $L_{\alpha+1}$ as our new universe of discourse the quantifiers

---

[6] Cf. Kutschera 1998a and 1998b.

[7] Cf. Plato's *Theaitetos*, 189e6-190a2.

change their meaning. Therefore we have to take s^{α} (s, restricted to L_{α}) as the name of an object in $L_{\alpha+1}$.

The difficulty is to define the class $D(L_{\alpha})$ of all sets s^{α}, where s is a class-term containing only free variables y with $y \varepsilon L_{\alpha}$. Fortunately, the problem was already solved by K.Goedel in (1940). $D(L_{\alpha})$ may be defined by way of an arithmetization of our set theoretical language S or by the Goedel-operations of forming, e.g., pairs and triples, set products, differences and unions. We have $D(x) \subseteq P(x)$ and we can set

$$L_{\alpha+1} = L_{\alpha} \cup D(L_{\alpha}), \text{ or, for } L_0 = \varnothing, L_{\alpha+1} = D(L_{\alpha}), \text{ and}$$

$$L_{\lambda} = \bigcup_{\alpha < \lambda} L_{\alpha}.$$

For $L = \bigcup_{\alpha} L_{\alpha}$, L is the class of all definable sets.

We can again assign to each set x an ordinal $O(x)$, the smallest α such that $x \varepsilon L_{\alpha}$. Then we again have

$$x \varepsilon y \supset O(x) < O(y),$$

but $O(x)$ is not, as in the collective approach, the smallest ordinal greater than all the orders of the elements of x. There may be subsets of L_{α} that are not elements of $L_{\alpha+1}$ but only elements of L_{β}'s with ordinals β much greater than $\alpha+1$. The order $O(x)$, therefore, does not only depend on the orders of its elements - the elements in case of $x \subseteq L_{\alpha}$ are of orders $\leq \alpha$, but $O(x)$ may be greater than $\alpha+1$.

3.3 Differences and Connections

An axiomatic system for this set theory may be formulated in close correspondence to Σ; let's call it Ω. I shall not discuss it here, but simply mention some relations between the two systems.

First we obviously have

$L_{\alpha} \subseteq V_{\alpha}$ and $L_{\alpha} = V_{\alpha}$ for all $\alpha \leq \omega$.

But after ω the sets L_{α} become smaller and smaller parts of the V_{α}. In Ω the principles of separation, union, pairing, sum and regularity (foundation) hold, too, but not the power set principle

P: $x \varepsilon V \supset P(x) \varepsilon V$.

Furthermore the axioms of infinity and replacement can be proven in Ω. The essential difference, then, is that Ω lacks the power set axiom.

On the other hand, in Σ (**ZFF**) Goedel's axiom of constructibility

K: V=L

cannot be proven which would be a theorem in Ω. Goedel, however, has shown that **K** is compatible with **ZFF** (or Σ), i.e. the axioms of **ZFF** are satisfiable over the class L of constructible sets.

Now $\Sigma+K$ is equivalent to $\Omega+P$.[8] P as we saw, is not a consequence of Ω, but the idea that for every L_α there is a $\beta>\alpha$ such that each subset of L_α is constructible in some L_γ for $\alpha<\gamma\leq\beta$, is not implausible. It is not a part of the constructive conception of set, but certainly not foreign to it, that for each L_α all the sets in $P(L_\alpha)$ will be constructible if you go up far enough in the hierarchy. So P, from the standpoint of constructible sets, is an higher existence axiom, a higher axiom of infinity, while K for collective sets is an axiom of restriction.

3.4 Ontological and Semantical Foundation

I want to close my paper by pointing out two arguments for preferring the constructive notion of set to the collective one.

The first, Fregean one was already mentioned: We know how to go about collecting stamps or sums of money, but how do you go about collecting sets, especially infinitely many sets? And it is far from evident that the product of such an activity is anything like what you need for set theory. How can a new definite object pop up if you collect nothing? Or something different from a penny if you collect just one penny? And why should the collection of two collections be different from what you get by simply collecting their elements? - Forming sets as sorts of things by distinguishing them according to their qualities is clearly a much better defined procedure.

The second argument is a semantical one. To guarantee that all of the infinitely many wellformed expressions of a logical language are assigned extensions we have to proceed inductively. In our set theoretical language, however, there is no suitable inductive parameter. The length or the degree (i.e. the number of occurrences of logical operators) of an expression won't work since we have to have, among others, a semantical rule, corresponding to the principle of abstraction, the rule (*) that a formula $s\varepsilon\lambda xA[x]$ is true iff $A[s]$ is true. Here the sentence $A[s]$ may be longer (or of higher degree) than the expression $s\varepsilon\lambda xA[x]$ interpreted by it. Let r be the Russell set, e.g., that is $\lambda x\neg(x\varepsilon x)$. Then according to our rule (*) $r\varepsilon r$ is true iff $\neg(r\varepsilon r)$ is true, and that, according to the rule of negation, is the case iff $r\varepsilon r$ is false. What we need to prevent such semantical circles, vitious or not, is that the relation $\rho(\phi,\psi)$ between wellformed expressions ϕ and ψ of $\mathbf{S}$, obtaining iff by the semantical rules of $\mathbf{S}$ the extension of ψ depends on the extension of ϕ, is founded, i.e. $\forall S'(\varnothing\neq S' \subseteq \mathbf{WF}(\mathbf{S}) \supset \exists\psi(\psi\varepsilon S' \wedge \rho[\psi]\cap S'=\varnothing)$, where $\mathbf{WF}(\mathbf{S})$ is the class of wellformed expressions of $\mathbf{S}$ and $\rho[\psi] = \{\phi: \rho(\phi,\psi)\}$. Foundedness of ρ, in view of its transitivity, means that there is no infinite sequence of (not necessarily different) expressions $\phi_1,\phi_2,...$ such that $\rho(\phi_{n+1},\phi_n)$, and that excludes semantical circles.

---

[8] The compatibility of Σ with K (if Σ is consistent) does not justify the use of Σ from a constructivist point of view, since the argument relies on Σ.

Now, as again Goedel has shown, we can recursively define a function $E(\phi A,x)$ in **ZFF**, the extension of the wellformed expression A in the set x, where ϕA is the Goedel number of A. $E(\phi A,x)$, then, is the extension of A relative to x, i.e. the extension A would have if x were the universe of discourse. In general absolute extensions can only be defined for restricted formulas and terms - otherwise it would be possible to reconstruct the semantical paradoxes in **ZFF**.

From the constructive point of view relative extensions are all that is to be expected. A predicate has an extension only with respect to an already existing domain of objects - in the heuristic construction of definable sets: only with respect to one of the L_α's. Relative extensions, furthermore, are all that is needed, if all sets are definable, since a definable set is expressible by a restricted class-term. Building the more and more inclusive universes of discourse L_α step by step you also define a sequence of appropriate languages with a recursive function determining the extensions of the wellformed expressions.

From a realistic point of view, on the other hand, absolute extensions would be expected as well as needed. And in the collective approach without an axiom of constructibility, finally, we need unrestricted terms like $P(L_\alpha)$ which cannot, in general, be interpreted inductively.

References

Boolos, G. 1971. The iterative concept of set, *Journal of Philosophy 68*: 215-232.

Frege, G. *BW. Wissenschaftlicher Briefwechsel*, ed. G. Gabriel, H. Hermes, F. Kambartel, C. Thiel, A. Veraart. Hamburg: Meiner, 1976.

Frege, G. 1884. *Grundlagen der Arithmetik*. Breslau: M. und H. Marcus.

Gödel, K. 1940. The consistency of the axiom of choice and the generalized continuum-hypothesis with the axioms of set theory, *Annals of Mathematics Studies* no.3, Princeton.

Gödel, K. 1944. Russell's mathematical logic. *The Philosophy of Bertrand Russell*, ed. P.A.Schilpp. Evanston: Open Court.

Jané, I. 1995. The role of the absolute infinite in Cantor's conception of set. *Erkenntnis 42*: 375-402.

Jech, T. 1978. *Set Theory*, New York: Academic Press.

Kutschera, F.v. 1989. *Gottlob Frege - Eine Einführung in sein Werk*, Berlin: W. de Gruyter

Kutschera, F.v. 1998a. *Die Teile der Philosophie und das Ganze der Wirklichkeit*, Berlin: W. de Gruyter

Kutschera, F.v. 1998b. Pragmatische Sprachauffassung, Bedeutungen und semantische Antinomien. *The Role of Pragmatics in Contemporary Philosophy*, ed. P.Weingartner, G.Schurz, G.Dorn. Vienna: Hölder-Pichler-Tempsky. 122-131

Scott, D. 1974. Axiomatizing set theory, *Proceedings of Symposia in Pure Mathematics*, vol.. XIII, pt. II: Axiomatic Set Theory. Providence.

17

Is Logic the Science of the Laws of Truth?

UWE MEIXNER

1 Frege's Characterization of Logic

In a paper published in 1918, 'Der Gedanke. Eine logische Untersuchung' ('Thought. A Logical Investigation'), Frege says (p. 30, my translation): 'As the word "beautiful" to esthetics and the word "good" to ethics, thus the word "true" is pointing out a direction to logic. All sciences have truth as their aim, logic, however, is, in addition, involved with truth in a quite special manner. ... It is the task of logic to cognize the laws of truth [*literally*: the laws of being true].' Frege makes this more precise. He distinguishes *normative* laws from *descriptive* laws. The laws of truth are, like the laws of nature, descriptive laws, although, of course, they can be taken as a basis for prescriptions, and thus as a basis for normative laws: for the laws of *rationally correct* thinking. The laws of truth must, in turn, according to Frege be distinguished from the laws of nature; the latter describe the invariant form of what is happening in time; the laws of truth, however, describe timeless *being*. Still fighting psychologism, Frege strongly emphasizes that logic is not concerned with the *psychological* laws of factual thinking; the task of logic is to discover the laws of truth, not the empirically descriptive laws of actually occurring believing or thinking (p. 31).

Frege arrives at a general characterization of what the laws of truth consist in (p. 31, my translation): 'In the laws of truth the meaning of the word "true" is unfolded.' However, it seems that there is not much of interest to be expected from an investigation of *such* laws of truth, for a few lines further down Frege declares (p. 32) that any attempt to define truth [*literally*: being true] is bound to fail, due to circularity, since, according to Frege, the concept of truth must already be given - given as a primitive - in order to decide whether the allegedly truth-defining concepts apply in any considered case: for the question whether they apply is the question *whether it is true* that they apply. He comes to the conclusion (p. 32, my translation): 'It is likely that the content of the word "true" is totally singular and indefinable.'

In a much earlier manuscript - the fragment 'Logik' from 1897 - Frege had already arrived at practically the same positions.[1] There he writes (p. 39, my translation): 'Truth apparently is something so primitive and simple as to be not reducible to anything yet simpler.' And: 'Logic is the science of the most general laws of truth [*literally*: of being true].' Frege adds apologetically: 'Perhaps one finds that one cannot think of anything totally determinate that is meant by these words. Inaptness of the author and of language may be the cause of this. But the intention was only to give a rough characterization of the aim [of logic]. What is missing must be supplemented by the carrying out [of logical investigations].' Now, Frege certainly carried out many logical investigations where he clarified many things in and around logic; but it can hardly be said that his very characterization of logic as *the science of the laws of truth* has been clarified by these investigations further than it is explicated by his rather scant remarks that he explicitly attaches to the characterization. At least, however, in the course of his logical investigations, Frege amply provided us with examples of what he thought *are* laws of truth. But are those examples indeed what Frege thought they are? Are even the axioms and theorems of a classical propositional calculus laws of truth? Note that if logic is to be the science of the laws of truth, it is not enough that those axioms and theorems can in some sense also be construed to be laws of truth. No, they must be primarily and essentially laws of truth - albeit that need not be obviously or trivially so.

---

[1] Already in the introduction to the first volume of *Grundgesetze der Arithmetik* (*Fundamental Laws of Arithmetic*) published in 1893, we find Frege asserting that logical laws are laws of truth (see p. XVI). But there (pp. XV-XVII) the attack against psychologism is paramount (logical laws, says Frege, are laws of *being true*, and *not* natural laws of *holding to be true*), and the definition of logic as the science of the laws of truth is only implicit, but nevertheless unmistakably implied. Thus, in the *Grundgesetze*, we find that definition coupled with Frege's assumption of having faultlessly shown (p. XXVI) that 'arithmetic is nothing but further developed logic' (p. VII) - *without* Frege being aware that there might be a problem in this coupling. See for this Section 1.4 below.

1.1   ... and Modern Logic

But let us first, before tackling the question just posed, look beyond the confines of classical Fregean logic. Let us consider logic with the very large scope it has acquired today. Logic in its modern form, as currently practiced, is certainly *not* the science of the laws of truth, nor is its relation to truth in any way special. Of course, like all sciences, modern logic too is aiming at truth, namely, like each and every science, at the particular truths it is interested in, for example: Is it true that formula F is provable in system S? Is it true that system S is deductively equivalent to system S'? Is it true that system S is sound and complete with respect to the model structures in set M? Indeed, there are many truths modern logic is interested in, but none of them is a law of truth in approximately the sense Frege seems to have in mind.

Moreover, modern logic is certainly interested in the axioms and theorems of logical calculi (as has just been said, at least some of those formulas are intended by Frege to be laws of truth); but modern logic is not interested in them *qua* laws of truth. In the first place, the word 'true' does not even occur in them. But this is not a serious objection, since we can insert 'it is true that' in front of any sentential part of any formula without changing its meaning. The second objection is decisive: Modern logic proceeds fairly close to the maxim: 'Give me the axiomatic system, *whatever it is*, and I give you its models (if there are any).' Or vice versa: 'Give me the models, *whatever they are*, and I give you the axiomatic system for them (if there is one).' Take a tense-logical principle like Fp⊃FFp. This formula (expressing the density of the temporal ordering) is logically valid with respect to an appropriate set of model structures. But it is not logically valid with respect to a certain other set of model structures; with respect to that set we find, on the contrary, the discreteness-formula Pq ∧ p ∧ ¬Fp ⊃ P(Fp ∧ ¬FFp) to be logically valid. The modern logician is happy to formulate two alternative systems, one in which Fp⊃FFp is provable, and one in which it isn't provable, but Pq ∧ p ∧ ¬Fp ⊃ P(Fp ∧ ¬FFp) is. Thus, although modern logicians are interested in formulating axiomatic systems, they are *qua modern logicians* not interested in assuring that those systems codify laws of truth or even *something true*. The truth *of* their axiomatic systems - contrary to the truth *about* them - does not matter to modern logicians *qua* modern logicians. It is enough if some interest attaches to the provable formulas - some interest derived from some envisaged application - be it artificial intelligence, the semantics of natural language, or even merely some puzzling argument in the history of philosophy.

1.2   ... and Logic as a Branch of Philosophy

From the modern point of view, Frege's characterization of the aims of logic is hopelessly outmoded and sounds quaintly philosophical. Although logic, alongside psychology, was the very last fledgling to leave the nest of philosophy, logic is today very much independent of its mother. Modern logicians do not much care about finding the laws of truth (or even the normative laws of correct reasoning); if logic is not practiced for its own sake (as the pure science of formal symbolic systems), it has - like applied mathematics - become a discipline of abstract engineering, catering indiscriminately to various special needs, among them those of philosophers. In the latter case, it is indeed called 'philosophical logic'; but this must not blind one to the fact that there is nothing intrinsically philosophical about so-called 'philosophical logic'.

If we take Frege in saying that *logic is the science of the laws of truth* as wanting to explicate the word 'logic', then our criticism will have to be that his explication departs too far from the *presently given* pre-explicatory, but nevertheless informed standard usage of the word, and is therefore not adequate according to the standards of adequacy for explications laid down by Rudolf Carnap. But this would certainly be unfair to Frege; for Frege intends to explicate the word 'logic' under the restraint that logic *has* to be a branch of philosophy. He took logic to be necessarily a philosophical discipline, a part of philosophy. Thus he is, rightly considered, not explicating the word 'logic', but the words 'logic as a branch of philosophy'. In saying that logic is the science of the laws of truth, Frege must today be taken to say that logic *as a branch of philosophy* is the science of the laws of truth; for him, the tag 'as a branch of philosophy' was simply redundant.

It is not *for us*. But what Frege *meant* to say may still be correct. There certainly exists a part of present-day logical activity - a small part, and unfortunately, it seems to me, a more and more diminishing one - which is at the same time a part of philosophy. Due to tradition - in the past all of logic was a part of philosophy - this small part of the sum total of present-day logical activity is still also simply called 'logic'; but nowadays it would serve clarity to call it 'logic as a branch of philosophy'.

1.3   ... and Classical vs. Non-Classical Logic

So it may be correct, as Frege holds, that logic - if taken as a branch of philosophy - is the science of the laws of truth. But *is* it in fact correct? Certainly not uncontroversially. Philosophically-minded logical intuitionists hold that logic is the science of the laws of *provability* or of *justified assertability*. From their point of view, logic could be the science of the laws of truth only if 'true' were co-extensional with 'provable' or with 'justifiedly assertable'. But, in the normal sense of the word, 'true' is certainly not co-extensional with 'provable' or with 'justifiedly assertable', and it seems to me that Frege and most other people would wish to hold on to this aspect of the normal sense of the word 'true'. So would most logical intuitionists, but they would add that they do not find the concept of truth - as distinguished from provability and justified assertability - to be a particularly useful one; they would urge us to get rid of it. For them, the axioms and theorems of their restricted - hence non-classical - calculi, e.g., of propositional logic, cannot be primarily or essentially laws of truth, and hence, for them, logic cannot be the science of the laws of truth.

Thus it is by no means philosophically uncontentious that logic is such a science. But again, it would be unfair to hold this against Frege's definition. For Frege is clearly explicating the word 'logic' under the further restraint that logic - as a branch of philosophy - is identical to *classical* logic. Like the restraint that logic must be a branch of philosophy, the restraint that logic is identical to classical logic was unrecognizable to Frege. The possibility that logic might offer alternatives to classical logic did not occur to him, just as the possibility did not occur to him that logic could be more than a branch of philosophy. Thus, when Frege says that *logic is the science of the laws of truth*, he must today be taken so say that *classical logic - as a branch of philosophy - is the science of the laws of truth*.

1.4 ... and Logicism vs. Elementary Logic

Obviously, Frege's explicatory thesis about the nature of logic is gaining in plausibility, once the restrictions are made explicit that Frege tacitly, and indeed unconsciously, deposited into its meaning. In fact, by now Frege's thesis seems so plausible as to appear trivial. Doesn't classical logic center on truth and falsity, where these two concepts are, in addition, obeying the principle of bivalence (or in other words, where each of these concepts is the negation of the other)? But even if it is so, is this enough to make classical logic, even within philosophy, the science of the laws of truth? For are such laws the *primary* objects of cognition for classical logic, or rather something else? Only if such laws are indeed the primary objects of cognition for classical logic, and not merely, as it were, by-products of its activities, can classical logic be indeed the science of the laws of truth.

At this point we should remember that Frege was also a philosopher of mathematics and went about - in the *Grundgesetze der Arithmetik* (*Fundamental Laws of Arithmetic*) - realizing the logicistic program of reducing arithmetic to logic. But the primary objects of arithmetical cognition are surely not laws of truth, but abstract structures: numbers and systems of numbers. Hence, from the point of view of logicism, it is incongruent to regard laws of truth as the primary objects of logical cognition. If logicism is right, logic - that is, for Frege, classical logic, a branch of philosophy - must at least sometimes be primarily concerned with other things than with laws of truth - namely with the object-related truths about certain 'logical objects', as Frege calls them. This difficulty for Frege's definition of logic, which arises from the very aspirations he had for logic, points us, however, to yet another restriction Frege can be taken to be tacitly assuming when he is speaking of logic as being the science of the laws of truth: At least later in his career, by the word 'logic' Frege may very well be merely intending *basic predicate logic*, which of course includes (truth-functional) propositional logic.

This further restriction is strongly suggested by the contents of the latest text in which his definition of logic occurs, the *Logische Untersuchungen* (*Logical Investigations*), published in three installments between 1918 and 1923 (I have quoted from the first installment above in Section 1). In the three published parts of *Logische Untersuchungen* Frege is *exclusively* concerned with central aspects of classical propositional logic. A fourth part, dedicated to classical predicate logic, and which would presumably have been mainly, if not merely, concerned with its more elementary aspects, was begun by Frege, but not finished. Since in the fragment of the fourth part he refers to the third part (which bears the title 'Logische Untersuchungen. Dritter Teil: Das Gedankengefüge' - 'Logical Investigations. Third Part: The Thought-Structure') as already published, Frege's work on the *Logische Untersuchungen* was apparently cut short only by his death in 1925.[2]

In order to give Frege's explicatory definition of logic the greatest chance of being correct or adequate, we may take him to be *ultimately* saying, in saying that logic is the science of the laws of truth, that classical *elementary* logic - as a branch of philosophy - is the science of the laws of truth. Indeed, at the end of his life, he *could* well have arrived at the conclusion that even if arithmetic is a part of some science which is a branch of philosophy, that science cannot properly speaking be called 'logic'.[3] And Frege would have been quite right in thinking so. Any science in which it is asserted (be it as an axiom or as a theorem) that there are infinitely many objects - a strange law of truth indeed! - cannot, properly speaking,[4] be called 'logic', no matter whether that assertion refers to a universe of objects which is divided into hierarchically ordered layers, or to one that does not have this hierarchical structure that is so satisfying to the order-loving

---

[2] See the introduction by Günther Patzig, the editor of *Logische Untersuchungen*, pp. 5-7.

[3] In the fragment 'Neuer Versuch der Grundlegung der Arithmetik' ('New Attempt to Found Arithmetic') from 1924/25 he begins to attempt a geometrical foundation of arithmetic. But he also makes two striking statements (p. 298, my translation): 'I had to give up the opinion that arithmetic is a branch of logic and that therefore in arithmetic everything has to be proved purely logically' and (p. 299) 'It seems that the logical source of cognition cannot by itself present us with objects'.

[4] 'properly speaking', that is: without missing the entrenched part of the meaning of the word.

minds of modern proponents of logicism.[5] And therefore, since arithmetic requires an infinity of objects, a science which is able to incorporate arithmetic cannot, properly speaking, be logic. If that science *is* to be a branch of philosophy, it must be *ontology*, or in other words: *general metaphysics*.[6]

1.5 ... and Frege's Elementary Oversight

Ironically, Frege's logicistic program - the high aspirations he had for logic - may be said to have failed precisely because Frege did not pay enough attention to the results of classical elementary logic, that is, to precisely those homely laws of truth he apparently in the end meant to be all that logic is concerned with. The following is a theorem-schema of elementary predicate logic: $\neg\exists y\forall x(R(x,y) \equiv \neg R(x,x))$. Russell's letter to Frege in which Russell formulated his famous antinomy, in effect, merely pointed out to Frege that he had violated this very law of truth, thus making his system in the *Grundgesetze der Arithmetik* logically inconsistent. Never before had a logician been so tragically punished as a logician for having been blinded by a metaphysical hope! For Frege, this hope - to which he entirely dedicated himself without realizing its metaphysical, non-logical character - had been the *ontological* reduction of arithmetic to his *ontological* theory of functions and objects, and in particular *Wertverläufe (courses of values)*. For the realization of this hope he threw away a logician's carefulness and wariness. I do not see how otherwise the inconsistency of his system could have remained hidden to him for such a long time.

1.6 ... and Intensionalism in Logic

But can we accept Frege's ultimate, modest claim that classical elementary logic as a branch of philosophy (and therefore *without* the heavy concentration on proof-theoretic and model-theoretic issues which is so characteristic of modern logic and which has almost entirely replaced interest in the contents of the logical systems themselves)[7], that logic *thus* regarded (I from now on leave tacit the modifier 'as a branch of philosophy') is the science of the laws of truth?

---

[5] Cf. e.g. Franz v. Kutschera who in Kutschera 1985 takes Zermelo-Fraenkel axiomatic set theory to be logic (p. 225) since it is provably equivalent to the overtly hierarchical (or 'inductive' - cf. pp. 210-212) system of Dana Scott (pp. 213-215, pp. 223-224).

[6] Frege *could* have arrived at this view - I am not saying that he did. Indeed it is rather unlikely that he ever realized the metaphysical nature of his so-called logicism. The reason for this is the predominant Neo-Kantian anti-metaphysical atmosphere in Germany in the second half of the 19th century: Metaphysics and ontology were banished from philosophy, and any self-respecting philosopher, imbued by that atmosphere, could not allow himself to regard his position as ontological and his practice as ontology.

[7] I am not saying that these issues are without philosophical interest. On the contrary, some results in this area are of the greatest philosophical importance *for epistemology*: the undecidability of predicate logic, the incompleteness of axiomatized arithmetic.

Since the scope of classical elementary logic is certainly too small to capture *all* laws of truth (laws of truth involving modalities, for example, are outside its ken), we have to replace the phrase 'the laws of truth' by the phrase 'the *most basic* laws of truth', as is indeed suggested by Frege himself: In the fragment 'Logik' from 1897 he had said (see the quote in Section 1 above) that logic is the science of the *most general* laws of truth. Presumably, what is most general is most basic, and vice versa.

Then there still remain two nagging closely related questions which we have already encountered in a modified form on the way to the present position: (1) Are the objects of cognition of classical elementary logic *primarily* laws of truth? (2) Are the axioms and theorems of a system of classical elementary logic - and in particular those of a system of classical propositional logic - *primarily* laws of truth? Since the axioms and theorems of a system of classical elementary logic are precisely the primary objects of cognition of classical elementary logic, the first question reduces to the second; this question is what we now must concern us with.

To a student of logic who, in the spirit of Frege, has been taught the meaning of the classical sentence-connectives 'and', 'or' and 'not' by truth-tables and who has then been made familiar with the utterly simple truth-value semantics for classical elementary predicate logic - a semantics that does without a universe of discourse - the answer to question (2) may seem to be obvious: 'Yes, the axioms and theorems of a calculus of classical elementary logic *are* primarily, essentially and naturally laws of truth, and indeed laws of truth without any ontological content whatsoever, albeit, *pace* Frege, they certainly contain more than a mere development of the meaning of the word "true".' However, even in Frege's own works we can find a massive hint that the answer 'Yes' to the question at issue is not necessarily correct. In the 'Ausführungen über Sinn und Bedeutung' ('Expositions on Sense and Reference', written between 1892 and 1895) we read (pp. 31-32, my translation): 'The logicians of content like only all too much to stop at the sense [the meaning]; for what they are calling content is, if not perception, so certainly sense. They do not consider that what matters in logic is not how thoughts [propositions] result from thoughts, without respect to the truth-value; they do not consider that the transition from the thought to the truth-value and - generally speaking - from the sense to the reference [*literally, but misleadingly*: the meaning] must be made, that the logical laws are primarily laws in the realm of reference and only secondarily pertain to sense.' Frege does not explain why the necessity of making the transition from the sense to the truth-value requires that logical laws are *primarily* laws in the realm of reference. Even if we agree with Frege that the truth-value of a sentence is its reference, there is no necessary connection between the two positions. Rather, a 'logician of content' - or in other words: a proponent of *intensionalism* in logic - can agree with Frege that the transition from the thought to the truth-value, from the sense to the reference *must* be made, and yet deny that the logical laws are primarily laws in the realm of reference. For an intensionalistic logician, logical laws are primarily laws in the realm of sense, and only *secondarily* do they pertain to reference and hence to truth.

2   The Intensionalistic Characterization of Logic

It follows that for an intensionalistic logician the axioms and theorems of a calculus of classical elementary logic are neither primarily nor essentially laws of truth, *although* their applicability in the realm of truth and reference is of course a highly important reason for our taking any interest at all in those axioms and theorems. Thus, regarding them as laws of truth is undoubtedly a natural, but nevertheless *secondary* perspective on them. If this secondary perspective is made the primary one (as is done by Frege), then, for the intensionalistic logician, this is comparable to declaring that the principles of physics are *primarily* laws for the building of rockets, televisions, and nuclear weapons. Thus, even if intensionalistic logicians accepted the highly restricted Fregean range of the word 'logic', they would certainly deny that logic is the science of the most basic laws of truth; this denial would be as obvious to them as denying that physics is the science of the most basic laws of technology is obvious to physicists. For the intensionalistic logician *logic is the science of the most basic meaning relations.*

3   Intensionalistic Logical Validity and Consequence

Is Frege right, or the 'logicians of content'? I will demonstrate for the simple case of classical propositional logic that the cause of the intensionalists is a strong one, making good the expectation Adolf Reinach voiced in his 1911 paper 'Zur Theorie des negativen Urteils' ('On the Theory of the Negative Judgment') (p. 251, my translation) 'that large parts of traditional logic will in their foundations prove to be general proposition theory [allgemeine Sachverhaltslehre]'.[8]

I have already mentioned that there is no mention of truth in the axioms and theorems of logical systems. Much more importantly, there need not be any mention of truth in the semantics for such systems: The fundamental semantic concepts of *logical validity* and *logical consequence* can be intuitively satisfactorily defined without making any use of the concept of truth at all. All of this is very well known under the heading of *algebraic seman-*

---

[8] If the foundations of logic are in question, it is more appropriate to translate Reinach's term 'Sachverhalt' by 'proposition' than by 'state of affairs'. Behind the intensionalist Reinach there stand the earlier intensionalists Husserl and Bolzano (as Wolfgang Künne emphasized in discussion).

tics; but let me rehearse that part of it that concerns classical propositional logic in order to show that even there Frege's definition of logic is not incontestable:

(1) Let L be a language of propositional logic, built in the usual manner on the basis of an infinity of propositional variables p, p′, p″, etc. by applying the sentence-connectives ¬, ∧, ∨, and brackets.

(2) An *interpretation* of L is a pair <W,V> consisting of a non-empty set of worlds W and a function V which assigns to every propositional variable of L a subset of W, and to all other formulas of L a subset of W according to the following stricture: For all formulas φ and ψ of L: $V(\neg\varphi) = W - V(\varphi)$, $V(\varphi \wedge \psi) = V(\varphi) \cap V(\psi)$, $V(\varphi \vee \psi) = V(\varphi) \cup V(\psi)$.

(3) φ is an L-logical consequence of $\psi_1,...,\psi_n := \varphi$, $\psi_1, ... ,\psi_n$ are formulas of L, and for all interpretations <W,V> of L: $V(\psi_1) \cap ... \cap V(\psi_n) \subseteq V(\varphi)$.

(4) φ is L-logically valid := φ is an L-logical consequence of $\neg\varphi$.

Intuitively, (3) says that a formula φ of L is a logical consequence of formulas $\psi_1,...,\psi_n$ of L if and only if the proposition expressed by φ is *intensionally contained* in the proposition the conjunction of $\psi_1,...,\psi_n$ expresses, *no matter* which particular propositions are expressed by φ and $\psi_1,...,\psi_n$. Thus (3) encodes an intensionalistic conception of logical consequence, a conception which the 'logicians of content' would undoubtedly favor and which undoubtedly is intuitively at least as satisfactory as the orthodox extensionalistic conception.[9] Note that there is no mention of truth in the definiens of (3); all that is talked about is the *propositional contents* of certain formulas and how those contents are related. Given (3), it is clear that in (4) also the logical validity of a formula of L is defined merely in terms of the propositional contents of certain formulas and how those contents are related. There is no need whatever of the concept of truth. Nevertheless, the very same formulas and inferences of L turn out to be logically valid that are logically valid according to the orthodox extensionalistic semantics for L, and these formulas, axiomatized by some adequate calculus or other, are precisely those that form the canon of classical propositional logic. Thus we have a clear demonstration that the laws in this canon have no unseparable relation to truth. They are not essentially laws of truth, and, in view of the

---

[9] Cf. the following remarkable passage from Reinach's 'Zur Theorie des negativen Urteils' (p. 222, my translation): 'All connections of justification encountered by us in science or in daily life are connections of propositions. This is also true of the connections that are generally subsumed under the name of "laws of inference": They are, rightly regarded, nothing else but general nomological relations of propositions. The fundamental consequences that result from this insight for the construction of the science of logic are obvious.'

intuitive satisfactoriness of definitions (3) and (4), it is more than doubtful whether they are at least primarily or naturally laws of truth.

4 Intensionalism with Truth Not Ignored

One might object that the intensionalistic conception of propositional logic is ontologically costly: Even if intensionalists who want to do propositional logic can get around assuming a plurality of possible worlds (in order to construe coarse-grained propositions simply as sets of worlds), they surely cannot get around positing propositions in some sense, together with an appropriate propositional algebra, as additional entities. To this I can merely say: So what? What is bad about propositions? And of course the ontological-economy-objection with respect to propositions is no objection Frege either would or could have raised. He was not an ontological scrooge. Ontological miserliness was not one of his vices, and, as we all know, his ontology comprises what he called *thoughts*, entities that, notwithstanding the word Frege used to designate them, have nothing to do with subjectivity, but are what we would call *fine-grained propositions*.

Indeed, it is hard to see what Frege could answer to a modern intensionalistic logician, contesting in the way presented above Frege's claim that logic is the science of the laws of truth. Presumably he would insist that the transition from sense to reference, from the thought to the truth-value *must* be effected. But modern intensionalistic logicians - whatever their forebears did, who according to Frege liked only all too much to stop at the sense[10] - would be quite ready to comply with Frege and bring truth into the game - although not quite in the manner Frege had in mind.

The above semantics for classical propositional logic can be made to yield laws of truth, and indeed not merely in the trivial sense that every sentential part of a principle of classical propositional logic can, without changing its meaning, be prefixed with the words 'it is true that' (or with a symbol having the meaning of this phrase). For this purpose we re-define what is an interpretation of the language L as follows:

(2*) An *interpretation* of L is a triplet <W,ω,V> consisting of a non-empty set of worlds W, a subset ω of W, and a function V which assigns to every propositional variable of L a subset of W, and to all other formulas of

---

[10] Adolf Reinach, at least, is a notable exception to Frege's allegation. Shortly before he (for the second time: cf. Section 3) envisions large parts of traditional logic as being founded on general proposition theory, he says ('Zur Theorie des negativen Urteils', p. 251, my translation): 'A sentence is true if the corresponding proposition obtains. And two contradictory sentences cannot both be true *because* two contradictory propositions cannot both obtain. Thus, also in this case the sentence-law leads back to a proposition-law. At the same time, we have here an example that illustrates in what sense we asserted above that large parts of traditional logic will in their foundations prove to be general proposition theory.'

L a subset of W according to the following stricture: For all formulas φ and ψ of L: $V(\neg\varphi) = W - V(\varphi)$, $V(\varphi \wedge \psi) = V(\varphi) \cap V(\psi)$, $V(\varphi \vee \psi) = V(\varphi) \cup V(\psi)$.[11]

We can then define the concept of *truth in an interpretation* for formulas φ of L as follows:

(5) φ is true in $<W,\omega,V>$:= $<W,\omega,V>$ is an interpretation of L, and $\omega \subseteq V(\varphi)$.

The intuitive meaning of this definition is the following: A formula φ of L is true (in an interpretation $<W,\omega,V>$ of L) if and only if the proposition that φ expresses (in that interpretation) is intensionally contained in the proposition which is the intersection (or *intensional sum*) of all *obtaining* propositions (for that interpretation). If we want to derive, on the basis of (5) and (2*), the classical truth-conditions for the propositional connectives, and indeed all the *metalinguistic* laws of truth one would normally assume for them (*these* metalinguistic laws, not certain object-language formulas, really deserve the designation '[logical] law of truth'!), then we need to add one extra condition for ω to (2*): ω *is a singleton set* (in other words: ω can be reduced to precisely one possible world in W). If we allow ω to be empty, then we cannot prove: *For all interpretations $<W,\omega,V>$ of L and formulas φ of L: φ or ¬φ is not true in $<W,\omega,V>$*. And if we allow ω to have more than one element, then we cannot, for example,[12] prove: *For all interpretations $<W,\omega,V>$ of L and formulas φ of L: φ or ¬φ is true in $<W,\omega,V>$*. But already if we simply take (2*) as it is, without any extra condition for ω, then we can prove *for all and only* the principles π of classical propositional logic (as formulated in L and as codified in an appropriate axiomatic system): *π is true in every interpretation $<W,\omega,V>$ of L*.

5   What is Primary: Intensional Containment or Truth?

The upshot of this is that Frege could not accuse the modern 'logicians of content' of disregarding the importance of truth for logic. Nevertheless, laws of truth, such as those presented above, are for the intensionalistic logician no more than a most welcome side-effect of logic, which, however, is *primarily* concerned with laws of meaning relations.

Whether Frege's view of logic is to be preferred or that of the intensionalists at this point crucially depends on the question whether the central concept of the intensionalists, the *intensional containment* of one proposi-

---

[11] Additional clauses can be added for *modal extensions* of L: $V(\Box\varphi)=W$, if $V(\varphi)=W$, and $V(\Box\varphi)=\varnothing$, if $V(\varphi)\neq W$; $V(\Box^*\varphi)=W$, if $\omega \subseteq V(\varphi)$, and $V(\Box^*\varphi)=\varnothing$, if not $\omega \subseteq V(\varphi)$.

[12] Another law of truth that is not provable if ω has more than one element is the following: *For all interpretations $<W,\omega,V>$ of L and formulas φ and ψ of L: if φ∨ψ is true in $<W,\omega,V>$, then φ or ψ is true in $<W,\omega,V>$*.

tion by another, can be understood without even tacitly presupposing the concept of truth. Now, the proposition *that the apple is colored* intensionally contains the proposition *that the apple is extended*.[13] Does this need any gloss in terms of truth? For example the gloss: the sentence 'the apple is colored' cannot be true without the sentence 'the apple is extended' being true? Or the alternative gloss: it cannot be true that the apple is colored without it being true that the apple is extended? It seems to me the intensionalists would be within their rights if they asserted the concept of intensional containment to be primitive and sufficiently clear, and if they added: 'The sentence "the apple is colored" cannot be true without the sentence "the apple is extended" being true *because* the proposition that the apple is colored intensionally contains the proposition that the apple is extended, and the direction of explanation *is not* the other way round, as is groundlessly presumed by the extensionalists.'

6   Frege and Three Uses of 'True'

Since Frege employed the concept of proposition (under the name of 'thought') and believed in the existence of propositions, Frege - even given the paramount importance he accorded to truth in logic - might have become reconciled with logical intensionalism, *if* he only could have seen a viable method of defining truth in an intensionalistic framework.[14] But he never succeeded in seeing *any* method of defining truth, he never even succeeded in seeing truth as an analyzable property. Frege really did not have any very clear idea of truth, and hence of laws of truth, at all.

The reason for this is that Frege never clearly distinguished the two fundamental and fundamentally different object-language uses of the word 'true' from each other (he *did* distinguish from them the *metalinguistic* use, where 'true' is applied as a predicate to sentences, but considered it *secondary* and did not pay much attention to it)[15]: the *ontological* use where 'true' is applied as a predicate to propositions, and that use where 'true' merely functions as a semantically redundant monadic sentence-connective (but is employed in order to make an assertion more emphatic). Listen to

---

[13] Both propositions concern the same apple and the same moment of time.

[14] Indeed (as Gottfried Gabriel pointed out in discussion) there are unmistakable intensionalistic leanings in Frege's last published work *Logische Untersuchungen*, especially in its third installment 'Gedankengefüge', where the connectives 'and' and 'not' are clearly taken to express *propositional* functions (functions that form propositions - *thoughts* - from propositions) - cf. pp. 72-73 - and *true and false as logical objects* play only a minor role. Apparently Frege's final move towards intensionalism is connected with his abandoning the logicistic program (or more generally speaking: with his abandoning his belief in *logical objects*; cf. Footnote 3).

[15] See 'Der Gedanke', p. 33 (my translation): 'And when we call a sentence true, we really mean its sense.'

this passage from 'Der Gedanke' (p. 34, my translation): 'It is also remarkable that the sentence "I smell the odor of violets" has the same content as the sentence "It is true that I smell the odor of violets". Thus nothing seems to be added to the thought [proposition] by my attributing the property of truth to it. And yet, is it not a great success when after long hesitation and arduous investigations the researcher can finally say "what I surmised is true"? The meaning of the word "true" seems to be completely singular. Could it be that we are here concerned with something that cannot be called a property in the ordinary sense at all? In spite of this doubt, I will for the time being in accordance with ordinary usage continue to express myself as if truth were a property until something more appropriate will have been found.' Here Frege does not realize that it makes a fundamental difference whether the sentence 'It is true that I smell the odor of violets' is parsed as (1) 'It is true that' + 'I smell the odor of violets', or as (2) 'It is true' + 'that I smell the odor of violets'. According to the first parsing, nothing, indeed, is added to the (cognitive) meaning of 'I smell the odor of violets', nor does the first parsing exhibit an attribution of a property to a thought. According to the second parsing, however, something is obviously added to the meaning of 'that I smell the odor of violets' - after all, the sentence 'it is true that I smell the odor of violets' is not synonymous to the phrase 'that I smell the odor of violets'; in fact, the second parsing, being a *subject-and-predicate* parsing, *does* exhibit an attribution of a property to a thought: The property of being true is attributed to the thought *that I smell the odor of violets*.[16] Frege could not see this because he kept confusing the second parsing with the first. In a passage parallel to the one cited above, in the much earlier (1892) paper 'Über Sinn und Bedeutung' ('On Sense and Reference'), he already insisted (p. 49, my translation) 'that the relationship of the thought to the true must not be compared with that of the subject to the predicate'. He really did not have any good reason for holding this.

7 The Definability of 'True', pace Frege, and *the True*

All three common uses of the word 'true' - the redundant, the ontological and the metalinguistic one - are easily definable for large fragments of natural language:

---

[16] Thus the sentence 'it is true that I smell the odor of violets' is indeed ambiguous: *It has two different meanings*, corresponding to the two different ways in which it can be parsed. Yet, 'it is true that <I smell the odor of violets>' must be true if 'it is true <that I smell the odor of violets>' is true, and vice versa. (But note that an ontological skeptic with respect to the existence of propositions could doubt the *vice versa*!) Hence the two disambiguated sentences resulting from 'it is true that I smell the odor of violets' stand in the same semantical relationship towards each other in which '*d* is an equilateral triangle' and '*d* is an equiangular triangle' stand: The latter two sentences have different meanings, but neither one of them can be true without the other being true.

For 'A' sentences are substitutable, for '*p*' names of propositions, for '*s*' names of sentences:

$$\text{It is true that } A := A.$$
$$\text{It is true}(p)^{17} := p \text{ is a fact } (p \text{ obtains, } p \text{ is the case}).^{18}$$
('that A' - being a name for a proposition - is substitutable for '*p*'!)
$$s \text{ is true} := \text{the proposition expressed by } s \text{ is a fact.}$$

Frege presumably would have objected what was mentioned above (in Section 1): that we already need to presuppose the notion of truth in order to apply the definiens of any definition of truth in any given case. But this is not a good objection. For instead of asking ourselves *whether it is true that the definiens applies* in any given case, we can simply ask ourselves *whether it applies*. Or Frege might have objected that the above definitions offer mere synonyma for 'true'? But this can hardly be the case since they make the concept of truth clearer than it was before, and certainly clearer than it was to Frege himself.

For him, curiously, laws of truth must be laws concerning a certain *object* (*Gegenstand*), *the true*, which is a *saturated* entity and hence cannot be a property.[19] It is not amiss to see how Frege's rather unnatural (but technically useful) notion of object truth-values, of truth and falsity *as objects*, can be fitted into an intensionalistic framework: If we employ a framework of coarsely individuated propositions, then we can quite naturally identify *the true* with the tautological proposition, and *the false* with the contradictory proposition (propositions, being saturated entities, are after all objects in Frege's sense).

8   What Remains

Frege's main motivation for claiming that logic is the science of the laws of truth was his opposition to psychologism. This is quite clear from the contexts in which his claim occurs. But psychologism being long since defeated, to what uses can we put today Frege's dictum that logic is the science of the laws of truth?

Even if it surely cannot serve as a generally acceptable characterization of logic, of its subject matter and its aims, even in its more elementary and traditional parts, Frege's definition of logic certainly draws our attention again to the fact that we are interested in logic to a high degree because its application in truth-directed investigations points us from truths to further

---

[17] That is: '*This* is true: *p*', or more idiomatically: '*p* is true'.

[18] Not all propositions are facts. For example, that Munich is the capital of Germany in 1998 is not a fact (this is much better than saying that it is a *non-existent* fact), and therefore, according to definition, that Munich is the capital of Germany in 1998 is not true.

[19] See 'Über Sinn und Bedeutung', pp. 48-49.

truths. This, certainly, is why money ought to be spent for logic. Moreover, what is not acceptable as a characterization of logic as a whole may nevertheless serve as a heading or slogan for a partisan movement or interesting research program *within* logic. Truth-value semantics and other approaches of ontological minimalism[20] could very well adopt this battle-cry against more ontologically-minded directions in logic: *Logic is the science of the laws of truth*, and of nothing else - or if it is not, let us see to what extent it can be treated in an ontologically neutral manner.

References

Frege, G. 1966 [1893/1903]. *Grundgesetze der Arithmetik*, 2 vols. in one, reprint of the 1893/1903 Jena edition, Hildesheim: Olms.

Frege, G. 1971a. Ausführungen über Sinn und Bedeutung. *Schriften zur Logik und Sprachphilosophie aus dem Nachlaß*: 25-34, ed. G. Gabriel, Hamburg: Meiner.

Frege, G. 1971b. Logik. *Schriften zur Logik und Sprachphilosophie aus dem Nachlaß*: 35-73.

Frege, G. 1976. Der Gedanke. Eine logische Untersuchung / Logische Untersuchungen. Dritter Teil: Das Gedankengefüge. *Logische Untersuchungen*: 30-53, 72-91, ed. G. Patzig, Göttingen: Vandenhoeck & Ruprecht.

Frege, G. 1975. Über Sinn und Bedeutung. *Funktion, Begriff, Bedeutung*: 40-65, ed. G. Patzig, Göttingen: Vandenhoeck & Ruprecht.

Frege, G. 1983. Neuer Versuch der Grundlegung der Arithmetik. *Nachgelassene Schriften*: 298-302, eds. H. Hermes et al., Hamburg: Meiner.[21]

Kutschera, F. v. 1985. *Der Satz vom ausgeschlossenen Dritten*, Berlin: De Gruyter.

Leblanc, H. 1983. Alternatives to Standard First-Order Semantics. *Handbook of Philosophical Logic*, vol. I: 189-274, eds. D. Gabbay and F. Guenthner, Dordrecht: Reidel.

Meixner, U. 1995. Ontologically Minimal Logical Semantics. *Notre Dame Journal of Formal Logic* 36: 279-298.

Reinach, A. 1911. Zur Theorie des negativen Urteils. *Münchener Philosophische Abhandlungen*: 196-254, ed. A. Pfänder, Leipzig: Barth. (A complete English translation by B. Smith can be found in *Parts and Moments*: 315-377, ed. B. Smith, München: Philosophia 1982.)

---

[20] See Meixner 1995. Concerning truth-value semantics, see Leblanc 1983, pp. 189-274, in particular p. 191.

[21] Translations into English of the cited papers by Frege can be found in: *Collected Papers on Mathematics, Logic, and Philosophy*, ed. B. McGuiness, Oxford: Blackwell 1984; *Posthumous Writings*, eds. H. Hermes et al., Oxford: Blackwell 1979.

Index

abstract 54, 56, 76-78, 84, 176
abstraction 54, 82, 259-261, 323
abundant 282f.
acquaintance 163, 184, 207, 259, 301
actual 36, 72, 79-80, 186, 189, 193, 270f.
actuality 270f.
algebra 339
algebraic 338
analytic 273
analytical philosophy 19-20, 25, 31f.
analyticity 53-57, 145, 157
a posteriori 53-85
a priori 53-85, 308
arithmetic 53-54, 57-58, 62, 64, 69-70, 83-85, 97-101, 106, 257, 333-335
   Peano – 83-84
arithmetization 83, 325
assertability 332, 333
assertion 120
   – sign 55
axiom 53, 59, 61-62, 67, 74-76, 79-83, 98-100, 107-109, 213, 330, 336
axiomatic system 331

Begriffsumfang 181
belief 116, 189, 198, 201f., 287, 294, 299
bivalence 333
Block's dilemma 289, 293, 296, 310-314

Cantor's paradox 320
character (semantic) 182, 199, 202f., 205, 209
   formal – 292f., 305-308
   objective – 291f., 305-308
   -theory 288-290
circularity 181f.
class 182f.
co-extensional 333
cogito 70-73, 84-85
cognition 61-62, 65, 70-72, 76-78, 80, 85
cognitive 136f.
   – process 48
   – value 92-94
collection 272, 279f., 319
colour term 304
communication 123, 125, 127-128, 135
composition (of functions) 186f., 189, 193

compositional 253
compositionality 114, 138, 169, 192, 232-233
comprehension 182, 319
concept 69, 77-78, 82, 119-121, 175, 177, 179-186, 235, 254, 256, 259, 267-283
   second-level – 235, 268
   subjective – 183, 190, 288, 292. 297-308
   universal – 267f.
   -word 175, 177f., 183f., 187, 194, 236, 244
conjunction 338
conjunctive 277f.
constituent 94-97, 142-143, 161-162, 168-173, 232, 244, 248, 267-283
constructibility 325
construction 77-78
constructive 327
content 142-145, 251, 254, 257, 267-283, 288, 336-339, 342
context 199, 202f., 251-252, 255, 260, 290
   -dependent 70, 85, 182
   -principle 14, 31f., 94, 232-233, 251-252, 258, 260
contextual 253-260, 264
continental philosophy 19-20, 25, 32
contingent 58, 64-65, 71
co-referential 182
count 60
countable 179
course of values 100-104, 182, 260, 263, 335
cumulation 323

deduction 61, 83, 98
default 204-206

deferential 201-207, 303f.
definition 53, 56-57, 65, 69, 76, 105, 120, 254-255
   contextual – 105, 255-264
   explicit – 259, 262-263
   implicit – 255
demonstrative 135, 199, 207
density 331
description 184, 192
   definite – 160, 162-165, 167-168, 185, 187, 211, 257
determinable 270
diagonal 292f., 305-308
direction (of a line) 260-261
discreteness 331
disjunct 271
disjunction 338
disjunctive 229, 277f.
division of linguistic labour 201-207, 291, 302f.
doxastic alternative 290, 294

EGO-mode of presentation 132, 137
empiricism 10, 41, 44, 60, 63, 67-68
empty
   – concept 69, 234-235
   – name 138, 238
   – set 69
epistemic 93, 96, 103, 107-109, 124-130, 192, 252-253, 260
   – value 147
epistemology 12, 21, 25f., 29, 35, 38, 41, 44-46, 53, 73, 80, 82, 159, 336
equality 179, 259-263
equation 259-260
equinumerous 180, 262
equinumerousity 259-260

equivalence 101-107, 183, 191, 259-263
equivalent 183, 260
essential 291, 304f.
esthetics 329
ethics 329
existence 4, 176, 182, 231f., 259-261
 – claims 231f.
experience 55, 59-66, 70-85
 intellectual – 70-71, 84-85
extension 69, 101, 180f., 184, 262, 267-283, 290, 324f.
extensionalistic 338-341
extensionality 319f., 323

fact 343
fine-grained 339
fission 227-229
Frege's axiom V 58, 83, 100-103, 106
function 68, 84, 91, 101, 175-179, 182f., 185f., 192, 257, 260-263
 constant – 170
 -theory 192f.
fusion 221-225

Gegebensein 91-110, 184
general 56f.
generality 53-85
generalization 70f.
 accidental – 67-68
 necessary – 67
genus, 270f.
geometrical 334
geometry 43, 53, 56-58, 61-62, 70, 73-83, 98, 106
 Euclidean – 53, 73-75, 77, 79, 81
 non-Euclidean – 70, 81

Gödel's incompleteness theorems 336
Goldbach's conjecture 283
grammaticality 177
grasp 35-50, 114, 123-130
grounded 57-58, 74, 80, 322

Haecceitism 159, 172-173, 213f.
hierarchical 335
holism 30-32, 296, 311-314

idea 36, 40, 46-50
idealism 5, 43-44
identitas indiscernibilium 279
identity 101-107, 141, 179f.
 criterion of – 184, 187, 258-263
 – of thoughts 93, 115f., 122, 191
implicit knowledge 216
incompleteness 336
index 182
indexical (expression) 113, 126, 128, 172, 292
indexicality 71-72, 85, 128-134, 199-203, 207, 292
indirect reference 245-246
individualism 287f., 295f., 309f.
individuation 180f., 183, 189, 191
induction 58-59
inductive 335
inference 53, 55, 61, 68-69, 71-72, 74, 79-80, 83, 95, 338
inferential
 – potential 198
infinite 334
infinity 325, 334
inner world 37, 44, 47
intension 160-161, 182f., 187, 191, 193, 214f., 290

intensionalism 335-341
intention 223f.
intentionalistic 95
intentionality 92, 100
intuition 57-58, 61-62, 64, 70, 72-83
   pure – 61, 73-83
intuitionist 332
inverse 269
iterative 321f.

judgement 54-59, 61, 66-67, 70, 78, 80, 253, 337
Julius-Caesar-problem 256, 259, 261-263
justifiability 91-110
justification 54-85, 91-110

language 42-43, 49, 189
   ideal – 159, 165-169
   private – 200
law 53-64, 67-70, 79, 187
   descriptive – 329
   empirical – 67-68
   general – 29, 53-85
   normative – 329
   – of thinking 6, 329
limit 182
linguistic 124
   – community 291f., 297, 306f.
   meta- 201-203, 207, 340, 342
logic, 11, 35, 46, 53-60, 64, 68-70, 72, 83, 85, 91-110, 329-335
   classical – 213, 332-336, 340
   free – 213
   first order – 239
   philosophical – 332

predicate – 103, 239, 334-336
propositional – 103, 334, 336, 340
second order – 84
logical, 183
   – consequence 68, 337-338
   – law 6, 49, 53-60, 68-70
   meta- 107
   – object 91-110, 334, 341
   – structure 55, 67
logician of content 336-338, 341
logicism 27, 53, 69, 81, 83-84, 99, 333-335
logicistic 333, 335

mark 65-66, 274-278
meaning 107-110, 135-138, 251-252, 255, 257, 287f., 291f., 337
   subjective – 183, 189, 293, 296
mental
   – file 198-200
   – process 48
mereological 271, 274-281
Merkmal 65, 274-278
metaphysics 159, 335
modal 64-68, 171, 340
modality 64-68, 336
mode of designation 147-148
mode of presentation 91-110, 117, 124, 136-138, 148, 184, 187f., 198-200, 202f., 275, 301
model 96, 331
   – theory 94, 230

name
   empty – 138, 212, 215, 219f., 238
   -using practice 212, 215-230, 291
necessary 58, 64-70, 85, 173, 252
necessity 64-70, 252-253
negation 280, 338
neo-Kantianism 10, 19-21, 24-30, 335
NINO 232-233, 235, 238-239, 242-248
normative 60, 78
number 58, 68-69, 83-85, 106, 176, 180-182, 184, 187, 253, 259-262, 333
numeral 180

object 57-58, 68-70, 74-85, 91-110, 137, 175f., 179f., 193, 257-261, 268, 335, 343
objective 8, 74, 81, 258
objectivity 23, 28, 36, 44, 50, 91-110, 258
ontic 252-253, 260
ontological 9, 176, 342
ontology 35, 44, 46, 160-161, 335
ordinal 321

paradox 166, 178
parse 342
part-whole relation 118, 271, 274-281
perception 64, 85, 199-200, 203, 207
permutation argument 261
perspectival 94
phenomenology 21, 24

philosophy of language 141, 159, 160-161
Platonic 95-96
Platonism 3, 10, 320
   Transcendental – 22
Port-Royal constraint 272f., 278
possible 56, 61-62, 66-68, 76-80, 186, 270f.
predicate 177f., 181f., 186f., 192, 194, 290f., 342
predicative 177, 188, 236
primitive 56, 59, 69, 71, 83-84
privacy 132-134
proof 55-59, 61-64, 67-70, 74-75, 79-80
proper name 113, 123-128, 159, 162-165, 167-173, 178f., 187, 193, 212, 238, 240-241, 244
   hybrid – 129
   ordinary – 159, 162-164, 167-168, 290f.
   logical – 162-163, 167
property 180f., 183, 229, 275, 342
proposition 44, 169-170, 189f., 336-344
   singular – 126, 161-162, 168-173
proprioception 199
provable 59, 63, 74
psychologism; anti- 14, 41-42, 49-50, 117-118, 329, 344
psychology 9, 46-47, 332

quantification 67-68, 79
quantifier 60

rational 55, 62, 70, 72, 81
rationalist 53, 59-60
realism 7

realistic 109
reality 23
reason 42-43, 56, 58, 69, 71-72, 76-78
   pure – 69, 85
reciprocity 267-283
recognition 206f., 257-259, 297-300
recursive 288-290
reference 113, 117, 137, 163, 170-172, 175f., 179, 187, 197-199, 211, 252-254, 260, 337
relation 91, 104-106
repetition problem 278-281
representation 14
representative 259-262
restriction 186 188, 323
rigid (designator) 169-173, 187
rigidity thesis 169-173
Russell's antinomy 335
Russell's constituent thesis 161-162, 168-173

saturate 241
saturated; un- 175-180, 193, 236, 343
Schiffer's problem 289, 296, 310
self-evidence 53, 61-62, 72, 81, 107-110
self-evident 55, 57-59, 67-68, 71, 80, 82, 85, 107-110, 282f.
semantic 108, 135-138, 338
   – content 135-138
sense 91-110, 123-128, 175, 177f., 183f., 190f., 193, 234, 245-246, 251-256, 260, 336
   -constituency 121-122
   -experience 55, 59-66, 70-85
   -impression 37-42, 44-45

-reference distinction 92, 144, 178, 187, 194, 197-199, 211f., 236-237
sensibility 64, 68, 74, 85
sentence-connective 194, 338
series 279
set 188, 281, 319f.
   null- 69
   – theory 184
simple 270f.
singular 57-59, 61, 68, 70-85
   – sentence 236-238
   – term 113, 179, 189f., 236-238
singularity 71, 74-75
solipsism 5
space 73-83
spatial 40, 57, 73-83, 258
   – intuition 58, 73-74, 76, 81-82
species 270f.
subjective 8, 258
subjectivity 36, 44, 50, 339
subject matter 68, 77, 147, 156
sufficiency 252-253
synonymous 184
synthesis 62, 79
synthetic 56-58, 62, 69-70, 73, 78-80
tense
   – logic 331
theorem 53, 74, 76, 330, 336
third realm 5, 36-37, 39, 44, 49
thought 35-50, 70, 73-74, 80, 94-97, 113-119, 177f., 183, 185-188, 191f., 211, 254, 336-342
token 199, 203, 205
   -reflexive 207
transcendental 62, 65, 78, 81
   – deduction 81

truth 8, 35, 49, 55, 64, 183, 329-331, 338-343
   -condition 135f., 193, 214
   -function 194
   – of fact 58, 64
   – of reason 58
   -table 109, 336
   -value 22, 30, 95, 100-105, 177, 179, 183f., 190, 253, 260-261, 263, 336
   -value semantics 336
twin-earth-story 291, 308
type 199, 202-205
   – theory 160, 182, 324

undecidability 336
uniqueness 256-262
unity (of propositions) 193
utterance 128, 136-138, 182

validity 21-28, 66, 68, 77-78, 81, 337
value 261, 263
   – theory 24f., 29f.
variable
   propositional – 338
vector theory of meaning 137-138

Wertverlauf 100-104, 335
wirklich 36, 270f.
Wirklichkeit 141, 270f.
World 182-189
Zermelo-Fraenkel set theory 323, 335